Flesh Cinema

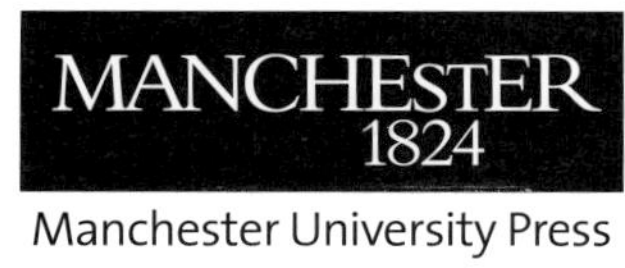

Manchester University Press

rethinking
art's histories

SERIES EDITORS
Amelia G. Jones, Marsha Meskimmon

Rethinking Art's Histories aims to open out art history from its most basic structures by foregrounding work that challenges the conventional periodisation and geographical subfields of traditional art history, and addressing a wide range of visual cultural forms from the early modern period to the present.

These books will acknowledge the impact of recent scholarship on our understanding of the complex temporalities and cartographies that have emerged through centuries of world-wide trade, political colonisation and the diasporic movement of people and ideas across national and continental borders.

Also available in the series

Art, museums and touch   Fiona Candlin

The 'do-it-yourself' artwork: Participation from fluxus to relational aesthetics
Anna Dezeuze (ed.)

After the event: New perspectives in art history   Charles Merewether and John Potts (eds)

Photography and documentary film in the making of modern Brazil   Luciana Martins

Women, the arts and globalization: Eccentric experience   Marsha Meskimmon
and Dorothy Rowe (eds)

After-affects|after-images: Trauma and aesthetic transformation in the virtual Feminist museum   Griselda Pollock

Vertiginous mirrors: The animation of the visual image and early modern travel
Rose Marie San Juan

The newspaper clipping: a modern paper object   Anke Te Heesen, translated by Lori Lantz

Screen/space: The projected image in contemporary art   Tamara Trodd (ed.)

Timed out: Art and the transnational Caribbean   Leon Wainwright

Performative monuments: Performance, photography, and the rematerialisation of public art   Mechtild Widrich

Flesh Cinema

The corporeal turn in
American avant-garde film

Ara Osterweil

Manchester University Press

Manchester and New York
distributed in the United States exclusively by Palgrave Macmillan

Published by Manchester University Press
Oxford Road, Manchester M13 9NR, UK
and Room 400, 175 Fifth Avenue, New York, NY 10010, USA
www.manchesteruniversitypress.co.uk

Distributed in the United States exclusively by
Palgrave Macmillan, 175 Fifth Avenue, New York,
NY 10010, USA

Distributed in Canada exclusively by
UBC Press, University of British Columbia, 2029 West Mall,
Vancouver, BC, Canada V6T 1Z2

British Library Cataloguing-in-Publication Data
A catalogue record for this book is available from the British Library

Library of Congress Cataloging-in-Publication Data applied for

ISBN   978 0 7190 8880 3   hardback
ISBN   978 0 7190 9191 9   paperback

First published 2014

Printed in Great Britain
by TJ International Ltd, Padstow

This book is dedicated to my mother Enid Weisman Osterweil (1944–2009), whose rebellious, indomitable spirit keeps me aloft even in her absence. (Ma, you were right: your love is enough to last a lifetime.)

Contents

Figures

Acknowledgments

This is a book about the profound and often conflicting demands that love, friendship, and art make upon us. How lucky I feel to have had the support of so many fellow travelers during the long process of this book's creation.

I will break custom and begin these acknowledgments by thanking my family for their extraordinary love. My deepest gratitude goes to David Baumflek, the love of my life, and my partner in all cosmic adventures. The greatest gift I was ever given was meeting you; let us always find new ways of being together and loving each other. To my beloved parents, Allan Osterweil and Enid Weisman Osterweil: though the world has never understood the odd ways in which our family operates, you have taught me that love is the supreme, and sometimes the only, answer. I have never witnessed any bond stronger than the one that you shared, and in its own idiosyncratic way, your relationship inspired me to ask the questions that led to the writing of this book. To my sister Elana, I have always admired your strength and honesty, and the unique person you are. I love you, and always shall. To my darling grandmother Beatrice Weinstein Osterweil Saltz (1912–2004), who offered me the least difficult form of love that I have ever known. Thank you Ross Diener for all of the support you have given me over the years, and also to Sylviane Baumflek for all of your kindness and generosity. And to my kids, Olivia and Picolo, who, more than anyone kept me company while writing this book, and who remind me every day how precious all embodied forms of being are.

This work could not have been completed without the dedicated guidance of so many incredible mentors. My deepest gratitude goes to Linda Williams, whose brilliant work on the representation of sex in moving images has guided me, like the North Star, since this book's early iteration as my dissertation. Thank you for being such an extraordinary teacher and friend, and for never losing faith in this project's potential.

I offer my tremendous thanks to Amelia Jones, for discovering this project and giving it a second life. For many editors, a book about avant-garde film *and* explicit sex would have two strikes against it. I love that, for you, this was a 'win-win.' Thank you for being such a wise and energetic mentor and inspiring friend throughout this process. And thank you to my editors at Manchester University Press, Emma Brennan and Marsha Meskimmon for your enthusiasm, and all the hard work you've done to give this book such a good home. It is such an honor to be part of such an excellent series.

I want to extend my deep appreciation to Perry Meisel, the late Michael Rogin, and Ronnie Landfield, the most profound teachers, outside of my family, that I have ever known. Not a day goes by that I am not humbled by your influence. Mike, you remain for me the epitome of what is good in this world, and you are so deeply and daily missed. I would also like to acknowledge my gratitude to the late Robert Sklar, into whose graduate course on American Film in the 1960s I snuck as an undergraduate and first discovered postwar American avant-garde cinema. I remember, with a twinge of embarrassment, ignorantly declaring that Andy Warhol's film *My Hustler* was 'not art.' Perhaps that is what you say when you've encountered something that is about to change your life. Thank you Bob for being patient while I grew up. Your kindness shall never be forgotten.

I would also like to thank Kaja Silverman and Carol Clover, who helped to shape this project when it was still a dissertation. Your work continues to resound with me in new and unexpected ways, and, Kaja, your *Flesh of My Flesh* was a great influence on this book's revision. Please forgive me for being stubborn and impossible when I was younger. I am older now and a little wiser I hope.

I am so grateful to the many people – too numerous to mention here – who shared memories and materials that helped me piece together the forgotten episodes of life and art contained herein. Tremendous thanks to the inimitable Ken and Flo Jacobs for sharing such colorful stories with me and being supportive of my work even though you did not always agree with my interpretations. I am in awe of the extraordinary energy you bring to your art and your love for each other. I also want to express my profound gratitude and admiration for Carolee Schneemann. Writing about your work has been a terrific challenge, but learning from you has changed my life.

Reflections by the following people have been indispensable to the development of this project: Jonas Mekas, P. Adams Sitney, the late Callie Angell, Amy Taubin, Christopher Sharits, Jim Hoberman, Steve Gebhardt, Rosebud Felieu, Kate Heliczer, Marilyn Brakhage, Gerard Malanga, Gordon Ball, and William Wees. Thank you for sharing your memories with me: I have tried, as best as I can, to honor their spirit. I also want to extend love and thanks to my dear comrades and fellow cinephiles Elena Gorfinkel, Federico Windhausen, Juan Suarez, and Marc Siegel. Film and writing are but a fraction of what is shared between us.

I am so grateful for the assistance of M.M. Serra at the Film-Makers' Cooperative; Andrew Lampert, Robert Haller, and Erik Piil at Anthology Film Archives; Claire Henry at the Andy Warhol Project at The Whitney Museum of American Art; Bradley Arnold at the James Stanley Brakhage Collection at University of Colorado, Boulder; Fred Camper; and Greg Pierce at The Warhol Museum for your knowledge and support. Each of you makes a tremendous contribution to the maintenance of experimental film culture, and I'm incredibly grateful for all that you do. I also want to thank Wayne State University Press for allowing me to reprint pieces of my article on Barbara Rubin from *Framework: The Journal of Cinema and Media* (51.1 (2010): 33–60) in Chapter One, as well as the British Film Institute, for allowing me to reprint pieces of my chapter 'On (and Off) the *Couch*' from *Warhol in Ten Takes* (2013) in Chapter Two.

The research for this book could not have been finished without the generous funding provided by Creative Capital / The Warhol Foundation, and the Social Sciences and Humanities Research Council. Both have opened new possibilities for my own research, including the opportunity to work with a host of emerging scholars whose diligent assistance greatly enhanced this project in its final stages. Many thanks to William Lockett, Julia Yudelman, Leah Pires, Patrick DeDauw, Thomas Pringle, Alex Weisler, and Cameron McKeich for your dedication, and to all of my avant-garde film students, but especially Pogo New and Anna Leocha, for helping me to experience these films anew with your inspired responses.

Friendship is at the very heart of this book, on and off the page.

I extend deep gratitude to Simon Stow, Omri Moses, Caroline Hanley, Jordan Weisman, Maki Narita, Brian Melman, Keith LaScalea, Adam Stracher, Cecily Hilsdale, and Jonathan Sachs for being such dear companions through the most wonderful and difficult times. I have learned so much from the enduring but nonetheless quixotic bonds between us. And to all of my dear friends who struggle so valiantly to balance the demands of art, work, and love, you are each a tremendous inspiration to me: Paul Gargagliano, Justin Glanville, Daniel Lichtman, Brian Ackerman, Lael Morgan, Amra Brooks, Amze Emmons, Iwonka Piotrowska, David Resnick, Noah Landfield, Nagisa Wada, and Erik Strand.

Finally, I would like to thank my new friends and colleagues in Montreal. To my kindred spirit Marielle Nitoslawska: your extraordinary film *Breaking the Frame* was a revelation to me, but your friendship has been even more so. Thank you also to Derek Nystrom, Manon Desrosiers, Alanna Thain, Paul Yachnin, Yuriko Furuhata, Marc Steinberg, Jonathan Sterne, Carrie Rentschler, Anya Zilberstein, Katharine Dempsey, and Patrick Turner for making Montreal seem like it just might one day feel like home. I couldn't imagine living here without you.

Introduction

> 'Give me a body then': this is the formula of philosophical reversal. The body
> is no longer the obstacle that separates thought from itself, that which it has to
> overcome to reach thinking. It is on the contrary that which it plunges into or
> must plunge into, in order to reach the unthought, that is life. Not that the body
> thinks, but, obstinate and stubborn, it forces us to think, and forces us to think
> what is concealed from thought, life… The categories of life are precisely the
> attitudes of the body, its postures.
>
> (Gilles Deleuze, The Time Image)

Like all turgid dreams, this one begins with bodies pressed against each other
in a dark room.

It was a cold night during the relentless Montreal winter when I screened
Ken Jacobs's 1963 film *Blonde Cobra* for my seminar on avant-garde cinema.
The film, which stars Jack Smith, is composed of the surviving footage of two
'catastrophic remakes'[1] of popular movies from the 1930s and 40s shot in the
late 1950s by Jacobs's friend Bob Fleischner. Described affectionately by critic
David James as 'the worst film ever made',[2] *Blonde Cobra* looks like outtakes
from a knockoff Dietrich picture made by a bunch of Martians. Punctuating
the decrepit remains of Fleischner's two abandoned parodies – one of Josef von
Sternberg's *Blonde Venus* (1932), the other of Robert Siodmak's *Cobra Woman*
(1944) – with periodic intrusions from a live radio, Jacobs distilled the relics of
these queer home movies into a euphoric elegy for things that fall apart – films,
dreams, friendships, and any stable notion of who we are or might like to be.

Costumed in the tropes of classical cinema, an unusual-looking group of
men sit, smoke, dance, ape, and masquerade in the crumbling tenements of
the Lower East Side. Other than Jack Smith, who convulses in the equally un-
convincing guises of gangster and goddess, their performances are attenuated
to the point of exhaustion. At different intervals throughout the film, we see
Smith festooned in sequin dress, silky headscarf, long dangling earrings, and
grotesquely applied lipstick, languishing in the debris that constitutes this film's
'set'. With his beaked nose and beady eyes, Smith is one part gypsy, one part
flapper, and one part whatsit. How incongruous this mutant Marlene seems in

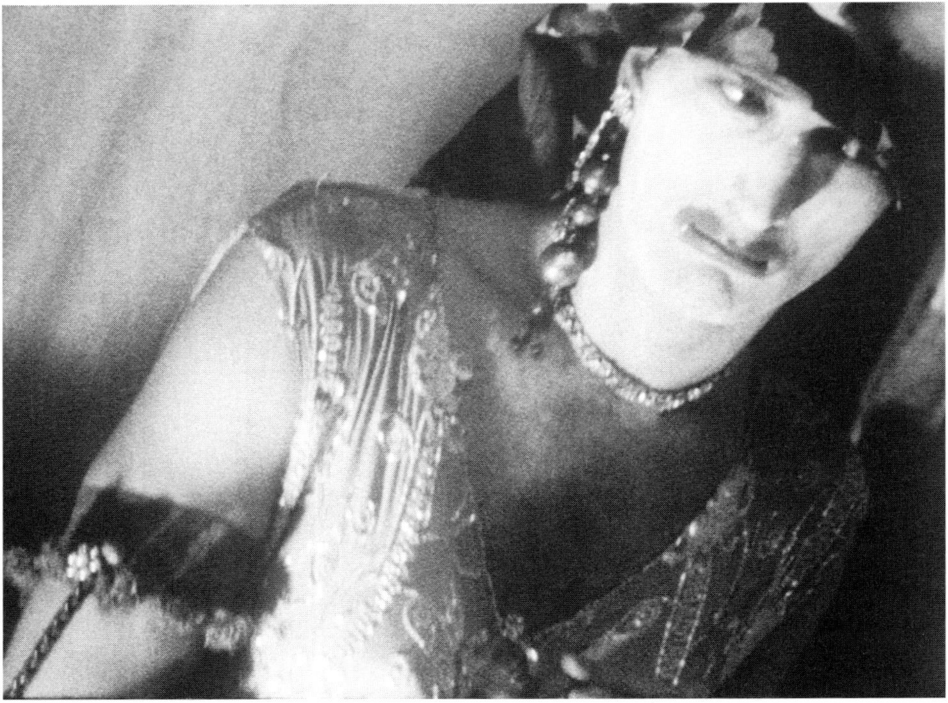

1   Jack Smith is one part flapper, one part gangster, and one part whatsit in Ken Jacobs's *Blonde Cobra* (1963). The film is composed of the outtakes from two failed film projects shot by Bob Fleischner and starring Jack Smith.

the cluttered apartment in which he lolls, indifferent to whatever absurd genre plot is plodding along.

Suddenly, the image blacks out. Disorientation, and – if you are in charge of the screening – panic. Is this blackout supposed to happen, or is it just the latest casualty of our precarious projection system? Though the image quickly returns (this time), it soon becomes clear that this is no mere technical error. Rather, failure is at the very core of this film; it is its *raison d'être*, its aesthetic sensibility, its politics. The entire film is a meditation on what happens when things go wrong, or what Judith Halberstam has described as 'the queer art of failure'.[3] Oscillating between the inept antics of its performers and the intermittent interruptions of a dark screen, *Blonde Cobra* appropriates failure as a means of detonating the slick fantasies of cultural capitalism. 'Why shave when I can't even think of a reason for living?' Jack Smith ponders, before stamping this aphorism with its inconsequential origin and authorship: 'Jack Smith, 1958. 6th Street.' In a 'heteronormative, capitalist society' in which success 'equates too easily to specific forms of reproductive maturity combined with wealth accumulation', Halberstam argues, 'failing, losing, forgetting, unmaking, un-doing, unbecoming, not knowing may offer more creative, more cooperative, more surprising ways of being in the world'.[4] Made in the margins of the culture industry by a band of misfits, *Blonde Cobra* opens up American cinema, and its audiences, to the radical potential of their undoing.

By celebrating perverse forms of instability that explode the most privileged myths of hegemonic culture, I argue that *Blonde Cobra* exposes the failure of America's movie-made aspirations to address the messiness of lived experience. During one of the film's many blackouts, we hear Smith's voice babbling in the background – the background of *what*? What constitutes the *background* when the *foreground* has *disappeared?* – but it takes a while to focus on what he is saying. Even in the dark, all is artificial, tawdry and cheap. Picture the glittery stucco sandcastles plopped upside-down on the ceiling of a Chinese restaurant and you will begin to imagine the grain of Smith's voice. But where is this voice coming from? In the typical theater, the speaker is located behind the screen so it seems as if the voices are emanating from, and grounded in, the bodies depicted on screen. Here, there are no visible bodies, and Smith's voice ricochets around the room with nowhere to land. Schizophrenically unmooring the voice from the body, the fictional world of the film collapses, throwing the audience back upon its own embodied particularities.

In the dark, Jack Smith ravishes us with a debauched tale that begins with a 'tweensy, microscopic little boy' who lives with his mother in a two-family house. This lonely little boy eventually befriends another (imaginary?) little boy, whose family lives in the upstairs apartment. As Smith describes the de-nouement of their nascent and potentially delusive friendship, he accidentally slips into the first person: 'The lonely little boy was less than seven, I know that because we didn't leave Columbus until I was seven, I know it, I was under seven and I took a match and I lit it and I pulled out the other little boy's penis and burnt his penis with a match!' As if to empirically test the reality of his friend – whose existence, much like the film itself, occasions no faith – the boy sears the other's genitals. With this 'obscene' confession – which remains, as the etymology of the word suggests, literally 'off-scene'[5] – the image snaps back and the Orientalist music resumes. But in a film in which even the characters don't believe in the 'reality' of the diegesis they inhabit, the illusory world of cinema crumbles. This sudden intrusion of biographical perversity ruptures the imaginary signification of the film and compels the audience to consider corporeal relations beyond its frame. By excavating the charged moments when biography seeps into and contaminates the illusion of cinema's hermetically sealed world, I argue that such leakages are essential to experimental film's corporeal mode of address. For in its failure to suture a universal subject into an idealized, self-contained fictional world, experimental cinema implicates the bodies of its spectator, performers, and creator as essential terms of its address.

Leaving this allegory of failed friendship behind, Smith begins to acoustically impersonate a certain 'Madame Nescience', a fortune-teller-cum-nun dreaming of her days as Mother Superior in a convent full of sex-starved girls. Around fourteen minutes into the film, the image blacks out again. This time we are sure that it is no mistake; we are ready to be lured into the blackness and the perverse pleasures it promises. In an unforgettable episode, Smith plays a gaggle of sex-starved nuns on the verge of nervous breakdown. We learn of their offenses from 'Sister Dexterity', whose voice Smith also ventriloquizes with demented glee. Accusing Sister Dexterity of lying, Madame Nescience commands her to drop her habit and 'bend over now!' Nescience delivers nineteen acoustic lashes to her inferior's ass. Amidst the frenzied sound of an (invisible) object striking an (invisible) surface, Jack Smith laughs demonically. 'What a turgid dream! What a turgid dream indeed!' he squeals as his alter ego Madame Nescience proceeds to the girls' dormitory to investigate. 'What does she find?' but a mob of insatiable young nuns caught throwing themselves on a plastic statue of Jesus.

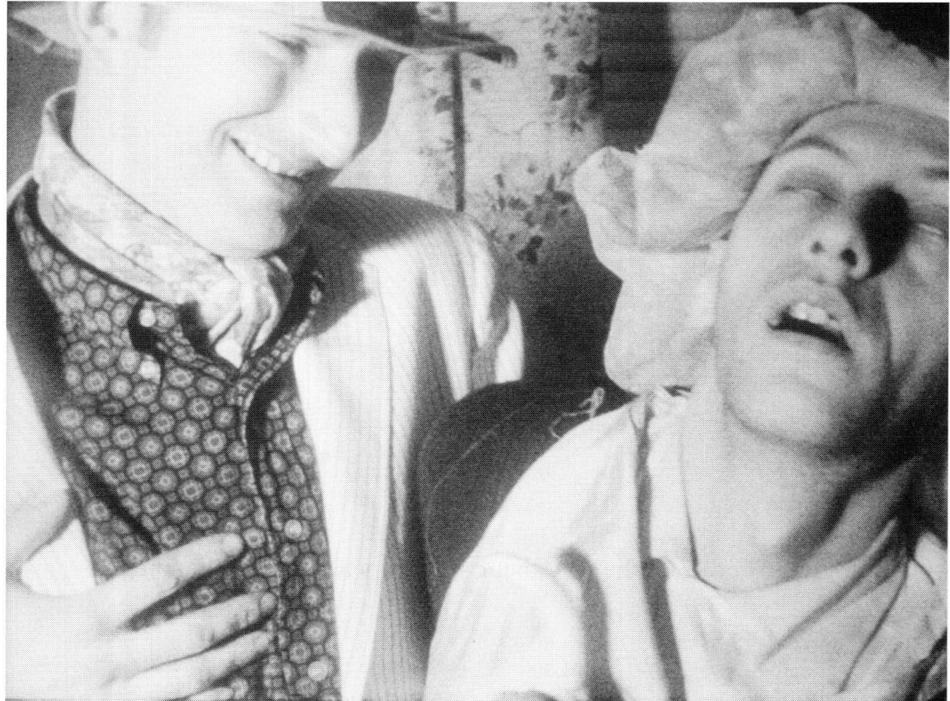

2 Jack Smith and Bob Fleischner cavort madly in the crumbling tenement that serves as *Blonde Cobra*'s makeshift set. Completed after Ken Jacobs and Jack Smith stopped speaking, the film allegorizes the necessity and failure of creative collaborations.

With this forbidden discovery, the unseen scene devolves into mayhem. 'The scene is a mad disorder of rosaries, and torn and tattered habits and cunts,' Smith reports. Outraged, Madame Nescience attempts to restore order: 'Girls I want all of you to bend over and all of you to drop your habits. I'm going to go down the line and paddle you with a cross, a silver cross.' And thus the concerto of screaming, yelping, laughing, whooping, and beating begins – all of which is improvised by Smith. If you have managed to stifle your giggle during the prelude to this orgy – as many of my students struggled to – it proves impossible to keep from cracking during Smith's masterful concatenation of virginal mob hysteria.

Animated by such hysteric energy, the blank screen in *Blonde Cobra* becomes a phantom limb. What we laugh at is not only what Smith *says*, but what we *see* and *feel*, the lurid *mise-en-scène* that each of us directs in our mind's eye and vicariously experiences. As Smith says in the very beginning of *Blonde Cobra*, 'We are drowning, drowning in a sea of nescience, completely soaked in an ocean of nescience, yes. And the whole world is nescient too.' Jacobs guides us through this oceanic feeling, reminding us that if we become re-attuned to our own bodies and each other we can experience a buoyancy that is in defiance of the heaviness of the world. The aim is not to drown in what Kaja Silverman has described as the 'unfathomable totality' of being-in-the-world,[6] but, as I will argue, to return to that nascent stage of *nescience* or *not knowing* in which it is possible to forge less scripted relations to our own and each other's bodies.

What happens to a film audience when there is no longer anything on the screen to look at? Confronted with the disintegration of filmic illusion, the fantasy of the audience as transfixed mob dissolves into a constellation of 'private symphonies of intensity exploding in the dark.'[7] One student appears catatonic while another fidgets in discomfort. A few sit riveted, others stupefied, a couple ironically amused. Someone laughs uncontrollably while others glance nervously or curiously around the room. I find myself drifting into hypnosis as the vibrating shades of the screen's darkness come to seem like the black planes of an Ad Reinhardt painting. As the noises of gurgling stomachs compete with Smith's mad elocution, one recognizes how we feel, see and even smell the sound of film in our bodies. Electrified by Smith's voice and our sensuous proximity to each other, we are unleashed from the cocoon of our respective solitudes into a fitful collective of bodies. In the synesthetic spaces opened up by experimental cinema's queer failures, we are transformed. Pitched into darkness, we become 'in-visible' – not in the superhero sense of being imperceptible, but in the sense that we become so intertwined with the film and each other that we can no longer distinguish between what French philosopher Maurice Merleau-Ponty describes as its 'flesh' and our own.[8]

Inviting each of us to corporeally experience the obscene events that its darkness occludes, *Blonde Cobra* is addressed to, and constitutive of, a counter-public. For when all of the elements of cinema fail – as they do here – we begin to recognize the embodied condition of spectatorship upon which movies have always depended. In their deliberate 'anti-artifactuality,' experimental films of the 1960s enable a 'sensuousness' of cinematic experience that engages the audience in the corporeality of the concrete world.[9] The film's blackout reminds us that the world is not a spectacle that one can simply observe, but a thick mesh in which we are profoundly and precariously entangled. We are not only the bodies to which cinema happens; we are cinema itself.

Working with the remains of two films that had been destroyed by fire, Ken Jacobs helps us to 'see' what American film culture had deemed obscene. Yet in an era in which the best definition of pornography circulating was Judge Potter Stewart's 'I know it when I see it,'[10] the provocation of *Blonde Cobra* lies in its vivid in-visibility. Yet the brilliance of the film is not merely its clever negotiation of the legal conundrum of how to know 'it' when one *can't* see it, but the way its embrace of failure creates a dynamic space for the viewer to experience contingency and unpredictability. Unlike pornography, which stages its sexual encounters for 'maximum visibility'[11] and, as I suggest in Chapter 2, sexual 'profit,' the corporeal avant-garde plunges its viewers into their own in-visibility. As this book argues, even the avant-garde's most explicit representations of the flesh deconstruct the 'it' of sexuality by obscuring the machinations of bodies in the thickness of perception. Rejecting a libidinal economy organized by visibility and the viewer's masterful, objectifying gaze (as are both Hollywood and hard-core pornography), the avant-garde interrogated the subject's blinding immersion in corporeality.

At the end of *Blonde Cobra*, Jack Smith wonders aloud 'what went wrong?' Clearly, the answer is *everything*. But by flaunting its own failure to play it straight, *Blonde Cobra* unravels the seamlessness of both cinema and identity. Refusing to buy into (or try to sell) heteronormative conventions for living or making art, Smith and Jacobs stabbed holes in the myths of the culture industry and the halted forms of human relations prescribed by it. Preferring 'pitiful' means of production to those engorged by capital, experimental filmmakers of the 1960s turned away from the 'art department perfected dream world'[12] of Hollywood to a cinema born of the radical messiness of corporeal experience.

Blonde Cobra had its public debut alongside Jack Smith's *Flaming Creatures* at New York's Bleecker Street Cinema in April 1963. While both were hailed by Jonas Mekas as inaugurating a 'Baudelairean' revolution in cinema,[13] within a few months *Flaming Creatures* would become Underground cinema's *cause célèbre* after screenings of the film were met with charges of obscenity, police seizures, theatre shut-downs, arrests, and a New York City court trial that brought public intellectuals such as Susan Sontag and Allen Ginsberg rushing to the film's defense.[14] Receiving more critical attention in the 1960s than almost any other experimental film, *Flaming Creatures* became synonymous with the outrageous corporeality of 'Underground' cinema. As it has also served as the rallying point for some of the best contemporary studies of postwar avant-garde cinema,[15] *Flaming Creatures* is not discussed in detail in this volume in spite of the fact that its production and reception were key events in the emergence of what I have termed 'Flesh Cinema.'

With its anarchic depiction of *déshabillé* drag queens, ecstatic gang-rape, and limp penises that hang, like last year's Christmas ornaments, in the nooks and crannies of impossibly entangled, androgynous bodies, *Flaming Creatures* troubles gender and careens sexuality away from what Freud had described as the 'normative' aim of heterosexual genital penetration.[16] *Flaming Creatures* not only celebrated the failure of anatomy to determine identity, but like *Blonde Cobra* relished the schizophrenic misalignment of corporeal acts and affects. Defying the organization of the polymorphous pleasures of the flesh under a strictly genital sexuality, *Flaming Creatures* affirmed the anarchy of undisciplined bodies. Yet even its subversion of what Frankfurt School philosopher and countercultural guru Herbert Marcuse decried as the 'supremacy' of genital sexuality[17] *Flaming Creatures* refused to offer unmediated access to sexuality. With its grainy film stock, out-of-focus and over-exposed images, bewildering compositions, and disorienting transitions, *Flaming Creatures* undermined the assumption that 'unrepressed' sexuality would be either visually transparent or unambiguously pleasurable. Like *Blonde Cobra*, *Flaming Creatures* equated the tyranny of a purely genital sexuality with the tyranny of a realist narrative form that privileged the pellucid presentation of bodies in space. I argue that, far from offering a sexual utopia to its audience, experimental cinema of the 1960s included 'unpleasure' alongside ecstasy as a key feature of its depiction of carnality. Though the avant-garde's corporeal mode of address certainly includes the explicitness of nudity and sex that we find in *Flaming Creatures*, it also embraces the kinds of opacity and synesthetic confusion that characterize *Blonde Cobra*.

By the time *Blonde Cobra* and *Flaming Creatures* debuted, Jack Smith and Ken Jacobs had not been speaking for nearly two years. In spite of the fact that Jacobs, his partner and soon-to-be-wife Florence Karpf, and Jonas Mekas were arrested for showing *Flaming Creatures* at the New Bowery Theater in February 1964,[18] hostilities between the once inseparable companions persisted until Smith's death from AIDS in 1989. Contrary to the story Smith narrates of the failed friendship between two lonely little boys in *Blonde Cobra*, these two did not terminate their six-year-long kinship because of a curious attempt by one to test the other's authenticity by mutilating his penis. Rather, Smith and Jacobs's falling out in 1961 on the shores of Provincetown, Massachusetts was due partially to the trouble that sexuality's supposedly 'normative aims' can bring to relationships explored in the margins of its purview: After both men fell in love with the same woman, their friendship didn't survive the summer.

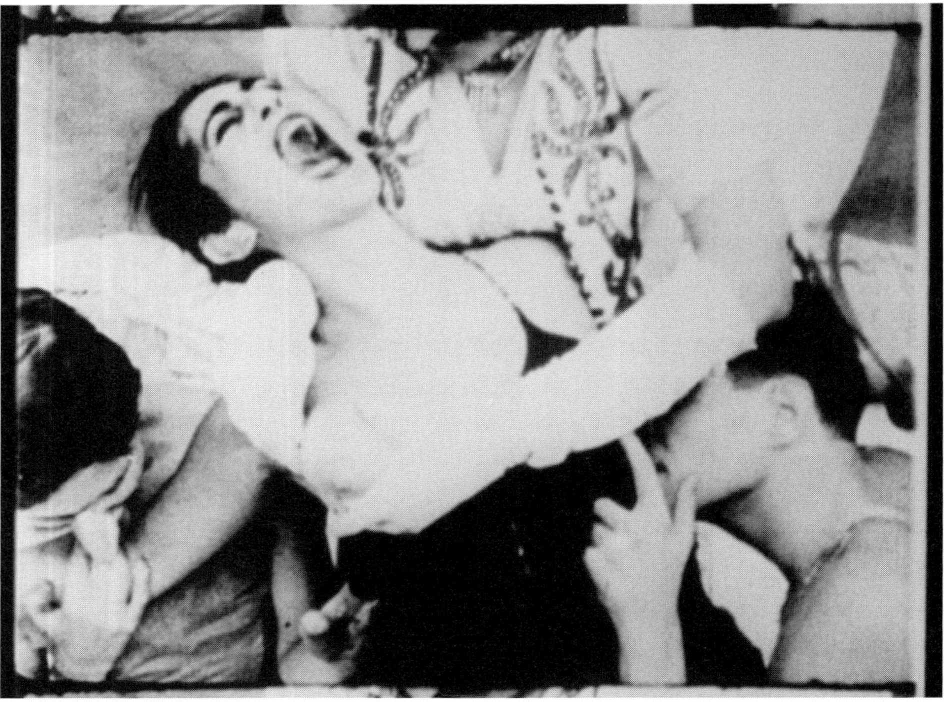

3   The anarchic depiction of sexual pleasure in Jack Smith's *Flaming Creatures* (1962–1963) inaugurated a new era in the representation of the body in American experimental film.

Behind a common enough romance plot, the main characters unpredictably fail to live up to their generic prototypes.

Like the lonely boys in the story of frustrated desire that Smith narrates, Ken Jacobs and Jack Smith lived, worked, and played in close, almost familial intimacy in the tenements of the Lower East Side. Though one was a 'midwestern Catholic queer,'[19] and the other a Jewish heterosexual misfit, their kinship was a form of survival. Born of their mutual alienation from the Eisenhower era, their friendship collapsed right at the moment when more eccentric forms of queer identity and artistic community were becoming available. Though the dissolution of their friendship was undoubtedly due to the conflicts that arise between two notoriously difficult personalities, it is also, I argue, a beacon of how individual idiosyncrasy fails to seamlessly conform to the grand transformations that we rely on to narrate history. The fact that Smith and Jacobs's rivalry over the same woman occurred simultaneously with Smith's growing identification with the newly visible gay communities in Provincetown and New York is not merely an apocryphal detail in the unwritten history of intimacy, but a sign of biography's irreducibility. For even in a world in the midst of radically re-imagining how kindred individuals of all kinds might identify and interact with each other, the demands that desire makes on us can be perilous. While we may prefer to theorize homosexuality and heterosexuality as two distinct forms of relationality that only coalesced in duress in the closet, such episodes suggest otherwise.

In this book, I contend that biography's queerness can illuminate much about the nuances, complexities, and contradictions of identity that history writ large can never teach us. Rather than offering up the artists discussed in this volume as universal subjects of history, I insist that their unpredictability matters as much as the sense of contingency produced in their films. The 'perverse embodiment' of experimental cinema that I theorize speaks as much to the events on screen and their effects on the audience, as it does to the lived experience of the artists who created them.

In what has become a mantra for my own method of historiography, David James reminds us that every film is an allegory of its own production.[20] Some films, I argue, are allegories of even more. I begin this study of the role of sexuality and the body within avant-garde cinema of the 1960s with *Blonde Cobra* because, in spite of its visual exclusion of the sexually explicit imagery it

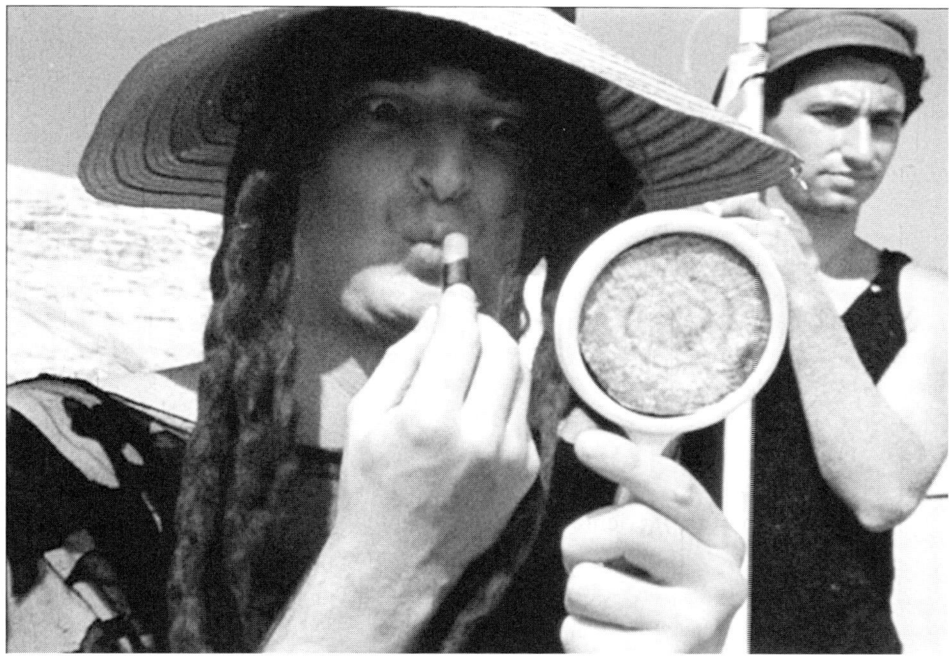

'What went wrong?' Jack Smith applies lipstick while Ken Jacobs gazes offscreen in　　**4**
The Death of P'Town (Ken Jacobs, 1961). Their friendship fell apart during the making of this film.

conjures, the film is both the beginning of an era of experimental cinema that would radically expand what it was possible to show on screen, and the end of a friendship whose own queer failure helped to produce seismic shifts in American visual culture. In its blissful fusions and evocative omissions, *Blonde Cobra* allegorizes the charged and improvisatory forms of collaboration that gave rise to an experimental cinema of the flesh capable of addressing but not reconciling the complexities of sexuality and desire. Mining the tension between corporeal revelation and concealment, *Blonde Cobra* helps inaugurate the 'invisible' sensibility that would come to characterize the corporeal avant-garde cinema of the 1960s and 70s. Yet by allegorizing the dissolution of the friendship from which it emerged – 'what went wrong?' – *Blonde Cobra* also inadvertently mourns the forms of nescience that dissipated as its creators' own identities began to coalesce around newly available subject positions that rejected the troublesome ambiguities that gave rise to these alliances in the first place.

Although *Blonde Cobra* does not produce an image of the outrageous entanglements of flesh it describes, many, many other experimental films of the era did. Celebrating perverse forms of corporeal intertwining and extension, experimental films pioneered new forms of relationality both for the people who created them and for the people who beheld them. For just as the boundaries between subject and object are transgressed in the experience of watching these films, the boundaries between friends often collapsed during their production. Yet, as this book shall argue, none of these films could have emerged without the peculiar, non-normative forms of kinship that inspired and sustained their creation. Simply put, we cannot approach the pioneering representation of alternative sexualities in American experimental cinema of the 1960s without recognizing how the off-screen struggles between artists of conflicting temperaments and complex identifications influenced and inspired them. These nescient, improvisational friendships are essential to understanding the explicit images of sexualized bodies that began to populate American experimental films in the 1960s.

Flesh Cinema

> The thickness of the body, far from rivaling that of the world, is on the contrary the sole means I have to go unto the heart of the things, by making myself a world and by making them flesh.
>
> (Maurice Merleau-Ponty, *The Visible and the Invisible*)

> The body which had been a neutral or invisible term of vision now was the thickness from which knowledge of vision derived.
>
> (Jonathan Crary, 'Modernizing Vision')

By the early 1960s, avant-garde cinema was the most sexually explicit form of American visual culture. Yet in addition to its transformative representations of bodies, experimental cinema also formed an inextricable part of a rich visual and political culture devoted to exploring the embodied experience of subjectivity. Concentrating on the sexually explicit work of several key filmmaker artists – Barbara Rubin, Andy Warhol, Stan Brakhage, Carolee Schneemann, Yoko Ono, and Paul Sharits – this book argues that experimental films of the 1960s approach the opacity of corporeality as a means of bio-political resistance to heteronormative, racist, capitalist, and imperial forms of power. Through the creation of provocative images of the body that move their audiences to dangerous, vertiginous forms of empathy, avant-garde cinema of this period detonates the boundaries between bodies, on, off, and around the screen. By privileging artists who habitually worked across diverse disciplines and media, *Flesh Cinema* imbeds its analysis of individual films within a study of the larger culture in order to articulate the new forms of relationality and resistance that were at stake in the expanded cinema practice of the period.

Situated outside of industrial cinematic practice, but on a continuum with other artistic movements of the period, including performance and body art, sculpture, painting, music, dance, and poetry, experimental cinema enables viewers to affectively overcome the boundaries between self and other through the haptic medium of the screen. Renouncing the scopophilic drive of Hollywood, avant-garde films challenge the fetishistic organization of bodies by formally acknowledging the occlusion of visual mastery that occurs in intimate corporeal encounters. As in Maurice Merleau-Ponty's phenomenological account of perception, avant-garde cinema of the 1960s treats the density of the flesh as the fundamental 'il y a,' or 'there is,' of existence, the substance which defined both the body and the world:

> The flesh is not matter, is not mind, is not substance. To designate it, we should need the old term 'element,' in the sense it was used to speak of water, air, earth, and fire, that is, in the sense of a general thing, midway between the spatio-temporal individual and the idea, a sort of incarnate principle that brings a style of being wherever there is a fragment of being.[21]

Since Merleau-Ponty considered body and world to be composed of the same 'element,' there can be no world without its apprehension through and in the flesh. Merleau-Ponty thus conceived of a relationship in which the 'flesh of the world' is constantly merging with the 'flesh of the body' in a perpetual state of 'reciprocal insertion' and 'chiasmic intertwining.'[22] Considering flesh the groundwork of inter-subjectivity or, more accurately, 'inter-corporeity,' Merleau-Pointy theorizes that a 'transitivity' between bodies serves as the basis for the subject's 'participation in and kinship with the visible.'[23] Yet Merleau-Ponty's complex notion of the 'visible' does not equate the visible with the seen, but rather theorizes visibility within a vibrating domain of materiality that is pregnant with the 'invisible.'

As Amelia Jones argues, Merleau-Ponty's insistence on embodied subjectivity performs a 'radical critique of the Cartesian subject,' which dissolved the 'metaphysical idealism embedded in the conception of modernism hegemonic in Europe and the United States in the postwar period.'[24] Beginning in the late 1950s, American experimental cinema initiated a profound investigation of corporeality that not only re-conceived the representational limits of American cinema and visual culture, but re-oriented aesthetics and subjectivity along an axis of radical contingency. Recognizing, as Merleau-Ponty did, that things in the world were 'inaccessible to a subject that would survey them from above,' experimental filmmakers created a thoroughly corporeal cinema that strove formally and affectively to acknowledge how the seer's body was 'caught up'[25] in the aesthetic of in-visibility. By inserting the beholder's body as an integral term in spectatorship, the corporeal avant-garde translated the embodiment of consciousness to the synergetic, transitive relationship between on- and off-screen bodies. The spectator was not addressed as a detached *cogito*, but as an embodied participant in a corporeal *mise-en-scène* that encompasses not only the activities documented by the camera, but the 'chiasmic intertwinings' of the bodies around and behind it.

Forged during the liminal period between the end of the stag-film era,[26] and the advent of hard-core feature-length pornography in the early 1970s, 'Flesh Cinema' took advantage of its own relative obscurity to redefine how bodies could be depicted on screen. In a cinematic culture circumscribed by the prohibition of the on-screen representation of nudity and sexual intercourse, the avant-garde's salacious solicitation of viewers and explicit focus on bodies offered titillating alternatives for viewers, and helped to transform American censorship laws. In spite of the significant aesthetic and political differences between mainstream pornography and the corporeal avant-garde, like all 'body genres,'[27] experimental cinema includes the viewer's body, and its range of involuntary responses, as an essential component of its address.

While experimental cinema's earliest critics tended to treat the avant-garde's exploration of the body either as a brief, 'infantile'[28] phase of Underground or 'Baudelairean'[29] cinema quickly surpassed by the more cognitive concerns of structural cinema, more recent critics have made equally myopic distinctions on the basis of filmmakers' gender or sexual preference. However, far from being a passing or peripheral concern of alternative cinema – or a realm explored only by female or queer filmmakers – the body was a defining, lasting, and central concern of avant-garde film (and video) in the postwar period, as well as the primary trope in the 1960s avant-garde's experiments with film form and film language.

My insistence on the corporeality of avant-garde cinema in the 1960s builds upon the groundbreaking work on American experimental film done by P.

Adams Sitney, David James, Scott Macdonald, Juan Suarez, Paul Arthur, and Annette Michelson, as well as many other studies of individual artists too numerous to mention here. It has also has been informed by the theoretical insights of many scholars who have helped map the corporeal and/or affective terrain of postwar art and film, including Sally Banes, Laura Marks, Linda Williams, Kaja Silverman, Douglas Crimp, Amelia Jones, Thomas Waugh, Kristine Stiles, Chrissie Iles, and Jennifer Doyle. Like many of these scholars, I aim to expand our perception of the body's role in postwar visual culture by helping to dismantle the distinctions between film and other art forms, as well as between high and low culture, which still persist within and between disciplines.

Like all historical transformations, the emergence of Flesh Cinema is over-determined. Taking advantage of the changing standards of decency, the demise of the studio system and the new (relative) permissiveness of Hollywood, the shifting attitudes of the emergent sexual revolution, and the mobile aesthetic codes proffered by art movements such as Pop and Fluxus, experimental film changed from the symbol-laden psychological cinema it had been in the 1940s and 50s into a corporeal, sexually explicit cinema. Rather than de-corporealizing the body in order to explore the dream states of the psyche, as experimental filmmakers of earlier eras had often done, avant-garde filmmakers of the 1960s depicted the body in all of its 'effervescence,' to borrow Sally Banes's key term.[30]

As I and other critics have described in more depth elsewhere,[31] the exhibition of avant-garde films also underwent significant changes during this period. From 1947 to 1963, the primary site of the exhibition and distribution of avant-garde cinema in the United States was Cinema 16 in New York City. Founded by Amos and Marcia Vogel, Cinema 16 educated a generation of *cinéastes* by providing the initial public presentation of American independent film.[32] Organized as a film society to avoid censorship and financial discrimination against individual experimental works, Cinema 16 eventually expanded its function as an exhibition site for mixed programs to include a separate distribution arm for the avant-garde.

The closure of Cinema 16 in 1963 announced the end of an era of avant-garde film culture and the dominant philosophy that had animated it for over fifteen years. The Film-Makers' Cooperative / New American Cinema Group,[33] which opened in New York in 1962, presented a significant alternative to Vogel's approach. As a collective run by filmmakers, without the intervention of an esteemed tastemaker, the Coop was non-exclusive and non-discriminatory, accepting all films submitted to it. Such a policy inevitably changed the character of experimental cinema in the period. As Jonas Mekas wrote, in the First Statement of the New American Cinema Group, 'We are for art, but not at the expense of life. We don't want false, polished, slick films – we prefer them rough, unpolished, but alive; we don't want rosy films – we want them the color of blood.'[34]

Mekas would serve as one of the primary witnesses, catalysts, and advocates for the transformation from a psychological to a corporeal avant-garde cinema. The other characters chronicled in this book played equally heterogeneous roles as creators, provocateurs, and organizers of an alternative public sphere organized around the production, distribution, and exhibition of experimental films. In large part through the efforts of individuals working in close collaboration with each other through cooperative communities and personal networks, experimental films steeped in the fluids of the body would move from their 'underground' screenings in private lofts and members-only events to 'aboveground' exhibition in independent theaters, art galleries, film festivals, college campuses, courthouses, and, by the end of the decade, commercial and porn theaters. Yet in its trajectory aboveground, experimental cinema sacrificed neither the daring nor the difficulty for which it had become notorious. The obstinate, stubborn bodies represented in *Flesh Cinema* not only plunged viewers into thought, as Gilles Deleuze promises in the epigraph to this volume, but would so trouble the extant 'categories of life' that those caught in its whirl would be, as I have been, turned inside out by their experience of them.

Rather than representing bodies as transparent signifiers, avant-garde cinema approached flesh as an endlessly variable substance that could come unbound from conventional ideologies of gender, identity, or subjectivity through shattering encounters with desire, sex, pain, birth, and death. Yet while the postwar shift of emphasis from a psychological to a corporeal notion of subjectivity was reflected in a variety of media, experimental cinema faced particular challenges of representation due to its specific ontology as a representational mode defined by what Christian Metz has famously described as 'imaginary' signification.[35] How could one represent the overwhelming, blinding tactility of corporeal encounters through a medium that insisted, above all, on two-dimensional visuality? By inventing new filmic languages to represent 'the thickness' of the body 'from which knowledge of vision derived,'[36] avant-garde filmmakers pioneered a cinema of what Laura Marks has so fruitfully described as 'haptic visuality.'[37] This involved not only an abrogation of any presumption toward optical mastery, but an attempt to visually and acoustically render tactility through various means of manipulating the 'skin' of the film. Yet while the haptic strategies of the corporeal avant-garde *expand* cinema's sensorium beyond the visual and acoustic transmission of imaginary signifiers, it also strives to acknowledge the radical *reduction* of visibility that results from being, as Merleau-Ponty theorized, deeply imbedded in, and intertwined with, the visible.

By couching its explorations of corporeality in a filmic language derived from the subject's 'in-visibility,' *Flesh Cinema* demonstrates how the mutual encrustment of tactility and vision complicates any facile notion of unmediated access to sexuality promised by the dissolution of legal censorship in the

1960s. As the films discussed in this volume instantiate, desire undoes us, and sex is, as Jack Smith jests in *Blonde Cobra,* 'a pain in the ass.' Embodiment was never a neutral strategy of representation or mode of cinematic address, but a complex dialectic that could cause distress for its makers and viewers alike. By touching the lived body of the beholder in their cinematic exploration of the flesh, avant-garde filmmakers re-invent spectatorship as a participatory realm of assault and seduction.

By foregrounding the 'in-visibility' of corporeality, 'flesh cinema' makes spectators physiologically aware of the difficulty of *seeing* the body through the blinding core of sexuality. Rejecting the ideological implications of Hollywood's cinematic apparatus, avant-garde cinema disrupts the 'seamless' conventions of editing and visual presentation favored by mainstream and later pornographic practice, and shatters the illusory naturalness of gender and sexuality. Foregrounding the roles that boredom, distraction, interruption, discomfort, tension, and ambivalence play in our attempts to intertwine with others, avant-garde cinema acknowledges the effects of the intrusion of the cinematographic apparatus onto the scene of intimacy, and the inevitable performativity of gender and sexuality. Yet through their creation of a thoroughly 'perverse' cinema that swerved away from what Freud had described as the 'normative' aims of sexuality,[38] experimental filmmakers use the body as a site of ideological resistance.

Queer bonds

Through its creation of a personal, domestic cinema, experimental film challenged Hollywood's industrial mode of production with alternative models of affective labor and creative collaboration. In doing so, it pioneered queer modes of friendship, work, sex, and intimacy that were as historically significant as the radical articulation of bodies taking place on screen. The films discussed in this volume not only allegorize the artistic collaborations and idiosyncratic working methods that inspired and sustained them, but also the 'shatterings,' to conjure Leo Bersani,[39] that their filmmakers experienced through messy, inter-corporeal relation with friends and lovers.

Insisting upon the inextricability of art and life, this volume gives equal consideration to the on- and off-screen models of corporeal relationality explored by film artists and their fellow travelers working in other media. Defying the critical taboo against 'biographical fallacy,' I approach the particular lived experience of the subjects of this book as an indispensable means of understanding their artistic practice. For, as this book argues, it is impossible to adequately theorize a personal, anti-industrial cinema devoted to the exploration of inter-corporeal encounters without taking into account the way such confrontations shatter and reconstitute their makers. Rejecting any facile notions of biographical transparency, this study nevertheless investigates types of knowledge and modes of discourse produced outside of, and often not authorized within, an industrial, corporate context. That this alternative circuit of knowledge should involve sentimental detours, material fragments, gossip, irreconcilable contradictions, and the necessarily imperfect recollections of 'key witnesses' should come as no surprise. Forms of eccentric embodiment that are capable of producing new forms of relationality can and should be messy.

Finally, this book insists that it is the critical and often critically troubled bonds of friendship – particularly the queer kinship between friends differently but analogously marginalized by their sex, gender, race, or class – that serves as the basis for the radical reconstitution of corporeal representation and relationality in experimental cinema. The films discussed in this volume engage, and were catalyzed by, the difficulties of sustaining friendship – between individuals who did or didn't fuck – against the tensions generated by attraction, political disagreement, and differences in identity. As this book chronicles, these friendships often struggled against the over-determined ideals of heterosexual love and romance in their search for more idiosyncratic and expansive ways of being and working together. Not only were these friendships often called upon to do art's work, but in many cases they laid the groundwork for the recognition of the types of ontological 'analogy,' in Kaja Silverman's sense of the term, that enable us to recognize the Other as an extension of our own flesh.[40] As Stan Brakhage wrote to Paul Sharits after their fraught collaboration on Brakhage's film *Lovemaking*, 'our quarrels are of that same quality called "family quarrels"; and I realize it is so with most of the film-makers: we have managed, all (or most) of us, to be that close despite the politics which would seek to separate us.' In an ode to the unbroken but unbinding bonds of their friendship, Brakhage concluded that the 'love of an art is very like the love of person, wherein "opposites attract" is surest blessing.'[41]

Chapter summary

The first chapter of the book, 'Saint Barbara: the apocryphal, ecstatic cinema of Barbara Rubin', explores the quixotic life of filmmaker Barbara Rubin, whose double-projection film *Christmas on Earth* (1963) is, I argue, the most sexually explicit film of the 1960s. By charting the filmmaker's startling biographical trajectory from eighteen-year-old filmic prodigy to Hasidic expatriate, this chapter explores the utopian vision of non-hierarchical group sexuality in Rubin's film against the backdrop of her eventual move towards fundamentalism and concomitant renunciation of the New York art world. Though Rubin was a close friend of Jonas Mekas and Andy Warhol, this essay privileges her long and intimate relationship with Allen Ginsberg in order to understand the ways in which different forms of 'queer coupling' and ethnic collectivity significantly influenced not only her film but the social, political, and sexual dynamics of the postwar avant-garde.

The second chapter, 'Andy Warhol, porn realist', explores two of Warhol's most sexually explicit films, *Couch* (1964) and *Blue Movie* (1968), in order to understand how the artist situates sex within capitalism. From the depiction of queer group sex in a film composed of discrete, unconnected reels to the development of a feature-length, commercially exhibited narrative film about heterosexual coupling, Warhol created an archive of sexual perversion that swerves sexuality from its normative aims. Paying close attention to the rare and historically innovative representation of interracial sexual intimacy in *Couch* as well as the emphasis on failure and obsolescence in *Blue Movie*, this chapter considers the way forms of 'dysfunctional' intercourse can deflect or otherwise refuse the ideological interpellation of sexuality.

Firmly committed to the relocation of cinema within the home and use of cinema to develop new ways of seeing, Stan Brakhage forged a truly domestic, personal cinema in startling opposition to the narrative, industrial machine of Hollywood. Yet while Brakhage's re-conception of the expressive capacity of the 'camera eye' constitutes one of the most singular contributions to the evolution of the medium, his resolute emphasis on heterosexuality, marriage and childrearing have made his place in the recent revival of postwar avant-garde cinema contentious. The third chapter, 'Stan Brakhage: acts of seeing' explores the tensions between defamiliarization and documentation generated in the artist's *oeuvre* by his shattering encounters with sex, birth, and death. By exploring the representation of bodies in *Window Water Baby Moving* (1959), *Lovemaking* (1968), and *The Act of Seeing With One's Own Eyes* (1971), this chapter argues that Brakhage's painstaking attempts to cleanse his cinematic style in the face of such transformative acts not only radically transform the artist's conception of embodied vision, but open his cinema up to a profound, queer engagement with otherness.

Chapter 4, 'Carolee Schneemann: meat joys', situates Schneemann's evolving notion of flesh as 'meat' within her articulation of a radical feminist politics deeply attuned to the stakes and limitations of heterosexual romance and collaboration. Beginning with an analysis of her collaboration with Robert Morris on *Site* (1964), this chapter goes on to consider Schneemann's individually authored film and performance work, as well as the personal relationships that both sustained and inspired it. Dissatisfied with the representation of her lovemaking in Brakhage's films *Loving* (1957) and *Cat's Cradle* (1959), Schneemann set out to make her own filmic document of the sex act, which culminated in the film *Fuses* (1964–1967). Breaking free of the constraints of male authorship with *Fuses*, as she had done in her groundbreaking performance piece *Meat Joy* (1964), Schneemann developed a complex ontology of the flesh to negotiate the violent instrumentalization of bodies by the imperial, patriarchal state. Delving into Schneemann's poignant personal reflections on her decades-long relation-ships with Jane and Stan Brakhage, this chapter explores the key artistic texts that emerged from, or partially in response to, these intimate friendships. In doing so, it investigates the way inter-personal struggles regarding the gendered division of labor, the respect accorded female artists, and the representation of the female body were profoundly constitutive of Schneemann's aesthetic and political project.

In the fifth chapter, 'Yoko Ono's body count,' I examine several films and performance pieces by Yoko Ono, including *Cut Piece* (1964), *No. 4* (a.k.a. *Bottoms* 1966), *Bed-In For Peace* (1969), and *Fly* (1970), the last two of which she made with her partner John Lennon. Examining the relationship between the perverse deployment of the gaze in Ono's work, and the body disciplined by the cinematic apparatus or performance injunctive, this chapter explores the political implications of Ono's strategic use of sadomasochistic structures of engagement. By looking at the ways in which the still, vulnerable, assaulted, or prone body is figured as a site of resistance within her work, this chapter investigates Ono's subversion of the gendered and racialized dynamics of look-ing. Finally, this chapter considers how the perception of Ono's own identity as an Asian female intoned both the racial politics and reception of her films and performances during the Vietnam era.

Like Yoko Ono, Paul Sharits was originally associated with Fluxus although he became better known for his 'structural' films and pioneering moving-image installations. The final chapter, 'Paul Sharits, beyond the pleasure principle,' focuses on several of Sharits's 'flicker' films, including *Piece Mandala / End War* (1966), *T,O,U,C,H,I,N,G* (1968), and *Epileptic Seizure Comparison* (1976), in which the abstract language of light and color associated with flicker is in-terspersed with explicit representational imagery of the convulsive body. By juxtaposing medical footage of eye surgery and epileptic seizures with images of coitus, self-mutilation and attempted suicide, Sharits puts typical strategies of structural film into productive dialogue with more taboo or pornographic representations of the body. In doing so, he forges a cinema practice based on a thoroughly corporealized notion of vision, in which the film apparatus is used to mimic the physiological responses of the body in pain. By contextualizing Sharits's aggressive fantasies of 'cinema touching' within his own acute experi-ence of suffering, occasioned through loss, physical assault, chronic anxiety, and depression, this chapter explores the way in which Sharits's cinema employs 'isotropic' film structure to manage the overstimulation associated with carnal pleasure and pain.

Notes on methodology

This study attempts to account for the complex, contradictory representations of the body in American experimental film of the 1960s and 70s by using formal analysis, historically informed discourses of pornography and censorship, theories of gender and sexuality, biographical information, and archival research. It also, however, strives to provide an account of what it *feels* like to watch films that have been designed to turn on, frustrate, and discipline the spectator. I recognize that my own attempts to experience the past anew through the medium of my own body are inevitably impregnated with what Walter Benjamin describes as the 'presence of the now.'[42] Indeed, it would have been impossible to imaginatively relive these marginalized but vital moments in the history of postwar art and cinema without present-day encounters (with other bodies, other artworks, other corporeal and political events) that made these artifacts come alive in urgent ways. If I have not labored under the illusion that my efforts to illuminate these films will guarantee an image of the past 'the way it really was,'[43] it is because my aim has always been to learn from these films through a process of empathy.

In his prophetic 'Theses on the Philosophy of History,' Walter Benjamin explains how affective collisions of the past with the present crystallize in the sudden, arresting appearance of what he describes as 'monads.' These monads enable us to 'blast a specific era out of the homogeneous course of history'[44] and thereby 'seize hold of a memory as it flashes up at a moment of danger.'[45] Yet such an approach to history is also, as Benjamin reminds us in a less quoted phrase, a 'process of *empathy* whose original is the indolence of the heart, *acedia*, which despairs of grasping and holding the genuine historical image as it flares up briefly.'[46] If to think historically is, at some level, to empathize, then Benjamin warns us that it is also to risk our own dissolution. What these films can teach us – about love, sex, intimacy, pain, and loss – threatens to undo and unmake us. But they can also teach and inspire us to find more creative, empathetic ways of living and loving.

Notes

1 David James, 'Underground Film: Leaping from the Grave,' in *Allegories of Cinema: American Film in the* Sixties (Princeton, NJ: Princeton University Press, 1989), p. 125.
2 Ibid., p. 127.
3 Judith Halberstam, *The Queer Art of Failure* (Durham, NC: Duke University Press, 2011).
4 Ibid., pp. 2, 3.

5 See Linda Williams's definition of obscenity and 'on-scenity' in 'Porn Studies: Proliferating Pornographies On/Scene: An Introduction,' in *Porn Studies*, ed. Linda Williams (Durham, NC: Duke University Press, 2004), pp. 1–23.

6 Kaja Silverman, *Flesh of My Flesh* (Stanford, CA: Stanford University Press, 2009), p. 26.

7 Chris Kraus, *I Love Dick*, Semiotext(e) Native Agents Series (Cambridge, MA: The MIT Press, 2006), p. 239.

8 Maurice Merleau-Ponty, *The Visible and the Invisible*, ed. Claude Lefort, trans. Alphonso Lingis (Evanston, IL: Northwestern University Press, 1968). The term that Merleau-Ponty develops is the 'flesh of the world.'

9 Charles Altieri, 'The Sensuous Dimension of Literary Experience: An Alternative to Materialist Theory,' *New Literary History*, 38 (2007): 71–98; and Charles Altieri, 'Contingency and Sociality in American Poetry of the Fifties,' in *Freedom and Form: Essays in Contemporary American Poetry*, ed. Esther Giger and Agnieska Salska (Lodz: Wydawnictwo University Press, 1998), pp. 27–35.

10 This phrase was famously used by Justice Potter Stewart to describe his threshold for pornography in the obscenity case *Jacobellis v. Ohio* (1964). Jon Lewis, *Hollywood v. Hard Core: How the Struggle over Censorship Saved the Modern Film Industry* (New York: New York University Press, 2000), pp. 127–134.

11 Linda Williams, *Hard Core: Power, Pleasure and the 'Frenzy of the Visible'* (Berkeley, CA: University of California Press, 1989).

12 Jack Smith, '"The Adorable and Pasty Creatures...": Journal Notes on the Uses of Pornography,' in *Wait for Me at the Bottom of the Pool: The Writings of Jack Smith*, ed. J. Hoberman and Edward Leffingwell (New York: High Risk Books, 1997), pp. 77–80; p. 78.

13 Jonas Mekas, 'Baudelairean Cinema,' in *Movie Journal: The Rise of New American Cinema* (New York: Collier Books, 1972), pp. 85–86.

14 J. Hoberman, 'Crimson Creatures: The Case Against *Flaming Creatures*,' in *On Jack Smith's Flaming Creatures (and Other Secret Flix of Cinemaroc)* (New York: Granary Books, 2001), pp. 35–50.

15 See Juan A. Suárez, *Bike Boys, Drag Queens and Superstars: Avant-Garde, Mass Culture, and Gay Identities in the 1960s Underground Cinema* (Bloomington, IN: Indiana University Press, 1996); Hoberman, *On Jack Smith's Flaming Creatures*; Dominic Johnson, *Glorious Catastrophe: Jack Smith, Performance and Visual Culture* (Manchester: Manchester University Press, 2012); Edward Leffingwell, Carole Kismaric, and Marvin Heiferman, eds, *Flaming Creature: Jack Smith, His Amazing Life and Times* (Long Island City, NY: The Institute for Contemporary Art, P.S. 1 Museum, 1997); and Marc Siegel, 'Documentary That Dare/Not Speak Its Name: Jack Smith's *Flaming Creatures*,' in *Between the Sheets, In the Streets: Queer, Lesbian, Gay Documentary* (Minneapolis, MN: University of Minnesota Press, 1997).

16 Sigmund Freud, *Three Essays on the Theory of Sexuality*, trans. James Strachey (New York: Basic Books, 2000), originally published as Sigmund Freud, *Drei Abhandlungen zur Sexualtheorie* (Frankfurt am Main: Fischer, 1905).

17 Herbert Marcuse, *Eros and Civilization: A Philosophical Inquiry into Freud* [1955] (Abingdon: Routledge, 1998).

18 J. Hoberman, 'The Making of *Flaming Creatures*: Up On the Roof' in *On Jack Smith's Flaming Creatures*, pp. 20–33.

19 Paul Arthur, '"A Panorama Compounded of Great Human Suffering and Ecstatic Filmic Representation": Texts on Ken Jacobs,' in *Optic Antics: The Cinema of Ken Jacobs*, ed. Michele Pierson, David E. James, and Paul Arthur (Oxford: Oxford University Press, 2011), pp. 25–37; p. 27.

20 James, *Allegories of Cinema*.

21 Maurice Merleau-Ponty, 'The Intertwining: The Chiasm,' in *The Visible and the Invisible*, p. 139.

22 Ibid., p. 138.

23 Ibid., pp. 141, 143, 138.

24 Amelia Jones, *Body Art/Performing the Subject* (Minneapolis, MN: University of Minnesota Press, 1998), 15, 37.

25 Merleau-Ponty, 'The Intertwining,' pp. 136, 139.

26 In the United States, stag films were made and distributed illegally from the beginning of the twentieth century until their demise in the 1970s. For an explanation of stag, see Linda Williams, 'The Stag Film: Genital Show and Genital Event,' in *Hard Core*, pp. 58–92.

27 Linda Williams, 'Film Bodies: Gender, Genre, and Excess,' in *Film Genre Reader II*, ed. Barry Keith Grant (Austin, TX: University of Texas Press, 1995), pp. 141–159; Carol Clover, *Men, Women and Chain Saws: Gender in Modern Horror Films* (Princeton, NJ: Princeton University Press, 1993).

28 Parker Tyler, 'Underground Infantilism: Surfacing Superstars,' in *Underground Film: A Critical History* (New York: Da Capo Press, 1995), pp. 45–60.

29 Mekas, 'Baudelairean Cinema.'

30 Sally Banes, *Greenwich Village 1963: Avant-Garde Performance and the Effervescent Body* (Durham, NC: Duke University Press, 1993).

31 Ara Osterweil, *Flesh Cinema: The Corporeal Avant-Garde, 1959–1979* (Ann Arbor, MI: UMI Dissertation Services, 2005); Scott MacDonald, *Cinema 16: Documents Toward a History of the Film Society* (Philadelphia, PA: Temple University Press, 2002); David E. James, ed., *To Free the Cinema: Jonas Mekas & The New York Underground* (Princeton, NJ: Princeton University Press, 1992); James, *Allegories of Cinema*.

32 James, *To Free the Cinema*, p. 6.

33 The Film-Makers' Cooperative was founded by Jonas Mekas, Shirley Clarke, Stan Brakhage, Gregory Markopolous and other filmmakers to distribute avant-garde films through a centralized archive.

34 Jonas Mekas, 'First Statement of New American Cinema Group,' in *Film Culture Reader*, ed. P. Adams Sitney (New York: Praeger Publisher, 1970), pp. 79–83, originally published in *Film Culture*, no. 22–23 (Summer 1961).

35 Christian Metz, *The Imaginary Signifier: Psychoanalysis and the Cinema*, trans. Ben Brewster (Bloomington, IN: Indiana University Press, 1986).

36 Jonathan Crary, 'Modernizing Vision,' in *Viewing Positions: Ways of Seeing Film*, ed. Linda Williams (New Brunswick, NJ: Rutgers University Press, 1994), pp. 23–35; p. 34.

37 Laura U. Marks, *The Skin of the Film: Intercultural Cinema, Embodiment, and the Senses* (Durham, NC: Duke University Press, 2000).

38 Sigmund Freud, *Three Essays on the Theory of Sexuality*, in *The Standard Edition of the Complete Psychological Works*, trans. James Strachey, Vol. 7 (London: Hogarth Press, 1953).

39 Leo Bersani, *Is the Rectum a Grave? And Other Essays* (Chicago, IL: University of Chicago Press, 2009).

40 Silverman, *Flesh of My Flesh*, pp. 1–16.

41 Quote from Brakhage, letter to Paul Sharits, April 6, 1974. Brakhage File, Anthology Film Archives.

42 Walter Benjamin, 'Theses on the Philosophy of History,' in *Illuminations: Essays and Reflections*, ed. Hannah Arendt (New York: Schocken Books, 1968), pp. 253–264. In this essay, Benjamin writes that 'History is the subject of a structure whose site is not homologous empty time, but time filled by the presence of the now' (p. 261).

43 Ibid., p. 255.

44 Ibid., p. 263.

45 Ibid., p. 255.

46 Ibid., p. 256. The first italics are mine; the second are Benjamin's.

Saint Barbara: the apocryphal, ecstatic cinema of Barbara Rubin

1

We're in the months of love; I'm seventeen years old. The time of hopes and dreams, as they say – and here I am, getting started – a child touched by the finger of the Muse – excuse me if that's trite – to express my fine beliefs, my yearnings, my feelings, all those things poets know – myself, I call them spring things.

(Arthur Rimbaud, letter to Théodore de Banville, Charleville, May 1870)[1]

I love you, but also isn't it time to discuss our limitlessness?

(Barbara Rubin, letter to Jonas Mekas, New York, June 1966)[2]

Barbara Rubin's notorious 1963 film *Christmas on Earth* may be the most sexually explicit film of the 1960s. It is certainly one of the most stunning. Shot with a borrowed 16mm Bolex camera when Rubin was only seventeen years old, the film transforms the sexual orgy it records into a kaleidoscopic, psychedelic, hallucinatory happening. Originally called *Cocks and Cunts* before being re-titled after a phrase from Arthur Rimbaud's epic poem 'A Season in Hell', *Christmas on Earth* consists of two twenty-nine-minute black-and-white reels projected simultaneously, one inside the other, in order to mimic the frenetic inter-penetration of bodies on screen. Projected through a random assortment of color filters held just in front of the lens, and amplified by an ad-hoc soundtrack culled from any available radio, *Christmas on Earth* detonates the conventional frames of cinema in order to expand the representation of lovemaking beyond its bounds. Pioneering the use of multi-media projection decades before it became the norm in installation art, *Christmas on Art* utilizes its overlapping frames to multiply and fuse the bodies it records. Experiencing this synesthetic burst of erotic energy for the first time when I was Rubin's age when she made it, my body was electrified. Shattered by its outrageous and profoundly contingent depiction of sexuality, I knew for the first time in my life that in the realm of desire anything is possible. For *Christmas on Earth* is not only the quintessence of the 'expanded cinema' practice of the 1960s, but a record of a particular moment in the postwar period when people of various kinds began to explore alternative sexualities in historically unprecedented public venues. This book

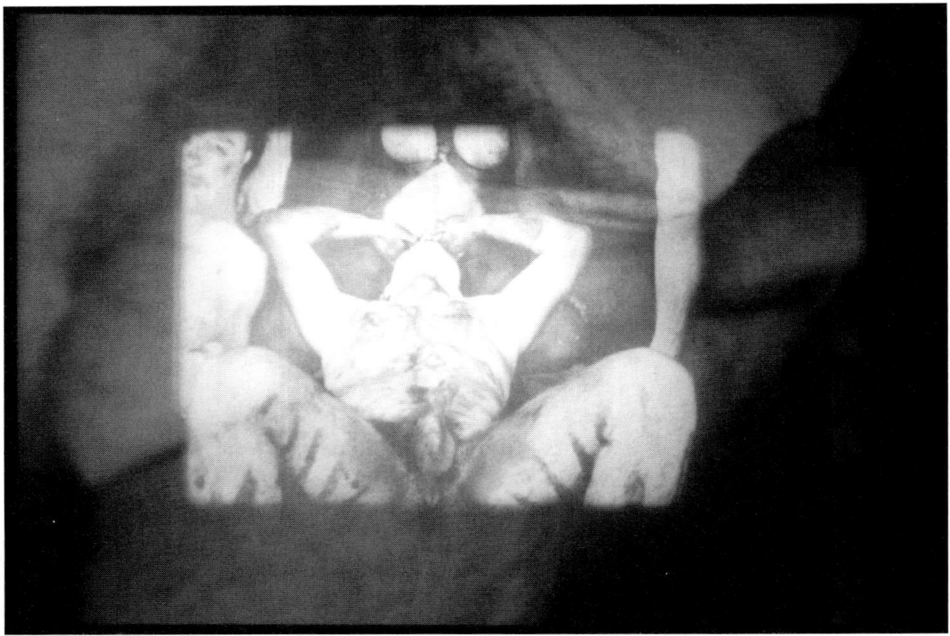

5   Barbara Rubin's use of double projection in *Christmas on Earth* (1963) is the
quintessence of the expanded cinema practice of the 1960s. Here, an orgy of bodies is
superimposed on a close up of ambiguously gendered flesh.

not only explores how both artists and observers were reconfigured by such
ecstatic encounters with film and sexuality, but also theorizes the queer forms
of love and friendship that catalyzed these revelatory experiences.

Like many of the artistic legends from the 1960s, Rubin died young, at age
35. Yet unlike many of the kindred spirits whose early deaths secured their exceptionality, Rubin's death all but erased her. Although she created one of the
most accomplished and innovative artworks of the period, Rubin was neither a
skilled practitioner nor a prolific director. As Stan Brakhage modestly claimed
about himself, Rubin was an 'amateur', in the etymological sense of being a
lover.[3] While Rubin was frequently seen wielding a camera at some of the most
outrageous media events and happenings of the 1960s, there was often no film
in her camera.[4] On the occasions when her camera *was* fully loaded, much
of the footage that has been attributed to Rubin appears strikingly unprofes-
sional – even by experimental film's alternative standards. More a woman with
a movie camera than a committed documentarian, Barbara Rubin nevertheless
transformed the role of the camera from its function as a recording apparatus
to a literal *agit-prop* with which to provoke her audiences. Challenging the presumed distinction between performer and observer, as well as the privileging

of the products of filmmaking above the process of manipulating a camera as a corporeal extension of the body, Rubin re-conceptualized what it meant to be a filmmaker.

Yet had Barbara Rubin never picked up a camera, or appeared in front of one, her contributions to the art, music, and literary countercultures of the time would still be considerable. Rubin's multiple roles an organizer, agitator, and innovator had profound effects on the artistic and musical worlds of the 1960s, and have had a prophetic influence of moving image media and installation practice ever since. Initially through her friendships with Jonas Mekas and Allen Ginsberg, and then through her own determination, Rubin infiltrated the Underground scene, serving as a catalyst for the interaction between individuals whom she regarded as the best minds of her generation.

Although Andy Warhol's first biographer Victor Bockris characterizes Rubin as a 'squirrel extraordinaire,'[5] she was, in fact, much more than a local emissary, in spite of the fact she frequently delivered musical celebrities such as Donovan, Bob Dylan, and the Byrds to Warhol's Factory. Yet although Rubin played an integral role in weaving together the different artistic strands of the 1960s counterculture, she has been virtually omitted from its history. Undoubtedly prey to the general marginalization of female artists decried by Linda Nochlin,[6] Rubin's obscurity is also partially attributable to the unusual circumstances of her biography. From the time of her discovery of Hasidism in the late 1960s to her death in 1980, Barbara Rubin never returned to the ethos of drug experimentation and free love that she previously epitomized. Although she pioneered multimedia, multiple projection extravaganzas decades before this became an art-world norm, Rubin's longing for the immigrant Yiddish culture of her ancestors drew her deeper into the religious traditions of the past. After Rubin severed nearly all of her ties to the New York avant-garde community and moved to a religious community in France in the early 1970s, the threads that tied her so closely to the cultural developments of the 1960s tapered off and eventually unraveled.

Yet the absence of critical attention paid to Rubin also reveals the extent to which Rubin's only known finished film challenges dominant preconceptions about the limits of representation in this period. While the sexually transgressive work of contemporaneous avant-garde filmmakers such as Andy Warhol, Jack Smith, and Kenneth Anger has been salvaged in the queer recuperation of Underground cinema of the 1960s, Rubin's work remains apocryphal. More sexually explicit than either *Flaming Creatures* (Jack Smith, 1963) or *Scorpio Rising* (Kenneth Anger, 1963), both of which were charged with obscenity,[7] *Christmas on Earth* neither suffered nor benefited from the notoriety associated with these films. This essay juxtaposes an analysis of *Christmas on Earth*'s incredibly fluid sexual representations with an investigation of the off-screen forms of queer coupling that inspired and were catalyzed by it in order to understand how truly expanded forms of cinema exist on a continuum with other forms of expanded relationality.

To Barbara With Love

As I write this, I am sitting here surrounded by a pile of books about to topple over where I have stacked them. I have scoured these materials for any reference about *her*. But she exists only in fragments. A glimpse of her, here and there. Mostly there. Massaging Dylan's curls on the back of the *Bringing it all Back Home* (1965) album cover[8] or hovering on the stairs in front of the Royal Albert Hall in London, where she organized the landmark International Poetry Congress in June 1965. I have a vision of Barbara standing behind the big boys, looming on the side of a photograph, a camera covering her face like a mask. She has been pushed aside to make way for the giants of poetry and prose, the *geniuses*. Or maybe not pushed aside, maybe self-effaced. Like the skull in Hans

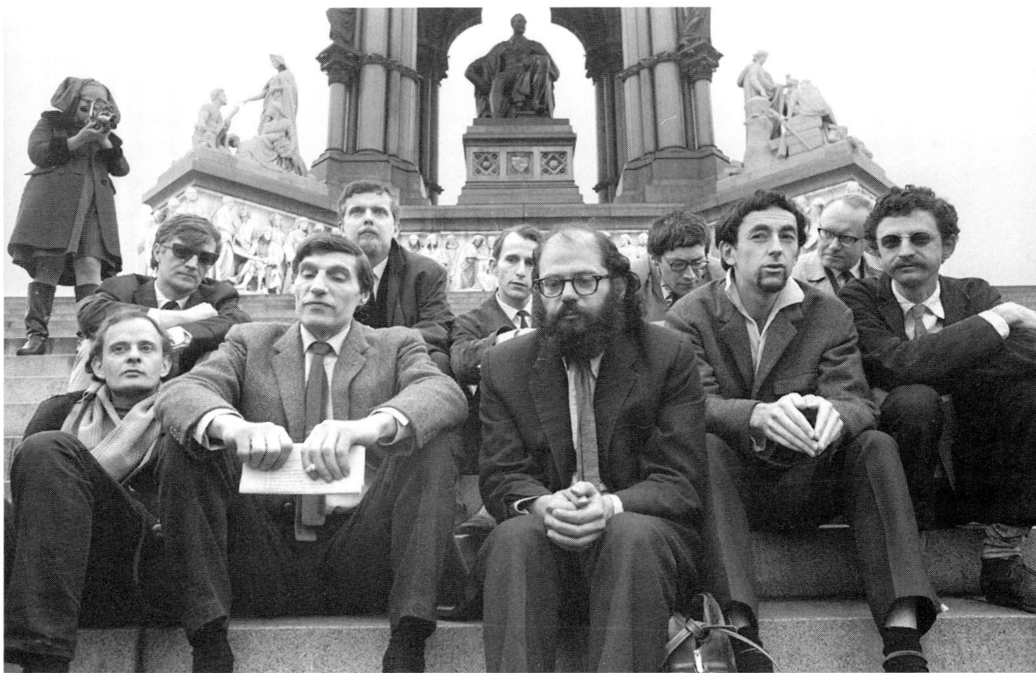

6   Barbara Rubin hovers with camera over the ambassadors of mid-century poetry. Back row, from left to right: Adrian Mitchell, Anselm Hollo, Marcus Field, Michale Horovitz, Ernst Jandl. Front row: Harry Fainlight, Alex Trocchi, Allen Ginsberg, John Esam, Dan Richter. Rubin organized the landmark International Poetry Congress and Feast on June 11, 1965, at the Royal Albert Hall in London.

Holbein's painting 'The Ambassadors,' she is the stain.[9] I no longer know what is real and what I have imagined, so I return to the pile of books to search for some confirmation of my vision. It collapses.

Each of the books is threaded with neon post-its, a scholar's version of Gretel's trail of cookie crumbs. They mark places where she is mentioned – always briefly: the 'filmmaker Barbara Rubin,' Allen Ginsberg's 'sometimes girlfriend,' the inspiration for Ophelia in Dylan's 'Desolation Row.' If Barbara Rubin is mentioned at all in these hefty homages, her life is reduced to a few swift strokes – repeated over and over again in the different versions. Drugs: many. Obsessions: Ginsberg. Downfall: Hasidism. Always, Ginsberg and Hasidism. Rejected by one, she turns to the other. Or, in alternate versions, her growing interest in Hasidism turns Ginsberg off. One serves as a remedy for the other, but it is a remedy that only makes the patient sicker. Her death in childbirth in 1980 proves the disease incurable.

Alternately, Rubin is the link between others to whom more attention is paid. She is a conduit. *So-and-so* met *so-and-so* through Barbara Rubin. And not just any old *so-and-so*. Dylan and Warhol. Warhol and the Velvets. These were not mere introductions, the busybody work of an amateur matchmaker. In another life, on the steppes of White Russia, Barbara Rubin must have been a *shadchen*.

Her image haunts me. Donning a turban over her shaved head, draped in flowing rags, and aglitter with bangles, Rubin was a hippie before it was acceptable or recognizable to be one. She is one part saint and one part babushka in Mekas's *Walden* (*Diaries, Notes, and Sketches*, US, 1969), her head covered by some sort of *schmata*, tied up by a long checkered scarf and crowned with a pair of sunglasses. Again, she is surrounded by the ambassadors: Allen Ginsberg, Peter Orlovsky, Ed Sanders, Tuli Kupferberg, Gerard Malanga, Andy Warhol. Barbara looks down, laughs, talks, looks away, listens. You can't hear what she is saying, but then another 'voice' steps in, filling the place of the absent one. 'It was Barbara who got us all together,' Mekas's inter-title informs us, and on this note, she vanishes.

Rubin also appears in Warhol's *Screen Tests* for the requisite three minutes. The *Screen Tests* are like an alternative *Who's Who of America*, circa 1965, but the personalities he catalogued are of course more important than the forgotten names in the official version. More than anything, this is undeniable proof that she existed. But it is also evidence of how she disappeared. Her face emerges – a pretty, somewhat plain face – but it blinks away into oblivion as the ghostly white leader overcomes her features. Is this where she has gone – into oblivion?

I long for sound, to hear her voice. I look up addresses. I write letters. I make phone calls. Not everyone wants to reminisce with a strange academic about lost youth. 'What was her voice like?' I ask. 'How did you know her?' 'Did she sleep with men? Women?' 'What were your impressions?' Unwittingly, you pick at the scab of memory. Your youth is an insult. You're a schmuck, a

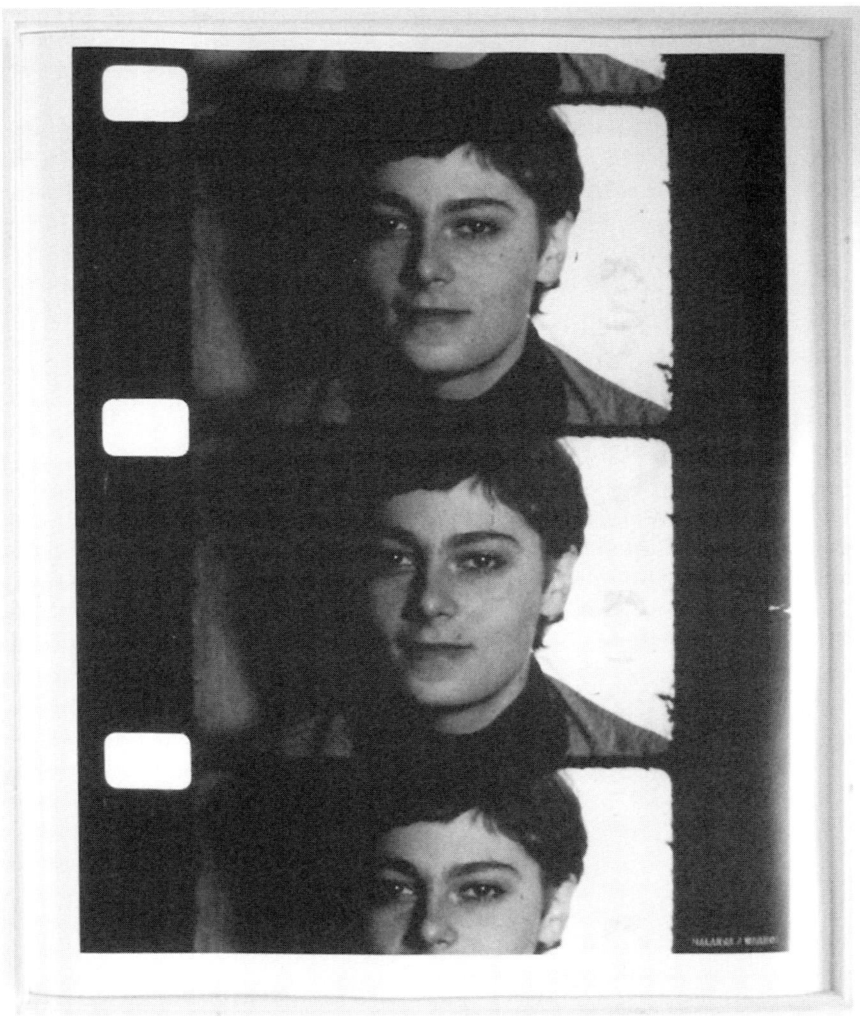

7   Andy Warhol. *Screen Test: Barbara Rubin*, 1965.

fool, an ass; you want to know the details of dead people's sex lives. Sometimes they retaliate. *In the 1960s, people fucked; didn't anyone tell you? Who do you think you are? What are you after? How* old *are you? Have you ever even seen a movie?* Always answer politely, like you don't get they are being rude. Unless you can make a joke.

'Like a yenta from Queens,' film critic Amy Taubin finally describes it – *her voice.* 'When I first met her, she was gabbing on the phone at the Filmmakers

Coop with her hair in rollers.'[10] Later, I hear Rubin's voice in Mekas's recent tribute to her, *To Barbara With Love* (US, 2007), a short film comprising snippets of ancient footage: Rubin swimming at the beach, 'filming' a young child in an apartment, dancing trance-like in some kind of street gathering or protest, wading into a public fountain fully clothed, riding passenger-side in a car, her fingers strumming her bare knees, her usually covered short hair exposed and windblown. She looks like a real girl here, a teenager.

Each 'genius' seems to have constructed Barbara Rubin in his own image. For Mekas, she was a saint. His was the post-asylum nest into which she fell, after being institutionalized as a teenager, and from which she later sprung, transformed from an overweight, troubled child into an Underground mover-and-shaker. Everybody says, 'Jonas loved her.' Some people say she took advantage of his affection for her. 'Did she love him?' The answer is unclear. It certainly *seems* as if she did, signing nearly every one of her letters to him, 'Love love love.' Is this part of the historian's job – to assess true love?

When you watch *To Barbara With Love*, you realize it is a love letter sent back in time; its heart still throbs in its mouth. In the film, they seem like a couple; it is the 1960s, it is warm, they are young. Jonas's face is taut and angular, his hair long, smooth and slightly greasy. She is *his* discovery, *his* angel, an unlikely Lolita, whose sexual provocations seduced older, more experienced men. And like Lolita, Barbara grew up, had kids, got fat, and became unrecognizable to the people who had been infatuated with her. She began the 1960s ahead of her time; she would end them behind it. And then she would die.

But there are always the cynics, who see ambition where others see love, who recall calculating selfishness where others describe immense generosity. I want to dismiss them, but their testimony is often the most compelling. Shit talk always is. Anyway, what do I know? I wasn't there. The past is not all roses – not even the 1960s. Tell yourself: The past reeked as noxiously as the present. She was an opportunist, a starfucker, a p.r. genius, out for nothing but herself, an appropriator, a manipulator. She took superimposition from Jerry Jofen, who couldn't afford to shoot with fresh film, and who believed that as long as you shot over the original footage in the same drug-addled state of euphoria, there would be an organic continuity between the layers of imagery.[11] And as for the spontaneous, 'live' radio soundtrack of *Christmas on Earth*: that was nothing Ken Jacobs hadn't done first in *Blonde Cobra* (1963).[12]

Everyone wants to talk about Barbara's Jewishness. Ask a few questions and before you know it, they are onto the notorious conversion to Hasidism. And once they get going, it's impossible to bring them back – to film, to the 1960s, to Warhol, to Ginsberg, to the cool Barbara who knew everyone, went everywhere, and organized everything. Secular Jews love to *kvetch* about religious ones; it's our favorite hobby. But it's the one thing I am not interested in; it's too sensational; it's not the point.

I collect the references to her stardom eagerly, not like a zealot, but like a simple fan, seeking her secular traces. Oh, but how I would swoon over one of those *schmatas*, to coil around my finger around a strand of the hair she repeatedly clipped off! But that would be too much. I am entering the dangerous territory of relics and saints. I am not a worshipper of fingernails and teeth. Here are the facts.

Sexual outlaw

A middle-class Jewish girl from Queens, Rubin came to the Underground film community in New York as a teenager. She had just been released from a juvenile correction facility for her vast experimentation with drugs that began after swallowing a handful of the diet pills that she had been prescribed to manage her weight.[13] Such treatment was not unusual at the time; middle- and upper-class families often tried to 'correct' the non-normative behavior of their queer offspring with psychiatric interventions. Spirited girls and homosexual boys were particularly vulnerable to these interventions. Being overweight and eccentric landed Barbara Rubin in an institution, where she, like Warhol Superstars Brigid Berlin and Edie Sedgwick, became addicted to amphetamines and other narcotics.

Refusing to assume a more conventional form, Barbara was sent away to cure her of her idiosyncrasies. It would not take long to realize that the cure had failed. Through her uncle, William Rubin – who then managed the Gramercy Arts Theater, where many avant-garde film screenings were held – the recently liberated teen was introduced to Jonas Mekas, the most important advocate of Underground cinema as well as the founder of the Film-Makers' Cooperative and, later, the Anthology Film Archives. Mekas hired Barbara to assist at the Coop.

In 1963, Rubin borrowed Mekas's crank-up 16mm Bell and Howell silent film camera. Over the course of a few days, she filmed *Christmas on Earth* in Tony Conrad and John Cale's Ludlow Street apartment[14] with Gerard Malanga, Arnold Rockwood (a.k.a. Pasty Arnold of *Flaming Creatures* fame), Johnny 'Jackie' Foster, a woman named Barbara Gladstone, and possibly a woman named Debbie Feiner.[15] According to playwright Richard Foreman, who, along with his then-wife Amy Taubin, was an intimate friend and early supporter of Rubin, *Christmas on Earth* was originally shown unedited. Originally featuring long, 'poignant' takes of lovemaking between painted and costumed figures as they fornicated in nearly every position imaginable, *Christmas on Earth* was continually re-edited for each performance. Foreman maintains that Rubin's exposure to the rapid montage of Gregory Markopoulos's films inspired her to slice the original into dynamic fragments that, from his perspective, enhanced the psychedelic effects of the film while diminishing its emotional affect. Although critics praised the re-edited film for its virtuoso, seemingly deliberate juxtapositions, her close friend Rosebud maintains that Rubin, bare-breasted and high on amphetamines, actually randomly parsed the film, dumped the fragments into a wastebasket, and mindlessly reconstructed it. Rubin's euphoric description of her method of production verifies Rosebud's account:

> A week out of nine months of mental hospital indoctrination and I meet Jonas and he gives me a camera and film love and trust and I shoot up down around back over under and shoot over and over speedily slow back and front end, the subject chosen by the creeping souls of the moment cocks and cunts, love supreme can believe to fantasy I then spent 3 months chopping the hours and hours of film up into a basket and then toss and toss flip and toss and one by one absently enchanted destined to put it together and separate onto two different reels and then project one reel half the size inside the other reel and then show it and someone tells me what a good editing job I did…[16]

In *Christmas on Earth*, at least five nude bodies are seen engaged in a variety of different sexual acts, including heterosexual genital penetration, homosexual anal sex, fellatio, cunnilingus, and masturbation. While Rubin's spontaneity in the filming and in the editing processes comes through in the film's unusual energy, it is nonetheless hard to fathom that the serendipitous juxtapositions of bodies were not more deliberately choreographed. Impossible corporeal fusions evolve and disappear through overlapping fields of illuminated color. Through Rubin's evocative use of superimposition, faces overlap with genitals, entwined couples penetrate vaginal and anal orifices, and corporeal appendages from one reel become entangled with limbs from the other. Enacted within, between and upon the separate reels, sex transcends the frame, moving the viewer towards a sense of love's limitlessness. Such dialectical images of lovemaking – in which close-ups of body parts from one reel prick and permeate wider shots of entwined bodies from the other – are among the extraordinary effects of the film's superimposed double projection, whose form critic Daniel Belasco compares to Josef Albers's *Homage to the Square* series.[17] As a result of the film's square within a square format, bodies exceed their spatial and temporal limits to merge with and penetrate each other in a writhing palimpsest of flesh. Transformed by high-contrast body paint into positive and negative forms, bodies are reshaped and reborn. Released from their anatomical vessels, the energies of the flesh deliquesce in hermaphroditic rapture. Dissolving the boundaries between male and female, subject and object, record and performance, and real and imaginary space, *Christmas on Earth* creates a kinesthetic spectacle whose startling effects are entirely contingent upon the unrepeatable fortuities of each screening. How fitting that such boundless bliss cannot be contained within the film canister.

Studying the reels individually on an ancient Steenbeck flatbed editor at the old Film-Makers' Cooperative, I can't help but feel like a surgeon partitioning

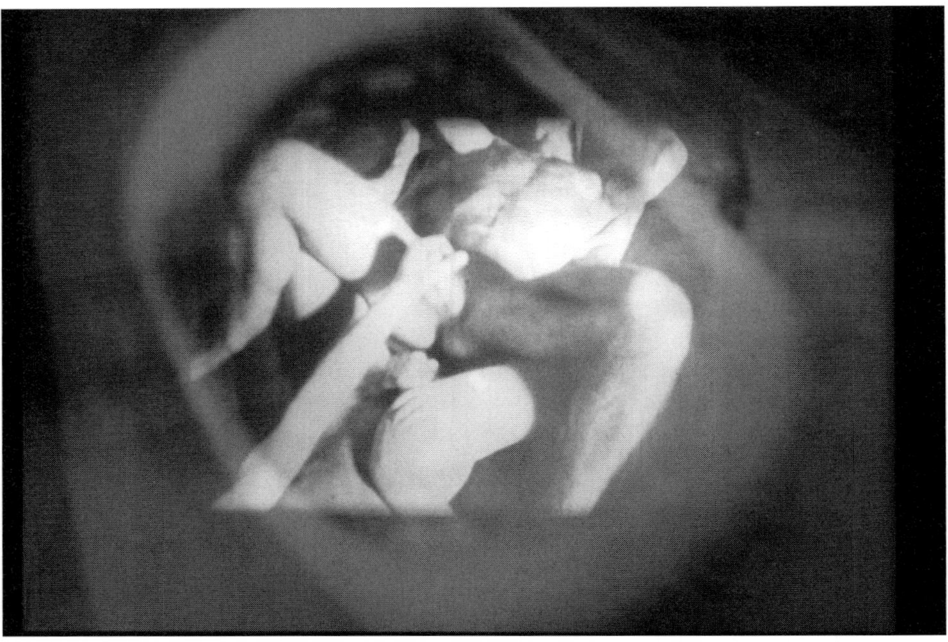

8   Entangled bodies from one reel penetrate an open mouth in the other in Barbara Rubin's *Christmas on Earth* (1963).

the impossible embrace of conjoined twins. Subjected to such cruel exposure, the 'disjunctive liquidity'[18] of the body resolves, its mysteries dissected. Liquescent forms coagulate; subjects re-assume recognizable forms. Significant differences between Reels A and B emerge that are obscured when the film is seen through Rubin's preferred method of double projection. Reel A, for instance, privileges corporeal fragments much more than Reel B, which is dominated by images of complete bodies. Commencing with a shot of a non-erect penis as it bobs up and down, Reel A delivers a startling sequence of extreme close-ups, including the face of a woman screaming (silently) in ecstasy, fingers spreading open the lips of a vagina, an anus puckering open and shut, and a penis as it grows tumescent. True to Rubin's original title, 'Cocks and Cunts,' Reel A presents a ravishing array of genitals. Vaginas and anuses are repeatedly spread open, as if inviting the camera and the observer to penetrate these tempting apertures.

Orifices, however, are not the only organs that shift shape in *Christmas on Earth*'s frenzied game of hide and seek. Presaging the work of film and video artist Vito Acconci, who recorded himself with his penis hidden between his thighs in a series aptly titled *Conversions* (1971), *Christmas on Earth* subjects

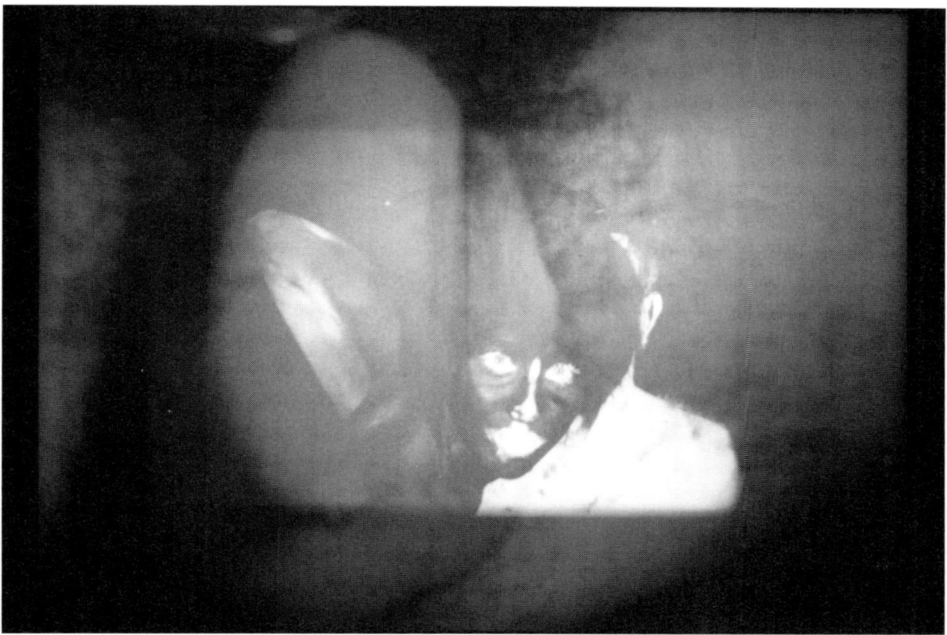

Originally titled *Cocks and Cunts*, *Christmas on Earth* (Barbara Rubin, 1963) displays images of both male and female genitals even as it resists what Herbert Marcuse described as 'genital supremacy.'   9

the male genitals to a sequence of dramatic transformations. In addition to presenting the marvels of swelling and diminishing erections, *Christmas on Earth* also includes images of genital masquerade. At a certain point in the film, a man pulls his testicles over his cock, hiding it beneath the bulge of his scrotum, before allowing it to pop out a few seconds later. As with the myriad images of spread orifices, this gesture is an insatiable swallowing, the body devouring itself.

At the end of the first reel, the camera extricates itself from the tangle of body parts to focus on a group shot of the performers, lavished in body paint. The main female character is painted almost entirely black, except for white regions covering her breasts and stomach, which transform her torso into a spectral mask. The four members of her male harem, who sit surrounding her on the floor, are painted white. Situating its sexual adventures in the ritual practices of the primitive 'Other,' Rubin's use of body-paint makes it difficult to distinguish between the participants, let alone decipher which body part belongs to whom.

Rather than inviting the spectator to identify with any of these performers, *Christmas on Earth* privileges the viewer's transitive, fleeting attractions to overlapping corporeal surfaces and impossible fusions of the flesh. At one point in the first reel, the camera rhythmically zooms in and out as the lips of a vagina are pulled open and shut. Scholars Sally Banes and David James have both articulated the ways in which Rubin's use of double projection simulates the act of sexual penetration.[19] What has not been noted is the way in which the thrusting motion of the camera acts as a surrogate for the viewer by enabling the desired penetration of the on-screen bodies. In this intensifying 'frenzy of the visible,'[20] Rubin's characteristically wild camera movements not only mimic the performer's corporeal immersion in the sexual act, but facilitate a nearly tactile interaction between the observer-participant and the screen. Like an enthralled lover, Rubin's camera pans and swerves, enters and retreats. As the first reel ends in a blur of flickering white blotches, the participants wave at the camera, breaking the established Hollywood taboo against directly addressing either the apparatus or the implied audience. Addressing us directly, the sexual players in *Christmas on Earth* do not merely acknowledge the artifice of their performance, but implicitly invite us to join their ecstatic masquerade. Yet even as they bid their audience farewell, and thereby recognize the temporal confines of their own performance – after all, the reel must end, 'Christmas' cannot last forever – their gesture opens the film outward, beyond the borders of the film frame towards the endlessly renewable off-screen participation of the audience. Marking its own limits as a point of departure for more limitless explorations of relationality, *Christmas on Earth* transforms the transitory pleasures experienced by a group of friends on a few fleeting days in 1963 into an invitation for its viewers to practice erotic boundlessness.

The epilogue of the first reel is the subject of the second reel. Panning over the supine figure of the lacquered woman, Rubin's camera, like Willard Maas's in *Geography of the Body* (1943) and Yoko Ono's in *Fly* (1970), explores the body as geographical terrain, while simultaneously insisting upon sexual congress as a rapturous game of role-playing. Through the de-familiarizing effects of paint, bodies become inscrutable juxtapositions of hill and valley, positive and negative space. Peering out from an inky expanse of torso, breasts become eyes, and the sensuous rolls of the stomach grin like a Cheshire cat. Although Reel B includes close-up images of body parts, it is significantly more oriented towards the representation of whole bodies and the performance of recognizable albeit taboo sexual acts. Whereas Reel A creates the impression of interpenetrating body parts largely through the technique of superimposition, Reel B offers diverse tableaus of non-simulated sex. Through double projection and superimposition, bodies blossom, fuse, and disappear. As Banes has observed, these techniques produce 'a seemingly endless array of breasts and penises, vulvas and exploring fingers – enough to belong to a crowd.'[21]

Like Eadweard Muybridge's late nineteenth-century chrono-photography, *Christmas on Earth* documents the metamorphoses of bodies engaged in various forms of 'locomotion.' Yet whereas Muybridge excluded the body's involuntary reactions to sexual stimulation from his compendium of corporeal motion, Rubin explores both voluntary and involuntary gestures of bodies engaged in a spectrum of sexual acts. At times, the performers in *Christmas* ostentatiously pose for the camera, as when the woman squeezes the folds of her stomach into a smile, or when one man spreads open the cheeks of his ass while lying with his legs spread above his head. At other times, however, the bodies in *Christmas on Earth* abstain from theatrical gestures, and instead permit the audience to glimpse unstaged, involuntary expressions of corporeal pleasure. At one moment, for example, ejaculate rushes from a man's trembling penis following a rather frenzied display of masturbation and anal sex between two male partners. While such 'confessional' moments suggest the authenticity of the enacted pleasures, they exist on a continuum with the film's exploration of sexuality as performance.

Instead of privileging this moment of corporeal 'truth' over the manifold displays of unverifiable sexual pleasure in the film, as hard-core porn films would begin to do a decade later, Rubin treats male sexual climax as only one of the myriad possibilities of bodily ecstasy. Instead of culminating the erotic explorations in *Christmas on Earth* with this shot, Rubin insists upon the continuity rather than the cessation of sexual pleasure implied by orgasm, by immediately cutting to images of undiminished sexual plenitude. Although shots of male orgasm would not dominate the representation of sexual pleasure until the explosion of hard-core pornography in 1972,[22] as a hard-core film *avant la lettre*, *Christmas on Earth* resists the kind of teleological impulse that would circumscribe later forms of visual pornography.

Porn scholar Linda Williams has argued that Muybridge's studies of human motion fetishize the female body through the addition of superfluous props that insist upon the constructed status of femininity.[23] Comparing Muybridge's photographs of women and men, Williams argues that male nudity is treated as natural or self-evident, while Muybridge's representation of female nudity is over-saturated with narrative meaning. Whereas male bodies are generally displayed without adornment, and are seen engaged in banal activities such as walking, catching, and throwing, women are often posed in intimate rituals of dressing and undressing, caressing and flirting. Frequently draped in diaphanous veils and accompanied by unnecessary props, Muybridge's women engage in primitive forms of striptease that both presuppose and *implant* the perceived artifice of the female gender.[24] Muybridge's visual construction of sexual difference, Williams argues, pre-structures the fetishized representation of women in feature-length narrative and pornographic film.

Like Muybridge, Rubin relies heavily on veils and other types of costumes that simultaneously mask and reveal the human figure. However, rather than merely ornamenting the female body, Rubin insists that masculinity too is a form of masquerade. Transformed into erotic objects through costume and make-up, here the male performers occupy what is typically considered the 'feminine' position by rendering their bodies serviceable for penetration. While critic Amy Taubin has observed that the 'dilemma' of *Christmas on Earth* 'is maternity and its place in a definition of female sexuality,'[25] the film as compellingly presents the related desire of the male to open himself and his body. In spite of the copious images of male genitalia, the structuring desire of the film is the ontology of the orifice, the urge to be spread, penetrated and occupied. In *Christmas on Earth*, binary oppositions cease to obtain as the relationship between anatomical difference and prescribed sexual roles collapses in an orgy of fluid exchanges.

As Sally Banes has argued, Rubin's creation of 'a fantastical, Orientalist sexual space' enables the white woman, 'recast as a woman of color,' to be 'sexually available in a way that white women are not supposed to be.'[26] Freed from the sexual guilt historically affixed to white womanhood, here woman partakes in the giving and receiving of a host of sexual favors without suffering the attendant social consequences of perceived promiscuity. Similarly, the men in Rubin's film pursue their own expansive sexuality. Painted to resemble primitive creatures, the men alternate between performing heterosexual and homosexual acts. Taking advantage of the widespread cultural double standard that persistently accepts provocative images of 'native' sexuality while prohibiting images of Western or Caucasian nudity, *Christmas on Earth* proffers the perceived 'innocence' of the native sexual encounter as one of many roles that can be taken up in the erotic adventure.

In addition to fetishizing the racial or ethnic Other, Rubin shamelessly objectifies the female body. Yet far from attesting to any essentialist notion of the hyper-sexuality of indigenous culture or femininity, the various masquerades in *Christmas on Earth* suggest the ways in which sex and gender always already involve being-as-performance. Several times during the film, the woman's body 'becomes configured as an abstraction of a face – her breasts become eyes, her pubis a mouth.'[27] Whereas the woman's actual face is transformed into a mask by the decorative paint, her sexual organs are presented as a substitute for the defining features of her visage. Like René Magritte's painting *The Rape* (*Le Viol*, 1934), Rubin's reconfiguration of the female body as face reduces woman to a notion of pure carnality at the same time that it analogizes the female genitals to an all-consuming, insatiable orifice. However, unlike the misogynist trope of the 'vagina dentata,' which conflates the mouth and the female genitals as a response to the male's fear of castration by the woman,[28] Rubin's visual conjunction of these two orifices suggests the polymorphous pleasures of eccentric embodiment. Since, as Banes observes, the female 'body itself has oxymoronically become a mask,' it can deflect the penetrating gaze of the spectator even as the camera 'unmasks' the body's most private parts.[29]

In Rubin's film, sexuality is never associated with violence or violation, even as bodies are exchanged between multiple partners. Much as in Jack Smith's *Flaming Creatures*, the outrageously costumed players in *Christmas on Earth* express conventionally taboo sexual desires through the use of both racial and sexual masquerade. Like Andy Warhol's *Couch* (1964), which exhibits a range of homosexual and heterosexual encounters on the eponymous piece of Factory furniture, *Christmas on Earth* queers sex by demonstrating how its infinitely unruly pleasures shatter the distinctions between bodies and genders. Yet unlike Warhol's *Couch*, whose constant exchange of sexual partners suggests the extension of the capitalist marketplace into the private sphere, as I discuss in the following chapter, Rubin's intimation of a pre-capitalist ritualistic domain of pleasure imagines a sexual utopia unpolluted by the political economy of late capitalism.

As David James and Sally Banes have argued, the projection technique of *Christmas on Earth* results in an inter-penetration that is analogous to the sex act itself. James has noted both Rubin's struggle as a female filmmaker in a cinematic vanguard largely dominated by men, and the way in which this struggle

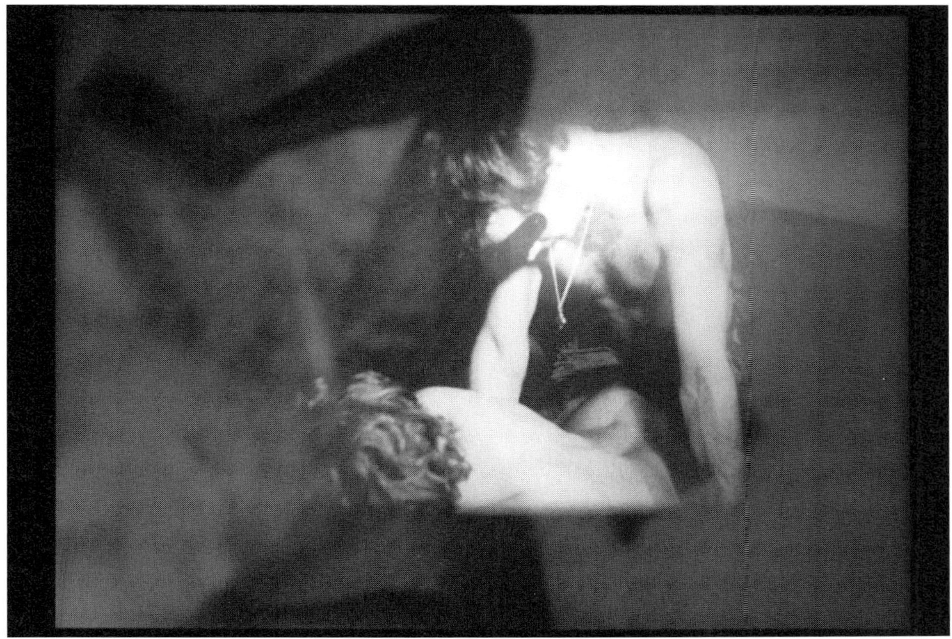

Two men have sex over a palimpsest of other ambiguous bodies in *Christmas on Earth*   **10**
(Barbara Rubin, 1963). Through its use of costume and body paint, the film presents
both femininity and masculinity as gender masquerades.

is allegorized formally through the 'labial' inter-penetration of Rubin's double projection. James writes,

> Figuring female bi-labialism both in its representation of the vagina and in the intercourse of one screen with other, it [*Christmas on Earth*] suggests allegorical readings of image production and re-production. It polemically asserts the double-ness, the plurality, moving towards the polymorphous-ness, of the female against the fetishizing of the male that is figured, filmically, in the phallomorphism of single projection and, socially, in the circle of filmmakers associated with the New York Cooperative at that time.[30]

Despite the undeniable difficulty of being a female filmmaker in a male-dominated experimental film community, the critical tendency to employ essentialist or anatomical notions of femininity, including 'bi-labialism,' 'plurality,' and 'doubleness,' in relation to experimental films by women is problematic. Rather than privileging the 'bi-labial' properties of female anatomy over the supposed 'oneness' of the male anatomy, *Christmas on Earth* de-essentializes the anatomical body of both sexes by depicting the flesh in a constant process of metamorphosis. Watching the fantastically morphologized bodies that emerge from the film's hallucinatory double projection, one becomes immersed in the rhapsodic folds of indistinct flesh. Shifting the color filters over the lens at a recent screening of the film for my class, I feel the film as a prosthetic extension of my own body.

According to her friend Rosebud, Barbara Rubin was fully aware of the effects that her film would have upon audiences of the day. For an eighteen-year-old girl, untutored in the arts of cinematography and editing, to make a film more explicit than any of the Underground films by established (male) experimental directors of her generation, quickly created a sensation. However, unlike Jack Smith, whose notorious *Flaming Creatures* propelled him to the center of numerous legal battles and earned him a reputation for obscenity, Barbara Rubin's sexual precociousness quickly transformed her into a beneficent, otherworldly innocent in the eyes of her public. In his review of the film in *Film Culture* in 1965, Mekas waxed elegantly about the cinematic candor with which Rubin approached the sex act:

> *Christmas on Earth*: A woman; a man; the black of the pubic hair; the cunt's moon mountains and canyons. As the film goes, image after image, the most private territories of the body are laid open for us. The first shock changes into silence then is transposed into amazement. We have seldom seen such down-to-body beauty, so real as only beauty (man) can be: terrible beauty that man, that woman is, are, that Love is.
>
> Do they have no more shame? This eighteen-year-old girl, she must have no shame, to look at and show the body so nakedly. Only angels have no shame.

But we do not believe in angels; we do not believe in Paradise any more, nor in Christmas; we have been Out for too long. 'Orpheus has been too long in Hell.' – Brakhage.

A syllogism: Barbara Rubin has no shame; angels have no shame; Barbara Rubin is an angel.

Yes, Barbara Rubin has no shame because she has been kissed by the angel of Love.[31]

While Jonas Mekas remains the most devout champion of Rubin's *oeuvre*, his ethereal syllogism disavows the carnality of Rubin's exploration of bodies. Although Underground film historian Parker Tyler himself was prone to characterizing Underground films as 'infantile,' primitive, and gimmicky, he astutely critiques Mekas for disavowing the 'stark erotic subject matter of the film' through a patently 'deliberate effort to replace black magic with white' and 'to saturate adult sexuality with a "childlike" innocence.'[32] Although Rubin promotes the stereotypes of both primitive sexual excess and the unselfconscious 'innocence' of native culture, she does so strategically. By appropriating these mythic tropes, Rubin negotiates an alternative space in which to disassemble the hegemonic notions of identity that such stereotypes help to maintain.

Underground rebel

With the exhibition of *Christmas on Earth*, Barbara Rubin quickly became one of the central figures of the emerging artistic vanguard. But the story of Rubin's significance does not end with her film. Rubin had an uncanny way of stumbling onto the defining scenes of her generation. Undoubtedly, many of Rubin's debuts were more than accidental (she was known to consciously seek out celebrity); others more serendipitous. From approximately 1963 to 1968, Rubin facilitated major exchanges and events whose impact extended far beyond their unique nature as happenings. On New Year's Eve (1963–1964), Rubin, along with Jonas Mekas and P. Adams Sitney, led the charge to show *Flaming Creatures* illegally at the Third International Experimental Film Exposition in Knokke-le-Zoute, Belgium. After smuggling the film into the projection booth in the canister of Stan Brakhage's *Dog Star Man* (1961–1964), Rubin and her associates tied up the secretly compliant projectionist, locked themselves in the room, seized control of the switchboard, cut the lights, and began to show the film. Even after the authorities arrived and attempted to halt the screening, Rubin remained undeterred. As a riot erupted, Rubin shouted encouragement to the audience while hurling curses at the police. Unrestrained by the probability that she could be prosecuted for showing the film (exhibitors in New York had already endured imprisonment and formidable legal battles), Rubin projected the film on the face of the Belgian Minister of Culture.[33]

Avant-garde film historian P. Adams Sitney recalls Barbara Rubin's zeal as she traveled from Belgium to Cannes, Paris, Munich, and Italy. While Sitney longed to find an established audience and suitable exhibition venues for avant-garde cinema, Barbara Rubin was more committed to 'showing films in the street and starting a revolution.'[34] Although they were both dedicated to gaining exposure for experimental cinema, Barbara Rubin was driven by the impulse to expand the meaning of cinema beyond the confines of the screening room and thus to eradicate artistic censorship in even its most benign manifestations. As she followed Sitney around Europe, Rubin frequently cancelled screenings that he had labored to organize, preferring to project films on the empty sky.

According to Rosebud, who hitchhiked around the country with Rubin in the early 1960s, the two teenaged girls just happened to arrive in Berkeley in 1964 at the height of the Free Speech movement. While Berkeley students rallied *en masse* to Mario Savio's rhetoric, Rubin recognized an opportunity to exercise her own personal freedom. In the midst of one of the most incendiary student rebellions in history, Rubin bought a razor at the local drugstore, chopped off all of her hair in the midst of Sproul Plaza, and threw the strands of it into the crowd in a gesture of defiance.

While many of her colleagues at the time remember Rubin as a nurturing, spiritual being, others recall Rubin's impieties with long-simmered acrimony. Often enraging her closest friends, Rubin's shock tactics used cinema as an instrument to challenge the bourgeois parameters of social etiquette as well as to expand the role of the media in the counterculture revolution. Conjuring the outrageous tactics of the Dadaists, Rubin used her camera to provoke and disturb, frequently transforming highbrow publicity events into carnivalesque debacles in which social hierarchies were inverted and ridiculed. In doing so, she created connections and communities within the counterculture that would retrospectively come to seem inevitable.

Rubin brought Warhol to Café Bizarre in Greenwich Village in 1965 to meet the Velvet Underground, and then helped to pioneer the multimedia assaults known as the Exploding Plastic Inevitable. Desperate to dance, Rubin dragged Warhol to the Dom, an old Ukrainian dance hall in the East Village. Ed Sanders and Tuli Kupferberg (later the Fugs) followed, as did Gerard Malanga, and a host of other poets and artists. 'Just as Barbara hoped, Warhol's Factory people mingled with the poets, and a new movement began in which music, art, and poetry were combined. Out of this union came rock venues like the Balloon Farm, later the Electric Circus, and suddenly the East Village became the New York center of the 1960s psychedelic rock-n-roll scene.'[35]

Did Barbara invent the East Village? Hardly. But at a time when Warhol's Factory was dominated by Harvard dropouts and the black sheep of some of the most blue-blooded American families, Barbara embraced the Old World ethnicity that flourished there – even if it was not her own. Filmmaker Ken

Jacobs remembers Barbara standing on a car, commanding a mass of people, like a hyperbolic figure from a French Revolution painting. On another occasion, Barbara decided to join the Polish State Parade in order to advertise the New American Cinema.[36]

As one of the primary organizers of the *Andy Warhol Up-Tight* series, Rubin both appalled and delighted audiences that had gathered for a glimpse of the New York Underground at various colleges and speaking venues. On January 13, 1966, Andy Warhol was invited to be the evening's entertainment at The New York Society for Clinical Psychiatry's 43rd annual dinner, held at Delmonico's Hotel. Bursting into the room with a camera, as the Velvet Underground acoustically tortured the guests and Gerard Malanga and Edie Sedgwick performed the 'whip dance' in the background, Rubin shouted obscene questions at the attending psychiatrists, extracting a morsel of delicious revenge from the profession that had once pathologized her. Casting blinding lights in their faces, Rubin hurled derogatory questions, including 'What does her vagina feel like? Is his penis big enough? Do you eat her out?'[37] As the horrified guests began to leave, Rubin continued her interrogation: 'Why are you getting embarrassed? You're a psychiatrist; you're not supposed to get embarrassed…'. The following day, the *New York Times* reported on the event; their chosen headline 'Shock Treatment for Psychiatrists' reveals the extent to which Rubin's guerrilla tactics had inverted the sanctioned relationship between patient and doctor, expert and amateur.

Rubin's contributions were not always so violent. She organized a multimedia event originally named the *Kreeping Kreplach*. (Someone with whom I spoke mistakenly referred to this as the Kreeping 'Ker-platch', making the sound a cartoon frog makes when it jumps off a two-dimensional lily pad into a sheaf of turquoise water. A *kreplach* is not a frog but a Jewish dumpling, like a wonton, but so doughy-dense that it might make a similar sound when it plunges into broth. For the record, I have never seen one 'kreep.') *Kreeping Kreplach* was soon re-christened, or *judenfrei*-ed, as *Caterpillar Changes*, a two-week-long multimedia event, which played in New York at the Cinematheque at 125 West 41st St. in February and March 1967. Participants included musicians such as the Gato Barbieri Quintet, the Free Spirits, Angus MacLise, and the Velvet Underground, the ethnomusicologist and film abstractionist Harry Smith, as well as Underground filmmakers Jack Smith, Ken Jacobs, Andy Warhol, Shirley Clarke, Storm de Hirsch, D.A. Pennebaker, Jerry Jofen, Marie Menken, Stan Vanderbeek, Willard Maas, Robert Breer, and Ed Emschwiller, to name just a few. It too, was a *Who's Who*, but unlike Warhol's *Screen Tests*, which individually entombed each participant in an isolated, straining silence, Rubin's event was a celebration, a free-for-all, a be-in, a happening.

London calling

Barbara's interventions weren't always welcomed or appreciated. Her brazenness was as much of a turn-off as it was a turn-on, often for the same people. Showing up uninvited in London for Allen Ginsberg's 39th birthday – he was reportedly displeased about it – she irritated her British hosts by troubling their stiff upper lips with her commune 'etiquette.' Carrying a camera with her, she often 'filmed' without filming, or produced cinematic images with so much superimposition and free-wheeling camera movements that they ceased to document the events she 'recorded' in all but the most subjective ways. That didn't prevent her from infuriating people with her in-your-face filming techniques. In London, Barbara alienated people who might have been considered fellow travelers. On one occasion, beat poet Gregory Corso threatened to throw her and her camera out the window.[38]

Ginsberg and Rubin were part of the first wave of Americans to come to London in the midst of the counterculture; by the end of the decade, the so-called

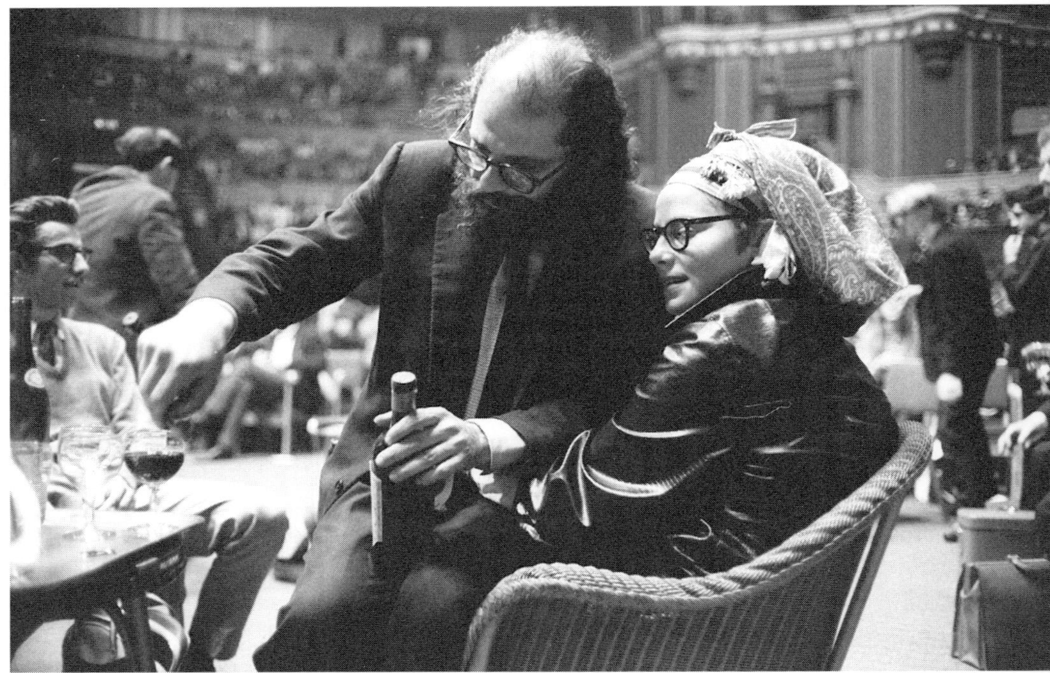

11   Allen Ginsberg sprinkles an unidentified substance into a glass while sitting on Barbara Rubin's lap at the First International Poetry Incarnation at the Royal Albert Hall in London, 1965. The beat poet and underground filmmaker were kindred spirits, roommates, occasional lovers, and queer friends.

British invasion would be mirrored by an American invasion. It represented a significant meeting of some of 'the best minds' of their generation, coming together from both sides of the Atlantic. Though Ginsberg was already an established force in American poetry and a well-known personality, like every teenaged girl from America, he wanted to meet the Beatles. So did Rubin. When John Lennon and George Harrison showed up at a party and talked with Ginsberg while she was off in another room doing drugs, and then disappeared before she returned, Barbara screamed at Ginsberg in a fury of disappointment.[39] She had already met Roman Polanski, Federico Fellini, Aldous Huxley, and countless other major talents; she had slept with Dylan and Ginsberg. Is it possible there is another category that we have forgotten in our endless revisions of Benjamin's notion of the Artist as Producer? Is there such a thing as the Artist as Groupie?

Not all of Rubin's encounters were missed. Some of Rubin's amphetamine-fueled whims were impossible to pull off; others created seismic shifts in the counterculture. An unwelcome guest at a Ginsberg birthday party, Rubin ended up organizing a much grander celebration. Memorialized in Peter Whitehead's documentary *Wholly Communion* (1965), the historic poetry reading at the Royal Albert Hall on June 11, 1965 featured nineteen poets, including Lawrence Ferlinghetti, Pablo Neruda, Andrei Voznesenski, Harry Fainlight, Ernst Jandl, and William Burroughs. The event drew 7,000 spectators, turned a generation of British youth on to Ginsberg's poetry, and inaugurated London's underground scene.

But who was Ginsberg's Rubin? It's hard to say. Kindred spirit? No doubt. They were friends on the Lower East Side. They went places together: the Kerista group, a hippie free-love commune that had been founded in San Francisco, and whose beliefs included 'polyfidelity' and polytheism. Barbara, Allen, and Peter Orlovsky.

Going up the country, 1968

Rubin moved into Ginsberg and Orlovsky's shared apartment on East 5th Street, between Avenues C and D in the East Village. Gerard Malanga lived across the hall; they regularly kept the doors open, allowing friends and sexual partners to move freely among them. Astonishingly, the rent was only $35 a month. Ginsberg biographer Bill Morgan describes the situation as follows: 'Before long Rubin moved into Allen's apartment, aggressively took over the space, and began planning her life with Allen. She said she wanted to have twelve children by a dozen different famous men, and the first of these was to be Allen. The apartment became quite chaotic with five or six people living in three and a half rooms, exactly the nightmare Allen had hoped to avoid.'[40]

The Ginsberg folks are fond of recalling Barbara's tyranny, which followed Ginsberg from his apartment on the Lower East Side to the home he purchased in upstate New York at Rubin's behest. In 1967, Rubin convinced Ginsberg to buy an old farmhouse in Cherry Valley, about eighty miles west of Albany. It would be a tax write-off for the newly formed Committee on Poetry, and Ginsberg imagined it as a kind of rehabilitation commune for poets grappling with addiction. Rubin chose the location after learning of a Jewish community in the nearby town of Sharon Springs.[41]

The hot springs at Sharon Springs had once been a refuge for German Jews who were unwelcome at nearby Saratoga Springs. Yet after Prohibition destroyed the market for hops, the local agricultural crop, and the building of the New York State Thruway diverted traffic away from the area, the resort town had fallen into decline. After World War II, Sharon Springs got a second wind when the West German government paid medical care reparations to Holocaust survivors, whose therapeutic needs included the spa treatments naturally available in the vicinity.[42] In the 1950s, while Ginsberg was busy expanding the role of the prodigal Jewish son with visionary flair – swooning over Jack Kerouac, sleeping with outlaw Neal Cassady and the patrician-cum-degenerate William Burroughs, writing the 'obscene' epic 'Howl,' experimenting with drugs, and traveling to Mexico, San Francisco, Morocco, and Paris – the very middle-class Jewishness that Ginsberg was trying to escape was overflowing in Sharon Springs, with its kosher hotels and Yiddish bingo games.

Barbara Rubin and Allen Ginsberg weren't part of the postwar wave of Holocaust survivors that moved to Sharon Springs in search of spiritual and physical healing. If anything, the queer arrival of these bohemian city folk recalled an earlier moment in the history of the area, when Oscar Wilde had stopped there in 1882 to do a reading on his literary tour of America. But in other ways, their journey was not completely dissimilar from the trajectory of Jewish immigrants seeking the chance for rebirth outside of the city. Like those traumatized subjects of history, these also sought healing and renewal. For Ginsberg, moving to Cherry Valley represented the possibility of getting Orlovksy, his lover, away from his drug addiction and out of the Lower East Side, whose filthy streets he had obsessively tried to clean with a toothbrush while strung out on methadrine.[43] For Rubin, moving to Cherry Valley meant the chance to marry Ginsberg, bear dozens of his children, and live out the rest of their days in idyllic Old World bliss. For many, this vision is the laughable fantasy that defines Barbara's intractability.

Ginsberg and Rubin arrived in Cherry Valley in late spring 1968. 'More kibbutz than commune,' the farm was designed as quiet retreat from the city.[44] Peter Orlovsky arrived with his mostly catatonic brother Julius in tow, and no intention of weaning himself off drugs. Letters from the early days of the farm manifest Ginsberg's frustration with his friends' dismissal of his 'no needles' policy; people would hide their needles and stash all over the farm. And the downside of Rubin's incredible ability to mobilize people into action turned out to be her penchant for bossing people around. On the farm, Barbara preferred directing others and was rarely up for physical labor that involved sweating profusely.[45] Yet from all accounts, the farm at Cherry Valley was one of the many sites where the poet outlaws of the Beat Generation interacted with, argued with, and lived with the younger generation of the Underground film, art, and music scene.

Nearly everyone with whom I have spoken insists that Rubin became more and more impossible to live with in Cherry Valley. She regularly visited a Hasidic community in Sharon Springs and would come home at night and proselytize about her newfound piety, particularly to the Jews in residence. This was particularly irksome to Ginsberg, who had consistently refused the label 'Jewish Poet.' Rubin and Ginsberg fought constantly. He defended himself against her tirades by screaming that he was a 'Buddhist Jew.'

Queer coupling

But there's more to the story than Rubin's supposed tyranny. True to the model of fluid sexuality in *Christmas on Earth*, in which sexual preference is less a permanent identity than a position that can be temporarily occupied and exchanged, Rubin's relationship with Ginsberg defied the rules of codified sexual behavior. By all accounts, Rubin was an energetic, enchanting figure, full of an unbelievable enthusiasm – some of it undeniably fueled by her voracious drug habits – for bringing people together. A woman under the influence, she also exerted an incredible influence on others. Ginsberg was not always as unreceptive to her charms as many of his friends claim. Ginsberg and Orlovsky were accustomed to having group sex. Yet, most of the women with whom they shared a bed were more interested in the beatific-looking Orlovsky than Ginsberg. This all changed with the arrival of Barbara Rubin. 'Now, in addition to Peter's current girlfriend, a great beauty named Annie Buchanan [a poet, whose involuntary tears are immortalized in my favorite of Warhol's *Screen Tests*] Allen had one of his own. He confided to [his friend poet Gary] Snyder at the time that he had learned the BIG heterosexual secret. All he had to was lie back passively and let a woman make love to him from nipples to knees. After that stimulation he didn't have any trouble getting it up and screwing her… .'[46]

Was Barbara Rubin Ginsberg's beard? Unlikely. Ginsberg had already out-ed himself in public on numerous occasions, 'married' Orlovsky, and defended the rights of persecuted gays in Castro's Cuba. Ginsberg was queer before Stonewall, and queer before 'gay.' He had long ago given up the idea of heteronormativity.

Was she Ginsberg's girlfriend? There's some debate. Everyone confirms they fucked at least one time: on the dark, green carpet of the Film-Makers' Coop. Allen had seen her film *Christmas on Earth* and was overwhelmed: 'It was a lot of porn, beauty, in which she made an art object out of her vagina. I thought that was in the right spirit. We got into a very funny rapport, we were just there alone, and we actually ended up screwing on the floor that very night. She was really young and pretty and I liked her.'[47]

In the 1950s, Allen Ginsberg had already achieved the kind of sexual freedom, artistic license, and community of friends, artists, and lovers that Barbara Rubin desired. But Rubin's film *Christmas on Earth* captured on film the sexual ecstasy and all-over desire for penetration that Ginsberg had only put into words. Ginsberg's frequently expressed desire to move beyond the confines of heterosexuality and homosexuality, and embrace the full sensual, contradictory fullness of being a 'complete person' found kindred recognition in *Christmas*'s explicit yet ambiguous images of throbbing genitals and other body parts. Yet in spite of this recognition, Ginsberg did not share Rubin's fantasy of getting married. In a letter to Gary Snyder in July 1968, Ginsberg writes 'Barbara Rubin pining for me (ugh!) (ouch I mean)'[48] in a way that assumes its reader's familiarity with Rubin's aggressive seductions. Everybody except Ginsberg seemed aware of Rubin's plan to marry the poet and have a dozen children with him.

In a lengthy interview with *Playboy* magazine in August 1968, just months after he moved into the farm with Rubin, Ginsberg is asked extensively about his sexual and romantic life.[49] He does not mention Rubin by name, but many of his answers seem to refer indirectly to their complex relationship and its troubling implications for his own identity. When asked to clarify his earlier admission to Timothy Leary that an LSD episode had opened 'the door to women and heterosexuality' through which he could see 'womanly body visions and family life ahead,' Ginsberg ascribes this sentiment, and his occasional interest in women to the mind-altering qualities of drugs and the perennial grip of the Oedipus complex:

> Well, I get those feelings every time I take acid … Naturally, you'll come upon old feelings you didn't know were there and were ashamed of, like loving your mother and realizing that you and she were one and that you'd separated from her because you couldn't stand the fear of being one with her. And realizing that all women and your mother are one – for myself, at least – I cut myself off from all women because I was afraid I'd discover my mother in them, or that I'd have the same problems with them that I had with her.[50]

But the family life that Rubin imagined was not completely without appeal for Ginsberg. Later in the same interview, Ginsberg admits that he had worked hard to renounce the idea of fathering children, which had been desirable to him in the past. At the urging of a 'long-haired Indian Vishnuite,' Ginsberg realized that he had to 'Give up attachment, compulsion to have children on account of you're a Jewish boy from New Jersey.'[51] In light of his desire to detach himself from all things that stank of middle-class Jewishness, Barbara Rubin's overtures must have seemed especially rancorous.

When Ginsberg is asked if he will ever marry – a seemingly strange question considering his publicly avowed homosexuality – Ginsberg replies: 'I don't yet feel enough of that erotic romance around the belly for a chick – not enough to want to contract to stick with one woman the rest of my life … Maybe if there were some chick I dug who had the same detachment as myself and who wouldn't suffer continually from being unsatisfied by my lack of erotic interest, a marriage would be all right.'[52]

Barbara Rubin was a kindred spirit, and might have been a contender for the kind of relationship with a woman that Ginsberg was considering. In addition to polyfidelity, one of the values endorsed by the Kerista group to which they both belonged was 'compersion,' which they defined as 'the opposite of jealousy, positive feelings about your partner's OTHER intimacies.'[53] There is no indication that Rubin was not an enthusiastic practitioner of both of these ideals.

In a failed attempt to exorcise madness, drugs were forbidden on the farm – an injunction to which hardly anybody paid attention. In the midst of his troubles with Peter, Allen could depend upon Barbara to take care of the extra-familial responsibilities he had amassed. He may have rhetorically rejected the yoke of the patriarchal middle-class family, but in other ways Ginsberg and Rubin fulfilled somewhat traditional roles. Ginsberg paid the bills; Rubin looked after the 'family.' By November 1967, Ginsberg reports to poet Robert Creeley that Julius Orlovsky was living with Barbara Rubin and her girlfriends on 3rd Avenue, and talking and socializing at last.[54] On other occasions, Allen assures Peter that he should leave Julius's care to Barbara: 'Let that responsibility slide off your shoulders, quit that as much as possible, let Barbara and others take care of him for the summer.'[55]

And she did. Rubin took care of Julius Orlovksy, protecting him from others' rage and his own, as Ginsberg's earlier disgruntled lover Elise Cowen had cared for Peter's other brother Lafcadio.[56] Rubin also cared for the children of rock-n-roll manager Al Aronowitz, and the children of the mystic poet and Kabbalah scholar Lionel Ziprin. She never took money for nurturing the young, the sick, or the insane, although she spent much of her time doing just that. As Jonas Mekas famously described, of all the people floating around the Cinematheque, Barbara would be the only person to 'take a bum off the street.'[57] As Al's daughter Brett Aronowitz recalls, there was something 'holy' about her. Somewhere between a big sister and a nanny, Barbara was 'the Mary Poppins of the Beat Generation.' Though it's hard to imagine Julie Andrews reading the Old Testament in bed, chanting with the Hare Krishnas, reading Tarot cards, or taking a couple of kids to hear jazz at night in Harlem, that's exactly what Barbara did.[58]

Varieties of religious experience

Rubin left the farm after approximately seven months. Disappointed by Ginsberg's rejection, Rubin grew more involved with the Satmar community at Sharon Springs, and her observance became fanatic. But what was the basis for her attraction to one of the most orthodox, most doctrinaire forms of Hasidism, in which women were not treated as equals and conversation with 'outsiders' was of no interest? For a woman who dared to make sexually explicit, formally outrageous films at a time when even the Underground cinema scene was male dominated, it was, at the very least, an unusual choice. And while Satmar certainly offered the kind of immersive community that Rubin had always sought – in the Film-Makers' Coop, at the farm – its exclusionary practice seemed as far as possible from her utopian ideal of bringing people of all backgrounds together.

Spiritual discovery was, to a degree, part of what you did in the 1960s. Before becoming a born-again Christian in the late 1970s, Bob Dylan had a Jewish phase – encouraged by Rubin – that included seeking guidance from the famed Rabbi Freifeld of Yeshiva Sh'or Yoshuv in Far Rockaway. The Beatles, followed by Donovan, had gone to India in 1968 to study with the Maharishi. Ginsberg embraced Buddhism. But if Eastern religion was cool, and the esoteric study of Kabbalah was part of the expanded perception – alongside hallucinogenic drugs, orgies, and experimental film – celebrated by the counterculture, then Hasidism remained decidedly uncool. Rubin's turn towards it in the late 1960s was particularly troubling for her secular Jewish friends who had struggled to free themselves from their grandparent's *shtetls* and their parents' split-levels.

Many of the people most irritated with Rubin's 'conversion' were Jewish themselves. Lenny Bruce, notorious logorrheic Jew, found Rubin a 'pushy big mouth, very demanding, not beyond deception in pursuit of her own goals, and very manipulative.'[59] Though Rubin's Jewishness may have seemed exotic to some, her *chutzpah* became more off-putting as she became more dogmatic in her religious views. After visiting Rubin in a Hasidic community in Brooklyn, latent feminist and secular Jew Amy Taubin hoped her friend's enchantment with orthodoxy would be short-lived.[60] It wasn't.

In the Underground film scene that developed around the Cinematheque and the Film-Makers' Cooperative, there were not an overwhelming number of Jews. But Jewishness, and its re-signification as a more intentional kind of other-ness – whether it be beat, hip, or avant-garde – was a significant, if underappre-ciated, aspect of the postwar Underground. Indeed, ethnic communities were often the background against which the Underground's antics were performed, and the models upon which new kinds of artistic and sexual communities were based. Yet while the Eastern European identity of the Lithuanian Mekas broth-ers, the Polish Warhol and the Russian Orlovsky brothers helped establish their other-worldly aura, the middle-class, suburban Jewishness of people such as Barbara Rubin, Allen Ginsberg, Bob Dylan, Lenny Bruce, and Lou Reed was a stain that had to be rubbed out. And though Ginsberg often acknowledged his cultural Jewishness, and saw affinities with the tradition of Jewish anarchism that would have included some of his other contemporaries, including Judith Malina, Julian Beck, Tuli Kupferberg, and Abbie Hoffman, he did not want to be associated with its postwar suburban incarnation.

Approximately eight months after leaving the farm over a dispute about the proper way to slaughter a cow,[61] Rubin called the farm and invited everyone to her wedding to Mordecai Levy, whom she had met at Rabbi Freifeld's famed *baal t'shuvah* congregation in Far Rockaway. Mordecai had explored alternative spirituality at Rabbi Schlomo Karvak's Jewish house of love and prayer in San Francisco's Haight-Ashbury neighborhood before coming to Far Rockaway. Their romance was the result of a *shittach*, an organized introduction.[62]

The return of the repressed

When I first heard descriptions of Barbara Rubin's wedding to Mordecai Levy in January 1971, it seemed like pure apocrypha. People who had attended were fond of describing how men and women were separated, as was the custom, and how many of the women stood on chairs to peek over the dividing wall to get a glimpse of Bob Dylan. But I now realize that Rubin and Levy's wedding was much more than an amusing footnote to the 1960s.

Though their marriage didn't last very long, their wedding was one of the few moments when the postwar underground reunited with representatives of a religious tradition that many of them had abandoned or shunned. Crammed into a brownstone, two alternative communities who had been living in op-posing worlds – despite their neighborly proximity – came uncomfortably to-gether. For some it was a vision of another world; for others, it was the return of the repressed.

In our present day world of mega-churches and the crusades of the Moral Majority, we don't tend to think of religious fundamentalists and avant-garde artists seeking mutual enlightenment from each other. Indeed, as journalist David Katz has suggested, 'Orthodox Judaism, with its grey-bearded con-gregants in pure white shirts, *tallissim*, long black coats and wide-brimmed fedoras, laying tefillin and softly dovening in dimly lit shuls, may seem ir-reconcilably opposed to the secular libertines of the mid-twentieth-century avant-garde, devotees of all that is modern and against the grain, practicing their own rituals at art openings, poetry readings, happenings and "scenes."'[63] And yet, as it turns out, these worlds were not always as estranged as they now seem. Indeed, many of the most influential figures of the postwar un-derground had one foot in the Old World and one foot in the New. With mystic scholar/poet Lionel Ziprin as the downtown answer to Rabbi Freifeld, the blend of underground radicalism and Old World spirituality was a central nexus in the postwar underground. In 1970, these worlds collided at Barbara Rubin's wedding.

While Rubin's turn toward Hasidism seems unthinkable in relation to her earlier polymorphous perversity, it becomes legible in light of these social and historical considerations. Yet try as I may, it is still difficult to imagine Rubin, whose relation to sexuality was both ambivalent and ambiguous, living within a system that defines gender difference as clearly and conservatively as orthodox Judaism does. An extremely maternal person, Barbara Rubin had mothered the Underground's lost children. Often surrounded by homosexual men, her longing for her own children went unfulfilled throughout the 1960s.

After divorcing Levy, Rubin married a French painter named Besancon; shortly afterwards, they moved to France and settled in a Hasidic community. After giving birth to half a dozen children in as many years (although she is rumored to have been warned by doctors not to have any more children due to her excessive weight gain and slight frame), Rubin died of a postnatal infection in 1980, two weeks after the birth of her youngest son. According to 'Preliminary Report of the Death of an American Citizen Abroad,' posted two years later by an American Vice Counsel in Lyon, Rubin was buried in the Jewish Cemetery in Ceffois-le-Bas, Haut Ruin, France.[64] In a note addressed to Leslie Trumbull, then director of the Film-Makers' Cooperative, Rubin, calling herself 'Bracha,' ordered the destruction of the only print of *Christmas on Earth*, a request that has thankfully not been fulfilled.[65]

Perhaps sleeping in a different bedroom from her second husband, who remarried only weeks after his wife's untimely death, was not as unthinkable for Rubin as it may seem to those of us outside the faith. For someone whose sexuality had been formed in a queer community that nonetheless had different rules for women and gay men, Rubin may have been accustomed to the separation of the genders and the alienation from normative heterosexual intimacy. After all, with the exception of Allen Ginsberg and Bob Dylan, Rubin had always been much closer to women than she had been to men. Perhaps the orthodox practice that linked heterosexual sex to copious procreation was not such a leap for a woman who had had her most intimate relationships with 'gay' men and 'straight' women.

Amy Taubin has suggested that had the timing been different, the second-wave feminist movement of the 1970s could have offered Rubin a different alternative. Rubin, who briefly stayed with Taubin and her then-husband, the playwright Richard Foreman, after leaving Cherry Valley in despair, had always relied upon a community to support her. Alternative artistic and sexual communities were prevalent during the 1960s, in the form of the Kerista group, the Cinematheque, Warhol's Factory, the Film-makers' Coop, Judson Church, and the St. Mark's poetry scene, to name just a few. But as the 1960s came to a close, these institutions became less viable means of support for the individuals who had participated in and depended upon them.

Certainly, new communities emerged at the end of the 1960s, but they may not have been as open to the fluid participation of 'queer' women. Stonewall certainly inaugurated a new era of visibility for homosexual men, but it did not even begin to address the fate of the queer women who were the most significant fellow travelers of gay men throughout the 1960s. In some ways, the gay rights movement that emerged from it was as male-centric as the Hasidic community to which Rubin turned.

Kaddish

Although Barbara Rubin conceived of many ambitious film projects, she only finished two films.[66] Completed after her conversion to Hasidism, Barbara Rubin's last film, *Emunah* (1972), which she co-directed with Pamela Mayo, is a mishmash of diverse footage, all related to her interest in spirituality. Juxtaposing footage of Allen Ginsberg with Hebrew text and photographs of concentration camps, *Emunah* attempts to reconcile Rubin's two seemingly incompatible worlds: the New York Underground art scene and the Hasidism towards which she later turned. Yet rather than illuminating the mysterious link between the corporeal materialism of *Christmas on Earth* and the spirituality of Rubin's religious quest, *Emunah* projects the filmmaker's sentimental longing on to the figure of Ginsberg, who is seen reading 'Kaddish' at the Royal Albert Hall in London and lingering at the gravestone of William Blake. Suffused with the pathos of lost things, the film is nevertheless a montage of Rubin's 1960s, a poignant collision of the past and the present. Like Jerry Jofen, whose techniques of superimposition she borrowed, Rubin created a palimpsest of the different layers of her identity in *Emunah*. Superimposition may have been an economic necessity for both of these artists, but it was also an innovative formal strategy for representing the duality of what it meant to live as an Old World child in Warhol's New World. *Emunah* was Rubin's way of saying Kaddish for the secular life she had left behind.

Rubin's Jewishness is superimposed in *Emunah*, forming a resplendent layer through which one literally cannot see the rest of the film. The title is the Hebrew word for 'faith,' a faith that every Jewish soul inherits from the patriarchs and matriarchs of the Jewish people. As an inherited trait, *emunah* is always present in every Jewish soul, though not necessarily conscious. 'Emunah' is also the name of Barbara Rubin's first child, a daughter who may have inherited those traits that made her mother so special, but who most likely grew up being unaware of her vast contributions to the cultural zeitgeist of the 1960s. Like these contributions, *Emunah* remains unpreserved and unremembered. But if

Jewishness has been scraped off of our memories of the postwar underground, it cannot be rubbed off of Rubin's filmic farewell.

Had Barbara Rubin disappeared from the Underground community immediately after completing her first film, *Christmas on Earth* would remain one of the most compelling testaments to the spirit of 1960s experimental cinema and the counterculture, as well as a work of unparalleled formal and aesthetic consequence. Yet it is only through an examination of Rubin's entire, apocryphal career that the uniqueness of her vision, and the attending difficulty of her struggles as artist, woman, and filmmaker, come into focus. In an environment in which it was nearly impossible for an untrained, under-aged woman to break into a world of established male *auteurs*, Rubin took flight, soared to unexpected heights, and offered unqualified glimpses of beauty along the way. In the process, Barbara Rubin answered the question that had been posed to her, generations before, by Rimbaud in 'The Impossible,' *A Season in Hell*:

> When are we going to take off, past the shores and the mountains, to greet the new task, the new wisdom, the defeat of tyrants and devils, the end of superstition – to worship – the first to do so! – Christmas on this earth!

Notes

1 Jean Nicholas Arthur Rimbaud, *Rimbaud: Complete Works, Selected Letters*, bilingual edition, trans. Wallace Fowlie (Chicago, IL: University of Chicago Press, 2005), p. 362.

2 Joseph Klarl, 'Barbara Rubin: *Christmas on Earth*', *The Brooklyn Rail* (February 2013), www.brooklynrail.org/2013/02/artseen/barbara-rubin-christmas-on-earth (accessed on August 8, 2013).

3 Stan Brakhage, 'In Defense of the Amateur Filmmaker,' *Filmmakers Newsletter*, 4, no. 9–10 (July–August 1971), pp. 20–25; p. 21.

4 Jonas Mekas, *Movie Journal: The Rise of a New American Cinema, 1959–1971* (New York: Macmillan, 1972), p. 248.

5 Victor Bockris, *The Life and Death of Andy Warhol* (New York: Bantam, 1989), p. 181.

6 Linda Nochlin, 'Why Have There Been No Great Women Artists?' *ARTnews* 69 (January 1971), pp. 22–39.

7 J. Hoberman, 'Crimson Creatures: The Case Against *Flaming Creatures*,' in *On Jack Smith's Flaming Creatures (and Other Secret Flix of Cinemaroc)* (New York: Granary Books, 2001), pp. 35–50.

8 Most of Dylan's biographers pay scant attention to the singer's friendship with Rubin, who helped nurse Dylan back to health after his devastating motorcycle accident in 1966. Nevertheless, it is rumored that Dylan wrote part of his song 'Desolation Row' about Barbara Rubin: 'Now Ophelia, she's 'neath the window / For her I feel so afraid / On her twenty-second birthday / She already is an old maid / To her, death is quite romantic / She wears an iron vest / Her profession's

her religion / Her sin is her lifelessness / And though her eyes are fixed upon / Noah's great rainbow / She spends her time peeking / Into Desolation Row.' Bob Dylan, 'Desolation Row,' *Highway 61 Revisited*, prod. Bob Johnston (Columbia Records, 1965).

9   Jacques Lacan, 'Of the Gaze as *Objet petit a*,' *The Four Fundamental Concepts of Psychoanalysis* (The Seminar of Jacques Lacan Book 11), ed. Jacques-Alain Miller, trans. Alan Sheridan (New York: W.W. Norton, 1998), pp. 67–122.

10 Amy Taubin, interview with the author, winter 2008–2009.

11 Stephen Bornstein, telephone interview with the author, February 2009.

12 Ken Jacobs, telephone interview with the author, January 2009.

13 Steven Watson, *Factory Made: Warhol and the Sixties* (New York: Pantheon, 2003), p. 99.

14 Daniel Belasco, 'A Vanished Prodigy,' *Barbara Rubin: Christmas on Earth* (New York: Boo Hooray Gallery, 2012), published in conjunction with an exhibition of the same name, New York, Boo Hooray Gallery, December 18, 2012 – January 15, 2013, originally published in *Art in America*, December 2005, pp. 61–67.

15 Gerard Malanga identified the first four participants in an email message to the author from July 12, 2012. Debbie Feiner, a.k.a. Debbie Fein or Fine, was identified by Ken and Flo Jacobs with the help of Jim and Shelley Hoberman. The Barbara Gladstone who participated was not the future proprietor of Barbara Gladstone Gallery in New York.

16 Quoted in Gordon Ball, *66 Frames* (Minneapolis, MN: Coffee House Press, 1999), p. 232.

17 Belasco, 'A Vanished Prodigy.'

18 Paul Sharits, '-UR(i)N(ul)LS:TREAM:S:S:ECTION:S:ECTION:-S:S:ECTIONED (A)(lysis)JO: "1968–70."' *Film Culture* no. 65–66 (1978), pp. 7–25 (p. 7). Sharits does not use this phrase in relation to *Christmas on Earth*.

19 Sally Banes, *Greenwich Village 1963: Avant-Garde Performance and the Effervescent Body* (Durham, NC: Duke University Press, 1993), p. 215; and see also David James, *Allegories of Cinema: American Film in the 1960s* (Princeton: Princeton University Press, 1989), pp. 316–317.

20 Jean-Louis Comolli, 'The Frenzy of the Visible,' *The Cinematic Apparatus*, ed. Teresa de Lauretis and Stephen Heath (New York: St. Martin's Press, 1980). This phrase is used by film scholar Linda Williams to describe the out-of-control movement of bodies in hard-core pornography. Williams, *Hard Core: Power, Pleasure, and the 'Frenzy of the Visible'* (Berkeley, CA: University of California Press, 1989).

21 Banes, *Greenwich Village 1963*, p. 215.

22 Williams, 'Fetishism and Hard Core: Marx, Freud, and the "Money Shot,"' in *Hard Core*, pp. 93–119.

23 Linda Williams, 'Film Body: An Implantation of Perversions,' in *Narrative, Apparatus, Ideology*, ed. Philip Rosen (New York: Columbia University Press, 1986.)

24 Williams, 'Prehistory: The "Frenzy of the Visible"' in *Hard Core*, pp. 34–57.

25 Amy Taubin, 'Christmas on Earth.' Barbara Rubin File, Anthology Film Archives.

26 Banes, *Greenwich Village 1963*, p. 224.

27 Ibid.

28 Melanie Klein, 'Early Stages of the Oedipus Conflict and of Super-Ego Formation,' in *The Psycho-Analysis of Children*, trans. Alix Strachey (New York: Delacorte Press, 1975), p. 136.

29 Banes, *Greenwich Village 1963*, p. 224.

30 James, *Allegories of Cinema*, p. 317.

31 Jonas Mekas, 'Notes on Some New Movies and Happiness,' in *Film Culture Reader*, ed. P. Adams Sitney (New York: Praeger, 1970), pp. 317–325; pp. 322–323.

32 Parker Tyler, *Underground Film: A Critical History* (New York: Da Capo Press, 1995), p. 99.

33 Mekas, *Movie Journal*, pp. 111–112.

34 P. Adams Sitney, telephone interview with the author, spring 2004.

35 Bill Morgan, *I Celebrate Myself: The Somewhat Private Life of Allen Ginsberg* (London: Penguin, 2006), p. 394.

36 Ken and Flo Jacobs, interview with the author, winter 2008.

37 Watson, *Factory Made*, p. 259.

38 Barry Miles, telephone interview with the author, February 2009.

39 Ibid.

40 Bill Morgan, *I Celebrate Myself*, p. 392.

41 Stephen Bornstein, telephone interview with the author, February 2009.

42 Michelle York, 'Sharon Springs Journal: Like the Water, Grand Plans Buoy Spirits at a Vacation Spot From a Bygone Era,' *New York Times*, June 5, 2008.

43 Barry Miles, *Ginsberg: A Biography* (New York: Simon & Schuster, 1989), p. 412.

44 Allen Ginsberg to Gary Snyder, July 1968, *The Letters of Allen Ginsberg*, ed. Bill Morgan (Philadelphia, PA: Da Capo Press, 2008), p. 343.

45 Gordon Ball, interview with the author, January 2009.

46 Morgan, *I Celebrate Myself*, p. 392.

47 Ginsberg, quoted in Miles, *Ginsberg: A Biography*, p. 334.

48 Allen Ginsberg to Gary Snyder, July 8, 1968, *The Letters of Allen Ginsberg*, p. 343.

49 Allen Ginsberg, interview with Paul Carroll, *Allen Ginsberg, Spontaneous Mind, Selected Interviews 1958–1996*, ed. David Carter (New York: Harper Collins, 2001), pp. 159–199, originally published as Allen Ginsberg, interview by Paul Carroll, 'The Playboy Interview: Allen Ginsberg,' *Playboy*, April 1969, pp. 81–92, 236–244.

50 Ginsberg, *Spontaneous Mind*, p. 166.

51 Ibid., p. 169.

52 Ibid., p. 170.

53 'Kerista Commune Home Page,' *Kerista Commune*, accessed September 5, 2012, www.kerista.com. Even, Eve, 'Glossary of Keristan English (abridged),' *Kerista: Scientific Utopianism and the Humanities*, 1, no. 4 (Spring 1985), part 1, www.kerista.com/kerdocs/glossary.html (accessed on August 8, 2013).

54 Ginsberg to Creeley, November 28, 1967, *The Letters of Allen Ginsberg*, pp. 336–337.

55 Ginsberg to Peter Orlovsky, August 10, 1967, *The Letters of Allen Ginsberg*, p. 334.

56 Joyce Johnson, *Minor Characters: A Beat Memoir* (New York: Penguin, 1999), p. 122.

57 Quoted in Ball, *66 Frames*, p. 134.

58 Brett Aronowitz, telephone interview with the author, summer 2004.

59 Rosebud (Pettet) Feliu, telephone interview with the author, summer 2004.

60 Amy Taubin, telephone interview with the author, winter 2009.

61 Ara Osterweil, 'Queer Coupling, or The Stain of the Bearded Woman,' *Framework* 51, no. 1 (Spring 2010), pp. 52–53.

62 Devora O'Brien, telephone interview with the author, February 2009. O'Brien is Mordecai Levy's sister.

63 David Katz, '"Angels are Just One More Species": David Katz Meets Lionel Ziprin, Mystic, Maven and Maverick of New York's Lower East Side,' *Jewish Quarterly*, no. 204 (Winter 2006/2007).

64 Bill Horrigan, 'Program Guide to the 5th New York Lesbian and Gay Experimental Film Festival,' 1991.

65 Belasco, 'A Vanished Prodigy,' p. 49.

66 *Christmas on Earth Continued* (1965), co-authored by Rubin's friend Rosebud Pettet, was conceived as a billion-dollar fantasy epic that required the construction of a massive fairy kingdom in Ireland and the casting of virtually every significant *enfant terrible* from the music, literary, cinema, and art worlds, including Jean Genet, Lenny Bruce, the Beatles, Bob Dylan, Marianne Faithfull, the Supremes, and Marlon Brando.

2 Andy Warhol, porn realist

After being alive, the next hardest work is having sex.
(Andy Warhol, *The Philosophy of Andy Warhol*)

Though not often recognized as such, Andy Warhol was one of the most innovative and prolific pornographers of the twentieth century. Conquering the visual taboo of hard-core sexuality in films such as *Couch* (1964) and *Blue Movie* (1968), Warhol insisted – against decades of censorship – that the representation of the sex act was not only a legitimate cinematic subject, but the culminating achievement of a medium devoted to the study of corporeal motion. However, far from representing sex as the individual's orgasmic respite from a repressive civilization, Warhol's films offered a much more realistic account of sex as both performance and labor.

By foregrounding the crucial roles that boredom, distraction, and interruption play in our sexual interactions, Warhol frustrated audience expectations. He also provided a model – alternately dystopic and liberatory – of what sex looked like within late capitalism. In this chapter, I look at two films whose attempts to conscript sex within capitalism are shattered by the obstinate, and ultimately unreadable, gestures of their performers: *Couch* was the first film with hard-core sex that Warhol made, *Blue Movie* the last. Charting a wide spectrum from queer group sex at the Factory to intimate heterosexual coupling in a bedroom, these films are among the most important cinematic documents of sexuality in the postwar period. They are also, however, keys to the way in which the pleasures and pains of sexuality resist documentation. Filmed exclusively on and around the couch in Warhol's Factory and including footage of un-simulated homosexual and heterosexual sex acts, *Couch* extols the perverse and potentially resistant pleasures of queer sex in a free market. With its depiction of heterosexual coupling as an imminently obsolescent ritual, *Blue Movie* explores the emotional and political labors of lovemaking in a society in which intimacy functions as a form of ideology. Situating a discussion of these films in the larger context of Warholian pornography, this essay re-thinks the sexual politics of Warhol's Factory.

Perversion

Brief as it was, Warhol's own cinematic *oeuvre* recapitulated and condensed the history of cinema, from his early recreation of primitive cinema (short, silent, black-and-white, non-edited, and non-narrative films) to his gradual incorporation of sound, color, editing, and camera movement, in the creation of a feature-length, star-studded narrative cinema. Warhol's interest in sex, and the difficulty of finding a cinematic language for it, was central to this project. From his early black-and-white films such as *Kiss* (1963), *Sleep* (1963), *Blow Job* (1964), and *Eating Too Fast* (1966), in which Warhol dissected sexuality into its component parts; to his color parodies of soft-core sexploitation *I, a Man* (1967), *Bike Boy* (1967–1968), *The Loves of Ondine* (1967–1968); *Imitation of Christ* (1967), *The Nude Restaurant* (1967), *Lonesome Cowboys* (1967–1968), and *San Diego Surf* (1968); to his final, narrative masterpiece *Blue Movie*, Warhol archived a catalogue of so-called perversions organized by the sustained act of looking. After all, pornography documents not sex *per se*, but sex made *to be looked at*, which, as hard-core's ubiquitous 'money shot' suggests, can have quite different priorities than sex that is geared towards *what it feels like*. Yet what distinguishes Warhol's emphasis on the visual aspects of sexuality from more conventional pornography are the objects, intensity and duration of his gaze. What is *Sleep* – Warhol's six-hour looping film of the poet John Giorno sleeping nude with his groin perennially out of the frame – but an experiment in blueball stamina? Warhol's camera stared fixedly and often for uncomfortable length not only at the genital objects that constitute hard-core's regime of maximum visibility – but at faces, other body parts, bananas.

Yet while this brief trajectory superficially parallels Freud's heteronormative account of sexuality's movement towards genital maturity, it fails to account for the radical undoing to which Warhol subjected sexuality at every stage. Though his film career ends with the onscreen achievement of heterosexual genital penetration in *Blue Movie* (1968), Warhol's cinema consistently swerved away from what Freud considered sexuality's 'normative' aims, even as his camera remain fixed upon the bodies enlisted to perform the hard work of having – or avoiding – sex. Sex, for Warhol, was not reducible to genital penetration but included all of the activities that surrounded and obstructed desire. 'It's as much work for an attractive person *not to have* sex as for an *un*attractive person to *have* sex,' Warhol mused, acknowledging the intense amount of labor involved in sex's failure.[1] Embracing this failure, Warhol refuses to satisfy the demands of either normative sexuality or conventional cinema. Contrary to the 'pornotopia' of commercial hard-core pornography, in which nearly all sexual activities once marked as 'deviant' are marketed as lucrative novelties, Warhol's cinema staged sex that was insistently, unprofitably perverse.

In his landmark study *Three Essays on the Theory of Sexuality*, published in 1905, Freud defined perversity as 'sexual activities which either (a) extend, in an anatomical sense, beyond the regions of the body that are designed for sexual union, or (b) linger over the intermediate relations to the sexual object which should normally be traversed rapidly on the path towards the final sexual aim.'[2] This sense of the geographic or temporal distension of the sexual act is essential for understanding Warhol's cinematic perversion. Mining the 'challenge perversion poses to the symbolic order,' Warhol's camera 'turns aside not only from hierarchy and genital sexuality' but from what Kaja Silverman has described as 'the paternal signifier' of dominant culture, which claims ultimate arbitration of what constitutes 'truth' or 'right.'[3]

Warhol's cinema not only de-prioritized what Freud regarded as the proper goal of mature sexuality (heterosexual genital penetration) but dissolved the sexual aim into an excruciating sense of aimlessness. His perverse approach to documenting sex was apparent not only in his choice of objects and the intensity and duration of his camera's gaze, but in its privileging of distraction over the deed. Saturated with the difficulty of erotic relations, Warhol's sex films foreground the failure of individuals to either get on or off together. Ever sentient of the camera's presence, Warhol's stars perform for it, often at the expense of engaging more intimately with each other.

Un-lubricated by heteronormative desire, Warhol's films refuse to move rapidly towards genital penetration – especially, but not only, when they involve an attractive male and female couple. For even in Warhol's extensive documentation of homosexual sex, there is a significant swerving away from, or queering of, the 'proper' aims of sexuality towards a more critical investigation of what it means to pursue Eros within capitalism. For Warhol, what Frankfurt School philosopher Herbert Marcuse had famously described in *Eros and Civilization* as the tyranny of 'genital supremacy'[4] merged with the tyranny of conventional narrative. Though Warhol had been obsessed with the documentation of genitals since the early 1950s,[5] their representation in cinema posed particular problems not only because of American censorship laws, but also because of the filmmaker's aim to disturb facile narrative and sexual resolution. Since, as Douglas Crimp has argued, one of the 'signal achievements of Warhol's cinema is that it avoids denouement,'[6] then the on-screen danger of the genitals is that they threaten to provoke the kinds of predictable climax that Warhol preferred to avoid.

Though Warhol's cinema experimented with both the representation of genital heterosexuality and narrative form, it strove to avoid colonization by either. Instead of rushing forward towards climax, Warhol tiptoed backwards to what Douglas Crimp has called the 'space of not coupling,'[7] where he stubbornly refused to represent a 'happy ending.' As anyone who has watched his films knows, Warhol developed ingenious ways of avoiding climax. In films such as *Sleep* and *Blow Job*, Warhol's frequent use of close-cropped shots and a resolutely immobile camera keep the desired sight of the genitals just outside of the frame – to the endless frustration of the audience. Such is his reputation, as Thomas Waugh has argued, for being a 'cockteaser.'[8]

Couch

Yet while sex permeates all of Warhol's films, *Couch* is the first of Warhol's film to depict genital penetration. By featuring a wide variety of sexual permutations among the usual group of suspects on the couch at Warhol's 47th Street Factory, *Couch* explored a spectrum of possibilities for sexual partnerships and groupings (homosexual, bisexual, interracial) that would have been unthinkable before the sexual revolution and the civil rights era. By delivering the sexual goods that many of Warhol's more notorious films withhold, *Couch* overcomes the tease for which Warhol's cinema was already becoming notorious. It is – *in perhaps only this way* – a 'real' porno.

Along with Jack Smith's *Flaming Creatures* (1963), and Barbara Rubin's *Christmas on Earth* (1963), *Couch* is one of the inaugural films of the sexually explicit, queer Underground cinema of the flesh that flourished in the United States nearly ten years before the incursion of hard-core pornography into mainstream American film culture. Nonetheless, even as *Couch* reveals ever more taboo forms of sexual congress, it simultaneously strives to disorganize sex and its productive resolution through distraction. For though genitals are visible in *Couch*, the rapt attention they would have otherwise commanded from its historically sex-starved American audience is disrupted by the theatrical posturing of the film's sexual players, and the intrusion of other objects and people in the frame.

Shot between July and December 1964, *Couch* was originally an open-ended cumulative series of 100-foot (approximately three-minute) reels of various people doing various things on and around the Factory couch. Many of Warhol's superstars, including Gerard Malanga, Baby Jane Holzer, Ivy Nicholson, Ondine, Taylor Mead, Billy Name (Linich), and Naomi Levine, as well as many notables from the art and literary worlds such as Allen Ginsberg, Robert Frank, Alfred Leslie, Gregory Corso, Jack Kerouac, Peter Orlovsky, Amy Taubin, John Palmer, Rufus Collins, Joseph LeSeuer, Binghamton Birdie, Mark Lancaster, and Gloria Wood appear in the film, clustering around the couch and engaging in different activities.[9] Of the thirty-seven original rolls, only five actually contain instances of sexual penetration, and only a handful more contain instances of people stripping or kissing. Although Warhol collaborator Ronald Tavel remembers that the film wasn't often shown in public because of the censorship laws, it was nonetheless viewed by many at the Factory: 'See, a lot of people would come up to see it … you debauch, you walk out and have coffee and then come back and watch the movie, which everyone did – because how much could you watch these people on a couch?'[10] The first known public screening of excerpts of the film occurred at the East Village's St. Mark's Church, located at the corner of East 10th Street and 2nd Avenue, in March 1965.[11] The next spring, on April 17, 1966, a substantially edited version was shown publicly at the Film-Makers' Cinematheque on East 44th Street; its running time was approximately an hour. Current versions in circulation range from 40 to 58 minutes.

Although both versions of *Couch* are much longer than customary stag films, Warhol's film shares certain features of its mode of address with this by-then nearly defunct genre. *Couch*'s obvious breaches of continuity and lack of narrative coherence, as well as its silence and lack of color, were typical features of the stag genre. As in a stag, the sexual encounters in *Couch* are random and unrehearsed, and they are organized out of chronological order. Furthermore, *Couch* privileges the exchangeability of sexual partners and seemingly random sexual acts over emotional intimacy or sustained acts of lovemaking.

Work

Like the proverbial couch in the psychoanalytic session, Warhol's Factory sofa functioned as a liminal space where desires that were unactionable in real life could be explored. As Annette Michelson has argued, Warhol's Factory functioned as a 'world in which the prohibitions and restrictions that determine and sustain the structures and order of production' were bracketed.[12] More than any of Warhol's other creations, the Factory was itself, as Michelson argues, the *gesamtkunstwerk* of late capitalism – an all-encompassing place where work, art, and life converged. As both the literal and symbolic center of this site of sexual, social, and aesthetic experimentation, the couch exemplified the Factory's 'swinging door' approach to both sexuality and identity.

Nevertheless, while the sexual prohibitions and taboos of mainstream society were often overcome at the Factory, the laws of capitalist production were not. Warhol's 'total work of art' crystallized around the laden symbol of the office couch, where repose, sexual play, and leisure became highly skilled, competitive forms of labor. Though *Couch* may appear to epitomize the ethos of the sexual revolution, its libidinal economy is driven not by free love but by the free market. By accommodating homosexuality, heterosexuality, bisexuality, and asexuality, the couch served as a showroom for the range of bodies on display in the Factory. To perch on the couch was not only to turn oneself into a commodity, but into a body poised for the camera's gaze, regardless of whether the apparatus was running. Though Warhol's couch is hardly the equivalent of Foucault's panopticon, celebrity was indeed constructed as a discipline upon and around its purview. In a 'factory' environment where leisure served as the most conspicuous form of labor, instances of repose became highly self-conscious performative acts.

The difficult of understanding the politics of Warhol's films arises from this very problematic: In the sexual free market epitomized by *Couch*, individual subjects are reified as objects, while the private rituals of intimacy are transformed into (semi-)public spectacles. While such a stance seems prototypical of a 'postmodern' sensibility, this commodification of both sex and subjectivity nevertheless seems to delimit the subversive potential of Warhol's groundbreaking approach to the body.

In its embrace of the ethos of late capitalism, Warhol's philosophy of sex diverged from other countercultural approaches of the 1960s, most notably Marcuse's influential vision of 'Eros' as a force capable of liberating man from the repression of capitalist society. Merging the theories of Freud and Marx in his landmark book *Eros and Civilization* (1955), Marcuse's proposed revolution involved subverting the erogenous body's conventional territorialization, and delivering mankind from the conditions of libidinal alienation and economic exploitation into a liberated, egalitarian society where Eros triumphed. Warhol was hardly such an idealist. Rather than flaunting the bliss of polymorphous perversity, Warhol actually embraced the 'thing-ification' of social and sexual relations that Marcuse despised. Though many of Warhol's films implicitly critique the tyranny of the genital through the rapt attention they pay to non-genital body parts, they also celebrate the reification of erotic experience. In *Couch*, Warhol fuses the libidinal and the financial economy, reminding us that sex in a factory can be as tiresome as other forms of alienated labor. As one *Variety* critic wrote about *Blue Movie* in 1969, 'Warhol makes even sex a bore.'[13]

Such a stance should not surprise us. Unlike Marcuse, Warhol embraced the concept of the artist as a 'One-Dimensional Man' whose methods of creation were no different than assembly production.[14] Rather than liberating man from the conditions of alienation, Warhol's 'revolution' has often been accused of delivering man – and art – into greater depths of objectification. Yet to what extent can Warhol's embrace of capitalism and commodity culture be regarded as a critique? Nearly fifty years after their production, the politics of Warhol's films remain notoriously difficult to gauge, even when they offer hard-core 'proof' of their engagement. This is perhaps most true in texts whose overt content are the most provocative, but whose relentlessly impassive tone diminishes the types of affect that could potentially sustain a collective political response to injustice. One wonders, with Isabelle Graw, whether Warhol's work is 'not part of the solution' but 'part of the problem.'[15]

Sex, for Warhol, was inseparable from capitalism. As Graw has argued, Warhol welcomed the neoliberal intrusion of market laws into the most private spheres of life, transforming all aspects of life into work.[16] Indeed, as Warhol noted, sex was 'the hardest work' after being alive.[17] Yet sex's propensity for failure implicitly resisted the economic logic of optimization. As the arduous work of sex involved waiting for it, thinking about it, having it, remembering it, and replaying it,[18] it was particularly troubling that the affective payoff of sex was never guaranteed.

But if sex was work for Warhol, then the opposite was true as well: work was sex. Indeed, work was even a more capacious category in Warhol's philosophy than sex:

> I suppose I have a really loose interpretation of 'work,' because I think that just being alive is so much work at something you don't always want to do. Being born is like being kidnapped. And then sold into slavery. People are working every minute. The machinery is always going. Even when you sleep.[19]

If the machinery of capitalism never ceases, then the very condition of life is enslavement. In such a world, the only way to avoid exploitation is to avoid being born. And so we turn to the question of queer sex.

Distraction

For Warhol, sex *was* distraction. In *The Philosophy of Andy Warhol*, the artist describes two kinds of sex, both of which divert attention from the reproductive function of penetration. The first was an impossible aesthetic/romantic ideal constructed by the movies, the lessons of which couldn't be applied to real life 'with any reasonable results.'[20] The second kind of sex was the kind one could imagine having on the Factory sofa. Warhol writes,

> The best love is not-to-think-about-it love. Some people can have sex and really let their minds go blank and fill up with the sex; other people can never let their minds go blank and fill up with the sex, so while they're having sex they're thinking, 'Can this really be me? Am I really doing this? This is very strange. Five minutes ago I wasn't doing this…'[21]

Time and time again, Warhol celebrated the superiority of imagined or cinematic sex over actual, physical intercourse. 'Sex is more exciting on the screen and the between the pages than between the sheets anyway,' Warhol reminds us, in the same way that 'never doing it is very exciting.'[22] In *Couch*, Warhol eschewed straightforward, mutually absorbing sex in order to investigate the second kind of sex, the *real* kind: sex queered by distraction.

Lovemaking on and off the Factory couch is about as fraught an image of America's so-called 'sexual revolution' as you can find. This, I am beginning to suspect, is the point. As Frankfurt School film critic Siegfried Kracauer argued about the 'distractions' of popular culture, *Couch* demonstrates that sex is not a respite from capitalism but an extension of it.[23] Kracauer, who argued even before Warhol that the true meaning of things could be found in 'surface-level expressions,' saw the corporeal spectacle of the 'mass ornament' as 'the aesthetic reflex of the rationality to which the prevailing economic system [capitalism] aspires.'[24] In *Couch*, the assembly of bodies making sex on the couch recalls the production of other commodities on the Factory floor. Like the Tiller Girls Kracauer theorized in the 1920s, the bodies in *Couch* have been symbolically inserted into the 'capitalist system of universal equivalence' that transforms all meaning and affect into exchange value.[25]

Confronted with Kracauer's dilemma, where the distractions from work are both modeled on and designed to revitalize exploitative labor, Warhol eroticizes capitalism itself. And yet unlike the Tiller Girls, Warhol's bodies neither maximize profit nor approach seamless mechanization. Though Warhol adulated post-Fordist production methods, the sex workers in *Couch* are defiantly unproductive. Stripping 'sexuality of its functionality,'[26] the perverse organization of bodies in *Couch* not only divorces sex from reproduction, but 'subverts the binary oppositions upon which the social order rests,' including those between work and leisure, public and private, heterosexual and homosexual, and, as we shall see later, whiteness and blackness.

Couch is temporally disjointed, and the 'sessions' on the couch often impede narrative progression by interrupting the erotic gusto of previous reels. Like bad sex or wasteful work, each reel ends abruptly and often without climax as the screen fades to white. Wayne Koestenbaum has described the effect of Warhol's typical inclusion of the white leader at the end of a reel as both a foreshadowing of death, and a metaphoric approximation of the orgasmic bliss that the images themselves withhold: 'Thus at the end of each segment, the viewers experience a miniature, spunk-white death, a blotto orgasm, a swooning obliteration of consciousness.'[27] Such interruptions may substitute for an orgasm that never comes, but these *petits morts* also cyclically bring the tally of 'sexual profit' back to zero.

If capitalism depends on the perennial generation of surplus, then *Couch* makes a spectacle of the wasteful surplus of bodies only to dispense with it at every change of reel. Because of its stag-like structure, *Couch* perennially erases its narrative progress and fails to reabsorb its own excess as profit. In this version of sex, waste is the very core of meaning. There is no profit in non-reproductive sex, only the blissful disorganization of resources. But it is this uselessness – of sex, bodies, art itself – that distinguishes and potentially redeems sex, and Warhol's work, from its troubling mirroring of capitalism.

The version of *Couch* that I know best is composed of thirteen antic-packed reels that Warhol's assistant Gerard Malanga selected from the larger compendium between 1965 and 1966.[28] Humor seems to have been the basis of selection. The set-up for each reel sounds like a parody of a homophobic or misogynist joke: How many queer poets does it take to screw in a banana? What's the difference between a woman and a vacuum cleaner? My sketches of *Couch* look like they've been torn from a ten-year's old notebook: stick figures twist into

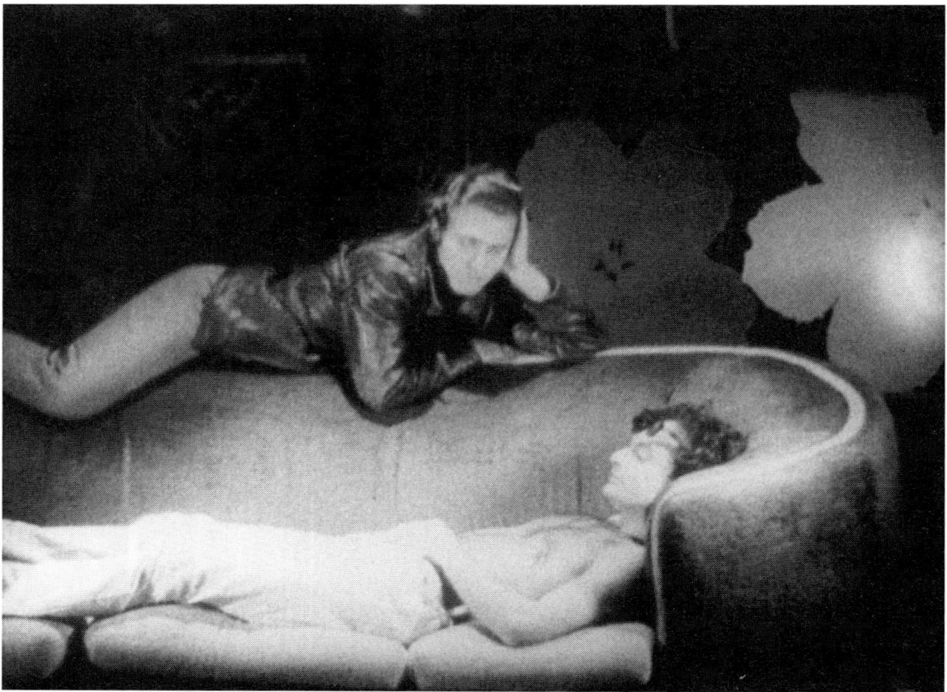

12   Gerard Malanga gazes longingly at Piero Heliczer, as he reclines on the eponymous piece of furniture in Andy Warhol's *Couch* (1964).

pretzel shapes, genital fruit bloom obscenely from every lap. Warhol was hardly the first pre-pubescent to joke about the analogy between penises and bananas but no filmmaker has pursued this absurdity with more tenacity.

The early reels of *Couch* are concerned with sexual posing and the staging of erotic gags. Desire ricochets between unresponsive non-participants. In the first reel, Gerard Malanga reclines vampire-like on the back edge of the couch, gazing at shirtless poet and experimental filmmaker Piero Heliczer, who lies 'asleep or dead'[29] on the cushions beneath him.

Despite Malanga's lustful gaze, neither man ever makes any attempt to breach the physical distance between them. For Warhol, who admitted that he felt depleted from trying to have sex,[30] 'just' looking suffices – at least for the moment.

In the next reel, desire again remains unrequited. If Soviet propaganda films staged the romance between a man, a woman, and a tractor, then Underground cinema's privileged mode of transporting desire was surely the motorcycle. In what seems a send-up of Kenneth Anger's *Scorpio Rising* (1963), a curvaceous nude Naomi Levine poses on the couch as an unidentified young man straddles

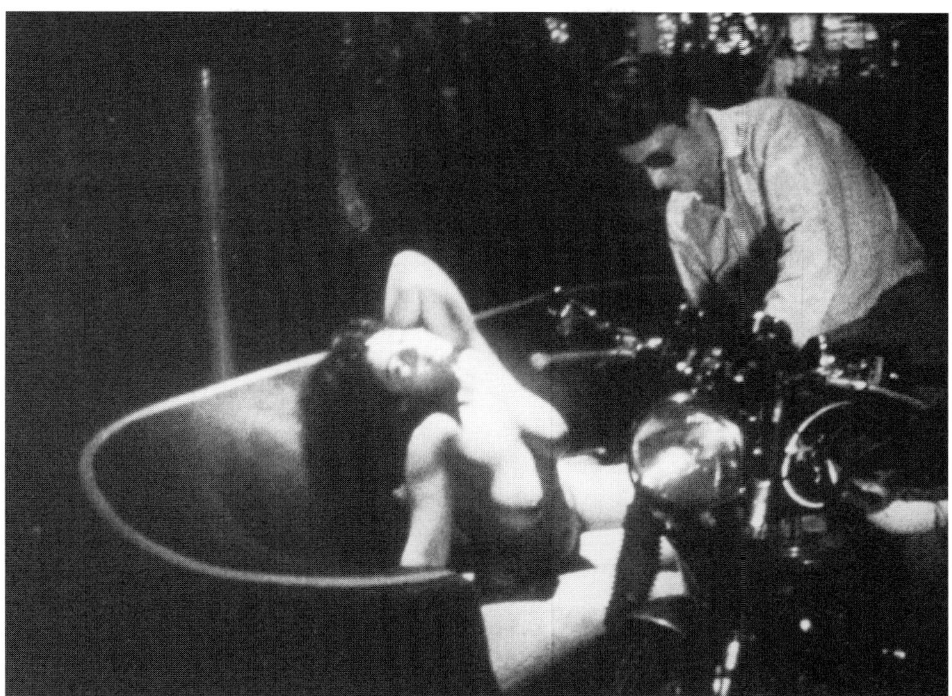

In a typical threesome from Andy Warhol's *Couch* (1964), women often play the '   **13**
'third wheel.'

his motorcycle beside her. She attempts to seduce him by jutting her breasts forward, staring longingly at the camera, and coyly twirling her hair. His gaze obscured by sunglasses, the motorcycle man remains cool and unresponsive, even when squeezing past her to fuss with his gear. As in Eduard Manet's famous painting *Le déjeuner sur l'herbe* (1862–1863), the woman's nudity is preposterous in contrast to the well-heeled dandy.

For Warhol viewers, this frustrated dynamic is a familiar one. On a date with a babe and a bike, woman is bound to be the third wheel. As Jennifer Doyle has argued, women are neglected objects in Warhol's films: positioned at the edge of the frame like inanimate clutter, they are not only excluded from the sexual activities but are often excoriated for being in the way. Aware that they are neither objects of the erotic gaze nor speaking subjects who anyone cares to listen to, they are abandoned to contemplate their own neglected status as objects that 'must be boring someone.'[31]

But there is more going on here than swish misogyny, the joke whose perennial butt is woman. His indifference is, after all, as stylized as her infatuation: framed by quotation marks, both performances parody gender norms. Even so, the woman's voluptuous body exceeds its negated exchange value. Yet as if to remind us of the wastefulness of femininity in a homoerotic economy of desire, Warhol refuses to excise the woman from his *mise-en-scène*. By rendering the woman's body obsolete, Warhol dispossesses heterosexuality of its greatest token of exchange, but he also bolsters the cult of the phallus that feminist artists and critics have struggled to demystify .

Queer sex, on and off the couch

Yet Warhol's emphasis on non-reproductive sex is not mere gynophobia. On the contrary, it is evidence of a radical politics that, as queer theorist Lee Edelman has argued, refuses 'reproductive futurism.'[32] Opposed to the absolute privilege of heteronormativity and its concomitant framing of the world's 'future children' as the discursive limit of thinkable politics, radical queerness resists every realization of futurity by assuming the place of the social order's death drive. This involves not only the refusal of 'every substantialization of identity' and 'history as linear narrative' (both of which are dismantled in *Couch*) but the thorough

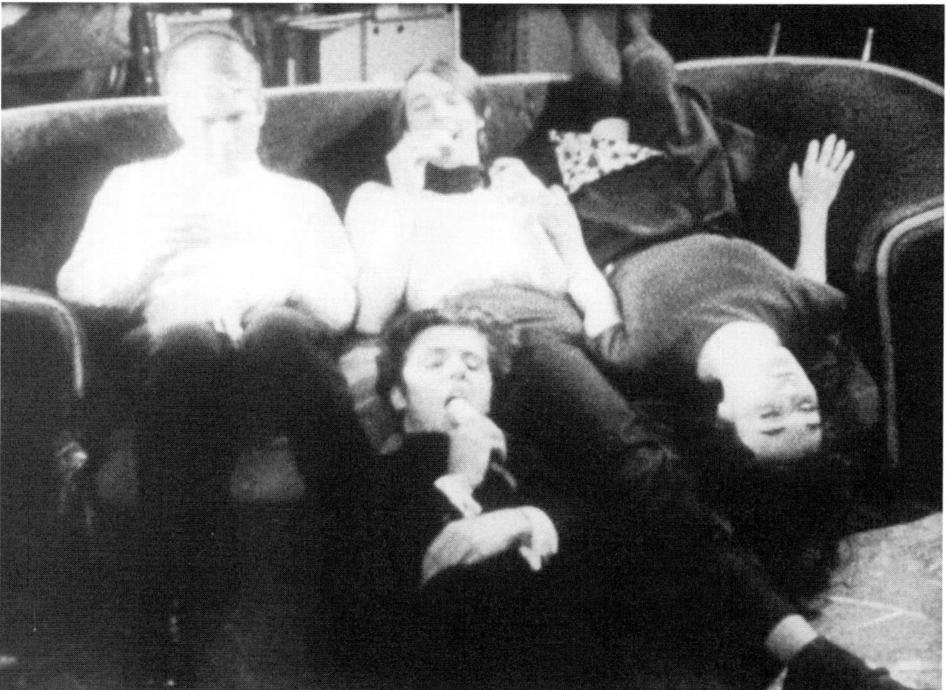

14   A group of men sit on the couch minding their bananas while Ivy Nicholson perches upside down like a catatonic bird. Andy Warhol, *Couch* (1964).

embrace of a negativity that, in severing our relation to ourselves, allows access to a total *jouissance*.[33] Withdrawing his allegiance from what Edelman calls the 'Ponzi scheme of reproductive futurism,' Warhol embraces queer sex and its 'negative' potential to obliterate identity and linear progress.

Sex in Warhol's cinema is as indifferent to ensuring the future of the labor force as it is to pleasing the customer. In all of the reels that follow, the traditional notion of heterosexual coupling is systematically undermined by the aggressive intrusion of other props and other bodies. In the fourth reel, for example, John Palmer and Joseph LeSueur sit on the couch while Gerard Malanga sits on the floor between them. They enact Warhol's favorite gag: all three of them peel and eat bananas, resulting in the appearance of erect phallic objects in their laps and mouths. Meanwhile, superstar Ivy Nicholson perches – like a catatonic bird – upside-down on the couch next to them.

Like the nude woman in the earlier reel, Nicholson is symbolically excluded from the scene. Deprived of both the literal penis, and the banana that both comically and ostentatiously stands in for it, the woman's body has no purchase. When this same group of actors appears three reels later in the same arrangement with replenished bananas, disrupting any sense of continuity, the still upended Nicholson fruitlessly attempts to compete for more attention by jutting her elbow in Malanga's face. Again, he ignores her.

In a world where one's sexual desirability determines one's value, this upended woman is the perfect sign of obstructed agency. Her bottoms-up bravado is also, however, an implicit critique of the phallocentrism that characterizes both heterosexual and homosexual culture. Excluded from *Couch*'s *mise-en-scène* of desire, she performs her uselessness. Yet in doing so, she discovers a perverse relation to her own body, as if celebrating the fact that nobody wants her. Dare we see signs of *jouissance* in such abjection? Cognizant that Warhol figures *her* defeat as a sign of *his* comic largesse, she is aware of her own futility. Strategically embracing her own negation, she disables her marginalization, and thus avoids the traps of both victimhood and masochism. It is certainly not the revolution Marcuse was hoping for, or that second-wave feminism would insist upon, but this performance of a subjectivity that has been doubly negated is *not nothing.*

However politically problematic, *Couch*'s dismissal of woman as an object of desire signals an important break from earlier visual cultures of male (homo) eroticism, which often incorporated female figures as a way of shoring up the 'epistemology of the closet'. The historically all-male audiences of stag films, for example, were enabled to bond with each other through the on-screen presence of an eroticized woman, whose virtual appearance may have provided sufficient 'cover' for more illicit homoerotic desires and interactions. Likewise, as Thomas Waugh has observed, even the gay spectators in Warhol's mixed audiences 'were begrudgingly willing to put up with Warhol's 'shotgun' approach – that is, a deliberate, commercially motivated, simultaneous appeal to both homo and hetero sensibilities.'[34]

In *Couch*, however, woman is no longer a necessary catalyst. Rather, her perversity calls attention to the double bind of femininity: in a patriarchal world in a which the woman's body can only signify as sexual currency, erotic disinterest further disables woman's access to meaning. But rather than aborting all possible relations between men and women, the absence of sexual desire serves in *Couch* as a point of departure for more perverse modes of relationality which, as Leo Bersani has argued, 'resist degenerating into a relationship.'[35] While 'received wisdom would have us imagine that friendships between men and women – and especially between gay men and straight women – are restricted by romantic burdens of expectation,'[36] *Couch*'s refusal of such expectations generates new possibilities. As Jennifer Doyle has argued in her ode to non-normative friendship, 'with a feminist ethic in place and a queer sensibility, the presence/absence of desire between friends seems less like a spoiler and more like a starting place.'[37]

Having queered normative relations between friends, *Couch* is free to move on to more candid explorations of sexual acts. It is only in the eighth reel that *Couch* actually approaches its reputation for being pornographic. In this segment, a fully dressed Gerard Malanga lies supine on the couch as Ondine, completely nude, kneels above him. As the reel progresses, the two men kiss and caress each other until finally they make out, perform oral sex and mount each other. Midway during their erotic activities, two other men, Walter Dainwood and Binghamton Birdie (a.k.a. Richard Stringer), enter the frame and attempt to distract the lovers by pouring beer on Malanga and putting a leather belt around his neck. When Dainwood shatters a mirror he has been using to spy on the couple, another man enters and vacuums up the shards on the floor. Though the film remains silent, one nonetheless cringes at the vacuum's irritating drone. As if this wasn't intrusive enough, the maid wielding the machine actually tries to 'vacuum' the couple entwined on the couch.

Of the thirteen reels, this is surely one of the most absurd. It is also, however, the one that most tellingly reveals the fusion of sex and work in *Couch*. As we learn from the *Philosophy*, maid work was hardly a neutral distraction for Warhol. On the contrary, it was an intensely cathected activity for the artist, who experienced a disproportionate amount of shame when compelled to bear witness to someone else cleaning up his mess. In the *Philosophy*, Warhol first celebrates, and then subtly challenges the American myth of a classless society. He writes, 'The idea of America is theoretically so great because we've gotten rid of maids and janitors, but then, somebody still has to do it … But there'll always be people who don't clean who think they're better than the people who do clean.'[38] A few pages later, however, Warhol admits to making the kind of affective distinction that he has just repudiated.

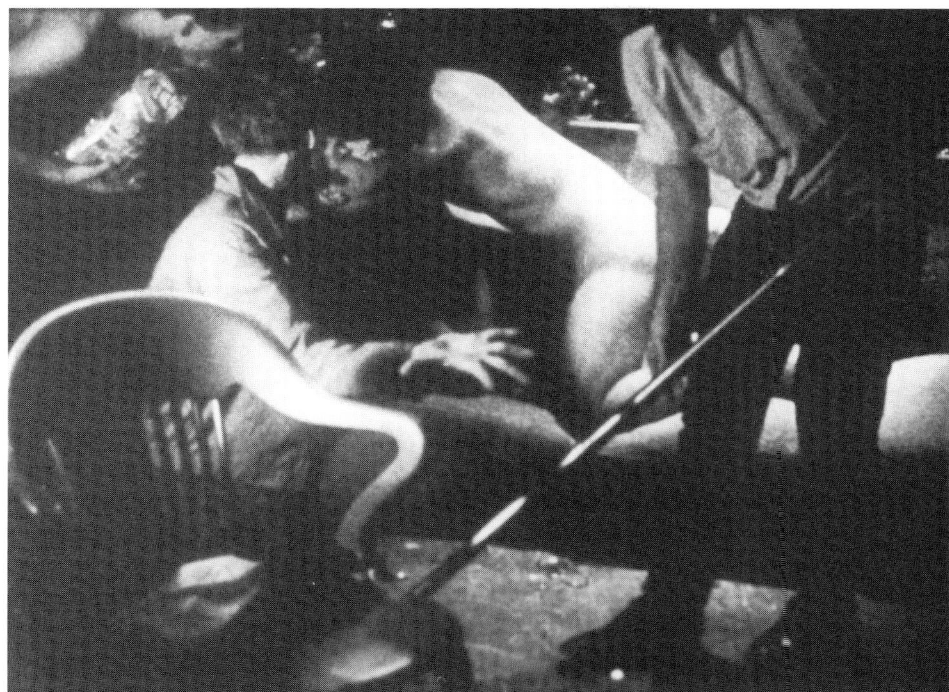

Someone vacuums in the foreground while Ondine and Gerard Malanga have sex in   **15**
the background in Warhol's film *Couch* (1964). Sex is not a respite but a continuation of
other forms of labor and distraction.

> It's so awkward when you come face to face with a maid … When I go to a ho-
> tel, I find myself trying to stay there all day so the maid can't come in. I make a
> point of it. Because I just don't know where to put my eyes, where to look, what
> to be doing while they're cleaning. It's actually a lot of work, avoiding the maid,
> when I think about it.[39]

Warhol was hardly the first person to be embarrassed by the maid's presence; in
certain circles, it is *de rigueur* to clean before her arrival. But it is an odd exception for a man who was never embarrassed when other people produced his
artwork for him, made public appearances for him, or went on dates for him.
Warhol even seemed to take pleasure in other people doing his dirty work: 'I
mean, everybody does something for everybody else … it's always an exchange,
and if it weren't for the stigma we give certain jobs, the exchange would always
be equal.'[40] So why was this particular service which, after all, wasn't 'any different from any other job'[41] so troubling?

Like watching sex work in pornography, watching maid work has traditionally entailed the viewing of feminine labor but without the erotic charge that naturalizes the male gaze. Warhol's musings on maid work remind us that what is most provocative about the maid's presence is *not* the fact of economic hierarchy, but the loaded question of where to put one's eyes. The maid, as a supposedly desexualized laborer in the bedroom, provokes a crisis of spectatorship. *Couch* presents Warhol's ludic solution to this dilemma: sex is what you can do when the maid is cleaning so that you don't have to watch her. Yet by situating maid work alongside (or in front of) sex work in *Couch*, Warhol not only puts these two forms of labor in dialogue, but also confuses their terms of value. This was not the only instance of Warhol eroticizing the work of cleaning and de-eroticizing the work of fucking: In an interview, Warhol admitted that he stopped watching daytime soaps because 'they don't have maids any more' – only people having sex who wear normal clothes.[42]

Typically, it is only once the maid leaves the hotel room that the purveyor of casual sex is free to resume their business. In *Couch*, such 'business' occurs regardless of the maid's presence. Reels nine through eleven are characterized by an unprecedented degree of intimacy between Gerard Malanga and 'Pope' Ondine (né Robert Olivo, 1937–1989) as they are interrupted by the antics of various intruders. Made five years before the Stonewall riots in June 1969, during a time in which sodomy laws made it illegal for men to have sex with each other in New York State (these laws were not repealed until 1980), these reels are remarkable for the candor and tenderness with which they approach gay lovemaking.

Reel nine opens with Malanga reclining nude on the back of the couch while Ondine lounges beside him. After so many 'tacky banana-fellatio jokes by drag queens,'[43] one is amazed when Ondine quite matter-of-factly removes his pants, mounts Malanga, and anally penetrates him. Overcoming the tease for which Warhol is best known,[44] the following three reels of *Couch* are among the most explicit examples of the 'taboo-shattering inscriptions of gay male bodies and desires'[45] that characterized Underground cinema of the 1960s. Yet both Ondine and Gerard Malanga seem completely unfazed by the significance of their groundbreaking performance. Their deliberately flat affect reminds us that there were plenty of men quite unabashedly having sex with each other in the 1960s, whether or not Hollywood was ready to acknowledge it.

Yet if the unselfconsciousness of these hard-core performances affectively minimizes the strength of the taboos they shatter, then the surrounding commotion underscores how truly remarkable they are. Within a few moments, Binghamton Birdie again enters the frame and does a handstand on a stool, while Walter Dainwood strips down to black bikini underwear and then undresses completely. In any other film from this period – even another made by Warhol – the sight of a man's cock would be enough to capture the attention of an audience. Considering the rarity of their onscreen appearance, it is hard to imagine the nude male genitals being upstaged. But that is exactly what happens here. Though one is originally startled by the appearance of erect and semi-erect penises on screen, one quickly grows accustomed to their ubiquity. Indifferent to the competing spectacle of this acrobatic young Adonis, Malanga hoists his legs in the air to facilitate deeper anal penetration. One cannot help but be moved by Malanga's willingness to be penetrated on-camera, the generosity of his bottomhood supplanting the mystique of the phallus that would become enshrined in hard-core porn.

Determined to sabotage the mesmerizing effect of watching two men have relaxed sex before the camera, Dainwood and Birdie stage a dance party in the foreground of the shot, effectively blocking the action. This pattern – of sexual revelation and obfuscation – continues. Reel ten, for example, opens upon Malanga and Ondine snuzzling on the couch in what seems like a post-coital embrace. A handful of other men come and go, attempting, somewhat unsuccessfully, to distract the viewer's gaze away from the couple. To inventory the

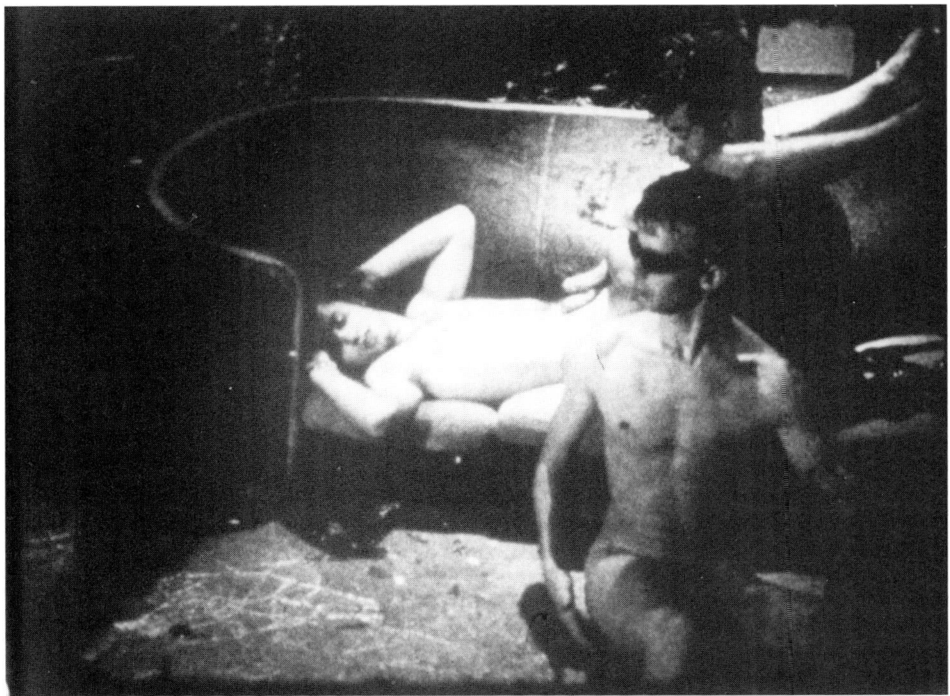

Ondine and Gerard Malanga having sex on the couch while another man sits in front of it. *Couch* (1964) is one of the first postwar films to depict explicit images of homosexual penetration.　　**16**

distractions to which Warhol subjects the lovers is no small feat; suffice it to say that this cockteaser employs almost every trick in the book.

After a while, however, they cease to matter. One stops trying to peer between the bodies to read the acts of love amongst the antics, and begins to enjoy the distractions as much as the deed. As Foucault has argued, 'homosexuality's threat to the dominant order has far less to do with the sodomitical sex act than it does with the queerness of the forms of relationality which surround the act.'[46] There is ample evidence of such queerness here. As a man enters the frame with an over-sized roll of plastic wrap (in order to fashion a full-body prophylactic?), Ondine nonchalantly flops Malanga's cock in his hand. This comic proximity of a flaccid penis to an erect tube of saran wrap reminds us of the thing-ness of flesh, its mutability and materiality. In staging such bizarre equivalences between bodies and other consumer goods – bananas and cocks, bikes and chicks – Warhol, like Duchamp before him, teaches us how to pervert bourgeois commodities for our own pleasure. *Couch* shows us, in other words, how to have queer and defiantly unproductive sex within capitalism.

Warhol may indeed be guilty of staging a variety of sexual taboos in *Couch* in order to capitalize upon their historical novelty, but this cannot account for the poignancy generated by these acts. Watching *Couch* now, nearly fifty years after it was filmed, I am struck anew by André Bazin's much critiqued insistence on the ontological equivalence between the photographic image and the object.[47] After the death of so many of the film's participants, and the devastation by AIDS of much of the community that Warhol's films document, it is hard not to be moved by what is in front of the camera. However staged these glimpses of illicit, unprotected, sex are, they seem paradoxically 'authentic' in their nonchalant, routine performativity. Is this the transcendent possibility of sex assembled at the Factory?

Legally impermissible at the time of *Couch*'s production, homosexual sex acts were officially decriminalized only at the beginning of the AIDS era. However Warhol may or may not have intended these images, retrospectively they cannot help but testify to a moment of liminal potentiality. Made four years before Warhol officially renounced filmmaking after being shot by Valerie Solanas, five years before the Stonewall riots inaugurated a bold new era of gay liberation, and fifteen years before the ravages of AIDS, *Couch* preserves a moment in which a group of people had enough courage to come out of their respective closets and onto the couch. However impossible such deceptively 'innocent' interactions have been rendered – by AIDS, by the codification of gay identities in the post-Stonewall era, or by the ubiquity of video and internet pornography – I can't help but be totally, tenderly and tragically in thrall to their indexicality. What could be a more powerful *punctum* than obsolescence?

Race

We cannot investigate the possibilities for perverse sex within capitalism without considering the challenge posed by another one of *Couch*'s most charged sexual moments: the *ménage à trois* that occurs between a white man, a white woman, and a black man in the second to last reel of the film. Warhol biographer Victor Bockris has described the scene as follows: 'Kate Heliczer was fucked in the ass by Gerard Malanga as she lay on top of the big black dancer Rufus Collins, while her husband, Piero, an underground filmmaker, ran out of the Factory and took a walk.'[48] Though it remains unheralded as such, this is one of the first interracial porn scenes in American cinema.[49] *Couch*'s explicit depiction of interracial sex not only significantly predates hard-core porn's foray into the same territory by a decade, but also avoids the fetishistic racism upon which mainstream interracial porn films would come to rely.[50] Rather than treating its interracial daisy chain sensationally, *Couch* presents the scene without ornamentation, approaching it with the characteristically flat affect of Warhol's stationary camera.

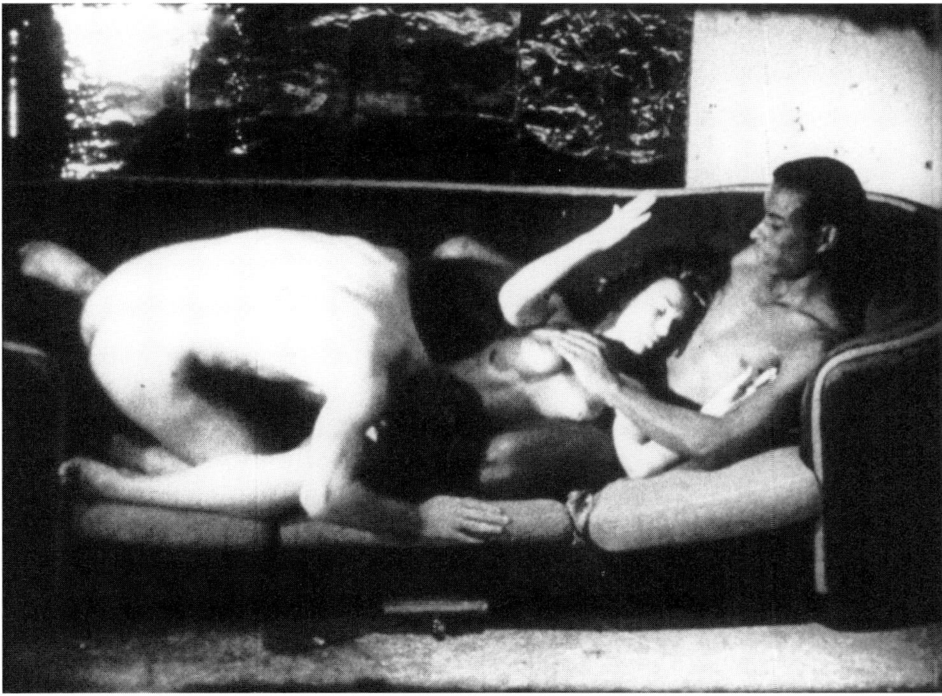

No errant bodies block the spectator's view of this interracial *menage à trois* between   **17**
Kate Heliczer, Gerard Malanga, and Rufus Collins in *Couch*, which was shot during one
of the most intense periods of crisis in the Civil Rights era.

In the context of the rest of the film, however, it is precisely this straightforwardness that distinguishes *Couch*'s interracial sex scene from all of the others. For while *Couch* does not emphasize the racial difference of its performers through costume or lighting, it does quietly announce the taboo it shatters by removing the 'quotation marks' that seem to frame sex in every other scene. Breaking *Couch*'s relentless pattern of revelation and concealment, this is the only uninterrupted sequence of sexual activity in the thirteen preserved reels of the film. In spite of the lurid tone of Bockris's description, this scene is *Couch*'s most intimate sexual encounter. Whereas in other sequences, the couch itself often obstructs the view of the sexual activity that occurs on it, here the couch is arranged frontally to optimally display its entwined bodies. Evincing a greater degree of harmony than any of the previous encounters, Warhol presents this groundbreaking interracial *ménage à trois* as suffused with shared sexual pleasure.

It is impossible to understand the politics of *Couch* – and their implications for racial, gender, and sexual identity – without attempting to understand why this scene has such a notably different charge than all of the other depicted sex acts. Considering the magnitude of the taboo against miscegenation in American cinema,[51] and the particularly tempestuous time in which the film was produced, *Couch*'s incorporation of an interracial sex scene is startling, in spite of the fact that, as Factory photographer Billy Name recalls, its racial dynamics were not considered particularly noteworthy by the scene's participants.[52] While this may indeed be true, it would be a mistake to treat this scene as just another instance of 'arbitrary coloring' in Warhol's *oeuvre*.[53] Even in the mid-1960s, blackness remained exceptional at Warhol's Factory. Of the 472 *Screen Tests* Warhol made in the mid-1960s, only four were of African-Americans: Rufus Collins, fashion model Donyale Lune,[54] her friend 'Kellie,' and Dorothy Dean.[55] Nonetheless, on the rare occasions when black performers actually appeared in front of Warhol's camera, they often played key roles: Dorothy Dean mysteriously gets the last word in Warhol's *My Hustler* (1965) before being rudely cut off by the termination of the film's last reel; Abigail Rosen, daughter of Harlem Renaissance poet Helene Johnson and the first black female bouncer at Max's Kansas City[56] – Dean was the third – inaugurates Warhol's soft-core film *Tub Girls* (1967) by eating watermelon with Viva (Susan Hoffmann) while sitting naked 'as a jay bird' in a clear glass bathtub.[57]

Unlike these two black female bouncers, who adjudicate the opening and closing of Warhol's films, dancer Rufus Collins (1935–1996) briefly became one of the director's main attractions. Collins was a member of the Living Theater who had been introduced to Warhol by their mutual friend Billy Name, and went on to star in Warhol's films *Batman Dracula* (1964) and *Suicide* (1965), as well as Jonas Mekas's *The Brig* (1964). Judging exclusively from Warhol's films, one could easily take Collins to be the single black male in circulation in the

Factory during the 1960s. He appeared first before Warhol's camera, locking lips with Warhol's 'first' (white) superstar Naomi Levine in *Kiss* (1963); their kiss was later expanded under the title *Naomi and Rufus Kiss* (1963) where, at fifty minutes, it held the Guinness record for the longest kiss every recorded on film.[58] Though it hasn't been critically acknowledged as such, it was also one of the first interracial kisses between a black man and a white woman to play on American screens.

But reaching 'first base' was only the beginning; in *Couch*, Warhol determined to go all the way. Shot midway through Freedom Summer, when young civil rights workers were explicitly going against the wait-and-see policies of the National Association for the Advancement of Colored People (NAACP) and the Southern Christian Leadership Committee (SCLC) in their attempt to re-enfranchise thousands of African-Americans throughout Mississippi, *Couch* broached the question of how far black and white intimacy could go. Filmed in the midst of the hunt for the bodies of three civil rights workers abducted and killed by the Ku Klux Klan,[59] Warhol's interracial *ménage à trois* was, in this respect, one of the most daring 'civil rights films' of the era.

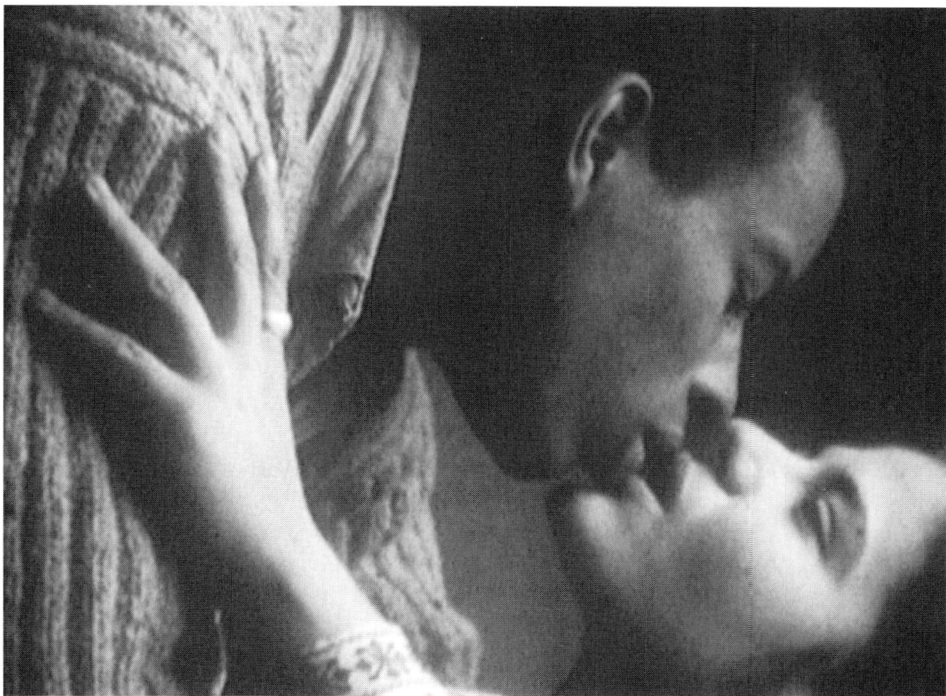

Interracial intimacy was one of many social taboos that Warhol broke in his films. Rufus   18
Collins and Naomi Levine make movie history in Warhol's *Kiss* (1963).

Yet beyond its daring display of interracial sex, how does *Couch* think the relationship between race, sex, and cinema? Like Warhol's silkscreen 'Birmingham Race Riot,'[60] also made in 1964, *Couch*'s inclusion of interracial sex acknowledged the incendiary context in which the film was made. Approaching interracial sex without shame, Warhol esteems it with a cool formalism: unlike some of the reels' more haphazard arrangements, this scene is notable for its compositional beauty and spatial integrity. Presented without distraction or interference from other bodies, this is the *only* scene in the film that resembles the kind of mutually absorbing erotic experience that Warhol called 'you-don't-think-about-it-sex.' Finally, we get to watch what looks like good sex – not hard work. But is 'make love not war' really the solution *Couch* poses to the question of racial strife?

Ultimately, Warhol seems far too cynical for me to believe this. As Warhol knew better than anyone, when a product was sufficiently novel, it didn't require expressionist ornamentation. Perhaps Warhol realized that what he had on his hands – or on his couch – was already so taboo that the best way to show it off was to simply to record it without interference. Such a stance may be opportunistic, but it does not lack political efficacy. After all, if sex and art could be subjected to the cold laws of the market, then perhaps racism could be too: exposure to a new product eventually diminishes its novelty. For radical documentary filmmaker Emile de Antonio, Warhol's famously cold, no-comment style was the most valid form of political critique.[61] Using skin tones rather than ink as his pigment, Warhol dares us to see this reel, with its own particular formal variations, as just another one in a series, simultaneously similar and singular.

Yet *Couch*'s interracial sex scene serves other purposes. Since the doubly non-normative *ménage à trois* explicitly dispensed with the notion of private, coupled sex that was so problematic for Warhol, there was no need to undermine it. In this way, the insertion of racial difference simultaneously eliminated the boredom generated by 'vanilla' heterosexual sex *and* resolved the quandary of the leftover third party. On the other hand, why should we assume that straightforwardly presented sex is any better than sex that is interrupted by distractions? Who is to say that best kind of sex is 'you-don't-think-about-it-sex?' To be absorbed by the spectacle of sex is, after all, to stop thinking about it. And to stop thinking about sex is to naturalize the 'concrete institutional forms of sexuality'[62] that, as Gayle Rubin has argued, are supplied by white supremacist, patriarchal, heteronormative, and capitalist culture. If movies had turned American citizens into an audience of uncritical spectators, then *Couch*'s use of Brechtian 'alienation effects'[63] had the potential to turn them back into critical observers.

Situated within the Factory's 'queer erotic economy'[64] *Couch*'s groundbreaking sexual and racial images are all the more remarkable because of Warhol's refusal to remark. Yet although Warhol did not sensationalize the interracial scene in *Couch*, he was well aware of the provocative nature of the image he had recorded. With the assistance of Billy Name, Warhol lent a still from the interracial sequence to poet and musician Ed Sanders, who placed it on the cover of the 'Mad Motherfucker' issue of *Fuck You Magazine* to celebrate its third anniversary.[65] But if Sanders underscored the magazine's oppositional stance through recourse to its incendiary cover image, as an editor, he seemed less concerned with its interracial content than with taunting fellow poet Gerard Malanga for his bisexual promiscuity. Sanders included an anonymous poem entitled 'Friends of GERARD MALANGA / (commissioned by Ronnie Tavel)' in which the word 'friends' signified 'men and women with whom Malanga presumably had some sort of sexual or otherwise entangled relationship.'[66] These names were arranged into two, gender-separated columns. The female column listed seventeen names, including Naomi Levine, Anne Buchanan, Barbara Rubin, and Rose Heliczer [sic], and concluded with a gesture towards 'thousands' more 'faces and snatches in the night.' The male column listed twenty-eight names, including Warhol, poets W.H. Auden, John Ashberry, Allen Ginsberg, Peter Orlovsky, and Kenneth Koch; Factory associates Ronald Tavel, Taylor Mead, Fred Herko, Rufus Collins, and Bob (Ondine) Olivo; and filmmakers Gregory Markopoulos and Willard Maas.

It is unclear whether the poem was authored by Sanders, or by notorious torturer Ronald Tavel, whose mastery of ridicule profoundly shaped the middle period of Warhol's cinema.[67] Regardless of its questionable authorship, the poem attempted to humiliate Malanga for practicing modes of friendship that, in contemporary parlance, come with sexual 'benefits.' Yet this is exactly the kind of sexual shaming that *Couch* refuses. Rather than distinguishing between platonic friendship and sexual love, homosexuality and heterosexuality, or sex and other forms of play, *Couch* rethinks 'friendship' as a form of intimacy that not only disturbs binary oppositions, but, as Jennifer Doyle has argued, nurtures forms of erotic 'relationality outside domestic and patriarchal structures.'[68] Prodding us to consider not only 'the importance and complexity of sex, but [of] everything else that surrounds it,' the distractions in *Couch* remind us how certain kinds of erotic 'friendship' are capable of queering the aims of both sex and work in late capitalism. Swerving away from ordained forms of genital penetration, *Couch* perverts what men and women, or men and men, are supposed to do together. In doing so, the film opens up a space where 'friends' of all colors and kinds could come out and get on or off.

Blue Movie

> The inaudibility of the visible will be redeemed.
>
> (Viva, *Blue Movie*)

> Sex is nostalgia for when you used to want it, sometimes.
> Sex is nostalgia for sex.
>
> (Andy Warhol, *The Philosophy of Andy Warhol*)

By the late 1960s, American popular culture had finally discovered that what couples did in their bedrooms mattered. Along with Stan Brakhage's film *Love-making* (1968), Yoko Ono and John Lennon's *Bed-In for Peace* (1969), and more popular texts such as Paul Mazursky's film *Bob & Carol & Ted & Alice* (1969), and John Updike's novel *Couples* (1968), Warhol's 1968 film *Blue Movie* aimed to expose the private rituals of coupling to the scrutiny of the American public. Although Warhol's films had already gained a controversial reputation for what Andrew Sarris derided as their 'tediously and fatalistically passive homosexuality' and 'nastily contrived anti-heterosexuality,'[69] *Blue Movie* actually explores the kind of intimate, heterosexual sex that Warhol's films customarily avoided. By foregrounding sex between a heterosexual couple in its poignant sketch of an afternoon tryst, *Blue Movie* excludes its homosexual author from the intimacy that it depicts.

Made four years after *Couch*, *Blue Movie* was not only the most sexually explicit feature-length, theatrically released American film of the 1960s, but also the first film of its kind to actually depict sexual intercourse.[70] It was the fulfillment of Warhol's career-long ambition to make a film about sex: 'I'd always wanted to do a movie that was pure fucking, nothing else, the way "Eat" had been just eating and "Sleep" had been just sleeping.'[71] According to Callie Angell, Warhol had initially tried to fulfill this goal in 1967 with the film *I, A Man*.[72] However, when his hope to cast Jim Morrison in the title role fell through, and Tom Baker was cast in his place, the stars refused to have un-simulated sex on film.[73]

Unlike *Couch*, *Blue Movie* is a color, sound, narrative, feature-length film that focuses exclusively on an intimate encounter between the film's only two actors: Viva (Susan Hoffmann) and Louis Waldon. Shot over three hours one late afternoon in October 1968 – a mere four months after Warhol was shot by Valerie Solanas,[74] – in art critic David Bourdon's Greenwich Village apartment, the film is, as Amy Taubin describes, 'categorically, literally and ethereally blue.'[75] Bathed in a blue tint that came from using tungsten indoor film that was ill suited for an interior streaming with light, *Blue Movie* is an homage to the 'blue' stag movies that Warhol's earlier sex films consciously imitate. Over the course of the languorous afternoon they spend together, Viva and Louis – who had played adversaries in Warhol's *Lonesome Cowboys* (1968) – have sex, hold each other, bicker, dress and undress, watch television, cook and have dinner, and shower together. They also talk, talk, talk – about everything from other lovers, to New York City politics, to the Vietnam war, to venereal disease. Indeed, their talking is so incessant that it is fair to say that although the actors do actually have sex in front of the camera – for only about fifteen minutes of the film's 105-minute running time – conversation is the privileged mode of intercourse in the film.

Originally titled *Fuck*, *Blue Movie* contains copious images of male and female nudity, images of genitals, and several sequences of sexual intercourse – including fellatio and vaginal penetration. Nevertheless, *Blue Movie* is not about 'pure fucking' and 'nothing else.' On the contrary, it is about sex and *everything* else. Although Warhol himself related the project of *Blue Movie* to *Sleep* (1963) and *Eat* (1964), it is quite distinct from the other two films in this 'trilogy.' Both *Eat* and *Sleep* remove their chosen activities from the normal contexts with which they are associated and thus compromise their verisimilitude. Furthermore, through the use of loop printing in the case of *Sleep* and the out-of-order sequencing of the reels in *Eat*, Warhol disturbs their normative temporality and thereby diminishes the documentary realism he claims to have been seeking. In sharp contrast, *Blue Movie* situates the sexual act in the context of heterosexual intimacy and domesticity, whose rituals unfurl slowly and tentatively in almost real time.

Unlike *Couch*, *Blue Movie* does not present sex in a Factory but sex in a home. The differences between the two locations, and the affective distinctions they generate, are tremendous. *Blue Movie* does not present sex as one alienated form of labor amongst others, but as an intimate negotiation of bodies and personalities, rituals, and habits. In contradistinction to the relentless interruptions in *Couch*, in *Blue Movie* nobody enters the frame or obstructs the view of the couple. Close-ups and medium shots of the actors predominate; this is, as Wayne Koestenbaum has argued, a film deeply invested in individual psychology.[76] Unlike the liminal, public space of the Factory couch, with its demand for visibility and swinging approach to sexuality, the bedroom has its own set of rules – about gender, privacy, and intimacy. By privileging the awkward interactions that happen before, after, during and between sexual acts, *Blue Movie* locates sex within the unfolding, anti-climactic temporality of domesticity. Other than a few minor adjustments – including a handful of zooms and a spattering of Warhol's signature strobe cuts – this is straight sex filmed straight. Indeed, *Blue Movie* is so straight that after its completion, Warhol never makes another film.

That being said, the film is not so straight after all. Not only does the film foreground a 'decidedly anti-normal heterosexual'[77] encounter, but it deconstructs heterosexuality nearly to the point of obsolescence. As Angell has observed, 'Given the pervasive ambience of impending but unconsummated sexuality which characterized so much of Warhol's earlier cinema, it seems appropriate that Warhol should have ended his career as a film director with *Blue Movie*.'[78] The film is, as Jonas Mekas described, an 'ethnography'[79] of the queer forms of coupling that happen when two people try to be together in a room. That they do so in spite of the obtrusive presence of the camera and its invisible operator, in spite of the pressures of other relationships beyond the frame, and in spite of the demands that masculinity and femininity and even the most transitive forms of coupledom make upon the individual, is what makes their efforts so poignant. Like most ethnographies, *Blue Movie* is a portrait of a lifestyle on the verge of extinction, in which the camera both preserves and destroys the rituals it records. Sex in such encroached-upon territory can only be, as Warhol writes, nostalgia for sex.

Steeped in nostalgia and melancholy, Warhol's farewell to cinema is, I argue, a eulogy for forms of intimacy that seemed increasingly anachronistic by the late 1960s. This final cinematic vision of coupling emphasizes the provisionary and contingent nature of forms of hetero-relationality that have been idealized,

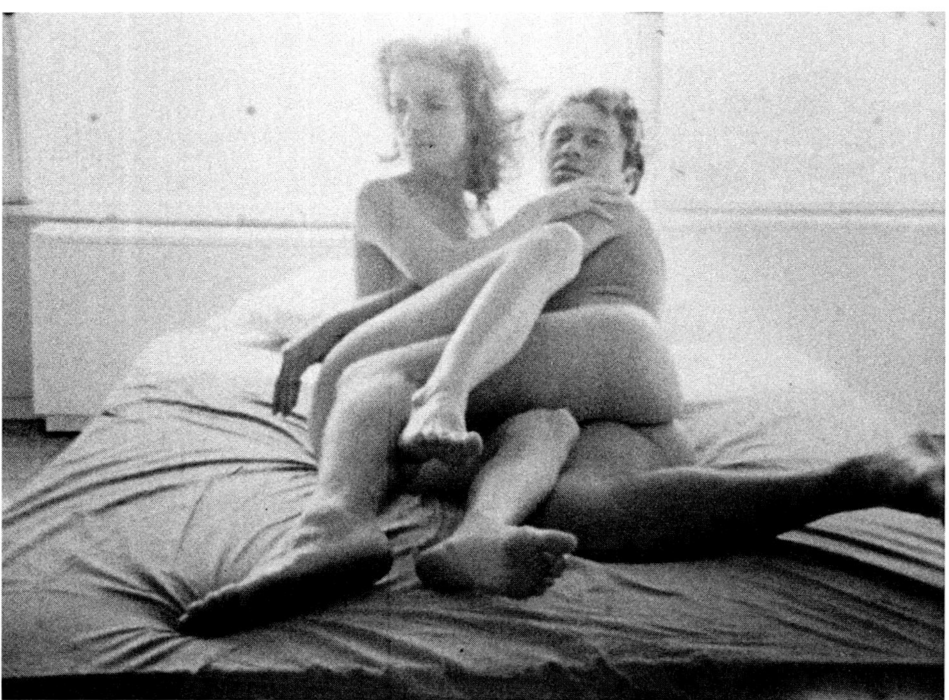

19   Viva and Louis Waldon negotiate the awkwardness of performing sexual intimacy for the camera. Though Warhol aspired to make a film that was just about 'fucking,' *Blue Movie* (1968) presents sex as one of many forms of discourse.

deconstructed, and unconvincingly reassembled. Though *New York Times* critic Vincent Canby derided the film as a 'put-on enacted by people who improvise their lives to fit the shape of fiction,'[80] it is precisely the improvisatory, performative nature of Viva and Louis's on-screen relations that makes their interactions so illuminating about the labors of intimacy. Negotiating the insistent publicity of Warhol's camera (and heterosexuality in general), and the consequent impossibility of ever truly being alone together, their relationship struggles to be performative and authentic simultaneously.

And yet, by foregrounding the way Viva and Louis Waldon attempt to evade the 'audibility' of the visible world, *Blue Movie* reminds us that as much as we may attempt to penetrate the secrets of the bedroom, the queer bonds between friends remain stubbornly illegible for outside spectators.

Blue Movie originally consisted of four 33-minute reels of film spliced together. It was shown like this throughout the winter of 1968 and spring of 1969 at the Factory, and once at a benefit screening for *Film Culture* magazine at the Elgin Theatre on June 12, 1969. On July 21, 1969, an abridged version of the film – cut from 133 to 105 minutes – made its commercial debut at the Andy Warhol Garrick Theatre at 152 Bleecker Street, where Warhol's *Lonesome Cowboys* was already playing. According to *Variety* magazine, the film made three times its production costs (which had been around $3,000) in its first week of exhibition in New York. Though the film had an uninterrupted run in Berkeley, California in the summer and fall of 1969, however, its exhibition in New York was plagued by controversy.

Although the national theatrical release of Warhol's *Chelsea Girls* in 1967 had catapulted Warhol the filmmaker into the limelight, it had also brought more intense scrutiny of the artist's growing reputation for demolishing sexual taboos. *Chelsea Girls* had provoked police censorship in both Boston and St. Louis; Warhol's later film *Lonesome Cowboys* – which played alongside *Blue Movie* in the summer of 1969 – was not only seized by police in Atlanta but actually inspired the FBI to open a file on the filmmaker.[81] Yet while these scandals were grist for the media, they also demonstrated that Underground films could be commercially viable. Provocateur that he was, Warhol was getting away with shattering the time-worn sexual taboos of American screen culture without serious penal consequence.[82]

In spite of having been rechristened from its original title *Fuck* in a failed attempt to avoid the censors, *Blue Movie* was seized by the New York City police on July 31, 1969. As with the famous 1964 police bust of Jack Smith's *Flaming Creatures*,[83] the theater manager, projectionist, and ticket seller were all arrested on charges of possessing obscene material.[84] In spite of expert testimony from a sociology professor at City College and film critic Parker Tyler,[85] when the film went to trial on September 17, 1969, the three-judge New York Criminal Court ruled unanimously that it was obscene and in violation of the penal code.

Arguing that *Blue Movie* 'graphically' depicted 'sexual activity between a male and female' with 'no redeeming social value,' the court dropped the charges against the projectionist and ticket seller but fined the theater manager $250.[86] Though Warhol retaliated by publishing the film as a book through Grove Press, with a complete transcription of the dialogue and lots of stills, he never directed another film again. Although the Supreme Court lifted the ban in 1973, the film was not re-released in New York until 2005, when it showed as part of the 'Views from the Avant-Garde Program' at the New York Film Festival.[87]

Redeeming social value?

In such a heated context, it is not surprising that the theatrical debut of *Blue Movie* was addressed by several mainstream publications, as opposed to most of Warhol's early films, which were rarely screened publicly and did not attract much critical attention at the time of their release. The media debate about *Blue Movie* coalesced around two related questions: whether its depiction of sex was titillating, and whether it could be said to have 'redeeming social value' – a phrase with significant legal consequence in the late 1960s.[88] *Variety*, which reviewed the film before its run-in with the police, saw these issues as inseparable. Arguing that 'Warhol makes even sex a bore,' *Variety* described *Blue Movie*'s action as follows: 'For two reels Viva and Louis Waldon sit, lie and roll about on a bed talking about things of redeeming social value and fondling.'[89] Describing the sex in the film as 'non-erotic' and 'mechanical,' Richard Corliss excoriated the film for capitalizing on the Supreme Court's recent ruling:

> some film-makers hide behind the Court definition of obscenity to show sex as being either ugly or boring, and thus redeemingly social. *Fuck* is exhibitable simply because, as in most Warholocausts, the performers take forever to do anything. The film is so excruciating to sit through that it can easily be used as 1) a scare film to uninitiated students of sex-education classes, 2) the subject of a *Partisan Review* essay, or 3) an example of a film that can pass unscathed, while far more accomplished and compassionate films like Stan Brakhage's *Love-Making* and Carolee Schneeman's *Fuses* are seized and censored.[90]

Implicit in these comments are the assumptions that a) the quotidian detail of heterosexuality is 'boring,' and b) that 'boring' sexual representations have more social value than entertaining or prurient ones.

Yet if *Blue Movie* seemed boring to mainstream critics, the avant-garde community esteemed it for achieving a rare kind of authenticity. *Expanded Cinema* author Gene Youngblood extolled the film as a 'most compassionate, human, real, unpretentious movie about physical love,'[91] while Jonas Mekas described it as 'the most touching, poetic "home" scene'[92] that he had seen in a long time. For the film's defenders, the film's authenticity was inseparable from its demystification of the sex act and its location of sex within discourse.

In spite of its candor regarding nudity and sexual acts, *Blue Movie* may be the least 'obscene' of all of Warhol's films. Not only are the machinations of lovemaking decidedly 'on-scene,'[93] but the film delivers a surplus of social value in the form of its unrelenting verbal discourse. While the characters discuss then-current political and social events, the film itself critiques the in-authenticity of pornography by offering a more complex and credible portrait of lovemaking. As Callie Angell has written, *Blue Movie* is 'almost a deconstruction of pornography, concentrating on the affectionate relationship between its stars' and presenting its 'climactic' scenes of sex quite casually, in the middle of what is 'basically four long reels of talk.' 'In retrospect,' Angell continues, 'the film seems to be more a documentary about life in the 1960s than a porno film.'[94]

Described as the 'undisputed queen of the unclad underground,'[95] for appearing nude in Warhol's *The Nude Restaurant* (1967), *Bike Boy* (1967), *Tub Girls* (1967), *The Loves of Ondine* (1967), and *Lonesome Cowboys* (1968), Viva is the engine of talk in this film. One of Warhol's most loquacious superstars, Viva drones on in her signature drawl about acting, auditions, dentistry, sexual diseases (after mentioning gonorrhea, she admits that her leotard is killing her crotch), the pressures of sexual performance, the failure of love, and the pitfalls of marriage. Taking note of the differences between her and Louis Waldon – she confesses to being the aristocratic daughter of a John Birch-er; he describes himself as part Native American – Viva insists that all blood (and therefore not only hers) is actually blue before it hits the air.

But if Viva and Louis engage in quotidian forms of bedroom banter, then they also demonstrate that politics are inseparable from pillow talk. There is no body outside of the body politic, and no bedroom immune from the incursions of imperial capital. Though both Viva and Louis claim disillusionment with the political process – he claims to have given up voting after the defeat of Democratic candidate Adlai Stevenson in 1956; she, since the assassination of President John F. Kennedy in 1963 – they mutually despair about the corruption of the war-mongering state. Weighing the difference between atomic weapons and chemical warfare, they bemoan the lack of a genuine alternative in the 1964 election between Texas Democrat Lyndon B. Johnson and conservative Republican Barry Goldwater, and express disappointment that then New York City Mayor John Lindsay had recently swung his support to Republic presidential candidate Richard Nixon over Democratic candidate Hubert Humphrey in the upcoming 1968 Presidential election. Though Warhol was mocked for claiming in the program notes that *Blue Movie* was 'about Vietnam and what we can do about it,'[96] the crisis in Vietnam is indeed a structuring force of this highly unstructured film. Viva offers the film's most powerful critique of the war when she says: 'We're paying destruction taxes. We're paying to hasten our debts and to hasten the extinction of the species … we're paying taxes to see ourselves obliterated.'

Indeed, the imminence of obliteration slips over the couple's interactions like shadows from the sinking sun. As the light fades from reel to reel, an air of melancholia seeps into the film, abetted by the film's blue tint. In a context in which the extinction of the human race by atomic warfare seemed inevitable, and participatory political action increasingly futile, Viva and Louis interrogate what types of political and sexual agency might remain in the face of constant encroachments on individual sovereignty by what Althusser famously termed the 'ideological state apparatuses.'[97] Though Vincent Canby sarcastically concluded that the characters demonstrated that there was 'nothing' they could do about Vietnam, he underestimates their power of negation. Hailed by Warhol's camera to create a credible portrait of lovemaking, Viva and Louis improvise a politics of refusal, in which they discursively reject their obligations as citizens, their obligations as performers, and the normative codes of heterosexuality. Not only do they advocate the refusal to vote, but in their rambling dissection of contemporary life, they also deny the obligation to go to war, to carry identification, to wear a brassiere, and to acquiesce to the police. Declaring military action 'over with,' 'finished,' 'old fashioned,' 'passé,' and a 'total waste,' Viva and Louis insist upon the obsolescence of modern warfare as well as the unsustainability of 'straight' or other institutional forms of relationality – including heterosexual monogamy.

Viva and Louis's political apathy is inseparable from their sexual disaffection. The first is a refusal to be implicated in what President Dwight Eisenhower described as the 'military industrial complex'; the second, a refusal to be interpellated by what Michel Foucault theorized as the 'power/knowledge' nexus of sexuality.[98] Viva, who complains that she can't 'keep up these long-term relationships … twenty-four-hour long-term relationships,' consistently deflates the myth of heterosexual romance that Louis parodies with his cheesy come-ons. Although Viva had apparently wanted to star in a Warhol sex film, she is 'decidedly uneager'[99] to make love in front of the camera. Throughout the afternoon, she complains about every aspect of Louis's sexual performance, including how terrible his penis looks when flaccid, his lack of foreplay, his failure to maintain an erection, how he is too rough and not romantic enough, and how boring it is to give him oral sex.

Instead of confirming the ecstasy of the sexual act, Viva and Louis's encounter foregrounds the awkwardness and discomfort involved in performing intimacy for the camera. Though the camera records their activities, it is not a welcome presence but an intrusive apparatus that the performers struggle to evade. Undressing becomes an ordeal as the lovers argue about who should remove which article of clothing first. Viva is apprehensive, often hiding her body from view or jerking her head from the pillow to look around suspiciously at the 'ghosts' of the film crew who invisibly populate the bedroom. She scolds Louis for putting his penis right in front of the lens – 'Nobody wants to see your ugly cock and balls!' – and then adjusts their position so that his genitals are no longer visible. Several times, Viva vocally calls attention to the presence of the camera and their consequent lack of privacy. But if Viva seems intent on avoiding the camera's gaze, she is also eager to evade the 'audibility' of Warhol's visible regime, which has been 'redeemed' by the addition of sound to his once silent cinema. After whispering something in Louis's ear that we spectators cannot overhear, Viva further excludes the imagined audience of the film by stating 'Maybe we should discuss it out loud at the next commercial break.' As the film continues, she becomes increasingly exasperated and demands, 'Why don't you ask everyone in here to leave?' After suggesting that they change positions in order to 'give a profile view' and ignoring Louis's comment that he's going to give her a baby, Viva seems momentarily reconciled to having sex in front the camera. But the sex cannot hold up to the pressure of performing in front of the camera. Anticipating critics' complaints that their lovemaking is 'mechanical,' Louis concludes that they should have 'organized orgasms,' in which everything is pre-planned.

But if Louis's attempt to synchronize their orgasms suggests the absurdity of transforming intimacy into spectacle, then his seduction techniques are equally pathetic. Though Louis maintains his bravado (though not his erection) in the face of Viva's ongoing humiliations, his romantic chivalry is conspicuous and unnatural. Not only do we not believe him when he tries to relax Viva by telling her that 'nobody is here but us,' (the film itself is proof that he is lying) but his romantic analogies – between her nipple and a dried apricot, the color of her tan and 'yellow jaundice' – parody the very conventions they have been conscripted to fulfill. When Louis promises to fuck Viva 'just like a cowboy,' viewers of Warhol's *Lonesome Cowboys* will find it difficult to forget just how inadequately cowboys fuck. (In that movie, Viva consistently refuses to make love to the cowboys, who then hump each other out of desperation.) Similarly, when Louis repeatedly tells Viva that he loves her near the end of the film, he sounds like an automaton poorly meeting the demands of post-coital intimacy: 'You're beautiful you're beautiful you're beautiful you're beautiful I love you I love you I love you I love you I love you…'

While *Variety* critiqued their performance for being 'more act than love,'[100] the magazine failed to acknowledge that the actors make no attempt to disguise the performative nature of their lovemaking. This, too, represents a refusal to adjust one's desire to the prescribed conditions of the apparatus: as Viva sings near the end of the film, 'I'm not in the mood for luuu-uhv, simply because you're near me…' For though the sex that Viva and Louis have is 'unsimulated' in the legal sense that actual genital penetration occurs in front of the camera, it cannot help but become, as Vincent Canby argues in a rare moment of insight,

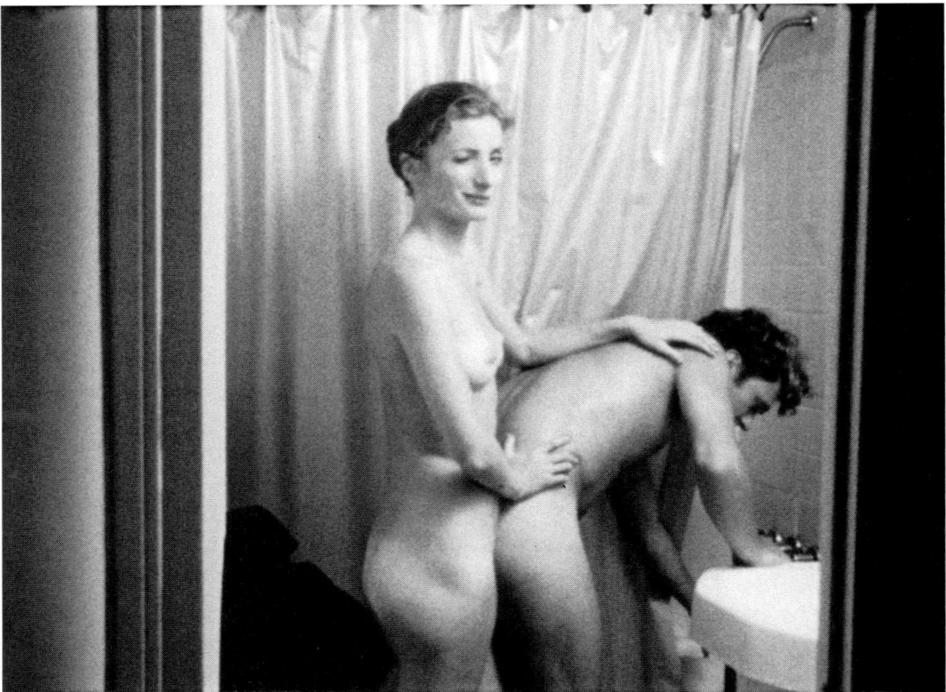

20   Captured by Warhol's camera, Viva and Louis Waldon nonetheless succeed in out-performing it. Andy Warhol, *Blue Movie* (1968).

a 'representation (and thus, not real) by the very process of recording.'[101] Canby goes on to describe *Blue Movie*'s representation of lovemaking as 'sex without passion, without love, without tenderness, without joy, something accomplished by the control of physical reflexes.'[102] But in spite of the fact that their intimacy has been transformed into a representation, it is not, as Canby claims, without tenderness. At a certain point in the film, Viva describes an episode in 'the Book of Love,' in which lovers 'brag about the ardor of the passion of their lovers by how deep the scratches are on their body.' With its staccato stop-and-start, fuck-and-duck rhythms, it's true that the sex in *Blue Movie* does not boast a lot of 'scratches.' Ever mindful of the camera's intrusion, the lovers do not proceed with the type of erotic abandon that could produce such incisions. Nor does its depiction of sex aim to scratch the prurient itch of the spectator.[103] Rather, in its prolongation of the unpleasurable tension of sexual stimulation, *Blue Movie* stimulates an 'itch' that, as Leo Bersani argues, 'seeks nothing better than its own prolongation, even its own intensification.'[104]

Yet *Blue Movie* is, nonetheless, a book of love. Spooning each other's bodies, or casually watching TV as if they themselves are not being watched, Viva and

Louis disable Warhol's intent to capture 'pure fucking' through anti-climactic acts of tenderness. Using visually untranslatable forms of tactility as a way of subverting Warhol's newly audible 'machine of the visible'[105] and its insistence on producing sex as spectacle, Viva and Louis compel Warhol's camera to surrender its optical mastery. In the last scene of the film, when Viva and Louis finally seem to enjoy themselves fucking and sucking in the shower – all the while parodying love songs, making animal noises, and finding ever-more ludic ways of evading the visual and acoustic discipline of the apparatus – Warhol's camera begins to caress their bodies. Panning over Viva's body as Louis tenderly washes her, the camera abrogates its visual mastery and attempts to join in on the fun it hasn't permitted its performers to have. For as much as it has strived to capture their bodies like butterflies under glass, the camera remains excluded from these moments of tenderness.

Yet as Amy Taubin argues, it is Viva's 'ambivalence about the very exhibitionism that has gotten her into this uncomfortable situation' that makes the film so fascinating.[106] In a culture that regarded the female body as a side of meat to be consumed – as the feminist protesters at the 1968 Miss America pageant insisted – Viva manages to take off her clothes without becoming disenfranchised. Outwitting the camera even as she becomes its object, Viva wriggles her way out from the place where Warhol has pinned her. Refusing to be excluded from the symbolic order, Viva thinks and talks. Rejecting the gendered restrictions of her own class, Viva not only helped to dismantle the taboos against sexuality in the late 1960s, but proved, in one Warhol movie after another, that she could out-talk the boys. Demeaned as a 'fag hag'[107] and 'slut'[108] by the mainstream press, Viva was nonetheless recognized by many of the viewers of Warhol's films as a new type of woman – a fashionable, educated, eloquent, irreverent, anti-war, pro-sex, anti-censorship feminist. As one female viewer wrote about the euphoric discovery of Viva as a 'livingbreathingflesh fantasy woman of now':

> I no longer sit there forced to empathize with Joan Crawford as she struggles with the complexities of adjustment to the life of a millionaire, the vicissitudes of the upper-middle-class pursuit of success, the agonies of suburban lust, or even how to mow a lawn. Now I can be myself, participating in a moving, pictured, now, a sense of my world, my environment, the pressures of my times.[109]

Negotiating the sexual politics of the bedroom with as much ingenuity as she outmaneuvers the police, Viva uses intercourse as a means of self-defense. Unlike that other late 1960s sex symbol Bonnie Parker, who wanted to play with boys' toys so badly that she was willing to die for it, Viva discredits the phallic order of guys and guns. While Bonnie shoots her way into oblivion, Viva talks her way out of extinction.

Notes

1 Andy Warhol, *The Philosophy of Andy Warhol (From A to B and Back Again)* (New York: Harcourt Brace Jovanovich, 1975), p. 98.

2 Sigmund Freud, *Three Essays on the Theory of Sexuality*, in *The Standard Edition of the Complete Psychological Works*, trans. James Strachey (London: Hogarth Press, 1953), Vol. 7, p. 150.

3 Kaja Silverman, *Male Subjectivity at the Margins* (New York: Routledge, 1992), p. 187.

4 In his 1955 book *Eros and Civilization*, Frankfurt school philosopher and 1960s guru Herbert Marcuse rallied against the 'genital supremacy' which supplanted the polymorphous perversity of childhood and delivered modern, one-dimensional man straight into the vice-grip of capitalism. Herbert Marcuse, *Eros and Civilization: A Philosophical Inquiry into Freud* (Abingdon: Routledge, 1998).

5 Jonathan Flatley, 'Like: Collecting and Collectivity,' *October* 132 (Spring 2010), pp. 71–98; Wayne Koestenbaum, *Andy Warhol* (New York: Viking Penguin, 2001).

6 Douglas Crimp, 'Spacious,' *October* 132 (Spring 2010), pp. 5–24; p. 24.

7 Ibid.

8 Thomas Waugh, 'Cockteaser,' *Pop Out: Queer Warhol*, ed. Jennifer Doyle, Jonathan Flatley and José Esteban Muñoz (Durham, NC: Duke University Press, 1996), Chapter 3.

9 Reva Wolf, *Andy Warhol, Poetry, and Gossip in the 1960s* (Chicago, IL: University of Chicago, 1997), pp. 134–138.

10 Ronald Tavel, interview by Patrick Smith, in *Andy Warhol's Art and Films* (Ann Arbor, MI: UMI Research Press, 1986), pp. 484–503; p. 489.

11 Screenings took place on March 19, 20, and 21. 'Andy Warhol's *Couch* at St. Marks Church,' Andy Warhol Chronology, *Warholstars.org*, www.warholstars.org/chron/couch.html (accessed July 7, 2010).

12 Annette Michelson, '"Where is Your Rupture?" Mass Culture and the *Gesamtkunstwerk*,' in *Andy Warhol*, ed. Annette Michelson (Cambridge, MA: The MIT Press, 2001), p. 101.

13 'Blue Movie, or F**K: Warhol Makes Even Sex a Bore,' *Variety*, June 25, 1969.

14 Benjamin H.D. Buchloh, 'Andy Warhol's One Dimensional Art: 1956–1966,' in *Andy Warhol*, ed. Michelson, pp. 1–48.

15 Isabelle Graw, 'When Life Goes to Work: Andy Warhol,' *October* 132 (Spring 2010), pp. 99–113; p. 102.

16 Ibid., p. 103.

17 Warhol, *Philosophy*, p. 97.

18 Koestenbaum, *Andy Warhol*, p. 80.

19 Warhol, *Philosophy*, p. 96.

20 Ibid., p. 47.

21 Ibid., pp. 48–49.

22 Ibid., p. 44.

23 Siegfried Kracauer, 'The Mass Ornament,' *The Mass Ornament: Weimar Essays*, ed. and trans. Thomas Y. Levin (Cambridge, MA: Harvard University Press, 1995), pp. 75–86.

24　Kracauer, 'Mass Ornament,' pp. 75, 79.

25　Flatley, 'Like,' p. 76.

26　Silverman, *Male Subjectivity*, p. 187.

27　Koestenbaum, *Andy Warhol*, p. 69.

28　In the 1980s, Malanga took the original material and re-organized the reels in a different order. Malanga sold this copy to the British Film Institute. Claire Henry, conversation with the author, May 25, 2012.

29　Wolf, *Andy Warhol, Poetry, and Gossip*, p. 115.

30　Warhol, *Philosophy*, pp. 97–98.

31　Jennifer Doyle "'I Must Be Boring Someone": Women in Warhol's Films,' in *Sex Objects: Art and the Dialectic of Desire* (Minneapolis, MI: University of Minnesota Press, 2006), pp. 71–96; p. 71.

32　Lee Edelman, *No Future: Queer Theory and the Death Drive* (Durham, NC: Duke University Press, 2004).

33　Ibid, pp. 1–5.

34　Thomas Waugh, *Hard to Imagine: Gay Male Eroticism in Photography and Film from Their Beginnings to Stonewall* (New York: Columbia University Press, 1996), p. 170.

35　Leo Bersani, 'Sociability and Cruising,' in *Is the Rectum a Grave? and Other Essays* (Chicago, IL: University of Chicago Press, 2009), p. 57. Bersani's concept of shattering forms of relationality is integral to Douglas Crimp's reading of Warhol's films in *'Our Kind of Movie': The Films of Andy Warhol* (Cambridge, MA: The MIT Press, 2012).

36　Jennifer Doyle, 'Between Friends,' in *A Companion to Lesbian, Gay, Bisexual, Transgender and Queer Studies*, ed. George E. Haggerty and Molly McGarry (Malden, MA: Blackwell, 2007), pp. 325–340; p. 329.

37　Ibid.

38　Warhol, *Philosophy*, pp. 99–100.

39　Ibid., p. 102.

40　Ibid., p. 100.

41　Ibid., p. 102.

42　Jordan Crandall, 'Andy Warhol' [1986], in *I'll Be Your Mirror: The Selected Andy Warhol Interviews 1962–1987. Thirty-Seven Conversations with the Pop Master*, ed. Kenneth Goldsmith (New York: Carroll & Graf Publishers, 2004) , pp. 348–381; p. 355.

43　Waugh, *Hard to Imagine*, p. 171.

44　Ibid., pp. 170–171.

45　Ibid., p. 141.

46　Doyle, 'Between Friends,' p. 329; Michel Foucault, interview by R. de Ceccaty, J. Danet and J. Le Bitoux, trans. John Johnston, *Ethics: Subjectivity and Truth*, ed. Paul Rabinow (New York: The New Press, 1994), pp. 135–140; pp. 136–137.

47　André Bazin, 'The Ontology of the Photographic Image,' in *What is Cinema?* ed. and trans. Hugh Gray, Vol. 1 (Berkeley: University of California Press, 1967), pp. 9–16.

48　Victor Bockris, *The Life and Death of Andy Warhol* (New York: Bantam, 1989), p. 203.

49 Porn scholar Linda Williams claims that the Mitchell Brothers' classic porn film *Behind the Green Door* (1972) was the 'first, American, feature-length hard-core film to include a major interracial sex scene.' Though it isn't feature-length and didn't have nearly as wide a reception as *Green Door*, *Couch* was made almost a decade before this. Linda Williams, 'Skin Flicks on the Racial Border: Pornography, Exploitation, and Interracial Lust,' in *Porn Studies*, ed. Linda Williams (Durham, NC: Duke University Press, 2004), pp. 271–308.

50 Ibid., pp. 299, 300.

51 The 1930 Motion Picture Production Code (which provided the skeleton for the 1934 enforcement agency, the Production Code Administration) explicitly prohibited scenes of miscegenation, amongst many other instances of sexual content. The Production Code was not changed until 1968. Jon Lewis, *American Film: A History* (New York: W.W. Norton, 2008); Susan Courtney, *Hollywood Fantasies of Miscegenation: Spectacular Narratives of Gender and Race 1903–1967* (Princeton, NJ: Princeton University Press, 2005).

52 Billy Name, phone conversation with the author, May 16, 2012.

53 David Antin, 'Warhol: The Silver Tenement,' *Art News* 65 (Summer 1966); Leo Steinberg, 'Reflections on the State of Criticism,' in *Robert Rauschenberg*, ed. Branden W. Joseph (Cambridge, MA: The MIT Press, 2002), p. 36.

54 Callie Angell, *Andy Warhol Screen Tests: The Films of Andy Warhol Catalogue Raisonné*, Vol. 1 (New York: Harry Abrams, 2006).

55 Yvonne Sewall-Ruskin, *High on Rebellion: Inside the Underground at Max's Kansas City* (New York: Thunders Mouth Press, 1998). Dean also appeared in Warhol's films *Space* (1965), *My Hustler* (1965) and *Afternoon* (1965), which was originally part of *The Chelsea Girls*.

56 'Interview with Abigail Rosen (McGrath),' interview by Gary Comenas, December 2007, *Warholstars.org*, www.warholstars.org/articles/abigailrosen/abigailrosen.html, accessed June 20, 2012.

57 Ibid.

58 RufusCollins.org, www.rufuscollins.org/little_known.html, accessed July 5, 2010.

59 On June 21, 1964, black CORE activist James Chaney, white CORE organizer Michael Schwerner and white summer volunteer Andrew Goodman were arrested, and then handed over to a waiting ambush of Klansmen who abducted and killed them.

60 Warhol appropriated journalist Charles Moore's photograph, which was originally featured in *Life* magazine on June 7, 1963. Michael Durham, *Powerful Days: The Civil Rights Photography of Charles Moore* (Tuscaloosa, AL: University of Alabama Press, 2005; New York: Stewart, Tabori & Chang, 1991).

61 Quoted in Branden Joseph, '1962,' *October* 132 (Spring 2010), pp. 114–134; pp. 125, 127.

62 Gayle S. Rubin, 'Thinking Sex: Notes for a Radical Theory of the Politics of Sexuality,' *The Lesbian and Gay Studies Reader*, ed. Henry Abelove, Michèle Aina Barale, and David M. Halperin (New York: Routledge, 1993), pp. 3–44; p. 4, originally published in *Pleasure and Danger: Exploring Female Sexuality*, ed. Carole S. Vance (Boston, MA: Routledge and Kegan Paul, 1984).

63 Bertolt Brecht, 'The Modern Theater is the Epic Theater' and 'Theater for Pleasure or Theater of Instruction,' *Brecht on Theater: The Development of an Aesthetic*, ed. and trans. John Willett (New York: Hill and Wang, 2001), pp. 33–42, pp. 69–76.

64 Flatley, 'Like,' p. 88.

65 *Fuck You* 8, no. 5 (March 1965). See Wolf, *Andy Warhol, Poetry, and Gossip*, p. 49.

66 Wolf, *Andy Warhol, Poetry, and Gossip*, p. 50.

67 Crimp, *'Our Kind of Movie,'* pp. 46–67.

68 Doyle, 'Between Friends,' p. 326.

69 Andrew Sarris, 'Westward Ho-Ho with Warhol,' *The Village Voice*, May 8, 1969.

70 'Warhol's "Blue Movie" The Bluest of 'Em All, If and When Released,' *Variety*, June 18, 1969.

71 Andy Warhol and Pat Hackett, *POPism: The Warhol Sixties* (New York: Harcourt Brace Jovanovich, 1980), p. 94.

72 Callie Angell, *The Films of Andy Warhol: Part II* (New York: Whitney Museum of American Art, 1994), 36, published in conjunction with an exhibition of the same name, New York, Whitney Museum of American Art, March 30 to April 24, 1994.

73 David Bourdon, *Warhol* (New York: Harry Abrams, 1989), p. 256.

74 Warhol was shot on June 3, 1968.

75 Amy Taubin, 'Afterglow,' *Film Comment*, 42, no. 1 (January 2006), pp. 58–59.

76 Koestenbaum, *Andy Warhol*, p. 154.

77 'Blue Movie, or F**K,' *Variety*, June 25, 1969.

78 Angell, *The Films of Andy Warhol: Part II*, p. 36.

79 Jonas Mekas, 'On Beaver Movies, Sex, and the Sense of Humor,' in *Movie Journal: The Rise of a New American Cinema, 1959–1971* (New York: Macmillan, 1972), pp. 352–354; p. 353; originally published in *Village Voice*, August 14, 1969.

80 Vincent Canby, 'Warhol's Red Hot and "Blue Movie,"' *The New York Times*, August 10, 1969.

81 Marcia Kramer, *Andy Warhol et al.: The FBI File on Andy Warhol* (New York: UnSub Press, 1988).

82 Angell, *The Films of Andy Warhol: Part II*, p. 36.

83 J. Hoberman, *On Jack Smith's Flaming Creatures (and Other Secret Flix of Cinemaroc)* (New York: Granary Books, 2001).

84 Morris Kaplan, 'New Warhol Film Seized by Police: Theater Staff Arrested After Showing of "Blue Movie,"' *The New York Times*, August 2, 1969.

85 Morris Kaplan, 'Professor Defends Warhol "Blue Movie" As "Not Stimulating,"' *The New York Times*, September 17, 1969.

86 Morris Kaplan, 'Film by Warhol is Ruled Obscene: 3 Judges Call "Blue Movie" Hard-Core Pornography,' *The New York Times*, September 18, 1969.

87 Until the re-screening of the film at the New York Film Festival, Viva's efforts to keep the film out of circulation made it impossible to watch *Blue Movie* anywhere save on videocassette at the Warhol Museum in Pittsburgh.

88 In *United States v. Roth* (1957), Supreme Court Justice William Brennan determined that hard-core pornography was 'utterly without redeeming social importance.' Jon Lewis, *Hollywood v. Hard Core: How the Struggle over Censorship*

Saved the Modern Film Industry (New York: New York University Press, 2000), pp. 261–262.

89 'Blue Movie, or F**K', *Variety*, June 25, 1969.

90 Richard Corliss, 'Film and Other Four-Letter Words', *National Review*, July 29, 1969, pp. 760–761.

91 Gene Youngblood, Intermedia, *Los Angeles Free Press*, March 7, 1969.

92 Mekas, 'On Beaver Movies, Sex, and the Sense of Humor', p. 353.

93 Linda Williams, 'Porn Studies: Proliferating Pornographies On/Scene: An Introduction', in *Porn Studies*, pp. 1–23.

94 Angell, *The Films of Andy Warhol: Part II*, p. 36.

95 Guy Flatley, 'How to Be Very Viva – A Bedroom Farce', *The New York Times*, November 9, 1969.

96 Canby, 'Warhol's Red Hot and "Blue Movie."'

97 Louis Althusser, 'Ideology and Ideological State Apparatuses', *Lenin and Philosophy and Other Essays*, trans. Ben Brewster (London: NLB, 1971), pp. 121–173.

98 President Dwight Eisenhower warned the United States about the threat of the nation's growing 'military industrial complex' in his televised farewell speech on January 17, 1961. *Public Papers of the Presidents*, Dwight D. Eisenhower, 1960, 1035–1040; Michel Foucault, *The History of Sexuality*, Volume 1: *An Introduction*, trans. Robert Hurley (New York: Vintage Press, 1990).

99 Taubin, 'Afterglow', pp. 58–59.

100 'Blue Movie, or F**K', *Variety*, June 25, 1969.

101 Canby, 'Warhol's Red Hot and "Blue Movie."'

102 Ibid.

103 Linda Williams, *Screening Sex* (Durham, NC: Duke University Press, 2008), p. 48; Leo Bersani, *The Freudian Body: Psychoanalysis and Art* (New York: Columbia University Press, 1986), p. 34.

104 Bersani, *The Freudian Body*, p. 34.

105 Jean-Louis Comolli, 'Machines of the Visible', in *The Cinematic Apparatus*, ed. Teresa De Lauretis and S. Heath (New York: St. Martin's Press, 1981).

106 Taubin, 'Afterglow', p. 59.

107 Sarris, 'Westward Ho-Ho with Warhol.'

108 Taubin, 'Afterglow', pp. 58–59.

109 Liza Williams, *Los Angeles Free Press*, November 7, 1969.

> Imagine an eye unruled by man-made laws of perspective, an eye unpreju-
> diced by compositional logic, an eye which does not respond to the name of
> everything but which must know each object encountered in life through an
> adventure of perception. How many colors are there in a field of grass to the
> crawling baby unaware of 'Green'? How many rainbows can light create for the
> untutored eye? How aware of variations in heat waves can that eye be? Imagine
> a world alive with incomprehensible objects and shimmering with an endless
> variety of movement and innumerable gradations of color. Imagine a world
> before the 'beginning was the word.'
>
> (Stan Brakhage, *Metaphors on Vision*)

Stan Brakhage taught a generation of experimental filmmakers how to see differently. His re-conception of the expressive capacity of the 'camera eye' not
only constituted one of the most singular contributions to the evolution of
the medium, but laid the foundation for an entire range of artistic practices
and inter-personal relations that coalesced around the demand to making embodiment visible. Firmly committed to the relocation of filmmaking within
the home and the use of the 'camera eye' to develop new ways of seeing, Stan
Brakhage forged a domestic, personal, and organic cinema practice in startling
opposition to the narrative, industrial machine of Hollywood.

Rejecting both the industrial cinema of the west coast, and the Underground
community in New York, Brakhage relocated with his family to the mountains
of Colorado in 1959. There, he transformed the home movie into 'the essential
practice of film' by documenting the depths of his psyche, the cycles of nature,
and his own personal experiences of childhood, love, sex, birth, and death.[1] Yet
since the earliest critical accounts of his work, Brakhage's romantic musings on
the self and nature were positioned at odds with the Underground sensibility
of filmmakers such as Andy Warhol and Jack Smith. Nevertheless, Brakhage
shared with these filmmakers a sense of the difficulty of representing corporeality through the conventional language of cinema. Though the emphasis on
the domestic everyday of heterosexuality, marriage, and childrearing in his
films seems at odds with the celebration of queer sex in Underground cinema,

Brakhage disassembled each of these heteronormative institutions with a battery of defamiliarizing effects.

The camera eye

As a filmmaker, Stan Brakhage was committed to the primacy of the visual. For Brakhage, understanding vision was unthinkable without recognizing its entrenchment in the flesh. Like Merleau-Ponty, Brakhage was constantly negotiating the collision of the 'flesh of the world' and the 'flesh of the body' on what might also be called the 'flesh' or 'skin' of celluloid. Brakhage's investigation of embodied vision entailed becoming conscious of those aspects of vision that human knowledge relegated to the unconscious, including the movements, shifts of focus, and dilations of the eye, 'the perpetual play of shapes and colors on the closed eyelid,'[2] and what the 'mind's eye' sees in visual memories and dreams. As Brakhage instructed a generation of avant-garde filmmakers:

> Allow so-called hallucination to enter the realm of perception, allowing that mankind always finds derogatory terminology for that which doesn't appear to be readily usable, accept dream visions, day-dreams or night-dreams, as you would so-called real scenes, even allowing that the abstractions which move so dynamically when closed-eye-lids are pressed are actually perceived.[3]

Brakhage's dedication to what he actually saw, rather than what he had been trained to see,[4] involved the virtual reinvention of film form and language. Challenging himself and his viewers to see differently from the impoverished ways in which their eyes had been disciplined, Brakhage's films strip the body of its conventional cultural associations through radical acts of defamiliarization. In this, as in many ways, Brakhage hailed back to the Russian and Soviet artistic movements of the early twentieth century.[5] Defamiliarization or estrangement (*ostranenie*) was the term coined by the Russian Formalists to describe the transformative perceptual effect of artistic devices that rendered the familiar unfamiliar or strange. By distorting an image of an otherwise recognizable object or sensation, critic Viktor Shklovsky argued, art could remove objects from the automatism of perception that arose from habitualization.[6]

By distorting the lens of the camera, obliterating perspective, altering camera speeds and film stocks, Brakhage adjusted cinema to the subjective and imperfect modalities of human vision.[7] Superimposing images of the body on other natural objects in his signature rapid-fire montage, Brakhage insisted on the body's relation to the flesh of the non-human world. By eliminating clear establishing shots in favor of extreme close-ups, out-of-focus and shaky camera work, and under- and over-exposed images, Brakhage enabled the viewer to re-discover bodies as unpredictably shifting, infinitely divisible, phosphorescent objects. Finally, by scratching, hand-painting, and chemically treating the celluloid, Brakhage insisted upon the tactility of vision by making physical impressions on the film's 'skin.'[8]

Brakhage constantly returned to images of the body in his work. Yet as he continued to explore the vicissitudes of corporeality, his attitudes towards its filmic representation transformed dramatically. After having refined his densely layered cinema of 'closed-eye' and hallucinatory vision, Brakhage began to re-orient his practice towards new forms of 'open-eye' vision in which the filmmaker's 'eyebody,'[9] to borrow Carolee Schneemann's term, became less conspicuous. Though only one aspect of Brakhage's incredibly prolific and diverse body of work, this reorientation from what Brakhage called a 'visible' to an 'invisible' art, involved, as scholar Marie Nesthus has chronicled,[10] a paring down of his methods of presentation, a painful repudiation of many of his earlier techniques, and a new investment in cinema's ontological capacity to photographically capture the profilmic event.[11] Inspired by a series of emotional shocks that informed an ongoing crisis of perception, Brakhage's approach to the body shifted from lyrical expressionism to what Hal Foster has described as 'traumatic realism.'[12] Yet whereas Nesthus situates the beginning of this transformation in the late 1960s, the coexistence of lyrical expressionism and traumatic realism is already evident in Brakhage's documentation of the birth of his first child in *Window Water Baby Moving* (1959).

By the early 1970s, Brakhage was describing his transformation as a new investment in the 'document' aspect of art-making. In a series of letters to an intimate circle of interlocutors that included critic and *October* founder Annette Michelson, fellow filmmakers Hollis Frampton and James Broughton, poets Robert Creeley and Ed Dorn, and filmmaker, journalist, and founder of Anthology Film Archives Jonas Mekas, Brakhage theorized the act of cinematic seeing in startling opposition to his earlier ideas in *Metaphors on Vision*. Defining 'document' in opposition to the term 'documentary,' Brakhage considered the first an attempt to get a 'naked fix' on what was transpiring in front of the camera.[13] In 1971, he wrote to Frampton, 'I am most concerned in my work at the moment with Document (as distinct, as I can make it, from Documentary – knocking that "airy" off the end giving me the sense I'm escaping that rhetoric and outright propaganda associated with "Old Doc" school of filmmaking.'[14]

Brakhage's establishment of a dialectical relationship between defamiliarization and documentation occurred in response to the demands made by certain corporeal 'actions' upon his subjectivity. These actions, which prompted 'ways-of-seeing so extremely different from most of [Brakhage's] earlier work as to constitute a counter-measure in the field of aesthetics,'[15] included the birth of his first child, sexual encounters with his wife and other intimate friends, the death of friends and loved ones, and his own witnessing of the medical evisceration of the body in open heart surgery and autopsy. Although Brakhage had been recording instances of birth, sex, and death since the earliest stages of his career, by the late 1960s, this urgency to 'document' the body so overwhelmed Brakhage that he attempted to purge his filmic language of adornment, abstraction and hallucination. Washing his films clean of many of the 'terribly visible signatures' that 'leak energy'[16] from the body and persona of the maker onto the celluloid in the form of effervescent traces, Brakhage aimed to take a 'good, hard look'[17] at those occasions of embodiment that have the greatest capacity to shatter and restructure our subjectivities. This involved consciously 'divesting' his films of the use of sound, paint, and other chemicals '(all use of them having been to express the inner, ego-centered, vision of myself),' multiple exposures and other specific laboratory effects, and 'Eisensteinian editing.'[18]

For Brakhage, the search for objectivity in the face of explicit corporeal trauma was not a defense against affect, as Foster has claimed about Warhol's *Death and Disaster* series,[19] but an opening up to the wounds of the world. Adjusting his vision in the face of (and in order to more honestly face) such traumatic action, Brakhage struggled to enable viewers to see extreme images of the body through their own eyes – rather than his. Of course, Brakhage was no naive realist. Though he invested new faith in the image's capacity to record the object as it is, he knew the impossibility of ever seeing things just as they are. As Nesthus has observed, 'the critical difference' between Brakhage's use of defamiliarization and documentation, 'seemed not to be in the presence or the absence of the artist's mark, but rather in the degree of its visibility.'[20]

Brakhage's 'return to the real' involved what Foster has described as 'a defiance of visual sublimation' towards a more direct engagement with the mechanics of the body.[21] It was also, in film-historical terms, a shift from an Eisensteinian notion of imagistic truth towards a Bazinian one. For Soviet film-maker Sergei Eisenstein, the truth of the cinematic image was subjective and could be manipulated through the deliberately orchestrated collision of shots in different forms of montage.[22] For André Bazin, who claimed in his famous 1945 essay 'The Ontology of the Photographic Image' that the 'image is the object,' the power of photographically based media inhered in their ability to capture an indexical record of what was in front of the camera. Though Bazin did not actually believe that photographs or movies were pure equivalents of reality – the often-overlooked last sentence of this essay makes this clear[23] – he thought that the art of film would be best served by, as Nesthus wrote of Brakhage, 'allowing the representation of the world to exist sufficiently within the work itself.'[24] Distinguishing between these two counter-traditions, which Brakhage traced even further back to the distinct approaches of the Lumière brothers and George Méliès, Brakhage described a tension in his own work between the 'natural reproductive magic of Film' and 'its theatrical-painterly-new-poetic-jigs.'[25]

This chapter explores the dialectical relationship and productive tensions between defamiliarization and documentation in an armful of films that Stan

Brakhage made about bodies transformed by birth, sex, and death: *Window Water Baby Moving* (1959), *Cat's Cradle* (1959), *Lovemaking* (1968) and *The Act of Seeing With One's Own Eyes* (1971). By arguing that as early as 1959 Brakhage had begun to explore a notion of 'clean-eyed' vision that complicated his use of expressionistic camerawork, I aim to unplug the 'leakages' of Brakhage's own desiring body on the scrubbed skin of these films.

Window Water Baby Moving (1959)

By his own admission, Brakhage was 'obsessed with childbirth.'[26] As an orphan, Brakhage couldn't help but feel that the details of his own birth were especially inaccessible. By obsessively documenting the births of his children with his first wife Mary Jane Collom (known as Jane Brakhage between 1959 and 1987, and now as Jane Wodening), Brakhage seized the opportunity to visually penetrate the hidden mechanics of the life-giving body. *Window Water Baby Moving*, which the Brakhages made in 1959, documents the birth of their first child, Myrrena. Neither a documentary nor a home movie in the conventional sense of these terms, *Window Water Baby Moving* extends domestic creativity to include the processes of filmmaking and childbirth. Shot by both Stan and Jane Brakhage,[27] the film is a collaborative artistic negotiation not only of one of the most charged corporeal experiences, but of the division of labor in a heterosexual marriage.

Window Water Baby Moving was a groundbreaking film. Made at a time when images of nudity, birth, and delivery were still forbidden by Hollywood's 1934 Production Code, *Window Water Baby Moving* offered an intimate and explicit portrait of childbirth. Although there were films about birth in limited circulation, these medical training films were geared towards technique and physiology. Focusing exclusively on 'a disembodied vaginal opening floating in space' that was 'mechanically tended, wiped, [and] tugged at by robot-like nurses and doctors,'[28] these films certainly did not include the visual perspective of the child-bearer herself. Rather, by visually reducing female bodies to their splayed genitals, these films strove to protect their subjects from potential designation as 'loose' women, and thereby sever the visual relationship between procreation and sexual desire. Yet even these sanitized educational films often came under attack by state government boards and local authorities.[29]

Combining an investigation of the corporeal and emotional aspects of childbirth, *Window Water Baby Moving* de-sanitizes and de-mystifies the mechanics of human reproduction. Like autopsy, which demanded of Brakhage an even greater visual candor in *The Act of Seeing With One's Own Eyes*, delivery presents an occasion for phenomenological 'in-visibility,' in which the fleshy secret that remained invisible during pregnancy suddenly becomes exteriorized into view. It is no wonder then that the Kodak lab where Brakhage processed the film

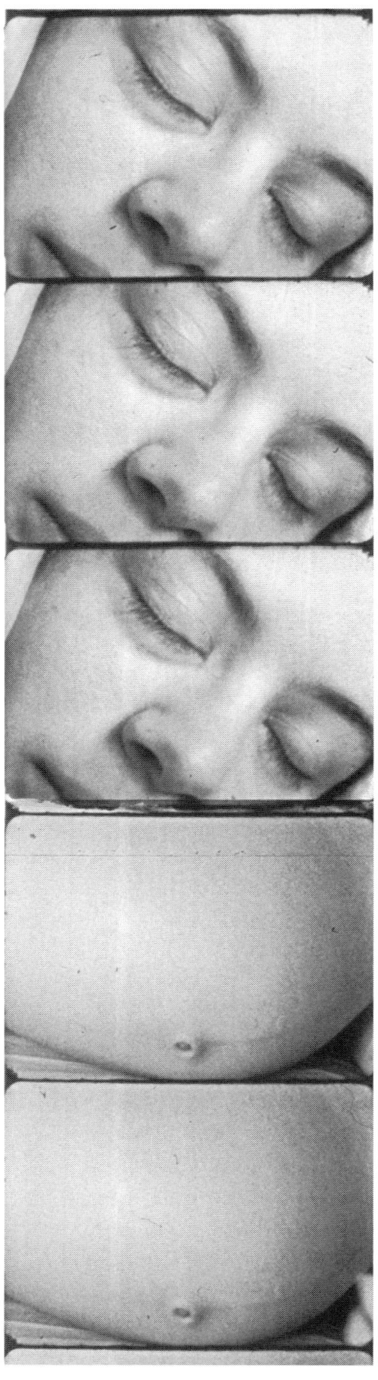

threatened to destroy the negative until the obstetrician 'promised that it would only be shown for purposes of childbirth instruction.'[30] For audiences in the late 1950s and early 1960s, the film was a viscerally shocking experience. Even the 'mother' of the post-war avant-garde Maya Deren, whose own partner Alexander Hammid had documented the birth of their feline companion in *The Private Life of a Cat* (1944),[31] was outraged by Brakhage's blasphemous intrusion into what she regarded as the most sacred female experience.[32] But if *Window Water Baby Moving* is the first postwar film to represent the *gestalt* of human childbirth, then it also signifies the moment when Brakhage first allows the naked, corporeal documentation of the body to overcome his more characteristic artisanal interventions on the surface of the film, as if to enable the birthing body to 'speak' for itself. The defamiliarization techniques that *are* visible in the film, such as the moments of upside-down, repeated, or canted footage, engage dialectically with the more unmediated images of the body, as if to illustrate the ways in which so-called 'objective' documentation is inseparable from 'subjective' impression.

Brakhage did not originally intend to film the birth. Yet in a culture where it was not yet acceptable for male partners to be on-site during childbirth – this trend began in the United States during the 1960s – the Brakhages hoped that filmmaking would provide an acceptable alibi for Stan's presence in the delivery room. Yet after finally finding a doctor enthusiastic to cooperate, the Brakhages failed to convince the hospital that either the father or his camera equipment should be allowed

21

Jane Brakhage's face in close-up followed by images of her pregnant belly in *Window Water Baby Moving* (1959), which Stan Brakhage made to document the birth of their first child.

in the delivery room. They decided on a home birth, so that Stan would have complete access to the delivery.

Filming the birth soon became a matter of desperate necessity. As the following quotation attests, recording the event through the camera became a form of psychic defense against the overwhelming affective charge of bearing witness to this most transformative event. As Jane Brakhage has described, Stan was so upset by her 'roaring and panting' that he momentarily stopped filming:

> He tells me to relax and pant. He needs to relax; I'm doing fine. I tell him how much I love him and ask him if he's got my face while I'm roaring and this sets him off again and reassures him, and he clickety-clackety-buzzes while I roar and pant, and we are both very happy, and it is like we are doing something together each with his own task, and each task is great and wonderful beyond telling.[33]

As Stan Brakhage later recalled, 'I knew for that first birth I could never have stood it in that room, without passing out or something, if I hadn't had a camera. … In fact, there's very little that's understandable to me about life, or even bearable, except the seeing of it. I have managed my whole sight by making films.'[34]

Window Water Baby Moving begins with shots of a window, framed diagonally, intercut with flashes of blackness. Jane moves in front of the window, her naked silhouette framed by incoming light. As she steps into a bathtub, reflected patterns of sunlight and shadow dissect Jane's pregnant belly into four quadrants. A rhythmic montage juxtaposes images of her placid face, wet and shimmering belly, and breasts with an image of Stan's face. Here, as on the other occasions when her husband is visible, it is possible that Jane operates the camera. We see the couple's interlocking hands as they rest on Jane's protruding stomach; moments later, they kiss.

After a long pause of blackness, the camera finds Jane on the delivery table; we see her breathing stomach and face, as well as a close-up of her vagina discharging water and blood. A hand presses down on Jane's belly with what seems like an excruciating amount of pressure. During a particularly painful moment in labor, we see a close-up of Jane's face with her mouth open in a muted scream. Though the film is silent, our bodies can't help but register this inaudible sound.

Brakhage cuts back to an image of Jane's smiling face from the earlier episode in the tub, followed by shots of the sunlit window. As the baby's head crowns, the film again returns to these earlier images, now rapidly edited and pitched upside-down. After images of the evacuation of the placenta and the cutting of the umbilical cord, the film ends with shots of the baby at Jane's breast and shaky, hand-held images of Stan's ecstatic face. Forgive me if this description makes the film sound clinical; let me try to explain, in another way, what it feels like to watch.

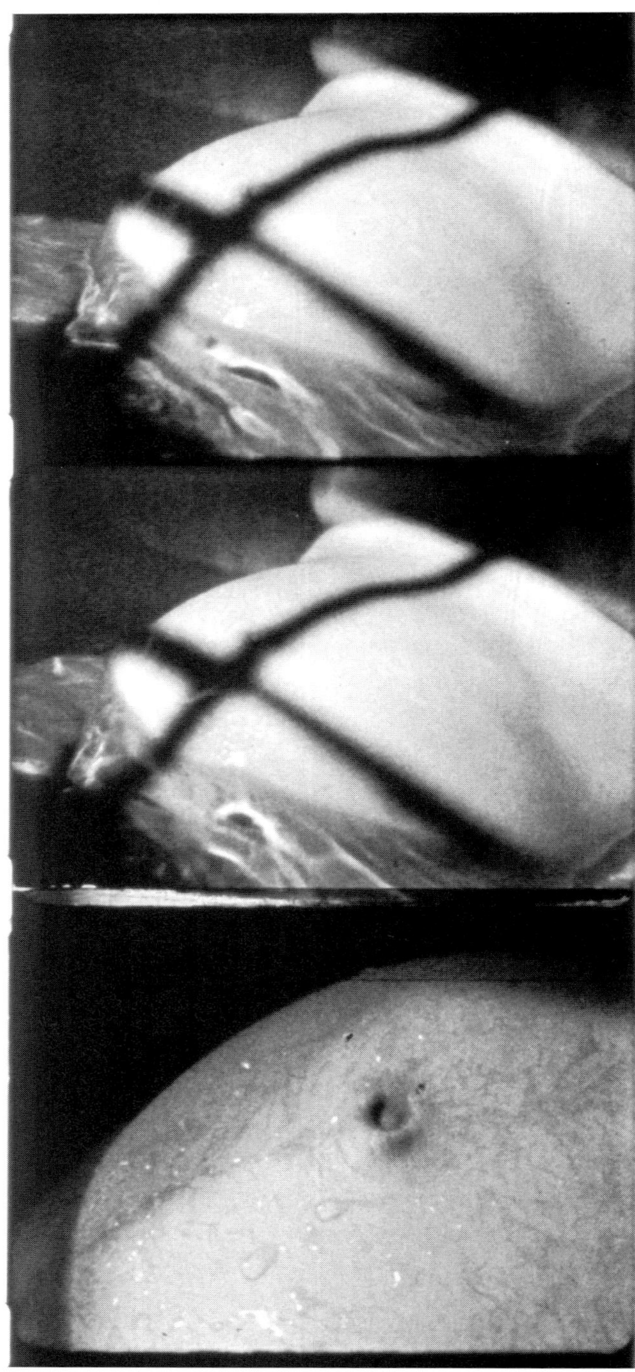

22
Even while Brakhage proffers atypically unmediated access to the body in *Window Water Baby Moving* (1959), we recognize his cinematic 'signatures' in the film's stunning lighting effects, which defamilarize Jane Brakhage's distended belly.

I show *Window Water Baby Moving* every year as a rite of initiation in an introductory course I teach on the poetics of cinema. Every year, I am astonished anew at the absolute hush that falls over the classroom as we watch; it is as if I can't remember what collective enthrallment feels like when it isn't actually happening. The film unravels my students, who tend to respond to it as either the 'most beautiful' or the 'most obscene' film they have ever seen. But where do these conflicting affects come from? Haven't these media-savvy students already seen and done everything?

Why *does* this old film so electrify and offend generations of viewers who have grown up in the visual abundance of the digital age? For even beyond the auratic traces of its antique, color-saturated celluloid, *Window Water Baby Moving* demands that one give oneself over to the image. This is not exclusively an effect of its explicitness, though this too is an essential aspect of the film's tendency to shatter the body of the beholder. Nor is it an effect of the poetic gestures with which Brakhage intersperses these images. Brakhage himself came to recognize these details as embellishment:

> The proven greatness of this film is not to be found in the inter-cut bath-tub and/or all those recapitulatory flashbacks throughout. These are fine-enough in themselves, structurally solid, and all-of-apiece with the total work; but 'Window Water Baby Moving' in all these times of its showing has proven that the heart of its matter is more subtly located than I had ever imagined.[35]

23
Window Water Baby Moving's (1959) explicit images of the opened body create visceral effects on the film's spectators. Even though the film is silent, we can 'hear' Jane Brakhage screaming as her baby crowns.

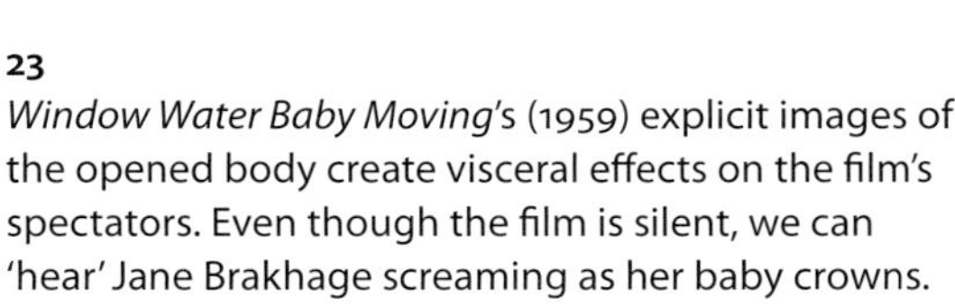

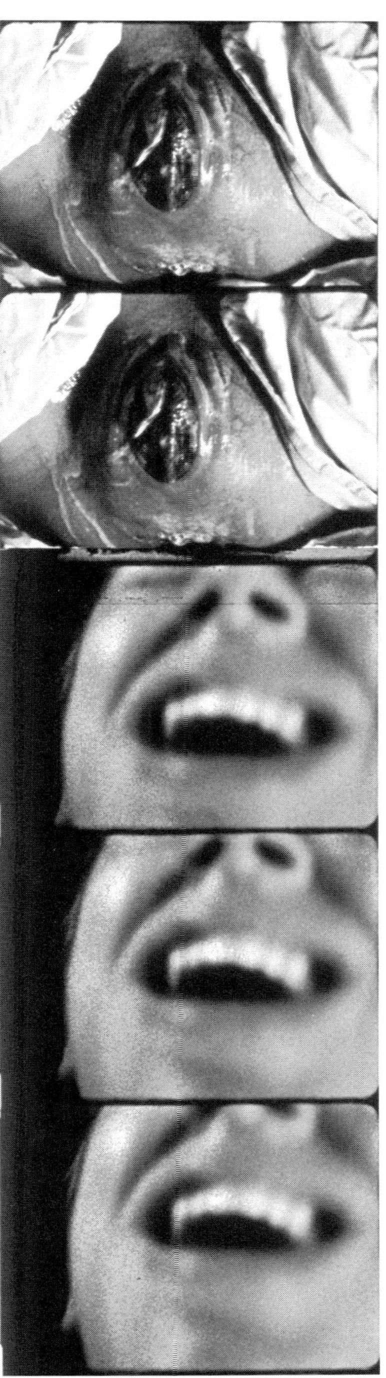

Watching the film each year, I find myself hypnotized by both the camera's insistence on the fact of the body *and* its poetic rendering. I have come to know intricacies of Jane Brakhage's body that I have never known about my mother's and will surely never know about my own. But it is not only *mechanics* that transfix here: it is the affective circuit that forms as the chiasms of our bodies intertwine. Jane's opened body opens the couple to a heightened form of intimacy that becomes visible in the fusion of these two, overlapping forms of creation. Such charged entanglements in turn open us.

In *Window Water Baby Moving*, art's 'invisible container' proves insufficient; Brakhage's corporeality makes itself visible in the dance of wondrous terror he does around his wife's bursting body. We recognize the 'Brakhage' we think we know in the camera's obsessive tendency to frame and reframe the body, in the way the filmmaker can't help but compare the protrusion of belly to the extension of light streaming through glass. The membrane of skin that conceals the baby stretches like a windowpane over the chasm between the visible and invisible flesh of the body. But like Jane's water, it breaks, allowing the insides of the 'in-visible container' of Jane's body to come rushing out. When we see Brakhage smiling at the end of the film, he is no longer the composed artist but the exuberant father addled into a state of discombobulated ecstasy. *Window Water Baby Moving* captures the fluids that spill from the body's seams, unstopping the leakages between artist and muse; father, mother, and child; wife and husband; infant and adult; amateur and professional.

Dissolving the ragged membranes between our bodies and what Laura Marks describes as 'the skin of the film,'[36] *Window Water Baby Moving* presses against us, stifles our breath, and churns and contracts our insides. I know by the way my students' shoulders seize up that their bodies register the different textures of skin and latex as the doctor's white clad fingers enter and disappear in Jane's vagina. And I can tell by their green faces that they can *feel* – analogically – the excruciating stretching of their own skin as the baby's head crowns. They have never *felt* film like this before. And even if they never see another experimental film again, I know they will never be the same.

The perils of heterosexuality

> We are either experiencing (copulating) or conceiving (procreating) or very rarely both are balancing in that moment of living, loving and creating, giving and receiving, which is so close to the imagined divine as to be more unmentionable than magic.
>
> (Stan Brakhage, 'The Camera Eye')

In spite of its formal innovations and affective assaults, *Window Water Baby Moving* nonetheless represents childbirth as the consummation of heterosexual lovemaking. In this way, it is, as Lee Edelman might argue, contingent on an ecstatic celebration of 'reproductive futurism' that treats childbirth as the ultimate act of meaning.[37] Throughout his career, however, Brakhage occasionally turned towards the documentation of sex acts that were not coextensive with reproduction. Several films, including *Flesh of Morning* (1956), and the *Sexual Meditation* series (1970–1972), are self-portraits of the artist longing for sexual fulfillment and finding relief in masturbation. Swerving away from copulation to concentrate on Brakhage's erotic isolation, these films insist on phallic sexuality even as they bemoan the radical solipsism of the individual, isolated within his own corporeal membrane.

For Brakhage, sex is not a facile aspect of human behavior, but a deeply mediated and inescapably performative staging of desire's impossible demands. In a 1967 essay called 'With Love,' which begins by acknowledging that 'there is no contemporary place for woman in art' because of art's historically phallic nature, Brakhage fantasizes about a time when 'male and female art may answer each other.' Yet quite phallo- and hetero-centrically, Brakhage imagines that this profound communion would probably happen:

> via sex at first … and furtively as in a lift of the skirt and some unzipping, but wherein the *bridge is an extension of penis*, as inspired at source, the opening of the form of woman as structured as her body, as sourced as her needs, and then, in time, as in love, the side-pockets will fall away, the hands of the masterbating [sic] man-shape of his medium be freed for embrace, their clothes in historical tatters from the workings of lust, be simply taken off and some art be reared in marriage, after all these poor bastards set adrift in the spaces of the imagination, some thus housed and finally homed, in love, growth of the union of these old arts inform them both thru its coming into maturity of their pasts, as do children always, for a being present of each in all.[38]

Imagining the history of art as a history of 'master-bation,' Brakhage dreams of a time when art – and the lonely, lusty bastards who make it – could be freed from their own phallic limitations and open up to more mature forms of being that acknowledge the profound connections between selves of different genders. Brakhage imagines that such an art could 'be reared in marriage,' an institution whose redemptive power had the capacity to house and finally home an art born of and sustained through love.

Whatever its limitations may have been, Brakhage's marriage to Jane Collom did indeed function as this kind of artistic home. Yet in Brakhage's films, sex is not as easy as his description of furtive skirt-lifting and unzipping suggests. Rather, Brakhage represents erotic intimacy as a crisis of relationality with shattering consequences for the artist's own identifications and ways of seeing. For an artist who rhetorically insists upon the distinction between the sexes, the bridge between men and women is not so easy to traverse – perhaps especially when conceived as an 'extension of penis.' Yet if the difficulty of recording the corporeal immersion of sex foregrounds the perils of heterosexuality, it also opens Brakhage up to desires and sensations that cannot be so easily housed in marriage.

To film sex between other people is not only to *see* it, but also to participate in it. For as this book insists, films that document sex are never only about the bodies of the performers in front of the camera, but inevitably include the body of the filmmaker behind it. As in Brakhage's films, the inevitable leakages of the artist's body not only shape the finished work, but impact the interpersonal dynamics of the profilmic event. Flooding the body with unactionable stimuli, sex overwhelms Brakhage's eye and queers his camera. But what are the consequences of such mediated, triangulated forms of intimacy? How does friendship proceed after such a radical dissolution of boundaries? As I argue in the following analysis of *Cat's Cradle*, the myth of heteronormativity crumbles under the burden that these bent forms of desire place on its wed-locked subjects. Exposing the fissures in the foundations of monogamy, Brakhage's films queer heterosexuality from the inside.

Cat's Cradle (1959)

Cat's Cradle represents the apotheosis of Brakhage's tendency towards romantic idealization of the heterosexual couple. Using his best friends James Tenney and Carolee Schneemann as alter-egos for him and his wife, Brakhage reduces their complex, egalitarian relationship to a form of poetic idealization. Shifting focus from the natural environment of their previous filmic collaboration together in *Loving* (1957), *Cat's Cradle* explores the sexual, psychological, and ideological aspects of heterosexual partnership within the home. Shot in Schneemann and Tenney's home in South Shaftsbury, Vermont, and saturated in red and magenta hues – as if drenched in menstrual blood? – *Cat's Cradle* entangles footage of both couples as well as a cat amidst picturesque details of the domestic environment. Rapid montage creates fleeting, tactile associations between the cat's fur, cut flowers, and the worn nub of a chenille bedspread. Streaming in through curtained windows and a cut-glass vase, light dances capriciously, silhouetting human bodies like dark stems amidst the baroque bursts of peonies that stain the wallpaper.

Yet even as the film captures the shimmering textures of what seems an ideal afternoon, the rapid montage of compulsively repeated gestures hint at underlying tension. Repeated footage of a disconcerted Brakhage entering the kitchen and unbuttoning the collar of his shirt seems an unintended parody of the famous 'Honey, I'm home!' moment of 1950s sitcoms. Men cross thresholds as if marking their territory, or brood at table with furrowed brows and endless cigarettes, while Brakhage's camera attempts to fix women's elusive form in a cat's cradle of color and light.

Lacking the mobility afforded by Brakhage's ever-shifting camera, Jane and Carolee seem entrapped within the home's cloying patterns and textiles. Insistent parallels between them essentialize the labor of chopping, darning, and rolling dough as feminine, while the intercutting of these images with the feline's slinky form congeal the mysteries of womanhood and nature. As in Eadweard Muybridge's early photographic studies of human locomotion, Brakhage's film genders the actions it records by the filmmaker's uneven distribution of costume and prop. An ornate apron worn by Schneemann equates her with the other decorations in the home, as if the tensions that underlay the foursome's often-fraught interactions could be displaced through such domestic clichés. While I can decipher the repeated image of Carolee's erect lurch as the painter's first tentative and then determined approach to the canvas, the staccato glimpses that we catch of her transform this meaningful action into unmotivated flamboyance. Systematically obstructed, repeated, and deconstructed gestures of cooking, cleaning, and undressing transform female artists into precious objects.

'Wed-locked' in the heteronormative myths of marriage and art, women are suspended in the prism of Brakhage's cinema. Were it not for Carolee Schneemann's later reflections, one would never guess that these women of synchronized small gestures – one a painter/performer and filmmaker; the other a writer – might have struggled, in their confinement to sink and stove, to make conversation with each other while their male partners debated theory and

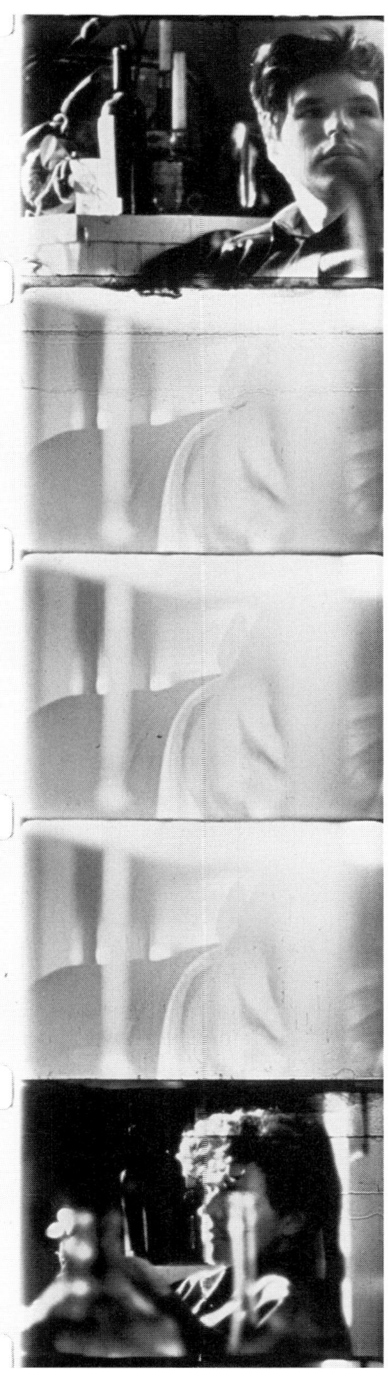

24
Stan Brakhage and James Tenney brood philosophically in Brakhage's *Cat's Cradle* (1959), which documents the tense interactions of the two couples in Carolee Schneemann and James Tenney's home.

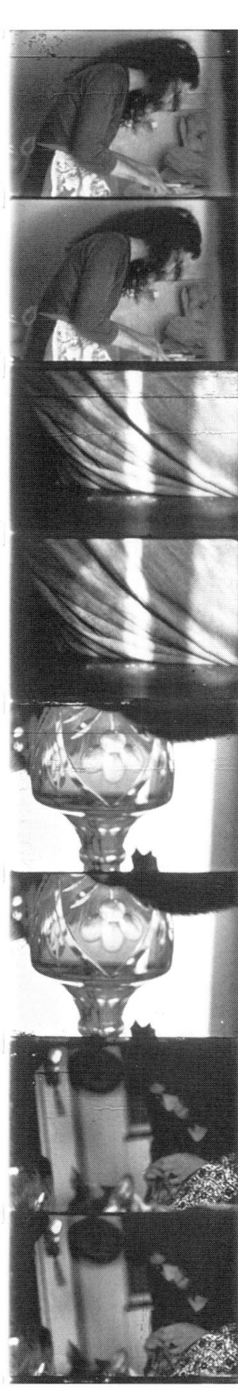

art. Although Brakhage memorably described *Cat's Cradle* as 'sexual witchcraft involving two couples and a "medium" cat,'[39] patriarchy is the witchcraft and the male artist the medium here. These are not the 'untutored' visions of a cat, but attempts to mystify gender inequality and aesthetically overcompensate for the insufficiencies of married bliss. Yet even as Brakhage's essentializing eye for detail insists upon what Betty Friedan would soon describe as 'the feminine mystique,'[40] the film cannot help but illustrate the desperate social construction of gender. Trapped within its own web of mid-century tropes, *Cat's Cradle* evidences the failure of Brakhage's artful vision to escape determination by the learned conventions of seeing. Puncturing the myth that the artist can ever document intimacy – even in the lowbrow, spontaneous form of the home-movie – Brakhage inadvertently reminds us that intercourse is always a discourse. In the following chapter, I discuss the impact of *Cat's Cradle* on the friendship between Brakhage and Schneemann, and its integral role in Schneemann's decision to make her own film *Fuses* (1964–1967), which in turn inspired Brakhage's attempt to see the body anew in *Lovemaking*.

Lovemaking (1968)

Though Brakhage's body leaks in from the behind the camera, *Lovemaking* is the sole film through which Brakhage bears witness to the sex act without spilling the occlusions of virtuoso technique onto the scene. Abjuring Brakhage's usual reliance on visual symbolism and cinematographic pyrotechnics, *Lovemaking* is a far more straightforward document of the sex act than many of his previous sex films. The film, which Brakhage described as an 'American Kama Sutra – Love's answer to filmic pornography'[41] may more realistically have been the artist's answer to Schneemann's charges that he had mystified her subjectivity and sexuality in *Loving* and *Cat's Cradle*.

25a & **25b**
In spite of the film's resplendent textures, Stan Brakhage entraps Carolee Schneemann and Jane Brakhage in a cat's cradle of gendered labor by cross-cutting between images of Carolee Schneemann chopping and Jane Brakhage sewing. Filmstrip from Stan Brakhage's *Cat's Cradle* (1959).

Lovemaking originally consisted of a single scene of heterosexual lovemaking between filmmaker Paul Sharits and his wife Frances, as they caress each other's bodies in a sun-splashed apartment. However, at the behest of family and friends, Brakhage ultimately expanded his focus to include non-heterosexual, non-human, and non-adult 'lovers.' Consequently, the final version of *Lovemaking* consists of four reels, each of which explores a different variety of sensual acts. According to Fred Camper, Brakhage's high school friend Robert Benson had propositioned Brakhage to include him in the film: 'You have used me as an actor in your films, but you haven't ever shown my greatest skill, which is cocksucking.'[42] But if Benson helped Brakhage to see non-heterosexual sex as a form of 'love,'[43] then it was the animal-lover Jane who encouraged Stan to expand the domain of lovemaking beyond homo sapiens when she asked, 'Why only humans?'[44]

The resultant film is far more comprehensive in its focus on diverse sexual acts and identities than Brakhage originally intended. The second part is focused on the activities of a group of dogs humping outside in nature. The third part explores, in intimate, lyrical close-up, a passionate homosexual encounter between Benson and his lover as they bring each other to orgasm through fellatio and masturbation. The fourth section, which features all of the Brakhage children at the time as well as a few neighborhood kids, documents seven or eight nude children, ranging in age from about three to twelve, as they play naked on a bed.

Although each of the four reels is linked thematically by the film's title, which indicates each of the various activities as forms of 'lovemaking,' the tone of each reel differs significantly. Nonetheless, all four episodes are bereft of the frenetic editing and hand-hewn interventions on the celluloid for which Brakhage is best known. For example, there is no painting, scratching, or moments of over- and under-exposure in the entire film. Far from the cosmological metaphors of *Dog Star Man* (1961–1964), the romantic proclivities of *Loving*, or the domestic idealization of *Cat's Cradle*, *Lovemaking* is the filmmaker's most candid and politically inclusive film about sexuality. As avant-garde film historian and Anthology Film Archives librarian Robert Haller has suggested, Brakhage 'made an important issue out of the difference of his two titles (*Loving* and *Lovemaking*), suggesting that the first film is more about affection and caring, whereas the second is more concerned with the physical imperatives for coupling (or just "fucking.")'[45]

Lovemaking is a key if underappreciated film in Brakhage's extensive *oeuvre*. Made in the era immediately preceding the explosion of pornography in mainstream cinema as the 1934 Production Code was in its death throes, *Lovemaking* is one of the most explicit documents of the sex act made in American cinema up until that point. Completed the same year as Warhol's *Blue Movie*, *Lovemaking* was as much of a departure from Brakhage's customary emphasis as the dramatic couple film was for Warhol. Merging Brakhage's ongoing concerns with the lyrical treatment of the body with a startling, hard-core emphasis on fucking, *Lovemaking* brings Brakhage's notion of documentation to new levels of sexual candor. If *Blue Movie* showed American audiences how prescient the queer Warhol could be about heterosexuality, then *Lovemaking* expands what we often mistakenly think of as Brakhage's exclusively heterosexual *métier*.

Not only is Brakhage's depiction of homosexual sex more explicit and more intimate than the filmic documents of homoerotic sex and desire made by many queer experimental filmmakers of the era (including Warhol, Jack Smith, and Kenneth Anger who confessed to being 'IN LOVE' with the film[46]) but it is the most sensual of all the four reels. Challenging any monolithic assumptions about Brakhage's supposed heteronormativity, *Lovemaking* demonstrates that Brakhage's commitment to dailiness included the recording of sexual acts by sexually marginalized individuals. It also suggests that it was partially due to Brakhage's recognition of different sexual practices that he decided to make a critical adjustment of his filmic grammar.

Yet in spite of the significant contribution *Lovemaking* makes to sex's cinematic history, and its unique role in Brakhage's *oeuvre*, the film remains all but forgotten in film scholarship. Undoubtedly, this is due to the controversy the film occasioned from the time of its original distribution in 1969 until 1982, when Brakhage decided, after much ado, to withdraw the film from circulation. For the thirteen years that the film was in distribution, its reception was plagued by conflict and misunderstanding. When the film was shown at the Huntington Hartford Museum in New York City in 1969, the outraged museum projectionist refused to project its second showing.[47] Interestingly, this initial controversy was elicited not because of its explicit depiction of homosexual sex or heterosexual sex – which included graphic images of fellatio and genital penetration – but due to its candid depiction of child nudity. In an interview between Jonas Mekas and *New York Times* film critic Vincent Canby in May 1969,[48] Mekas expresses his outrage over the film's censorship at a gallery that had been one of the homes of the Film-Makers' Cinematheque:

> How does a gallery dare call itself a gallery 'of modern art' when in reality it's the enemy of modern art? What they objected to, I think, was a sequence about child molesting. They said that it was particularly intolerable since the gallery is just across the street from Central Park. I think they thought that everybody who saw the film would run out and molest a child.[49]

Yet even in his defense of the film, Mekas stumbles in his description of the childhood sequence. In a letter to the editor written on the same day as the article's release, Mekas attempts to clarify his 'unfortunate mistake' of having referred to the scene in question as one of 'child molesting':

> The screening of Stan Brakhage's film 'Love Making' was cancelled by the Gallery of Modern Art not because there actually was a scene of child molesting in it; it was cancelled only because the Gallery thought that there was such a scene in the film. In actuality, the scene … is a simple and beautiful scene of children playing in a room and jumping up and down on a bed. It's couldn't be more innocent an occupation … Since he lives on top of a mountain, 9000 feet high, he has no distractions, and the sick preoccupations and perversions of the rest of humanity are far below him. He can concentrate on reality around him with a naked and innocent eye. … In short: if you hear the word 'obscene' used in connection with the Avantgarde Film, be on your guard … Obscenity can be found only in the commercial cinema. In the Avantgarde you can find only celebrations, adorations, and loving songs. There is a big difference between singing of nakedness, and pushing nakedness into people's eyes to blind them to get their money, money, money.[50]

Brakhage's innocence, and financial incorruptibility, were common motifs in critical defenses of the film. Guy Davenport, who after effusively describing the film's representation of 'the veined and knotty stalk' of the cock,[51] unconvincingly defends the film as a 'triumph of innocence.' Arguing that pornography 'has rarely been considered an art form of integrity for the simple reason that it is not in the service of art but in the service of the passion and frequently of money,' Davenport insists that *Lovemaking* is 'in nowise salacious … There is no coy disrobing, no romanticism, no flaunting of nudity as something to stare at. He is interested solely in the sexual engagement of a young wife and husband. His camera, let us note, is remarkably chaste; it does not pry; it *simply watches.*'[52]

One can only wonder whether Davenport would have made the same defense had he seen more than the first part of the film. For many of the film's more comprehensive viewers, it was the juxtaposition of the scenes, rather than the scenes themselves, which undermined the film's 'innocence.' As Peter Michelson has observed,

> The difficulty with *Lovemaking* is that it is caught between celebration of eros and exposition … I suspect, for example, that the reason viewers like the *New York Times* reviewer can misperceive the children sequence is its juxtaposition with the homosexuals, which implies an expository connection between the two scenes. Thus the viewer so disposed can see the children as objects for pederasty.[53]

In other words, the juxtaposition of the two reels functioned as a form of Eisensteinian 'intellectual montage,'[54] in which the collision of two different elements (adult homosexual sex + children playing) produced a third meaning or concept (= child molestation) that was not inherent in either image.

Such reactions transformed Brakhage's own initially ecstatic attitudes towards the film. In a letter written to his friend and fellow South Denver High School alumni Paul Sharits in April 1968, Brakhage anticipated that the film 'could possibly be as perfected, as edited,' as his 1963 film *Mothlight*.[55] Sharits, who had appeared in the *Lovemaking*'s light-drenched heterosexual scene with his wife, was also initially delighted with the film: 'fran & i are proud as children of "our" LOVEMAKING film & show it to everyone – the FIRST erotic film – Vermeer could not have done a more beautiful job.'[56] 'I, too, care very much for "Love Making":' Brakhage responded, 'it is a young prince among my film-children; and it moves strongly into the world already.'[57]

Both of their responses to *Lovemaking* would change drastically. By October 1969, Sharits felt 'compelled to "admit"' a few criticisms of Brakhage's cinematic treatment of his lovemaking with Frances, from whom he had recently separated:

> – 1st, yes, our fucking was 'authentic' in that that was how we 'did it that way that day' & often, in our own moments, our fucking was that simple & gentle –however:
>
> fran's morality … made her very apprehensive of sharing our 'intimacy' with even the art of cinema and so the whole thing was rather inhibited –
>
> fran & i have, at our highest moments of BLISS, performed very 'theatric'/ inspired ACTS ('blow jobs' & 'eating snatch' were normative, as was fran 'mounting' me [i am not a 'female suppressor'], to 'answer' that young lady's question about who gets to be 'on top' – – fran RODE HIGH a good deal of the time) … at times we approached near baroque flights (meat allegories of train rides, cartoon sado-masochisms, 'weird' insertions & even yogic meditational postures – which are of great interest to me) – these intimacies could not be released, not because we didn't trust you but because of a failing in our relationship – the film is not, from our 'end', dishonest, it is simply not a TOTAL image – my sense of sex is quite different, philosophically, than fran's – … someday perhaps we can do another more open & spiritual lovemaking film – … i am not ashamed… there is nothing which needs to be hidden –

Sharits's dissatisfaction with Brakhage's conventional treatment of his lovemaking, or perhaps more accurately, of his constricted performance for the camera, eventually inspired Sharits to make *Celestial Linearity*, his own 'unabashed' film about sex with his then girlfriend Dagny.[58]

Lovemaking remains a constant point of reference and a frequent source of contention in the increasingly unanswered letters Sharits sent to Brakhage between 1969 and 1974. Nonetheless the film maintained special currency between the two friends, who achieved new levels of intimacy with (and without) each other as a result of its production. Sharits, who described the film as a 'breakthru' for both himself and Brakhage, was amazed that the film allowed them 'to share on such a high level.'[59] Having made his own document of love-making, Sharits empathized with the 'difficulties of filming the sexual act.'[60] By 1971, Sharits, who had determined that Brakhage's film failed to turn him on 'erotically' because it was 'so domestic a vision,' wonders whether it was even 'possible to make a film which is "good film" and "very erotic."' Surmising that the scene of gay sex in *Lovemaking* might be a turn-on for 'homosexuals, or for women, or bisexuals,' Sharits wonders whether the film's greatest use value might be ironically, as an expository text for children.[61]

This special 'currency' of the film, however, turned out to be both a blessing and a curse. What first seemed like the promise of the film's sale-ability turned quickly into the kind of commercial nightmare which Mekas and Davenport were so eager to disavow. By the time Brakhage made *Lovemaking*, Grove Press, which had published some of the most controversial, sexually explicit writers in twentieth-century literature, had decided to capitalize on several recent Supreme Court cases that transformed the regulation of pornographic materials[62] by selling 8mm copies of sexually explicit experimental films for home use.[63] Through Grove, Brakhage decided to sell and distribute copies of only the first part of *Lovemaking*,[64] presumably because the homosexual and childhood scenes would have been less palatable to heterosexual audiences and more vulnerable to censorship.[65] Even Guy Davenport, who had praised the first part, had admitted that he was so 'apprehensive about the homosexual (ugly word!) passage' that he was afraid he might react to it 'as the President of the Daughters of the American Revolution' might have responded to the first section – or at the very least, be compelled to 'pop out' his contact lenses.[66]

Authorities did not find Brakhage's film quite so innocent. The film was confiscated in the UK, obstructed from screening in Paris in 1969,[67] and seized by the police when it showed in Berkeley, California in 1972.[68] It was also, according to Brakhage, the primary reason why the Internal Revenue Service conducted an ultimately unsuccessful investigation of the impoverished film-maker on charges of tax evasion.[69] Indeed, the question of profit turned out to be a key issue in the exhibition and distribution of *Lovemaking*. As both Viviana Zelizer and Kathryn Bond Stockton have argued, the discursive invention of childhood innocence is separable from evolving estimations of their financial value.[70] On several occasions, potential buyers approached Brakhage with thinly disguised pleas for images of child pornography. Among the most vivid of these correspondences are letters from a certain Eugene Verrier, whose stationery is adorned with a nude drawing of an elfin young boy who looks like he is about to leap into a body of water. After telling Brakhage how much he enjoyed the pictures of the filmmaker's own children, Verrier

> wondered if you [Brakhage] also do other work in films besides your own and had in mind an 8mm color, silent film of nude children swimming or playing or

> candid, etc. just showing them enjoying and occupying themselves in the 'fifth
> freedom' or freedom of clothes. Clothes date the films. I'm starting and have
> a small library of films along this line but only have young boys (pre-teens) at
> present showing them swimming in various areas. Naturally, your fee would be
> paid with an advancement if you cared to consider such a candid film.[71]

Over the next few months, Verrier's requests and promises for remuneration became more insistent. By December 1969, Brakhage was compelled to reject Verrier's appeals, and return his check: 'Please understand! I am not particularly interested in the nudity of children – mine or anyone else's … The children are seen, both naked and clothed, as the occasion happened to find them, throughout the majority of my work.' Although Brakhage supposed that he might send more photographs of naked children 'if [he] had any' – the issue being 'nothing' to him 'one way or the other' – Brakhage was averse to the fact that Verrier was 'not interested in any art of the film … nor any nudity as it might happen naturally in either art OR life … but, rather, only in naked children.'[72]

According to Mekas's logic – in which obscenity can only exist in relation to capital – Verrier's desire to commission 'innocent' images of naked children betrays his prurience, while Brakhage's refusal of money assures his purity. Interestingly, the law seemed to support these conclusions. When a New York City schoolteacher was investigated in 1974 for showing *Lovemaking* to his biology classes, he was legally acquitted (although reprimanded and transferred within the school system) because there had been no admission charges for the screenings. The district attorney considered it a 'weakness in the law' that showing a sex film in an educational context without charge was not considered a crime, whereas showing a sex film to a minor for money was regarded as a certain misdemeanor.[73] Of course, legally permissible free screenings also meant that the artist was not being paid for his work.[74]

Brakhage was no stranger to the agonies of film censorship. For years, he had difficulty finding labs that were willing to print his more explicit films. Nonetheless, ongoing criticism weakened Brakhage's resolve to the point of illness. In a letter to the co-founder of the Anthology Film Archives, Jerome Hill, Brakhage cited the psychological and physical suffering he endured as a result of *Lovemaking*'s controversial reception. Having ended up in a hospital after 'suffering specifically from "non-specific ureathritis, prostatitis" and non-specifically from the most complete psychological exhaustion I have ever felt,' Brakhage claims that both he and his doctor:

> suspect it is brought on by guilt feelings sexually which are, in my case, most
> probably 'caused', that is – by the abuse and resultant shame heaped on me
> these last several months because of my film 'Lovemaking' … (to name just
> a few of the crisis moments in this matter: Jonas' 2nd showing at Huntington
> Hartford museum was stopped and then the N.Y. Times – a paper that does get

to Colo. – stated that it was a film encouraging child molestation: the Omaha police arrived with full patrol cars front and back and stopped my second showing there: Willard Van Dyke refused to show it at the Museum of Modern Art, despite my pleading need of that institutional sanction: Grove refused to extend to me the usual protective legal clause in contract, leaving me so economically vulnerable as to be in an impossible situation should it ever go to court: many friends, almost all friends, attacked it with incredible irrationality – oddly each person choosing one or another, finally every, section of it – and many insisting I must withdraw it: P. Adams attacked it in print, in a nationally distributed 'teen age' magazine, calling it 'the first serious pitfall of his mature years,' but not really stating why he finds it such … a terrible hurt and, really, very deep betrayal to me).[75]

It is impossible to guess how Brakhage's own thoughts about *Lovemaking* would have evolved in the absence of such criticism. By 1974, Sharits, who had been harassed by a feminist colleague about how 'catastrophic' *Lovemaking I* was,[76] was in turn haranguing Brakhage about the author's own growing ambivalence towards the work:

i wonder why you don't just destroy it if you have such deep apprehensions. to me, it's a fine work; it does not matter if it is not an ultimately true statement about the totality of fran & my (former) sex life (i can't imagine anyone having such a static sex life that ALL OF IT could be captured in a single document … if it is a question of 'Truthfulness': (1) film is a lie 24 fps, by nature; (2) how can an artist hope to be any more truthful about his representations than the quantum physicist can be with his descriptions of particles, which have to be modified by observation or not be observed at all?????[77]

Brakhage decided to withdraw the film from circulation in 1982:

In the light of the Supreme Court decision, this date, regarding child pornography, I've decided to withdraw the film 'Lovemaking' from distribution – NOT because I regard it, in any sense, pornographic … but rather, simply, because I am afraid that those who have been exploiting children sexually will be tempted to use that old ploy of bringing something into court which they CAN defend as 'work of art' and batter the law therewith so as to continue their hideous trade. I don't want this film of lovers, including these children in loving play, EVER to be used for such purpose. Accordingly, I want you to put Anthology's print into the deepest recess of your vault (and not to show it publically anymore); and we'll hope it can be preserved for a time of greater clarity, a time when love is distinguished from currencies, enslavement and horror.[78]

More than thirty years later, *Lovemaking* remains in the 'deepest recess' of the vault. After writing Brakhage's widow Marilyn that 'I have come to believe that watching *Lovemaking* is essential to a fuller understanding of Brakhage's evolving cinematic – and philosophical – treatment of the body,[79] I was able to arrange a private screening of the film at the Museum of Modern Art. As Foucault might have predicted, I presumed that this most earnest document of sexual pleasure might provide essential knowledge about Brakhage's attitudes towards the flesh. After furiously scribbling down my usually cryptic observations – 'mustache armpit rococo [or is it Rocco?]' – I ask the projectionist to screen it again. He does. Too embarrassed to request a third viewing, I thank him. Upon leaving, the projectionist tells me that he didn't think he could 'take it' if I had asked to watch it again. But what exactly couldn't he – or I – 'take?'

The film begins and ends with the phallus – or rather, the penis that, as we learn from the last section, can only sometimes stand in as the bodily referent for patriarchal power and privilege. The first shot of the film is a close-up of Sharits's erect penis. Indeed, close-ups predominate to such an extent that it is often difficult to distinguish between male and female flesh, so entwined are the bodies to which it belongs. Though there are occasionally telltale signs of gender, like the wool of the woman's labia, the first sequence is truly concerned with light. Light streams and splashes, catching, illuminating, and silhouetting bodies in its course. Turning the delicate hairs (of an arm? a leg?) into a field of gold, light makes flesh ethereal. In my notes, I have twice underlined the word 'divine.'

What the first reel does to light, the second – the dog reel – does to fur. Sexual actions can be equally difficult to discern here, but then again, I didn't experience quite the same desire to see. The camera moves quickly, and the dogs have sex – some of the time. Mostly, however, they run through fields of flowers, or lie in the dust under an old car. Beautiful abstract shots of raindrops remind me that this is a Brakhage film, and not the kind of dated documentary about the birds and the bees that one endures in high school. Though I am slightly disgusted when I watch the dogs hump each other's faces, it is not as if I haven't seen similarly unsightly pleas for fellatio in the dog park. Watching what looks like two females nuzzling together, I wonder whether these androgynous creatures are supposed to stand in for the lesbians conspicuously absent from the film? Apparently, sex between women is not something Brakhage was interested in documenting. Judging from the sarcasm of my notes – 'dog's pink erect penis licking himself close up gross looks like Sharits's!' – I seem to have gotten bored with Brakhage's insights into the animal kingdom, but then one of the dogs gives birth to a litter of 'tiny wet pups' and I am happy again. The reel ends.

Of all of the reels, I am most moved by the third, which shows two men making passionate, unabashed love to each other. Unlike the heterosexual reel of Paul and Frances Sharits, which takes place in an empty room bathed in white light, this scene has an abundance of cultural information – what Roland Barthes would describe as the 'studium.'[80] Other than the make of the car and the particular saturation of the film stock, the dogs could have been filmed in any wooded where, at any time. But the third reel is unmistakably the late 1960s. Hair hangs long and greasy, faces bear beards and mustaches, a leather wristband is a cryptograph I haven't the key to decode. There is a houseplant in the window, patterned curtains in the window. I have recorded these details between notes about 'unkempt toes' and 'calloused heels,' noting how the room wears its age as much as the body.

The men tenderly undress, kiss, embrace, and fellate each other. The fact that the camera is so proximate to the bodies (and occasionally out of focus) that I often can't tell where one begins and ends makes it all the more startling when I suddenly realize that the bobbing mound of darkness and light that I've been curiously watching is a face buried in the crevice of the buttocks. 'Rimming!' I have written as if it's 'Eureka!' Think what you will, you can't pull anything over on me.

Benson wasn't lying when he told Brakhage he was good at giving head. 'WOW!' I exclaim in my notes, and then, in a more scholarly tone: 'very rare.' He takes his partner's flaccid cock into his hairy face (a 'Fassbinder look') and sucks it vigorously until it is hard. Brakhage's camera seems to find interest in his partner's sensitive face, which is shown in close-up, first smiling peacefully and then wincing in pleasure. Owing to the body's pose and the camera's foreshortening angle, a particular shot formally reminds me of Warhol's image of his lover John Giorno's face in *Sleep* – that face we looked and looked at because we couldn't see anything else. But unlike Warhol's *Sleep* and *Blow Job*, *Lovemaking* actually allows us to see not only the genitals but also the more intimate interactions between bodies. If Warhol's early films are often about the filmmaker's voyeuristic detachment, then *Lovemaking* is about what it feels like to bring the camera so close to other bodies that you can touch them.

It is hard not to wonder where Brakhage is in all of this. How are we to read his visual absence from the frame in relation to the touching contiguity of his camera? Surely, by now we are used to Brakhage filming his loved ones in tender proximity, rhythmically moving his own body in relation to theirs. Recalling the filming of his *Lovemaking I*, Sharits remembered how Brakhage was 'a mixture of nervousness and outgoingness, sweating, thinking & feeling intensely, merging in and out of our fucking.'[81] Judging from the intensity of the shots, one can only presume that Brakhage was equally, if not more involved in the interactions of the lovers in *Lovemaking III*. But how does such involvement complicate what we have come to understand about Brakhage as a desiring subject? How was Brakhage's own body queered by his proximity to the sexual acts his camera witnesses, and how is this 'queering' evident in the way he chooses to record it? For although the film sets up an equivalence between all kinds of sexuality in its 'birds do it, bees do it' approach, each reel is remarkably different in tone. Without a doubt, reel three is the most corporeally engaged – and least equanimous – portrait of lovemaking in the entire film.

If the third reel is the most intensely erotic, than the fourth is the most disturbing. Let me clarify. I don't mean 'disturbing' in the colloquial way that this word is so indiscriminately affixed to potentially prurient images of children: I was not morally 'offended' or 'made uncomfortable' by it. Reel four 'disturbs' us in the sense that it *interrupts* and *disarranges* our usual patterns of looking at children. And it does this first by showing the bodies of children as a frenzy of moving flesh, and then by perhaps unwittingly rearranging these bodies according to the corporeal hierarchies of patriarchal culture. In other words, Brakhage's portrait of childhood's polymorphous perversity first seems to dissolve what Marcuse had theorized as the tyranny of the genital, only to re-implant the perversion of phallocentrism.

Lovemaking IV revels in the unhampered, dizzying motion of little children. Boys and girls jump on the bed, strut, scramble, wrestle, cuddle, and collapse. They tumble with a plush alligator, chew on baby dolls, churn up the bedsheets, play on drums and flutes (though we can't hear them), shake tambourines, trample and get trampled, and, eventually, tire. The kids, who range from toddlers to pre-teens, are tan, fop-headed, and unkempt.

Just to clarify, there is no 'lovemaking' in reel four, if what is meant by lovemaking is sex. Certainly, there are moments when the kids mindlessly touch themselves, tugging at their own genitals the way they will scratch or adjust other parts of their bodies. But there is, one supposes, another kind of lovemaking here. Like the dogs, the children are not interested in coupling but in performing collective rituals of intimacy. One cannot help but be struck by the unthinking tenderness the children show to each other amidst other acts of equally unthinking disregard. Their play, which pivots on various forms of bodily contact and stimulation, reminds the beholder of the incessant tactility of childhood, of what it felt like to be embodied before we were disciplined, *en route* to adulthood, to look with our eyes, and not with our hands.

What then, do I find 'disturbing' about these joyful images? Within a few minutes of the film, I notice what seems like the special attention Brakhage pays to the children's genitals. Of course, they *are* fascinating! One can't help but be curious about these little parts, so like and yet unlike our own. Who remembers having such alien forms?! Though the kids are for the most part indifferent to each other's genitals, however, Brakhage is not. Though heads are often excised as the children bob and bounce out of the frame, Brakhage makes an effort to keep the genitals in focus. Certainly, they are not the only visually interesting parts of the body, and his camera also waylays on other strange little knots of flesh, including one particularly sore looking red belly button. But after a while, I couldn't help but note how the camera moves in search of the genitals, capturing the different sizes and forms of the boy's penises. Though girls' genitals are also occasionally in view, there is, quite honestly, not nearly as much to look at; the immature slits of their vaginas could easily be mistaken for the folds of knees or elbows. Judging from their behavior – and in contradistinction to Freud's claims – these children have not yet fixated upon the anatomical distinction between the sexes. Yet seen through adult eyes (mine and Brakhage's), their bodies can't help but mark the visual signs of sexual difference.

It is hard to tell where Brakhage's curiosity ends and mine begins; they overlap in this intriguing spectacle of incipient flesh. Is it possible that *I* was the one searching out images of the genitals, while Brakhage's camera remained indiscriminate? Perhaps. Critic Donald Richie, for example, saw the film completely differently, though his comments are not specifically directed to the children's scene: In *Lovemaking*, he writes, 'genitals are always seen, and shown, as examples of what is basic to life. They are never symbolic … but are always to be associated with that which is most living-giving. In this he is particularly free from that which almost always in America tends to disguise the appearance on the screen of the sexual organs.'[82] Such subjective discrepancies aside, how can we distinguish the act of seeing through one's *own* eyes, when we can't help but see through Brakhage's? Even showing the most 'innocent' images of naked children has been rendered taboo in our pedophilia-obsessed culture. Though Brakhage attempts to document the children as neutrally as possible, washing the lens of his camera eye clean, one cannot help but witness these images through eyes that have been trained to territorialize the body. Certainly the fact that the film is silent abets my sense of its voyeurism; judging from the amount of giggling, laughing, and shouting that one sees but cannot hear, any synchronous soundtrack would have significantly distracted from one's ability to focus on *anything*.

But if Brakhage is, as I contend, consciously or unconsciously more interested in composing shots of the genitals than any other single body part, then it is surely not because of any pedophilic tendencies. For an adult, seeing through one's own eyes involves seeing through the lens of our learned hierarchies. As Brakhage mourned in *Metaphors on Vision*, it is impossible to recapture the innocence of the eye of the child who cannot yet name difference:

> Once vision may have been given – that which seems inherent in the infant's eye, an eye which reflects the loss of innocence more eloquently than any other human feature, an eye which soon learns to classify sights, an eye which mirrors the movement of the individual toward death by its increasing inability to see.
>
> But one can never go back, not even in imagination. After the loss of innocence, only the ultimate knowledge can balance the wobbling pivot.[83]

In Brakhage's conception, only knowledge can compensate for the inevitable loss of infinite visual splendor that the untutored eye of the infant can perceive.

'Yet in this contemporary time,' he wrote, 'how many of us even struggle to deeply perceive our own children?'[84] Still, even in his own relentless struggle to perceive children, Brakhage recognized how the phallocentric logic of Western culture both prevented true vision and prevented the subject from knowing itself. This 'is a time,' he wrote, 'haunted by sexual sterility yet almost universally incapable of perceiving the phallic nature of every destructive manifestation of itself.'[85] Writing to poet Robert Creeley, Brakhage suggested the paradox of not being able to document bodies neutrally without recourse to the visual logic of patriarchy. 'I have found myself moved increasingly through those following three "Lovemakings" *toward voyeurism via Document*. All that might be easily regarded as Self-Expression (or what we have come to most easily recognize as Art in this century) became (in the later "Lovemakings") an invisible container. This proclivity has increased in most of my work since.'[86] In Brakhage's formulation, even the most objective documents cannot help but give way to voyeurism. Though the self-expression of the artist may be 'invisible,' it remains the only 'container' through which *Lovemaking*'s images can be accessed.

Before he made *Lovemaking*, Brakhage was gaining a reputation for imbedding images of the body in densely layered visual fields that were in such constant flux that it was often impossible to distinguish human parts from fragments of other wriggling matter. As Davenport described, 'Brakhage WILL not let you SEE anything.'[87] Of course, Brakhage's intensely collaged palimpsests were his most innovative contribution to the medium. For all of its inevitably partial visions, *Lovemaking* is, according to Davenport, the filmmaker's greatest 'vindication.'[88] In its vindication of seeing the body without expressive ornament, *Lovemaking* pursues Brakhage's relentless attempt to create a corporeal 'document.' It also marks a pivotal turn from the hallucinatory palimpsests of closed-eye vision to the opened eye vision required to view the dissected body.

Brakhage's desire to de-territorialize the body by splitting it irrevocably into pieces involves a radical re-imagining of cinematic spectatorship. From the mid-1950s, Brakhage rejected what seemed to him like the absurd idea of disinterested viewing; for him, vision was always inevitably embodied, idiosyncratic, flawed and subjective. After *Lovemaking*, however, Brakhage began to tiptoe back towards the possibility of detached or objective viewing. His aim was not to confirm or recapture the Kantian ideal of disembodied viewing against which his films and writings rallied. Rather, Brakhage's attempts to approach a 'lack of engagement' and a 'termination'[89] of personal reference in his work evidence a profound (if not total) re-adjustment of his own artistic priorities when confronted with the vicissitudes of the flesh. He wanted his films to 'feel' bodies without telling viewers *how* to feel about them.[90]

In his 1971 film *The Act of Seeing With One's Own Eyes*, Brakhage shifts from the stylistic dissection of the body – through use of close-up, hyperbolic montage, and the suppression of establishing shots – to its literal correlative. In the actual 'manual dismembering of the human cadaver,' Brakhage's inclination to represent the body-in-pieces reaches its apotheosis.[91]

'The Act of Seeing THE ACT OF SEEING WITH ONE'S OWN EYES with one's own eyes'[92]

> In that compelling, raw, insolent thing in the morgue's full sunlight, in that thing that no longer matches and therefore no longer signifies anything, I behold the breaking down of a world that has erased its borders: fainting away. The corpse, seen without God and outside of science, is the utmost of abjection. It is death infecting life.
>
> (Julia Kristeva, *Powers of Horror*)

> This is an age which has no symbol for death other than the skull and bones of one stage of decomposition ... and it is an age which lives in fear of total annihilation.
>
> (Stan Brakhage, *Metaphors on Vision*)[93]

On December 29, 1970, filmmaker Marie Menken died at the age of sixty-one after a short illness and much despair. Brakhage had known Menken and her husband Willard Maas since the 1950s, and considered her, along with Gertrude Stein and Jane, one of the three greatest influences on his artistic life. Seeing Menken's hand-held camera work in films like *Visual Variations of Noguchi* (1945) was, for Brakhage, an 'OPEN SESAME' that unsealed the door to greater perceptual and corporeal freedom in his own films.[94] For Brakhage, Menken's tendency to record 'her whole body's reaction to what she is seeing through the camera' generated 'exquisite maxims of the physiology which made them.'[95]

Yet in spite of the fact that Menken had been an artistic mother figure to him – as well as to many other young artists like Kenneth Anger and Gerard Malanga – Brakhage was not informed of her death for over a week. When he finally heard in early January 1971, he was devastated. Brakhage described the news as 'the last straw to my system' that 'came like a sledge hammer.' Suspended in deep 'physical mourning' Brakhage felt 'a terrible social disintegration' in addition to the immense grief of Menken's death. Brakhage was particularly troubled by the anonymity of her death, which 'grotesquely symbolized' the de-personalization of 'American 20th Century living' against which Menken and Maas had so creatively struggled. 'One of the very greatest film-makers of our Time dies and is buried in the style of Mozart: what else is there to say? ... I am sick, sick with the social mean-and-meaningless-ness and the sadness of her death – not that she die ... but that she died amidst such estrangement as she did.'[96]

Brakhage was in the middle of making a trilogy of films in Pittsburgh, Pennsylvania when he received the shocking news of Menken's death. During this time, Pittsburgh had become the 'third center of avant-garde film in America' through its substantial support of making, screening, and discussing opportunities for experimental filmmakers.[97] Under the guidance of curator Sally Dixon, the Museum of Art of the Carnegie Institute established a community of resident filmmakers that opened the doors for filmmakers who wanted to shoot in the city. Brakhage had already shot a film about the police, *eyes* (1971), and a film about open-heart surgery, *Deus Ex* (1971), and was considering football and newspapers as possible subjects for the third film in the trilogy. Instead, Brakhage decided to film in a morgue. Although this decision was inspired by fellow filmmaker Hollis Frampton, who had shot footage of autopsy for his long, ultimately unfinished work, *The Clouds of Magellan*,[98] I can't help but think that his desire to penetrate the physiological geographies of the opened body was, in some way, 'inhabited' by Menken's deeply 'somatic' vision,[99] and his own shock of losing this most idiosyncratic mentor to the de-individuation of death.

After seeing *The Act of Seeing With One's Own Eyes* with his own eyes, Frampton came to see Brakhage as the most important contemporary visual poet of human anatomy. Tracing the history of the visual culture of anatomy back to Renaissance physician and author Andreas Vesalius, Frampton writes

> A second long dissolve, then, to Stan Brakhage, entering, with his camera, one of the forbidden, terrific locations of our culture, the autopsy room. It is a place wherein, inversely, life is cherished, for it exists to affirm that no one of us may die without our knowing exactly why. All of us, in the person of the coroner, must see that, for ourselves, with our own eyes. It is a room full of appalling particular intimacies, the last ditch of individuation. Here our vague nightmare of mortality acquires the names and faces of others.
>
> This last is a process that requires a witness: and what 'idea' may finally have inserted itself into the sensible world we can still scarcely guess, for the camera would seem the perfect Eidetic Witness, staring with perfect compassion where we can scarcely bear to glance.[100]

To make *The Act of Seeing*, Brakhage spent three days in September 1971 filming in the Allegheny county morgue.[101] The experience affected the filmmaker profoundly. On the first day, Brakhage filmed:

> what's called an external autopsy, that is, where they don't cut anybody open. And so that day that's all I did, and that was hard enough for me to take; I'd never been that close a dead human being before. Then the next morning turned out to be … Sunday morning, and they had told me, you should come down Sunday morning because there's so many people that die on Saturday night. So I was more of less obligated; that's the way I felt about it; actually I was driven, for my own desperate reasons, to go down that Sunday morning, early, and

suddenly walk into a room where there are several murder victims, some sui-
cides, people who died by violent accident; I walked into this room where the
day before I had only photographed a… and everywhere I turned… suddenly
I was surrounded by… slaughter! And so I just began photographing desperately. I really overshot because I was so desperate to keep always the camera
going; every moment I stopped photographing I really felt like I might faint, or
burst into tears, or come apart, or something like that.[102]

In a letter to Jane, Brakhage described the act of filming autopsy as 'something
terrible to face': 'The dead, cut open in autopsy, looks like two incongruities:
dress dummies and meat. … The body gapes. It is a chasm attached to model
limbs.'[103] Even six weeks after returning from Pittsburgh, Brakhage was so troubled by what he had witnessed that he found it impossible to begin editing.[104]
Writing to Paul Sharits, he confessed, 'I thought, day after day of it, I would go
crazy… I'm back now and sweating through nightmares almost every time I fall
asleep.'[105] The nightmares did not go away once he commenced editing: 'Every
instant at my work-table,' Brakhage wrote, 'there is the temptation to make a
clever cut – cut away from all this corpse.'[106]

Brakhage originally intended to 'escape' from the morgue images by inter-
weaving them with consoling symbols like 'mountain-ranges, moons, suns,
snow, clouds, etc.' However, after 'one good look at the footage,' Brakhage 'knew
it was impossible (for me now anyway) to interrupt THIS parade of the dead
with ANYthing whatsoever, any "escape" a blasphemy, even the "escape" of Art
as I *had* come to know it. This gathering of images (rather than editing) had
to be *straight*.'[107]

Hewn from the horror of directly confronting the dead without recourse to
the escapism of art, Brakhage's newfound sense of urgent obligation inspired the
film's title. Derived from the Greek word 'autopsis,' the title of *The Act of Seeing
With One's Own Eyes* suggests the necessity of encountering the human corpse
in order to bear firsthand witness to the otherwise obscured complexities of
the body cavity. 'I had to go through, mind you, the *act* of seeing, something
different than just seeing, in fact something, I wouldn't say opposite, but quite
other than The Art of Vision.'[108]

For Brakhage, the distinctions between *Act of Seeing* and his earlier films
were immense. Whereas his earlier films about death, including *Anticipation of
the Night* (1958), *Sirius Remembered* (1959) and *The Dead* (1960) are concerned
with 'ideas,' his later documents are concerned with 'acts.'[109] Whereas *Sirius*
shows the corpse of Brakhage's pet dog organically decaying in the neighboring
forest, *The Act of Seeing* documents the extremely abrupt, seemingly violent
excavation of the body as a result of direct human intervention. Unlike *Sirius Remembered*, whose punning title and non-linear editing offer hope for suturing or
're-membering' the body, *Act of Seeing* insists upon the absolute finitude of both

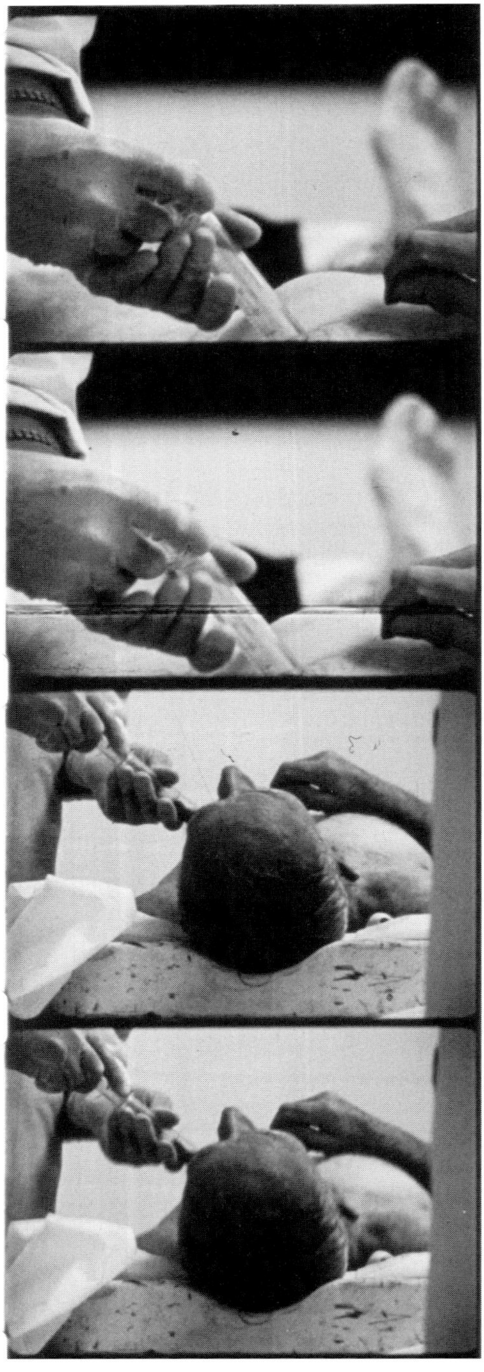

consciousness and corporeal wholeness in death. By choosing not to show the cosmetic reconstruction of the bodies for funereal display, Brakhage shows autopsies as an ontologically irreversible dismembering. Brakhage's refusal to make the body whole again through the magic of cinema – which could, as early filmmaker and magician Georges Méliès knew, easily overcome the limits of time and space – involved coming to terms with the radical finitude of being. Brakhage had warned Frampton that *The Act of Seeing* was not 'infinite cinema.'[110] Life is not composed of infinite vistas of immortal being, but rather, as poet Charles Olson might have insisted, singular acts of perception that prehend particular and immediate experiences:

> There are no hierarchies, no infinite, no such many as mass, there are only eyes in all heads to be looked out of.[111]

Undertaking the act of seeing with his own (newly washed) eyes entailed a revision not only of what it means to look, but also of what constitutes an 'act.' Contrary to the common notion of 'acts' as artificial gestures made by professional Hollywood stars, Brakhage embraced a notion of action wrest free from intentionality. Understanding that 'action' is what bodies *do* regardless of whether they meant to, Brakhage dilated the concept of the 'act' to include

26
Close-ups cinematically partition images of corpses in Stan Brakhage's *The Act of Seeing With One's Own Eyes* (1971). The title is an etymological translation of the word 'autopsy.'

both the involuntary motions and paralyzed immobility of the dead. Speaking of the postures of the bodies vivisected on the table, Brakhage affirms:

> Yes, these are acts. These people are all acting. In fact, the dead on the table are frozen in postures of act, action; that's a nice pun, considering that they're dead. But their last postures are there as solid as a photograph; they're so solid in fact that … as part of the autopsy they cut the back of the head, and they lift the scalp completely over the face, and bend the face almost in half, in order to cut open the skull, and get the brain out…[112]

In fact, as Brakhage describes, the apparatus that recorded action even better than his own camera was the pineal gland lodged inside the human brain. The pineal gland, which the 'mystics all say is the door that you push out to get the third eye,' in fact 'contains the most information of any part of the body on most people's deaths, as to the exact cause of it.' He explains,

> The dead are so frozen in that last posture that they've done all this, then they pull… they reach over and they pull the scalp back into place, unbend the face, the face flips absolutely back into that posture it had before they did all this. So that I had the immediate perception that the first masks made in the world must have been the actual faces of the dead, by perhaps the victors, or maybe even the relatives, because this face is so rigid and so rubbery that you can lift it off and clearly wear it. And what's that but the supreme and final act, and it's so whether the people died in their sleep or died violently or whatever. A man shot in the chest with a shotgun blast carried the whole impact of the horror of that on his face, and it remained there after they had bent the face in half and then put it back…[113]

Startling as these descriptions are, they are nothing compared to the film itself. Watching *The Act of Seeing* is an experience from which I have never fully recovered. The last time I screened it for a class, I consoled some of my more anxious students by telling them they didn't have to stay through the entire screening if they couldn't 'take it.' As it turns out, I was the only person to leave. I couldn't watch the film without supplanting an image of my mother's body for those being eviscerated on screen. She had died a year earlier and the association was terrible.

What is most indigestible about the experience is the palpable absence of affect. Accompanied by no musical score or explanatory dialogue, the film lacks the characteristically lyrical manifestations of Brakhage's vision. Nothing is concealed or ornamented; there is nowhere to hide. When the film begins, one is struck by the limpness of a male cadaver as a technician manipulates its arms and other appendages. When a fingernail is shown making an impression in the cadaver's arm, it becomes clear that the body's flesh has lost its resiliency. Time distends with such uncanny realizations; the few seconds it takes for the

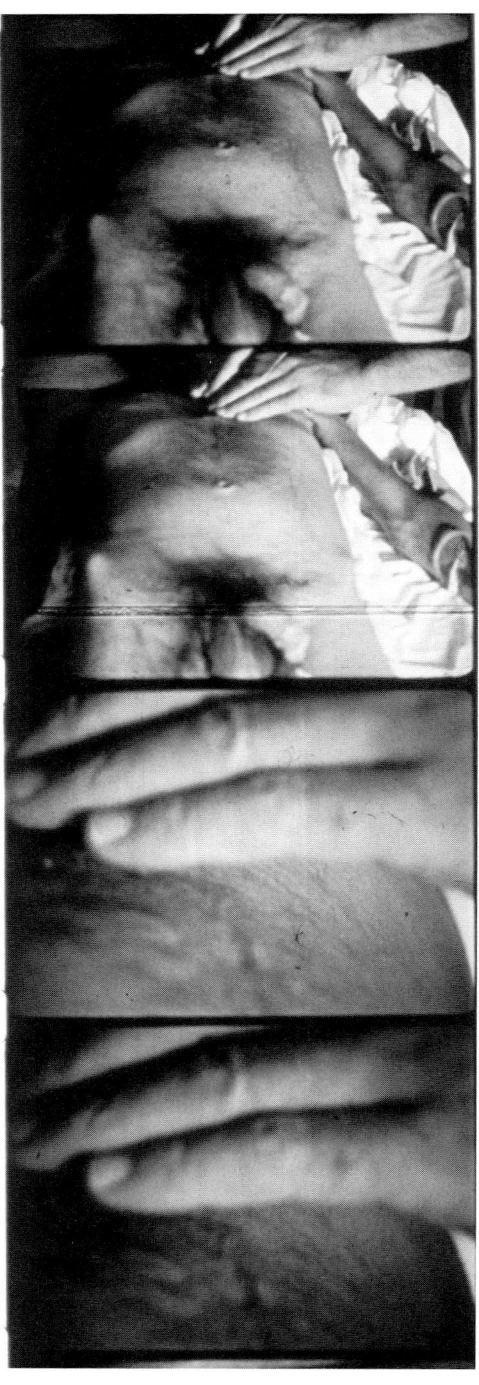

skin to resume its familiar shape feel unbearable. This is but the first assault.

A hand presses the cadaver's sternum, and the corpse's abdomen expands – as if in search of a final breath. But this, we discover, is just an involuntary motion of the body, which can be coaxed to respond even after death. Shots of the man's flaccid, immobile penis 'at last at peace' can't help but capture the viewer's attention, in spite of the body's grim location on the dissecting table.[114] Compared to the virile, indomitable hard-ons depicted in the mainstream porn films that debuted the same year, the sight of the limp, defunct penis radically undercuts any lingering affiliation of the male genitals with virility.

When a fly alights on the man's pallid foot, the body offers no resistance. Unlike Yoko Ono's film *Fly* (1970) (discussed in detail in Chapter 5), which tracks the exploratory movements of the eponymous insect as it traverses the geography of a nude woman's body, Brakhage's image is devoid of all corporeal tension. A woman is shown half-undressed with bloodstained clothes and her hands wrapped in clear plastic bags, apparently preserving significant forensic evidence. In contrast with the robust, bronze-complected body of the previous sequence, the woman's body

27
Made simultaneous with the legal, American debut of feature-length hard-core pornography, Stan Brakhage's *The Act of Seeing With One's Own Eyes* (1971) presents an alternative but no less explicit compendium of corporeal images and 'acts.'

reveals the remarkable pallor more conventionally associated with the cadaver. In yet another sequence, Brakhage juxtaposes images of another blood-covered female body with an examination of her clothes, most notably a pale blue and white gingham dress and a sensible white bra, which are held up and photographed by a still camera. These are but a few casualties of an ordinary Saturday night.

One of the most charged autopsies we see is that of a young, beautiful brunette woman. Writer Sharon Doubiago, who named one of her books of short stories after this film,[115] recalled her own reaction in 1973, when she saw it at the Stan Brakhage Film Festival at Goddard College in Vermont. High on poet Charles Olson – and LSD – Doubiago was 'looking forward to an autopsy film' because she 'was curious as to how a great artist would handle such a subject.' She was not, however, prepared for the images to come:

> When the second body is wheeled in and the sheet removed, we, the audience, gasp … She is the star of this movie, a famous movie star without a name. The white lines of her bikini are in such sharp contrast to the deep tan of her beautiful skin, one thinks for an instant that she is wearing it. Perhaps she drowned today at the beach, so recently she bathed in the sun, walked her perfect body for us.
>
> But this is a story of the Dead. This body is who she is.[116]

Neither was Brakhage: 'In the case of that girl that almost reduced me to… I mean I almost fainted when I first saw them cutting her open, and she died from having three drinks, came home, was restless, took a few pills, and died in her sleep.'[117] Like Edgar Allan Poe, who describes the death of a beautiful woman as 'unquestionably, the most poetical topic in the world,'[118] Brakhage is struck dumb by the spectacle of the comely eviscerated body.

Nearly ten years earlier, Doubiago had been spiritually paralyzed by the experience of reading the details of President John F. Kennedy's autopsy in the Warren Commission's report on his assassination. 'Knowing exactly how much his brain weighed, that he had an "unremarkable bony cage," were facts demonic to her psyche.'[119] By her own admission, Doubiago never recovered from such details. Neither have I from the following 'action,' which Doubiago describes as follows: 'Her face … falls down around the neck, then is turned inside out. Later, when they put it back on, they stretch it over the remains of her skull which they have battered with hammers, just like a rubber Halloween mask.'[120] And yet unlike the slasher films that typically debut around Halloween, Brakhage's film explores the secrets of the opened body without any assistance from make-up artists, special effects sorcerers or editing wizards. By cutting away the 'thin membrane' that separates the 'visible, knowable outside of the body and its secret insides,' the autopsies presented in *The Act of Seeing* overcome the 'collective taboo against [the body's] violation.'[121] Innumerable bodies of all hues and vintages are sliced, carved, and disemboweled. Flesh and bone are cleaved with steel scissors, scalps are peeled and brains removed. Flesh falls away like heaps of gelatinous fabric under the surgeon's knife, intestines are unfurled squid-like, fluids are extracted with pumps and tubes. 'Everything,' as Doubiago writes, 'oozes, is slush, the myths broken in a marshland.'[122]

Eventually, bodies are evacuated of all of their insides and hosed down. Some are redistributed into plastic garbage bags; others are packed into glass jars like preserves. It comes as an immeasurable relief when white sheets are pulled over the useless remains of corpses, the act of *not* seeing suddenly the most precious balm to one's death-ravaged eyes.

As Brakhage was legally required to not show any identifiable faces,[123] very few are glimpsed throughout the entire film. When they are shown, they are so particulated by the use of extreme close-ups and disorienting camera angles that they are unrecognizable. But if one is able to exert the discipline required to see *beyond* the film's unspeakable subject, certain corporeal differences begin to stand out as markers of individualization. Old flesh folds and droops where young flesh remains taut. Blackened insides seem to connote cancer and disease, while charred skin speaks of death by fire. Some bodies are fat; others lithe. The few black bodies that are glimpsed resonate among the all-white staff, though their difference is unremarked by Brakhage's camera. Reminiscent of Warhol's flat documentation of interracial lovemaking in *Couch*, Brakhage's matter-of-fact treatment of racial difference insists that death's egalitarianism trumps the social and political inequalities of the era.

Nonetheless, given the racial and sexual hierarchies that continue to inflect the reception context, the film's black and female bodies seem burdened by an excess of social and historical meaning. Although there is not always evidence that these individuals have died of anything but 'natural causes,' it is particularly hard to imagine these bodies outside of their inscription in culture. How quickly the mind piles these bodies alongside the iconic victims of racial, sexual, and imperial violence in the period: Kitty Genovese, Fred Hampton, Kim Phuc. In a patriarchal, racist, imperialist, and heterosexist culture like that of the United States, pain is inevitably feminized, raced, classed, and queered. In such a culture, it is unthinkable to suppose that the marginalized are capable of dying innocent deaths. Then again, who is? In his book *The Return of the Real*, Hal Foster writes, 'If there is a subject of history for the cult of abjection at all, it is not the Worker, the Woman, or the Person of Color, but the Corpse.'[124] But what happens when the corpse is also a woman, a worker, a person of color? Why do we presume that even this most abject body must be white, male, and upper class?

Foster has argued that, for much of contemporary culture, 'truth resides in the traumatic or abject subject, in the diseased and damaged body. To be sure, this body is the evidentiary basis of important witnessings to truth.'[125] But how many different kinds of truth can the body be compelled to speak? When the

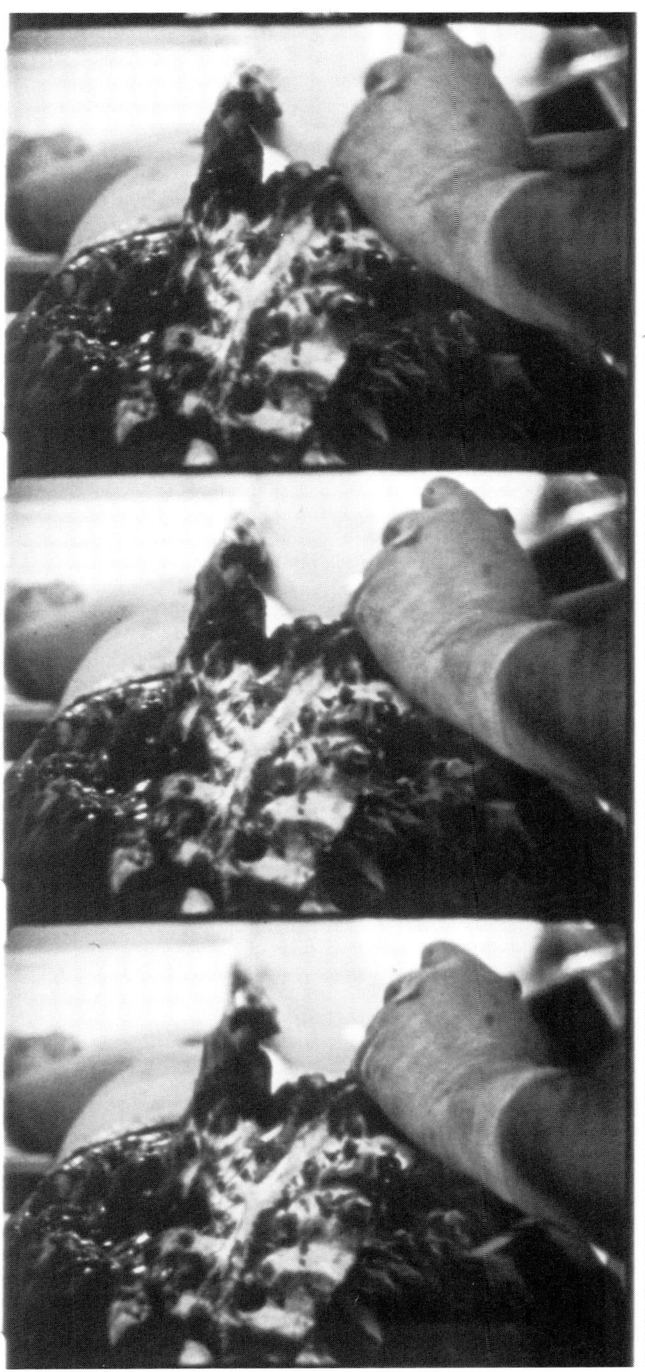

28
Images of an opened
human chest cavity
from Stan Brakhage's
*The Act of Seeing With
One's Own Eyes* (1971)
are chilling reminders
of the meatiness of our
flesh. Courtesy of the
Estate of Stan Brakhage
and Fred Camper
(www.fredcamper.com)

corpse is overwritten with the visual signifiers of race, gender, and class, the abject body becomes a knowledge spectacle. Foster has argued that in contemporary visual culture, trauma is often treated as an event that 'guarantees the subject,'[126] but in *The Act of Seeing*, the traumatic encoding of these doubly and triply marginalized bodies threatens to transform the subject into an object. While body artists of the 1960s and 1970s 'used "the body itself" to contest the ideological inscription of bodies,'[127]as I have argued elsewhere, then *The Act of Seeing* presents corpses that are compelled to reveal the secrets of their corporeality and can thus no longer resist these inscriptions. Subpoenaed to represent not only death, but also blackness and femininity, these bodies are not only de-individuated and essentialized but, as Giorgio Agamben has described about the medieval bandit, ontologically banished from 'a civilized order in which the body is granted some degree of sacred capital.'[128] Furthermore, their evisceration within the depersonalized space of the morgue further undermines the conditions of identification that are necessary for our acknowledgement of each other as 'the bone of my bones and flesh of my flesh.'[129]

Yet even though *Act of Seeing* is an epistemology of bodies that can no longer resist penetration, it is also, I would argue, an invitation to radically identify with the corpse. Sharon Doubiago takes up this radical invitation when she claims that, after watching Brakhage's film, she 'remembered being dead.' Her astonishingly visceral description of what it felt like for her corpse to be handled is not only a testament to her knife-sharp skills as a writer, but to the extraordinary capacity of Brakhage's film to serve as a bridge between the living and the dead: 'Flop me on the table, do your work. Drain my blood, weigh my brain, finger my heart, my cunt, remove everything, liver, intestines, kidneys, clitoris, muscles, my white fat, my bones. You are so desperate to find out. You believe that you can.'[130]

As the film comes to an end, Brakhage's approach to filming becomes more frenetic, as the rapidity of camera movement increases in sync with the pace of the editing. Corporeal fragments become blurry and out of focus as whizzing pan shots attempt to register the filmmaker's final impressions. The film finally ends with shots of a man wearing a white lab coat mouthing verbal descriptions into a hand-held recording device. Cadavers are no longer visible and the sense of cleanliness and order is restored. Yet the few dark spots that besmirch the autopsist's coat and equipment serve as visual reminders of the dissections we have just witnessed – as if we needed to be reminded. We may be, as Doubiago writes, 'anesthetized to the present, but our insides, our inner being gutted wide open to the world, for all time, for anyone, always knows, always remembers.'[131]

Notes

1 David James, *Allegories of Cinema: American Film in the Sixties* (Princeton, NJ: Princeton University Press, 1989), p. 35.

2 P. Adams Sitney, *Visionary Film: The American Avant-Garde, 1943–2000*, 3rd ed. (Oxford: Oxford University Press, 2002), p. 150.

3 Stan Brakhage, 'Metaphors on Vision,' in *The Essential Brakhage: Selected Writings on Filmmaking*, ed. Bruce McPherson (Kingston, NY: McPherson & Company / Documentext, 2001), p. 13.

4 Sitney, *Visionary Film*, p. 150.

5 Annette Michelson, 'Camera Lucida/Camera Obscura,' *ArtForum*, 10, no. 5 (January 1973), pp. 30–37.

6 Viktor Shklovsky, 'Art as Technique,' *Art in Theory 1900–1990: An Anthology of Changing Ideas*, ed. Charles Harrison and Paul Wood (Oxford: Blackwell, 1992), pp. 274–278; pp. 276–277.

7 Sitney, *Visionary Film*, p. 150.

8 Laura U. Marks, *The Skin of the Film: Intercultural Cinema, Embodiment and the Senses* (Durham, NC: Duke University Press, 2000).

9 Carolee Schneemann, 'Eye Body: 36 Transformative Actions,' in *Imagining Her Erotics*, ed. Carolee Schneemann (Cambridge, MA: The MIT Press, 2003), pp. 55–59.

10 Marie Nesthus, 'The "Document" Correspondences of Stan Brakhage,' *Chicago Review* 47, no. 4 (Winter 2001), pp. 133–156; pp. 133, 134.

11 Ibid., pp. 133–156.

12 Hal Foster, *The Return of the Real: The Avant-Garde at the End of the Century* (Cambridge, MA: The MIT Press, 1996), pp. 130–136.

13 Stan Brakhage, 'Interview with Stan Brakhage,' by Richard Grossinger, in *Brakhage Scrapbook: Collected Writings*, ed. Robert A. Haller (New Paltz, NY: Documentext, 1982), p. 192, originally published in *Io Magazine*, 14 (1973), p. 354.

14 Brakhage to Hollis Frampton, November 22, 1971, box 6A, folder 'Frampton, Hollis 1971–9/72,' James Stanley Brakhage Collection, University of Colorado at Boulder Libraries.

15 Brakhage to Annette Michelson, November 8, 1971, box 12A, folder 'Michelson, Annette 1969–1985,' James Stanley Brakhage Collection, University of Colorado at Boulder Libraries.

16 Brakhage to Robert Creeley, November 22, 1971, box 4, folder 'Creeley, Robert 1966–1973,' James Stanley Brakhage Collection, University of Colorado at Boulder Libraries. Brakhage is referring to Ezra Pound's poetry.

17 Ibid.

18 Stan Brakhage to James Broughton, November 10, 1971, box 2A, folder 'Broughton, James 1955–1972,' James Stanley Brakhage Collection, University of Colorado at Boulder Libraries.

19 Foster, *Return of the Real*, p. 131.

20 Nesthus, 'The "Document" Correspondence of Stan Brakhage,' p. 142.

21 Foster, *Return of the Real*, p. 161.

22 Sergei Eisenstein, 'Methods of Montage,' in *Film Form: Essays in Film Theory*, trans. and ed. Jay Leyda (New York: Harcourt Brace & Company, 1949), pp. 72–83.

23 Bazin's final sentence reads: 'On the other hand, of course, cinema is also a language.' André Bazin, 'The Ontology of the Photographic Image,' in *What is Cinema?*, ed. and trans. Hugh Gray, Vol. 1 (Berkeley: University of California Press, 1967), p. 16.

24 Brakhage to Creeley, November 22, 1971, box 4, James Stanley Brakhage Collection, University of Colorado at Boulder Libraries, quoted in Nesthus, 'The "Document" Correspondences of Stan Brakhage,' p. 143.

25 Brakhage to Annette Michelson, November 8, 1971, box 12A, folder 'Michelson, Annette 1969–1985', James Stanley Brakhage Collection, University of Colorado at Boulder Libraries.

26 Stan Brakhage, 'Interview with Stan Brakhage,' by Richard Grossinger, in *Brakhage Scrapbook*, p. 196.

27 The degree to which Jane Brakhage participated as a filmmaker is a matter of some dispute. Marilyn Brakhage has raised doubts about the assumption that Jane had filmed the images of Stan Brakhage that we see in the film. It is possible that Stan set up the camera to film himself in some shots, or that the doctor occasionally held the camera. Marilyn Brakhage, email message to the author, February 11, 2013.

28 Amos Vogel, *Film as a Subversive Art* (New York, Random House, 1974), p. 258.

29 Edward DeGrazia and Roger K. Newman, *Banned Films: Movies, Censors & The First Amendment* (New York: R. R. Bowker Company, 1982).

30 Peter Michelson, *Speaking the Unspeakable: A Poetics of Obscenity*, SUNY Series, The Margins of Literature (Albany, NY: State University of New York Press), p. 247.

31 Vogel, *Film as a Subversive Art*, p. 262.

32 According to Jonas Mekas, Deren 'shouted that night on the stage of the Living Theater against your own film Window Water Baby Moving. She was very upset and very angry. She accused you of touching & exposing or using one of the most private, most sacred moments of humans: the birth.' Mekas to Brakhage, November 30, 1977, box 12, folder 5, James Stanley Brakhage Collection, University of Colorado at Boulder Libraries.

33 Jane Brakhage, 'The Birth Film,' in *The Film Culture Reader*, ed. P. Adams Sitney (New York: Praeger, 1970), pp. 230–233.

34 Brakhage, 'Interview with Richard Grossinger' in *Brakhage Scrapbook*, pp. 190–200, p. 196.

35 Brakhage to Annette Michelson, November 8, 1971, box 12A, folder 'Michelson, Annette 1969–1985', James Stanley Brakhage Collection, University of Colorado at Boulder Libraries.

36 Marks, *The Skin of the Film*.

37 Lee Edelman, *No Future, Queer Theory and the Death Drive* (Durham, NC: Duke University Press, 2004), p. 27.

38 Stan Brakhage, 'With Love,' in *Brakhage Scrapbook*, pp. 118–119, emphasis added, originally published in *Harbinger* 1, no. 1 (July, 1967), pp. 4–5.

39 Stan Brakhage, description of *Cat's Cradle* in Film-Makers' Cooperative catalogue. http://film-makerscoop.com/rentals-sales/search-results?fmc_filmid=298 (accessed on August 13, 2013).

40 Betty Friedan, *The Feminine Mystique* (New York: W.W. Norton, 1963).

41 'Dixon papers,' 1969, private collection, quoted in Wheeler Winston Dixon, *The Exploding Eye: Re-Visionary History of 1960s American Experimental Cinema* (Albany: SUNY Press, 1997), p. 29.

42 Fred Camper, email message to author, February 22, 2012.

43 Ibid.

44 P. Adams Sitney, telephone conversation with the author, February 22, 2012.

45 Robert Haller to Carolee Schneemann, October 28, 1977, in *Correspondence Course: An Epistolary History of Carolee Schneemann and Her Circle*, ed. Kristine Stiles (Durham, NC: Duke University Press, 2010), p. 289.

46 Kenneth Anger to Stan Brakhage, September 26, 1972, box 1, folder 12, James Stanley Brakhage Collection, University of Colorado at Boulder Libraries.

47 Peter Michelson, 'The Avant-Garde Cinema of Sexuality,' in *Speaking the Unspeakable*, p. 249.

48 Vincent Canby, 'Where the Naked Truth Was Born' (includes an interview with Jonas Mekas), *The New York Times*, May 18, 1969, p. 24.

49 Jonas Mekas, interview by Vincent Canby, ibid.

50 Jonas Mekas, 'To the Editor. Motion Pictures. NY Times,' May 19, 1969, box 12, James Stanley Brakhage Collection, University of Colorado at Boulder Libraries.

51 Guy Davenport to Stan Brakhage, 13 July 1968, box 1, James Stanley Brakhage Collection, University of Colorado at Boulder Libraries.

52 Guy Davenport, 'Statement Concerning Stan Brakhage's Film Love-Making,' box 4, folder 6, James Stanley Brakhage Collection, University of Colorado at Boulder Libraries, emphasis added.

53 Peter Michelson, *Speaking the Unspeakable*, pp. 249–250.

54 Eisenstein, 'Methods of Montage,' pp. 82–83.

55 Stan Brakhage to Paul Sharits, dated 'near end April, 1968,' Brakhage File, Anthology Film Archives.

56 Sharits to Brakhage, dated 'Friday' 1968. Brakhage File, Anthology Film Archives.

57 Brakhage to Sharits, dated 'early August' 1968, Brakhage File, Anthology Film Archives.

58 Sharits to Brakhage, February 11, 1971, Brakhage File, Anthology Film Archives.

59 Ibid.

60 Ibid.

61 Ibid.

62 Linda Williams, *Hard Core: Power, Pleasure, and the 'Frenzy of the Visible'* (Berkeley, CA: University of California Press, 1989), pp. 88–89; Jon Lewis, *Hollywood v. Hard Core: How the Struggle over Censorship Saved the Modern Film Industry* (New York: New York University Press, 2000), p. 258.

63 Grove Press director Barney Rosset had an interest in sexually explicit cinema; he had acquired the American distribution rights to the Swedish film *I Am Curious Yellow*, and took over Cinema 16 after Amos Vogel closed it. See Scott MacDonald, *Cinema 16: Documents Toward a History of the Film Society* (Philadelphia, PA: Temple University Press, 2002).

64 Brakhage to Sharits, dated 'early August' 1968, Brakhage File, Anthology Film Archives.

65 The *Roth* test (whereby obscene material qualified as 'utterly without redeeming social importance') remained in effect until 1973, when the ruling in *Miller v. California* changed pornography legislation by effectively returning the task of content regulation to the states, according to their individual statutes designed to regulate materials. In doing so, the Supreme Court 'left the dirty work of content censorship to ambitious local prosecutors and anti-porn activists' (Lewis, *Hollywood v. Hard Core*, p. 261). Similarly, *Paris Adult Theater I v. Slaton* made it difficult to use restrictive admission policies as a means of avoiding local bans and prosecutions [...] *United States v. 12 200' Reels of Super 8 mm Film* and *United States v. Orito* [...] made it all the more difficult to move potentially pornographic products in from overseas or from state to state. Altogether, the four decisions functionally outlawed the public exhibition of hard core' (Lewis, *Hollywood v. Hard Core*), pp. 262–3.

66 Guy Davenport to Stan and Jane Brakhage, dated 'Birthday of Joyce Cary' 1968, box 4, folder 6, James Stanley Brakhage Collection, University of Colorado at Boulder Libraries.

67 Jimmy Vaughan to Stan Brakhage, 24 September [1969 or 1972], box 29, folder 7, James Stanley Brakhage Collection, University of Colorado at Boulder Libraries.

68 Brakhage to Jonas Mekas, June 30, 1973, box 12, folder 6, James Stanley Brakhage Collection, University of Colorado at Boulder Libraries.

69 John Furlong to Stan Brakhage, August 1974, box 17a (unprocessed at the time of writing), James Stanley Brakhage Collection, University of Colorado at Boulder Libraries; Dennis Kennedy, transcription of telephone conversation with Gloria Bartek, June 21, 1974, box 17a (unprocessed at the time of writing), James Stanley Brakhage Collection, University of Colorado at Boulder Libraries; Stan Brakhage to Barney Rosset, June 23, 1974, box 23, folder 11 'Grove Press Correspondence', James Stanley Brakhage Collection, University of Colorado at Boulder Libraries.

70 Kathryn Bond Stockton, *The Queer Child: Or Growing Sideways in the Twentieth Century* (Durham, NC: Duke University Press, 2009); and Viviana Zelizer, *Pricing the Priceless Child: The Changing Social Value of Children* (Princeton, NJ: Princeton University Press, 1985).

71 Eugene Verrier to Stan Brakhage, June 17, 1969, box 30, folders 14–15, James Stanley Stan Brakhage Collection, University of Colorado at Boulder Libraries.

72 Stan Brakhage to Eugene Verrier, dated 'early' December 1969, box 30, folders 14–15, James Stanley Brakhage Collection, University of Colorado at Boulder Libraries

73 'Sex-Film Showing OKd for Teacher', *Denver Post*, May 23, 1974. See newspaper clipping, box 18, folder 2, James Stanley Brakhage Collection, University of Colorado at Boulder Libraries.

74 Forrest Williams to Stan Brakhage, dated only 'August 23', box 18, folder 2, James Stanley Brakhage Collection, University of Colorado at Boulder Libraries.

75 Stan Brakhage to Jerome Hill, dated only 'near end June 1969', box 8, James Stanley Brakhage Collection, University of Colorado at Boulder Libraries.

76 Paul Sharits to Stan Brakhage, January 14, 1974, Brakhage Files, Anthology Film Archives.

77 Ibid.

78 Stan Brakhage to Jonas Mekas, July 2, 1982, box 12a, James Stanley Brakhage Archive, University of Colorado at Boulder Libraries.

79 Author email message to Marilyn Brakhage, December 6, 2011.

80 Roland Barthes, *Camera Lucida: Reflections on Photography*, (New York: Hill and Wang, 1981).

81 Sharits to Brakhage, 11 February 1971, Brakhage Files Anthology Film Archives.

82 Donald Richie, titled only 'Brakhage/Richie,' n.d., Brakhage File, Anthology Film Archives.

83 Brakhage, 'Metaphors on Vision,' p. 12; Marjorie Keller, 'Stan Brakhage: The Family Romance,' in *The Untutored Eye: Childhood in the Films of Cocteau, Cornell, and Brakhage* (Rutherford, NJ: Fairleigh Dickinson University Press), pp. 179–229.

84 Brakhage, 'Metaphors on Vision,' p. 13.

85 Ibid.

86 Stan Brakhage to Robert Creeley, November 22, 1971, box 4, James Stanley Brakhage Collection, University of Colorado at Boulder Libraries, quoted in Nesthus, 'The "Document" Correspondences of Stan Brakhage,' pp. 143–144, emphasis added.

87 Guy Davenport to Stan Brakhage, dated 'Birthday of John Clare,' 1968, box 4, folder 6, James Stanley Brakhage Collection, University of Colorado at Boulder Libraries.

88 Ibid.

89 Nesthus, 'The "Document" Correspondences of Stan Brakhage,' p. 148. Stan Brakhage to Ed Dorn, November 24, 1971, box 5A, folder 11, James Stanley Brakhage Collection, University of Colorado at Boulder Libraries quoted in Nesthus, 'The "Document" Correspondences of Stan Brakhage,' pp. 145–149.

90 'In a word documentary is always careful to tell us HOW TO FEEL about what we see. / Such aesthetic coercion is foreign to document, which reposes complete faith in the perfect fullness and sufficiency of the unrehearsed film image itself.' Hollis Frampton, 'Some Film Documents: Notes for a screening on 3/23/72 at Hunter College' (lecture, Hunter College, New York, NY, March 23, 1972), quoted in Nesthus, 'The "Document" Correspondences of Stan Brakhage,' p. 154.

91 Annette Michelson, '"Where is Your Rupture?" Mass Culture and the *Gesamtkunstwerk*,' in *Andy Warhol*, ed. Annette Michelson (Cambridge, MA: The MIT Press, 2001), p. 96.

92 Hollis Frampton coins this phrase in a letter to Stan Brakhage. Frampton to Brakhage, January 26, 1972, James Stanley Brakhage Collection, University of Colorado at Boulder Libraries.

93 Brakhage, 'Metaphors on Vision,' p. 13.

94 Stan Brakhage, 'On Marie Menken,' in *Brakhage Scrapbook*, p. 91, originally published as a reprint of a letter to Gerard Malanga, *Filmwise* 5–6 (1967).

95 Stan Brakhage, 'Inspirations', in *Essential Brakhage*, p. 210.

96 Stan Brakhage to Sally Dixon, dated 'early' January 1971, box 5, folder 'Dixon, Sally 1970–1971', James Stanley Brakhage Collection, University of Colorado at Boulder Libraries.

97   Robert Haller, *Crossroads: Avant-Garde Film in Pittsburgh in the 1970s* (New York: Anthology Film Archives, 2005), p. 7.

98   Stan Brakhage, 'Interview with Stan Brakhage,' by Richard Grossinger, in *Brakhage Scrapbook*, p. 194.

99   P. Adams Sitney, 'Marie Menken and the Somatic Camera,' in *Eyes Upside Down: Visionary Filmmakers and the Heritage of Emerson* (Oxford: Oxford University Press, 2008), pp. 21–47.

100 Frampton to Brakhage, January 26, 1972, James Stanley Brakhage Collection, University of Colorado at Boulder Libraries.

101 Nesthus, 'The "Document" Correspondences of Stan Brakhage,' p. 135.

102 Brakhage, 'Interview with Stan Brakhage,' by Richard Grossinger, in *Brakhage Scrapbook*, p. 195.

103 Stan Brakhage to Jane Brakhage, dated '2nd Tues in Pittsburgh' September 71, box 36, folder 10, James Stanley Brakhage Collection, University of Colorado at Boulder Libraries.

104 Nesthus, 'The "Document" Correspondences of Stan Brakhage,' p. 135.

105 Stan Brakhage to Paul Sharits, 8 October 1971, quoted in Haller, *Crossroads*, p. 21.

106 Stan Brakhage to Ed Dorn, November 24, 1971, box 5A, folder 11, James Stanley Brakhage Collection, University of Colorado at Boulder Libraries.

107 Stan Brakhage to Robert Creeley, November 22, 1973, box 4, folder 'Creeley, Robert 1966–1973,' James Stanley Brakhage Collection, University at Colorado at Boulder Libraries.

108 Brakhage, 'Interview with Stan Brakhage,' by Richard Grossinger, in *Brakhage Scrapbook*, p. 198.

109 Ibid., p. 199.

110 Stan Brakhage to Hollis Frampton, November 22, 1971, quoted in Nesthus, 'The "Document" Correspondences of Stan Brakhage,' p. 146.

111 Charles Olson, *The Maximus Poems*, ed. George F. Butterick (Berkeley, CA: University of California Press, 1984), p. 33, quoted in Shachar Bram, *Charles Olson and Alfred North Whitehead: An Essay on Poetry* (Lewisburg, PA: Bucknell University Press, 2004), p. 50.

112 Brakhage, 'Interview with Stan Brakhage,' by Richard Grossinger, in *Brakhage Scrapbook*, p. 199.

113 Ibid., pp. 199–200.

114 Vogel, *Film as a Subversive Art*, p. 267.

115 Sharon Doubiago, 'The Art of Seeing with One's Own Eyes,' in *The Book of Seeing with One's Own Eyes* (Saint Paul, MN: Graywolf Press, 1988), pp. 76–97.

116 Ibid., p. 84.

117 Brakhage, 'Interview with Stan Brakhage,' by Richard Grossinger, in *Brakhage Scrapbook*, p. 200.

118 Edgar Allan Poe, 'A Philosophy of Composition,' *Graham's Magazine*, 28, no. 4 (April 1846), pp. 163–167; p. 165.

119 Doubiago, 'The Art of Seeing with One's Own Eyes,' p. 80.

120 Ibid., p. 84.

121 Clover, *Men, Women, and Chain Saws*, p. 32.

122 Doubiago, 'The Art of Seeing with One's Own Eyes,' p. 84.

123 Fred Camper, 'About the Films,' liner notes for *by Brakhage: An Anthology*, Vol. 1 (Criterion Collection, 2003), DVD.

124 Foster, *Return of the Real*, p. 166.

125 Ibid.

126 Ibid. p. 168.

127 Ara Osterweil and David Baumflek, 'Emergent Bodies: Human, All Too Human, Posthuman,' in *The Anatomy of Body Worlds: Critical Essays on the Plastinated Cadavers of Gunther von Hagens*, ed. T. Christine Jespersen, Alicita Rodríguez, and Joseph Starr (London: McFarland & Company, 2009), pp. 240–258; p. 241.

128 Ibid., p. 254; Giorgio Agamben, *Homo Sacer: Sovereign Power and Bare Life*, trans. Daniel Heller-Roazen (Stanford, CA: Stanford University Press, 1998).

129 Genesis 2:23.

130 Doubiago, 'The Art of Seeing with One's Own Eyes,' pp. 84–85.

131 Ibid., p. 85.

4 Carolee Schneemann: meat joys

By the early 1960s, meat was everywhere. Whether limp or hard, fatty or lean, fresh or decayed, meat was becoming increasingly visible as a substance that could be used to reflect and critique the hierarchies of postwar American culture. As French structural anthropologist Claude Lévi-Strauss argued in his landmark 1964 study *The Raw and the Cooked*, how a society prepared their meat was the key to understanding the myths of that culture.[1] What then to make of the sudden profusion of meat in Roy Lichtenstein's cartoon paintings of steaks and turkeys, Claes Oldenburg's display cases of prime cuts, or the SPAM cans that adorned the Pop canvases of Andy Warhol and Edward Ruscha in New York's 'American Supermarket' show in 1964?[2] While these Pop artists fetishized the branding and packaging of animal flesh, their images also explored what such popular products might tell us about American consumer culture, and the period of incredible social and economic transformation that followed the Second World War.

Yet while these artists focused on meat as an exchange commodity, Carolee Schneemann utilized the meat of the body as material through which to enact alternative models of relationality that could not be conscripted within capitalism. While this is nowhere more evident than in the anarchic juxtapositions of human and animal flesh in Schneemann's groundbreaking 1964 performance piece *Meat Joy*, emphasis on the pleasures and pains of embodiment remained a significant vein of Schneemann's work throughout the 1960s and 1970s.

Recognizing corporeality as the basis for a profound similitude among all beings, Schneemann used the meaty body in a variety of films and performances to represent profound relations of analogy between subjects, regardless of whether they were male or female, animal or human, or alive or dead. By foregrounding the links between differently enfleshed subjects and thereby shattering the binary oppositions upon which patriarchal culture is founded, Schneemann re-oriented the history of twentieth-century Western art towards a radical engagement with the flesh. How such a re-orientation was lived and experienced in Schneemann's art and life is the subject of this chapter.

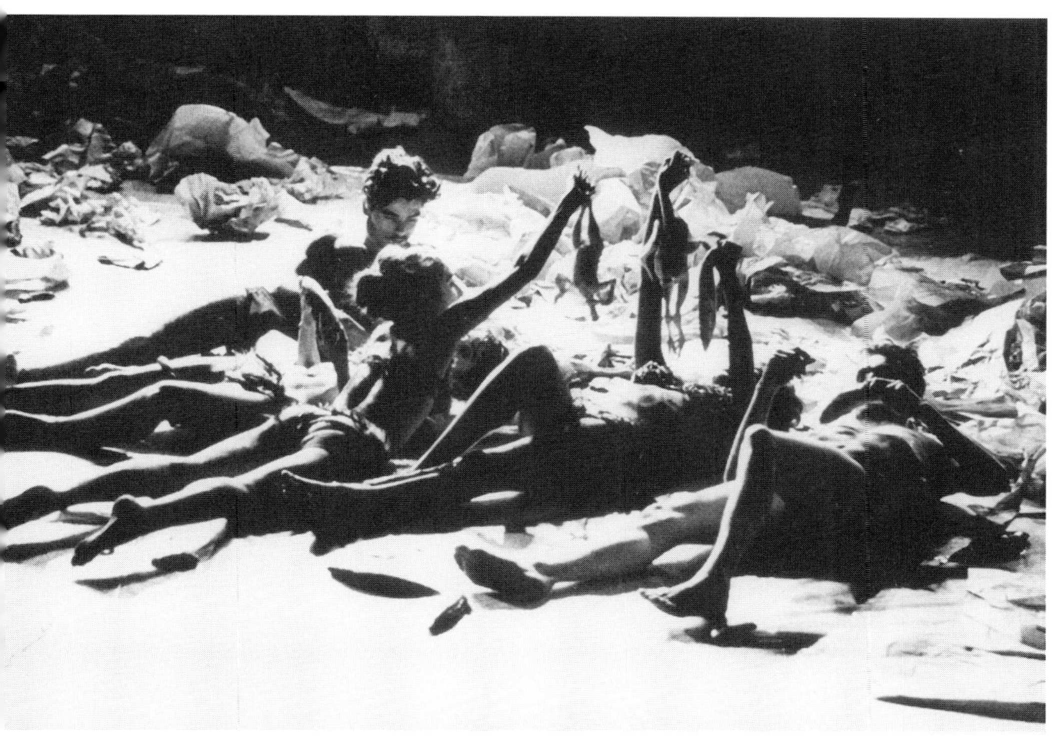

One of the pioneering pieces of body and performance art in the postwar period, Carolee Schneemann's *Meat Joy* (1964) juxtaposes human and animal bodies in an ecstatic orgy of the flesh. James Tenney and Carolee Schneemann are visible on the left. Courtesy of Carolee Schneemann. Photograph by Tony Ray Jones.

29

Though Schneemann has always identified as a painter, since the early 1960s her explorations of embodiment frequently fused the corporeal idiom of dance with the 'hand-touch sensibility'[3] of painting in durational media like film and performance. This corporeal turn necessarily involved a shift away from the fixed, two-dimensional 'frozen' image towards a sustained acknowledgment of 'the thickness of vision'[4] and the 'effervescence'[5] of the mortal body. As art historian Amelia Jones has argued, the body art practices that Schneemann pioneered in the early 1960s dramatize a 'profound shift in the conception and experience of subjectivity,' which posit the individual as fundamentally 'intersubjective (contingent on the other) rather than complete within itself.'[6]

Yet while flesh forms the basis of our essential but contingent relation to others, then meat reveals the precarity of embodiment. As Carolee Schneemann's work demonstrates, this precarity links male and female, human and animal, and live and dead bodies in a thickset consortium of the flesh. Yet while the 'incomprehensible vulnerability'[7] of the flesh functioned as a radical equalizer in Schneemann's poetics, it did not erase differences of subjectivity. Whereas Lévi-Strauss argued that weighty binary oppositions determine cultural meaning, Schneemann used the meat of the body to oppose the very distinction between obscene and sacred upon which patriarchy depended.[8] Schneemann perceived culture through a sensual economy of the flesh that was as attuned to the patriarchal territorialization of the body as it was to the body's ability to resist such systematic organization through erotic, ritualized motion.

Through its exploration of the flesh as the 'physiological source' of our 'ontological kinship'[9] with others – be they of different genders, races, nationalities, or even species – Schneemann's haptic, participatory aesthetics also provide the basis for an ethic based upon profound empathy. As Kaja Silverman argues in *Flesh of My Flesh*, the notion that the flesh of one's own body corresponds not only to the flesh of other bodies, but to the flesh of the world from which we all emerge, has the potential to bind us together in terms of mutual identification.[10] 'These correspondences,' Silverman writes, 'connect us to both ourselves and others, promoting transformation rather than stasis, equality rather than hierarchy, and an "unfinished universality" rather than a closed order.'[11] Though Schneemann's mixed-media practices strive to overcome social inequalities, they do not attempt to deny the differences that are constitutive of our individual identities. Simultaneously acknowledging the similarity and alterity of oneself and one's 'others,' Schneemann uses the erotic body as a vehicle of social transformation capable of engaging difference as the basis for more expansive forms of relationality.

The ethics of Schneemann's aesthetic are based upon the notion of a primordial and unbreakable kinship between bodies that persists throughout disagreement, estrangement, and even death. These 'mortal coils'[12] are constantly, viscerally apprehensible in Schneemann's work. They are visible in the sensual nurturing of both human and animal bodies in her films *Fuses* (1964–1967) and *Kitch's Last Meal* (1975), the first of which documents her beloved cat Kitch's vision of Schneemann's lovemaking, and the second of which marks Kitch's demise, as well as in Schneemann's decision to situate Kitch's corpse on a plinth during the 1974 New York performance of *Up To And Including Her Limits*.[13] The strength of these affective bonds has also sustained and energized the many requiems Schneemann has produced for departed friends, including *Homage to Ana Mendieta* (1988)[14] and *Mortal Coils* (1995), a sculptural installation that mourns the wrenching loss of seventeen friends between 1992 and 1995, including John Cage, Derek Jarman, Joe Jones, Marjorie Keller, Barbara Lehmann, Peter Moore, Charlotte Moorman, Paul Sharits, and Hannah Wilke.

As Schneemann's work reminds us, the 'mortal coils' that bind us to other people are not erased by mortality. On the contrary, as Silverman argues, it is precisely the acknowledgement of mortality's inevitability that has the potential to open us up to a sense of boundlessness: 'Since finitude marks the point where we end and others begin, spatially and temporally, it is also what makes room for them – and acknowledging these limits allows us to experience the expansiveness for which we yearn, because it gives us a powerful sense of our emplacement within a larger Whole.'[15] While finitude involves the recognition of oneself as spatially and temporally bounded, loss also has the potential to shatter any superficial boundaries between Self and Other. Schneemann acknowledges the potential of finitude to expand individual consciousness: 'each death,' she writes in reference to the friends eulogized in *Mortal Coils*, 'altered the interchange of our work, our lives.'[16] Yet even 'as the cherished body is dematerializing,' Schneemann writes, we 'cherish the container, the imbued physical shards of dissolving connection.'[17]

And yet even as the bodies of loved ones decay, corporeality remains the key to what Schneemann has described as a 'confirming' sensation of 'archaic affinity'[18] or, what Silverman calls the 'psychic affirmation' of 'our primordial kinship'[19] with others. 'Mourning rituals are inadequate,' Schneemann has written, 'if they don't involve our bodies, if we are not held, clutched, touched, contacted.'[20] 'Once my dead were in projection and motion,' Schneemann writes of *Mortal Coils*, 'they offered a spirit of simultaneous release and presence. They were active, layered, dissolving into one another, filling the space, enveloping the visitors.'[21]

Following Nietzche, Freud, Rilke, Lou Andreas Salomé and others, Silverman has described this feeling 'of simultaneous release and presence' as 'oceanic.' The 'oceanic feeling,' which pivots upon a 'sensation of "contact" between ourselves and other beings,'[22] is founded upon the seeming paradox that a sense of boundlessness can only emerge through the apprehension of our bodies' limits. Derived from a sense of being 'libidinally bound together,'[23] the oceanic feelings produced by Schneemann's work surge in confrontations between love and death. In her life and work, Schneemann has activated forms of Eros that are capable not only of acknowledging Thanatos, but of merging and dissolving the narcissistic, egoic conflicts of subjectivity. It is this oceanic feeling that makes the intimacies exchanged in Schneemann's work between human and animal bodies, as well as the other material elements of the earth, feel like a form of 'infinity.'[24]

Given Schneemann's commitment to exploring more equitable and expansive forms of relationality, it is fitting that much the artist's practice during the 1960s and 1970s was inspired by collaborative relationships between friends and lovers. Indeed, her work from this time pivots upon the physical and psychical forms of identification with various other artists, including her life-long friend Stan Brakhage, sculptor Robert Morris, and her long-term partners James Tenney and Anthony McCall. Utopian as Schneemann's recognition of corporeal kinship might be, however, these collaborations were never experienced in a historical vacuum, but were often troubled by social inequities which impacted the 'radicality and reciprocity' of identification with each other.[25]

Such generative tensions are nowhere more evident than in the nearly fifty-year friendship between Schneemann and fellow filmmaker, collaborator, and sometimes adversary Stan Brakhage. Though scholars have largely overlooked Schneemann's influence on Brakhage in favor of assuming his influence upon *her*, Schneemann's early paintings and approach to corporeality were integral to the development of Brakhage signature, hand-painted cinema, as well as his decision, in *Lovemaking*, to focus less on artistic pyrotechnics, and more on the flesh of bodies. Their fraught friendship not only serves as an allegory of the difficulties for a feminist artist working both within and outside the structures of heterosexuality and patriarchy, but also helps to contextualize the development of Schneemann's own performative ontology of the flesh.

Meat Joy (1964)

Meat Joy remains the privileged example of utopian bodily communion that Schneemann has pioneered for the last fifty years. Lasting over an hour, the original performance featured a group of men and women decked out in tiny fur-lined bikinis, who wrapped themselves in paper, rolled around on the floor, painted each other, and formed kaleidoscopic patterns with their writhing bodies in an orgiastic jubilation of the flesh. Towards the end of this rigorous rite, a 'Serving Maid' entered the scene, carrying a large tray of raw meat, including fish, plucked chickens, and hot dogs, which she strewed on the wriggling bodies, who had to somehow incorporate them into their kinetic, erotic performances.

In its concatenation of raw meat, wet paint, transparent plastic, rope, brushes, and paper scrap, *Meat Joy* celebrated the tactility of material elements. The entire piece was performed to a score collaged from audio fragments that included popular songs of the time, street sounds, Schneemann's voice reading her notes on the project, an audio recording of beginning French exercises, and a ticking clock.[26]

Schneemann's orchestration of anarchic bodies rejoiced in the collective corporeality of human and animal flesh, while implicitly challenging the patriarchal insistence that nudity was acceptable only when it belongs to sanitized, female bodies. By signifying the carnal body as a site of abundant sensual gratification, *Meat Joy* liberated sexuality from the constraints of gender distinctions. Such liberation involved new types of embodied vision, which often included prolonged instances of haptic 'blindness.' Noting her own inability to 'see' the entirety of the performance she had choreographed, Schneemann wrote to her partner James Tenney on the evening of *Meat Joy*'s May 30, 1964 debut in Paris:

> The impossible French audience I'd come to know & fear so well, hypnotized into a silence which no one ever had experienced before! … Beautiful to be in it – I didn't see it the way I 'didn't see' Chromodeon, but I *was* in it and alive in the

center of this radiant, fierce organism and a pleasure to me unprecedented in my theatre/dance pieces. You and me in it – what the telegram said – to make this possible our love, our life like a buried nervous system, a blood stream. I didn't see the audience (felt them as some huge enveloping beast and my body, our eight bodies strong, vital in the space and time we transformed).[27]

Schneemann's notion of embodied vision, in which there is no sight outside of the body, acknowledged the 'eyebody' as an imperfect organ. Eschewing Renaissance painting's construction of a stable subject whose eye was uniquely privileged to take in everything at once, there was no optimal perspective from which to view *Meat Joy*. As her remarks suggest, even Schneemann herself could not *see* the performance, so inside the visible was she. In a profound rejection

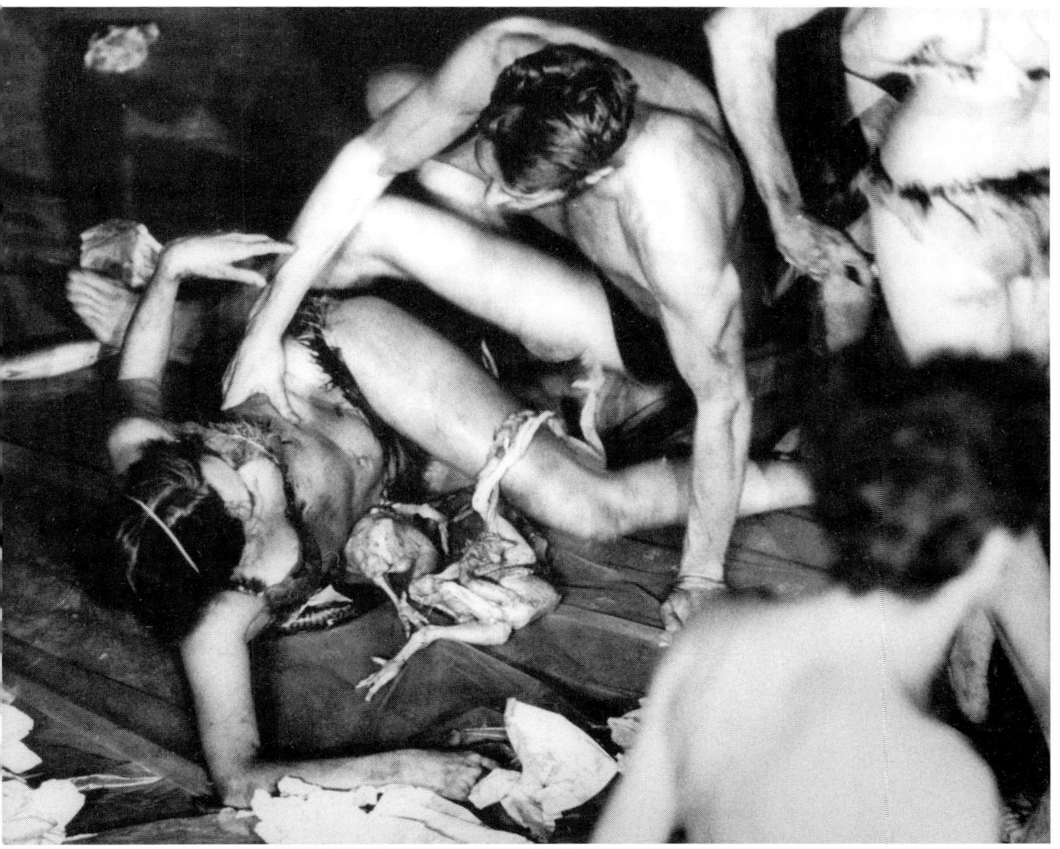

Entangled performers improvise interactions with the animal carcasses that are   30
poured on to them by the Serving Maid in Carolee Schneemann's *Meat Joy* (1964).

of the Kantian ideal of detached spectatorship, *Meat Joy* celebrated what it felt like to be a body immersed in flesh, ecstatic amongst other in-visible beings.

Schneemann has described *Meat Joy*'s 'celebration of flesh as material' as an 'erotic rite' capable of bringing members of a community into intense corporeal relation with each other:

> Its propulsion is toward the ecstatic, shifting and turning between tenderness, wildness, precision, abandon – qualities that could at any moment be sensual, comic, joyous, repellent. Physical equivalences are enacted as a psychic and imagistic stream in which the layered elements mesh and gain intensity by the energy complement of the audience… Our proximity heightened the sense of community, transgressing the polarity between performer and audience.[28]

These transgressions could be as messy off-stage as they were on; in a letter to artist Wolf Vostell, Schneemann noted with delight that somebody had vomited during *Meat Joy*'s New York debut.[29]

Following the notoriety of *Meat Joy*, the notion of 'meat' 'spread like an eroticizing flash fire.' As Schneemann recalls, 'things began to be called 'Meat'… this and that.'[30] Schneemann's inspiration for the title *Meat Joy* had actually been borrowed from beat poet Michael McClure,[31] a close friend of Allen Ginsberg, Jack Kerouac, Bob Dylan, and Stan Brakhage, who helped create a bridge between the poetry scene of the 1950s and San Francisco's hippie counterculture of the late 1960s. In 1963, McClure had published *Meat Science Essays* with City Lights Books. In an essay ironically titled 'Phi Upsilon Kappa' (the acronym of which would be an homophone of the word 'FUCK'), McClure extolled the virtues of the 'fleshmeat' which unites man and animal, originates language, and nourishes creativity through the satisfaction of its basic hungers for food and sex. Commanding his readers to 'free the word fuck from its chains and strictures,' McClure explicitly denied the Cartesian separation of mind from body by insisting that the 'body is all.'[32] He also implicitly challenged the Saussurian emphasis on the arbitrariness of language signs by insisting that words themselves were 'part of physiology,'[33] made by 'real meat lips and throat.'[34] 'Words are the body as they float from tongue to air to other meatspirit or listener,' McClure wrote.[35] Quoting a stanza of his own poem *Dark Brown*, he enlivened his readers to: 'be real, show organs, show blood.'[36] Encouraging artists to defy the limitations of censorship and bring the obscene 'on-scene,'[37] McClure wrote:

> The body was ignored, removed-from, twisted, distorted, and great spiritual beauties without human body have been laid down in paint, writing, and music. Now there is a return to the body with all previously repressed virtues of human lovely beast spirit animal that were uncovered by the experiments incorporated into it. A new vivid completeness enters in the arts with all splashes, drips, and chance and abstract autobiographies of spiritmeat taken whole

within a new portrait of man. Without change, that too will become a frozen imagevision of dead-meat.[38]

Moving through the two-dimensional surfaces of Abstract Expressionism, Schneemann expanded the domain of its 'abstract autobiography' beyond the limits of the canvas to an engagement with the sexual politics of meat. Even before encountering McClure's theory, in which the poet theorized all human beings as 'bags of meat,' Schneemann had already begun to explore a nascent ontology of 'meat.' As the daughter of a country doctor, Schneemann had witnessed the fleshy vicissitudes of living and dying bodies at an early age. She had not only grown accustomed to people coming into her house 'with bloody limbs in their arms,' but had been trained to wrap and tend to wounds.[39] 'There was always physicality around us – leaking, spilling out of boundaries, wounded farmers with bleeding limbs, broken bones, hemorrhages, infections, bodies that were not intact. No fantasy of the sanitized body in this household…'[40]

Schneemann had also experienced the excruciating transformation of her own body into meat. Before either modern birth control was legalized in the United States in 1960 or *Roe v. Wade* (1973) extended a woman's right to privacy to include her decision to terminate her pregnancy, Schneemann travelled, in the late 1950s, to both pre-Castro Cuba and rural Pennsylvania, to arrange illicit abortions. Schneemann described the process of having her own body partitioned like meat:

> Silvery clamps and pinchers, the sensation of being meat or wood held for chopping. And the 'inside' pain for which I find no correlatives. He [the doctor] punches a hole in me, he pulls me apart, I am splitting, twisting, pulled apart, mysterious islands of flesh scream in my head, suddenly singular with pain, blood, scrapings and pullings over and over.[41]

Such experiences undoubtedly influenced Schneemann's radical corporeal intervention in the history of postwar art. For though Schneemann acknowledged the momentous influence of De Kooning and Pollock on her work, she also recognized early on that the body's 'limitless' capacity to break through the conventionalizing language of abstraction was far more extensive than that of the brush.[42] Much like the fingerprint theorized by realist film theorist André Bazin in 'The Ontology of the Photographic Image,'[43] the tumultuous marks left by the pigment-laden brushes of Abstract Expressionist painters served as ontological evidence of the human bodies that had produced them. Yet by privileging the exquisite traces of inspired painterly 'action' over the bodies that made them, the heroic, masculine culture of Abstract Expressionism redeemed the painted canvas from its potential association with the stain of menstrual blood, shit, and urine. While Abstract Expressionism kept the body proximate but safely out of reach, Schneemann foregrounded the actual meat of the body rather than just the marks it left. As early as 1963's *Eye Body: 36 Transformative Actions*, Schneemann used her nude body as an extension of her painting-constructions, provocations that would continually earn her wrath, derision, and degradation by the phallocentric art world.[44] In a letter to Clayton Eshleman from 1975, Schneemann defended herself, for the umpteenth time, against implicit charges of narcissism and exhibitionism: 'In your earlier letter you write about my using temporal experience "must to a great extend hinge upon the necessity for you to show your naked body" … I do not "show" my naked body! I AM BEING MY BODY.'[45]

Schneemann's crucial distinction between 'having' versus 'being' a body grounded her use of the flesh as a vehicle for political resistance and social transformation. Though Schneemann was painfully cognizant of the capacity of the patriarchal apparatuses of medicine and war to rupture the body's flesh and transform it into meat, she also recognized the subject's capacity for resistance. 'The body writhes and crumples and twists,' Schneemann wrote in response to her abortion, but 'the head is filled with joy, exaltant, it is free.'[46] Even when trapped in the abattoir of an imperialist, racist, misogynist nation determined to make mince of its most marginalized subjects, the body could mobilize its defiance in erotic ritual and corporeal performance.

Meat Joy invited the subject to fully participate in sensual rituals of the flesh that had been rendered taboo by the Cartesian privileging of cerebral subjectivity. Celebrating the joys of meat threatened the state's symbolic power to lay waste to the subject through its violent penetration of the flesh. As Schneemann would demonstrate when training people how to resist the Vietnam draft,[47] the meat-like qualities of the flesh could also be used to defy the regulatory instruction demanded by military commandments. For even as the state exploited individuals, the flesh retained its 'votive'[48] capacity.

Yet homologous as it might be with other types of mammalian flesh, the meat of the human body could never be isolated from its role as a signifier of sex and gender within patriarchal culture. Meat was hardly neutral. Contemporaneous with Schneemann and McClure's use of the word 'meat,' another, powerful connotation of the word insisted upon its genitality. In her groundbreaking study of moving image pornography, film scholar Linda Williams explains how close-up images of genital penetration, referred to as 'meat shots,' were the culminating point of visual pleasure in stag films.[49] Mute proof that hard-core activity was taking place in the mostly silent, single-reel stag films that formed the lexicon of moving-image pornography from the 1910s to the 1960s, meat shots permitted a 'clinical, objectifying scrutiny of the female body' to their historically all-male audiences.[50]

By the time Schneemann performed *Interior Scroll* – first in 1975 for a mostly female audience in the 'Women Here and Now' festival in East Hampton, New York and then again in 1977 at the Telluride Film Festival in Colorado,[51]

– the 'meat' of stag films had been replaced by the 'money shot' that began to dominate hard-core moving image pornography after the success of Gerard Damiano's 1972 film *Deep Throat*.[52] These suddenly obligatory shots of male ejaculation had 'assumed the narrative function of signaling the climax of a genital event' by offering visual proof of male orgasm.[53] Yet as Williams argued, 'this new visibility' of 'the hydraulics of male ejaculation,' served to disguise and disavow knowledge of female pleasure, whose in-visible specificity elided hard-core's insistence on visual clarity.

Schneemann's orchestration of meat pushed against pornography's articulation of genital meaning. Deploying the word 'meat' to designate the entire flesh of the body, instead of just the female genitals, Schneemann challenged the instrumentalization of the female body – as both meat *and* money – by patriarchy. In *Interior Scroll*, first performed three years after the legal debut of hard-core, feature-length American pornography and its concomitant replacement of 'meat' with 'money,' Schneemann posed naked on a stage, with her body painted in quick stripes, as she pulled a long thin coil of paper from her vagina and unrolled it to read a narrative to the audience.

Citing an encounter with a 'happy man / a structuralist filmmaker,'[54] Schneemann described the rejection of her film from the avant-garde film community, which refused to consider her anything but 'a dancer.'[55]

> he said we are fond of you
> you are charming
> but don't ask us
> to look at your films
> we cannot
> there are certain films
> we cannot look at
> the personal clutter
> the persistence of feelings
> the hand-touch sensibility
> the diaristic indulgence
> the painterly mess
> the dense gestalt
> the primitive techniques.[56]

Foretelling the critique of patriarchal film language in Laura Mulvey's influential essay 'Visual Pleasure and Narrative Cinema' – also from 1975 – Schneemann charged her audience to 'PAY ATTENTION TO CRITICAL / AND PRACTICAL FILM LANGUAGE, IT EXISTS FOR AND IN ONLY / ONE GENDER.'[57] Yet rather than dismantle the phallocentric, fetishistic grammar of cinema through the patriarchal language of psychoanalysis, as Mulvey would do, Schneemann returned to the 'meat systems' of the body. Recognizing how

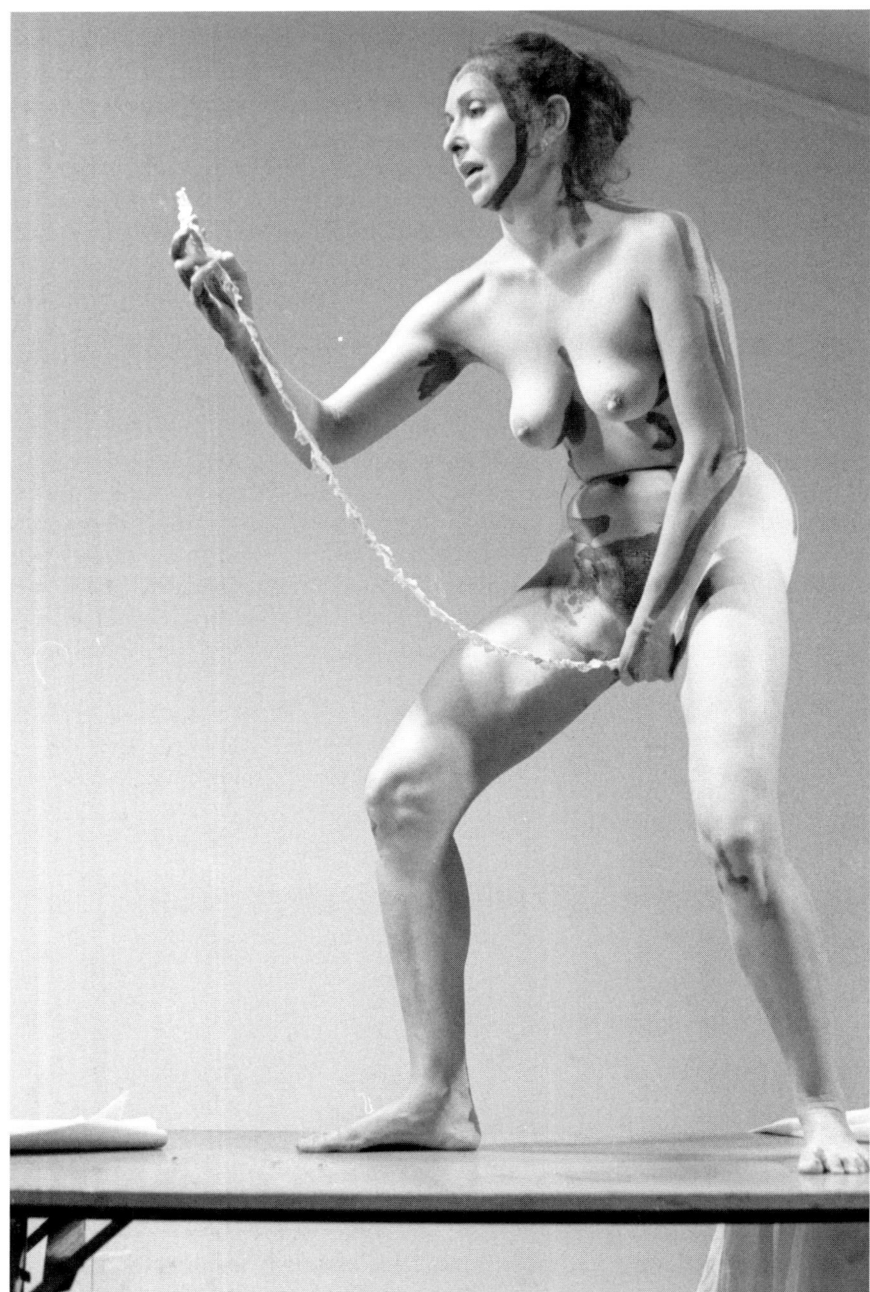

31   Carolee Schneemann collapses the distinction between body and mind as she
unravels and then reads a written monologue from her vagina in *Interior Scroll* (1975).

the transformation of food through the body's digestive system parallels the journey of each individual towards finitude, Schneemann's loquacious vulva proposes a cinema concerned instead with 'DIET AND DIGESTION.'[58] There is 'die in diet,'[59] she declares, reminding her audience that meaning lies within, rather than beyond, our mortality. Distinguishing her work from the metaphorical tendencies of other experimental filmmakers, Schneemann asserts, 'you are back to metaphors / and meanings / my work has no meaning beyond / the logic of its systems.'[60]

Assaulting the Cartesian distinction between body and mind with its bold assertion of genital thought, *Interior Scroll* not only insists that there can be no mind without meat, but that meat is mind itself. Enacting the vulvic as a deep, in-visible space, Schneemann transformed the 'occluded interior of the female body'[61] into a 'translucent chamber'[62] capable of producing its own discourse. Daring to make the unseen meat of the genitals think and speak, Schneemann rejects the dismissal of the female artist as 'sculptress' or 'film-makeress' while nonetheless insisting on the specificity of female bodies. In this way, *Interior Scroll* 'confronts' and 'dismantles the convention of the genital being "obscene"'[63] by finding a mode of representation that makes the in-visible legible. In doing so, it dramatizes 'an ethic about knowledge itself – received from and in the body.'[64]

Let us keep this ethic in mind as we meander through one of the defining encounters between minimalist form and the nude body in the early 1960s.

Site (1964)

Before moving on to an analysis of Schneemann's friendship with Brakhage, and its impact on the development of her oceanic film *Fuses* (1965), I would like to detour through *Site*, a 1964 performance piece in which the artist collaborated with Minimalist sculptor Robert Morris. I am aware that to dare to look back at this collaboration is to transform the white cube for which Morris is best known into a veritable Pandora's box. My aim is not to pick at old wounds. As an artist, I know that the success of any given piece is far less important than the process activated and worked through by partial failures. Yet in spite of my reluctance to eternalize a flawed object, *Site* remains a telling allegory of the difficulties engendered within heterosexual collaborations during a period in which the hard-won, necessary alliances between leftist artists were often deeply troubled by gender, class, and/or racial politics.

In 1964, both Robert Morris and Carolee Schneemann were involved with the Judson Dance Theater, an alternative space for the performing arts located in New York's Greenwich Village. Schneemann had brought *Meat Joy* to Judson in November 1964 after debuting it that same year in Paris and London.[65] Occasioning a raucous response from the European press, *Meat Joy* was already on its way to becoming one of the defining performances of the postwar era. Both Morris and Schneemann's interest in dance and performance had emerged from their work as painters. As Hans Namuth's photos of Jackson Pollock demonstrated to a generation of young artists,[66] painting was itself a form of dance, a way of negotiating the force of the body and other objects in space. Of all his male contemporaries, Morris exemplified Michael Fried's claims that Minimalist sculpture was fundamentally 'theatrical' because of its concern 'with the actual circumstances in which the beholder encounters the work.'[67] Upon first glance, Morris's early installations might have appeared like 'physically' and 'psychically' distancing fields of large-scale, geometric volumes. However, as Fried makes explicit, these volumes were an invitation for the corporeal participation of the beholder.

> 'the entire situation' means exactly that: all of it – including, it seems, the beholder's *body*. There is nothing within his field of vision – nothing that he takes note of in any way – that, as it were declares its irrelevance to the situation, and therefore to the experience, in question. On the contrary, for something to be perceived at all is for it to be perceived as part of that situation. Everything counts.[68]

Considering their shared investment in participatory forms of art, it is no wonder that Schneemann and Morris were drawn to collaborate. Schneemann recalls:

> What I wanted was a lot of muscular interchange in the space, to explore each other's weights and balances. I was working on exercisers concerning exchanges of gravity and weight, who was more physically powerful, how you yield, how you exchange pushing, pulling, grabbing, how you take responsibilities for one another's bodies, and we were doing that. Bob came to rehearse one day and said, 'Come on down to Grand Street, to my studio, I have another idea.'

Morris's idea involved the creation of a living tableau based upon Edouard Manet's famous painting of *Olympia* (1863). As Schneemann recalls,

> [Morris] had me lying on this little board, while he moved the 6' by 8' plywood panels around. And it had a vivid surprise because the initial image you saw was very minimalist and formal, you just saw a 6' × 8' board. But there were actually three boards, and I was hidden behind them naked, balanced on this little rack. So my job was just to keep my head down, so I wasn't sticking up over the panels, when they were horizontal. And as he lifted the last one I raised myself on the small shelf to be revealed, stained white with a little black cat collar on my neck.[69]

Morris's citation of Manet both invoked and repressed a rich history of representational controversy. Both *Site* and *Olympia* documented the relationship between a male and female artist. Inspired by Titian's 1538 *Venus of Urbino* (itself informed by Giorgione's 1510 *Sleeping Venus*), Manet's controversial painting of fellow painter Victorine Meurent[70] depicted its heroine not as a mythical goddess or odalisque but as a confrontational prostitute waiting for a client. Nodding to Jean Auguste Dominique Ingres's *Odalisque with a Slave* (1842), Léon Benouville's *Esther with Odalisque* (1844) and Charles Jalabert's *Odalisque* (1842), Manet's painting included a black female servant who appeared behind her mistress displaying a bouquet of flowers that had presumably been sent by an admirer.

In Manet's painting, Olympia looks neither at her servant nor at the fertile offering, but defiantly forward at the invisible but presumably male spectator/client around whose gaze, John Berger argues, traditional Western oil painting is organized.[71] We know from her gaze that this is a woman devoid of illusion and shame; she knowingly exchanges her body for capital. (Manet's replacement of the little dog in Titian's painting with a witchy black cat seems, in retrospect, an open invitation for the feline-smitten Schneemann to assume her place as the inheritor of Olympia's subversive discourse.) Yet if Olympia's refusal of innocence challenged the *de facto* possession of her body, her forward gaze also negated the possibility for a meaningful exchange of glances between white mistress and black servant. Compelled by her inferior racial status to remain on the margins of both Manet's painting and her mistress's resistance, Olympia's maid is, as artist Lorraine O'Grady has argued, a 'peripheral Negro,' 'a robot conveniently made to disappear into the background drapery.'[72]

Made one hundred years later, *Site*'s white-on-white *mise-en-scène* eliminates the presence of Olympia's maid entirely, in spite of the fact that the representation of this potent interracial alliance may have illuminated the politics of this most violent period of the Civil Rights era. That this omission of the black body silently echoed the negation of black artists from the canon of Western art can hardly be blamed on Morris. But it reminds us that Minimalism's emphasis on idealized 'primary structures'[73] or what Donald Judd described as 'specific objects,'[74] may have unintentionally effaced the corporeal specificity of subjects who may have required less 'universal' objects through which to enact their resistance. In spite of what may have been the radical intent of Morris's practice, *Site* makes clear that the body of Minimalism's 'beholder' was presumed to be white, male, and Western.

The most enduring documents of *Site* are black-and-white photographs of Schneemann's nude body reclining on a vertical white board in the background of a stage while Morris, dressed as a construction worker in white pants, white muscle shirt, and work gloves, bustles in the foreground, manipulating large sheets of white plywood. Unlike the constantly shifting vantage points of *Meat*

Joy, Site exhibited Schneemann's body as a frozen object distanced from the viewer by her remote position in the proscenium, and framed safely within the optical perspective of Western easel painting. Indeed, were it not for her eyes, collar, nipples, and the dark hair on her head and pubis, Schneemann would recede completely in the white box so fetishized by Minimalist installations of the period. Like the columns situated in Morris's early sculptural performance at the Living Theater, the most Schneemann can do is tip over.[75]

Schneemann was disappointed by *Site*'s failure to explore the weighted tensions between two differently sexed and gendered bodies. Rather than taking responsibility for each other through the terms of mutual give and take, Morris transformed Schneemann into an object whose 'specificity' – to deliberately misread Donald Judd – was inextricable from patriarchy's insistence upon sexual difference. If Minimalist art claimed to demystify the art object's manufacture of illusion, then *Site* re-mystified the female body as a cipher in the system of signification: 'For me,' Schneemann has recalled, 'this was another fated collaboration with a male friend … and I went into it to see how it would be, and with Olympia as the Site, I was unexpectedly immobilized and historicized.'[76] While Morris's activity situated his mobile body within the everyday, lived experience of the artist-worker, Schneemann assumed the position of one more alabaster Aphrodite in the archive. In its attempt to theatricalize the 'anxiety of influence'[77] between the male artist and his forebears, *Site* foregrounded male labor while erasing the subversive potential of female camaraderie. Furthermore, *Site*'s framing of Schneemann as a nude dancer had the unintended effect of detracting critical attention from her own kinetic work.[78]

Yet as all still photos of live performances, these images fail to capture the dynamic vitality of *Site*. For the meaning of *Site* depends not on the fact of Schneemann's nudity – art history is full of nudes – but upon the durational process of the performance, which unfolded to reveal a live woman defined by lifelessness. To the careful observer, however, there are two fleeting instances in which Schneemann's live body breaks free of her dead pose. In the recordings of the 1964 performance that I have seen, there are two moments when the camera catches Schneemann lifting and ducking her head in order to hide between the plywood sheets that are removed and then replaced by Morris. Watching these minor adjustments of Schneemann's inevitably aching neck, I finally begin to *feel* the way this piece is *sited* upon the body. Like the generations of anonymous women who contorted their bodies to appear magically 'sawed in half' by the celebrated male magicians with whom they worked,[79] Schneemann's corporeal labor is effaced, while Morris's is both seen and cited.

Yet *Site* is not quite the feminist disaster it has often been made out to be. Dressed as a construction worker, Morris reminded audiences how artistic processes that culminate in the pristine gallery show exist on a continuum with other kinds of labor including, implicitly, the work he himself had done in the railyards.[80] Transforming the typical, task-like movements of art handling into a type of minimalist dance performance, Morris used his own body to enact the kinetic performance required by the art worker. Bridging the new, site-specific practice of the 1960s with the construction sites in which many of its practitioners still or recently toiled, Morris strove to find a performative language capable of broaching the effects that class politics had on his own embodiment of masculinity – whose transparency he simultaneously deconstructed by wearing a mask of his own face during the performance.[81] Thin, and already sporting a receding hairline, Morris was hardly the epitome of hardhat masculinity. In this respect, his impeccable, close-fit white uniform suggested his own sartorial negotiation of the tensions generated between site and *Site*, between the locales of hard labor and elitist institutions of display.

Not necessarily at home in either environment, the male working-class artist situated himself on the borders of masculine realms of production. However problematic, Schneemann's inclusion was strategic, for it naturalized an ill-fitting masculinity whose performance might have otherwise appeared as facetious drag à la the Village People. If, as Sally Banes has argued, '*Site* recuperated the male artist's activity as safely masculine';[82] then it did so by fetishizing Schneemann, whose presence allowed Morris the freedom to dance with plywood without compromising his masculinity. But what kinds of discursive politics disabled Morris from recognizing Schneemann's own formidable muscular labors as existing on a continuum with his own?

In retrospect, *Site* unwittingly suppresses the very types of analogy that Schneemann privileges in her work. Founded upon Morris's projective identification with Manet-the-father, *Site* allegorized not only the artist's recognition of himself within the art historical past, but also his misrecognition of his own kinship with the female Other. In its attempt to clear a site where the principles of hard-edge Minimalism could illuminate the engendering of the body within industrial labor relations, sexual difference proved an ideological blind spot. The poignant limitations of *Site* serve as a point of departure for the rest of this chapter, which explores the equivalent 'blindings' that emerge when we try to see each other from inside acts of love.

Towards blindness: collaboration with Stan Brakhage

Throughout her career, Schneemann has struggled to bridge the spheres of sex, labor, and art within heterosexual intimacy. 'My work,' Schneemann has written, 'was dependent on my sexuality – its satisfaction, integrity. I couldn't work without a coherent sexual relationship – that fueled my imagination, my energies. My mind works out of the knowledge of the body.'[83] Yet as early as 1960, Schneemann had begun to realize the difficulty of sustaining this necessary fusion between art and lovemaking: 'The absorption of one identity into another being at best a glorious dream, a romantic fantasy and at worst – what it really is – an economic and social convention.'[84] Though she identified with the '[m]any others [who] are also trying to be this very difficult thing of two people with creative lives in themselves uniquely, sharing this together,' Schneemann could not help but see 'that the woman of these couples is always in the position to be "asking."'[85]

The tumultuous friendship between Carolee Schneemann and Stan Brakhage helped to generate the emergence of the most highly individualistic, anti-industrial model of personal, corporeal filmmaking in the postwar era. Before Brakhage met Schneemann in the mid-1950s, he was making black-and-white 'trance films' that, like Maya Deren's work from the mid-1940s, were characterized by their existential focus on a psychologically splintering protagonist. Borrowing chiaroscuro lighting from *film noir*, such overwrought psychodramas as *Interim* (1952, with music by James Tenney) and *Desistfilm* (1954) were parts of a wrenching process of post-adolescent self-discovery that included serious consideration of suicide by the artist at the age of 26.[86]

Contemporaneous with meeting both Schneemann and Jane Collum, whom Brakhage married in 1957, Brakhage's work turned away from the agonies of the psyche towards the representation of the body. Shifting from a Freudian conception of the self towards an investigation of embodied vision, Brakhage began to theorize the visionary capacities of the 'untutored eye' in ways that are remarkably consistent with Schneemann's contemporaneous notion of the 'eyebody.' Rejecting the ocularcentrism of Western culture, Schneemann's concept of the 'eyebody' embraced the ways in which vision was immersed in, and thereby inextricable from, corporeality. Pioneering what critic Kristine Stiles describes as 'an *aesthetic of the transitive eye*' by moving between 'the bodily eye' and 'the body-as-eye,'[87] Schneemann created painted and constructed environments designed to activate the 'trancelike state' occasioned by the 'physical transformations' of her body in ritual.[88] Brakhage, who published *Metaphors on Vision* in 1963, the same year that Schneemann created *Eye Body: 36 Transformative Actions*, was also interested in expanding vision beyond the limitations imposed by '19th century Western compositional perspective.'[89]

This shift from an interrogation of the unconscious towards an investigation of embodied vision involved what film theorist Laura Marks has described as a move towards 'haptic visuality.'[90] Following Alois Riegl's and Gilles Deleuze's related but not identical distinctions between 'optical' and 'haptical' modes of perception, Marks's concept of haptic visuality emphasizes 'the way vision itself can be tactile, as though one were touching a film with one's eyes.'[91] Influenced by the 'tactile activity'[92] of Schneemann's early painting-constructions, which incorporated material elements like cloth, paper, wood, nails, and glass, Brakhage increased the dimensionality of the celluloid strip through collage, and shifted his palette from black and white to vibrant color. Most innovatively,

Brakhage's embrace of haptic visuality involved the tactile interrogation of the 'skin' of the film through painting and scratching its surface.

I argue that it is impossible to understand the merging of painting, film, flesh, and collage in either Brakhage or Schneemann's work without contextualizing these innovations within their friendship. As Schneemann has attested, 'The condition of affinity, mutual influence and response are more consistent between Stan's and my work than is normally understood.'[93] Schneemann first met Brakhage in 1956 through her first husband, the American composer James Tenney (1934–2006). Tenney had gone to high school with Brakhage in Denver, Colorado; along with their other high school classmates filmmaker Larry Jordan and musician Morton Subotnick, they had formed a drama group called the Gadflies, the first of many artistic collaborations they would pursue until Brakhage's death in 2003. In the mid-to-late 1950s, Schneemann and Tenney were in constant communication with the Brakhages, visiting each other in Colorado, Vermont and Illinois,[94] and chronicling their stormy alliance in frequent letters. Although many of Brakhage's letters to Schneemann were either burnt by Brakhage or stolen,[95] the remaining letters reveal a sustained, meaningful dialogue that was nonetheless troubled by the inequitable gender politics of mid-century America.

By 1975, the year she performed *Interior Scroll* at the Telluride Film Festival at Brakhage's invitation, Schneemann described their friendship as being 'more mixed with appreciation, apprehension, closeness, despair, bitter hurt, fragmented love than any other.'[96] Theirs was a momentous relationship, based upon their shared engagement with embodied vision, and a commitment to incorporate the textures of heterosexual intimacy into their work. Yet unlike the many friendships with women that Schneemann had, in which she did not habitually feel 'embattled, put-upon, fogged-over,' or her relationships with male lovers, her friendship with Brakhage benefited neither from the affinity of gender nor the kinship generated by sexual intimacy.

The friendship between Schneemann and Brakhage had a momentous influence on the development of postwar aesthetics. As Brakhage moved towards an investigation of Eros in his cinema of the late 1950s, Schneemann and Tenney played pivotal roles as both filmic doubles and provocative alternatives for Stan and Jane. Allowing Brakhage to film them performing intimate, sexually explicit acts in *Loving* (1957) and *Cat's Cradle* (1959) – which, along with Brakhage's films *Daybreak* (1957) and *Whiteye* (1957), were shot in Schneemann and Tenney's Vermont home – they became sensual conduits through which Brakhage could explore the relationship between sex and cinema as two, intricately related forms of embodied experience.

Both *Cat's Cradle* and *Loving* fantasize a utopian sexual symbiosis of man and woman. As P. Adams Sitney has claimed, Brakhage's fluid treatment of bodies suggests the interpenetration of male and female, creating an androgynous being out of discrete individuals.[97] Nonetheless, this hermaphroditic merging was replicated neither off-screen in the film's mode of production nor in the couples' interminglings. By diverting attention away from inter-subjective conflict towards the sumptuous rhythms of natural light, Brakhage evaded the gendered issues that made the friendships between the couples so problematic. Though Schneemann had willingly participated in Brakhage's pursuit of his own 'visualized sexual self-definition,'[98] she would come to disavow Brakhage's representation of her in both films. 'Like *Cat's Cradle*,' Schneemann wrote, '*Loving* was an extremely frustrating event, in which I felt repressed, witnessed, appreciated but constrained.'[99]

For Schneemann, the repressed tensions of the foursome were epitomized by details of the film's *mise-en-scène* that willfully distorted the more egalitarian terms of domestic life practiced by Schneemann and Tenney. For Schneemann, the entire filming of *Cat's Cradle* turned out to be:

> a nightmare of willful distortion and destruction. Stan wanting me to paint in the apron & Jim posed like a decoy, their nervous jumping, skin crawling actions in the house so that all was chance in it and all that was intent by us become a melodramatic trapping as a trap for them.[100]

Particularly incensed that Brakhage had made her appear in stereotypically domestic garb regardless of whether she was peeling onions or painting, Schneemann joined other feminists of her generation in finding the apron a loaded symbol of gender inequity. Railing at Brakhage's translation of her subjectivity into clichés of 'ideal' domesticity, Schneemann felt deformed by the production.[101] Feeling like a mere prop, Schneemann had a sense not only 'of being superfluous' but also of reminding Brakhage of 'what he doesn't want to need as a woman as M.J. [Mary Jane Collum Brakhage Wodening] becomes all woman for him.'[102]

Schneemann's perceptions of Jane Brakhage – whom she regarded alternately as ally, adversary, and mystery – are crucial to the development and articulation of the artist's feminist consciousness. Equally significant to her revelatory discovery of Simone de Beauvoir's *The Second Sex* were Schneemann's surging first-hand impressions of the inequities she perceived in the Brakhages' marriage. Following a visit by Stan and Jane in 1958 – after the cordial filming of *Loving*, but before the agonies of *Cat's Cradle* – Schneemann described her visceral response to the 'intermangling' of the two couples.[103] Schneemann both identified and radically dis-identified with Jane Brakhage, whom she witnessed disappear under the cloak of Stan's art, and the dutiful fulfillment of her roles as wife and mother. Written in a fury after the visit, the following recollection articulates the pathos of feminist rage:

> Establishing herself for the future life … she sews great gowns to grow pregnant in and insists on nine children, with great natural joy but also, and this

is so sad, with wide-eyed fear, like an animal trapped from the pleasures of its free movement…[104]

In the same letter, Schneemann described Jane Brakhage as 'already a configuration – a family … in a process of transferring individualization, that is, nothing is just for "herself," for her discarding.'[105] Ascribing Jane's de-individualization to her dependence on Stan, Schneemann reflected upon the wife's paradoxical embrace of traditional domestic duties in the midst of the postwar struggle to redefine femininity on equal terms with masculinity:

> When there were no pies it was significant to produce one. When life depended on children it was a disgrace not to further the generations and by this the socio-economic foundations of living … There is no longer the physical-economic as primal conditions, as necessities to 'produce' children or anything else. Rather we assume reasons personal, emotional, individuation of choice. Now woman 'chooses' the natural it is not truly to be 'chosen,' for the process itself is one of selfless non-individualization, it is forever GIVEN. … Then to extend the boundaries of all 'hoods' – parenthood, wifehood, lifehood. (Hood – as what covers.) … For him she is another vast enterprise of his feeling, his needs and his will. He is 'everything' for her. For M.J. all she desires and needs depends on him and when one needs a great deal one *takes*. … His teaching her, his preparing her for what he Needs: a nurse, a mother, a wife, lover, child, domestic, maid, teacher for the children…
>
> This is a beautiful and terrifying amount of 'need' and an ennobling amount to her but here is the treachery that it comes all in *his terms*.[106]

Schneemann rejected the mantle of motherhood whose reflection she found so distressing in Jane. 'Embattled'[107] to protect her work as an artist, Schneemann fought against all forces that had the potential to derail her concentration, including procreation. On the occasions when Schneemann became pregnant, Tenney supported her decision to have abortions. Writing to Brakhage about the 'covert' preparations to terminate Schneemann's pregnancy in 1957, Tenney felt 'assured of the absolute necessity of selfishness' implied by their decision:

> A body cannot nourish many things at once – and yet we have a need to nourish – as we were nourished. The question is: which parasite do you prefer? Answer: our children are on paper and canvas. And if the other question is asked – what is the 'purpose' in loving – the answer is obviously *not* 'to make babies.' But this attitude is unlawful – inhuman – un-natural.[108]

Brakhage, however, was less amenable. In Schneemann's words, he 'rage[d]' at her abortion, arguing – astonishingly – that 'that baby belongs to Jim and to me.'[109] Brakhage's 'moralistic' reaction was so vexing that Tenney cited it as grounds for the necessary redefinition of their friendship:

> I must insist on a somewhat different relationship with you – not something
> I can define quite – but a relationship which precludes these shadow images
> you make of us. It's really no relationship at all as long as you obscure the real
> individuals we are and construct something of your own imagining instead.[110]

On what possible grounds could Brakhage have made such an outrageous claim
to co-paternity of Schneemann's unborn child? At first glance, his comments
suggest a monstrous sense of patriarchal possession that includes not only his
own wife and children, but those of his close friends. Surely this is an example
of what Lévi-Strauss theorized as the 'elementary structures' of kinship, in which
the circulation of women among men forms the basis for exchange within
patriarchy.[111] With further consideration, might we read Brakhage's sense of
ownership over Schneemann's fetus as an extension of the repressed homoerotic
bond he may have felt with Tenney, and was able to virtually satisfy through
the intimate, erotic communion of *Loving* and *Cat's Cradle*?

Frustrating as their visions of domesticity were to both Schneemann and
Tenney, the productions of these films served as an outlet to satisfy the homosocial forms desire 'between men'[112] that, as Eve Kosofsky Sedgwick has argued,
are prohibited by the taboos against same-sex intimacy between heterosexual
friends. Through Schneemann's body, Brakhage and Tenney were able to explore
forms of sensual communion with each other that neither of them could admit
to desiring. Though it has not diminished her sense of having been instrumen-
talized in *Loving* and *Cat's Cradle*, Schneemann came to recognize the role she
played as a queer conduit between her male lover and his best friend:

> Since Stan was Jim's closest friend and identified with the progress of his life
> since High School, there was ambiguity as to which of us was the sexual focus
> of his conscious/ unconscious desires and identifications; did Stan come closer
> to Jim through his sexual acceptance of me with Him?; did he feel any erotic
> bond to me through his affection for Jim? Were we together symbolic of some-
> thing as yet unrealized in his own experience?
>
> The genital taboos between the men were stronger than any for me, or than for
> me and Jim. I became the vehicle through which the men revealed as much as
> possible of their developing erotic natures.[113]

Was it possible that in filming *Loving*, Brakhage came to unconsciously believe
that he – fusing with Tenney's body – had entered Schneemann and fertilized
her? Or that Tenney had entered his own body through the open orifice of his
camera's eye? Might film make possible such eccentric, impossible forms of
embodiment? For all of the heteronormative ornamentation with which he
smothered Schneemann and Tenney in his films, Brakhage couldn't help but
be impregnated by the shattering force of their desire.

Fuses (1965)

Dissatisfied with Brakhage's representation of her subjectivity, Carolee Schneemann set to work on *Fuses*, an erotic film essay of her and Tenney's lovemaking that she shot and edited between 1964 and 1967. Schneemann was explicit about her decision to make the film as a reaction against Brakhage's misrepresentation of her own sexuality, as well as his appropriation of the female experience of child-bearing in his classic film *Window Water Baby Moving* (1959).[114] 'I wanted to see "the fuck,"' she writes, 'lovemaking's erotic blinding core apart from maternity/paternity.'[115] In its explicit documentation of sexuality unbound by either phallocentric conventions or the ideology of what Lee Edelman has termed 're-productive futurism,'[116] *Fuses* explores the sensual pleasures of inter-subjective interpenetration that could be activated within an egalitarian, heterosexual relationship. In doing so, the film posits a utopian alternative to the types of frozen, idealized forms of gender and sexuality explored by both Morris and Brakhage in their representations of hetero-relationality.

The first film Schneemann made after inheriting the seventeenth-century farmhouse in which she still lives and works, *Fuses* is evidence of the kind of expansiveness that a female artist can perhaps only articulate in a room of her own. Though Schneemann has referred to it as a 'genital landscape film'[117] – presumably because the way in which it juxtaposes unabashed images of penises and vaginas against vistas of the body and natural environment – *Fuses* evaporates the perception of distance necessary for the contemplation of landscape. An ever-shifting kaleidoscope of color, texture, light, and flesh, *Fuses* immerses the spectator within erotic ecstasy. Treating the camera as a mobile, tactile participant in the action, the film proffers not just an image, but an experience of sensuous abandonment. The bodies of Schneemann and Tenney writhe and commingle amongst washes of hand-painted crimson and indigo while fireworks of scratches and dots explode upon the celluloid. Gliding over breast, abdomen, and thigh, the camera caresses the lovers' bodies, thrusting in and out of their fusion. Painted, collaged, scratched, dyed, baked, stamped, and dipped in acid, the skin of the celluloid bristles and bursts with the affective contagion of desire. Genitals burst in and out of focus so proximate to the camera that we can almost feel the pulsing contractions of labia and scrotum. Fingers disappear in orifices and eyes roll back in pleasure; bodies pound each other so vigorously that the frame is itself upended by their force.

Though we are submerged in what Amelia Jones describes as the film's 'skeins' of color,[118] *Fuses*' celebration of egalitarian, non-reproductive sexuality liberates its performers from the cat's cradle of patriarchy and its domestic entrapment of women. Binary oppositions dissolve as warm and cool colors merge in the frame. As in Robert Rauschenberg's sculptural 'Combines' from the mid-1950s, fragments of the everyday world abut in the film's dense collage,

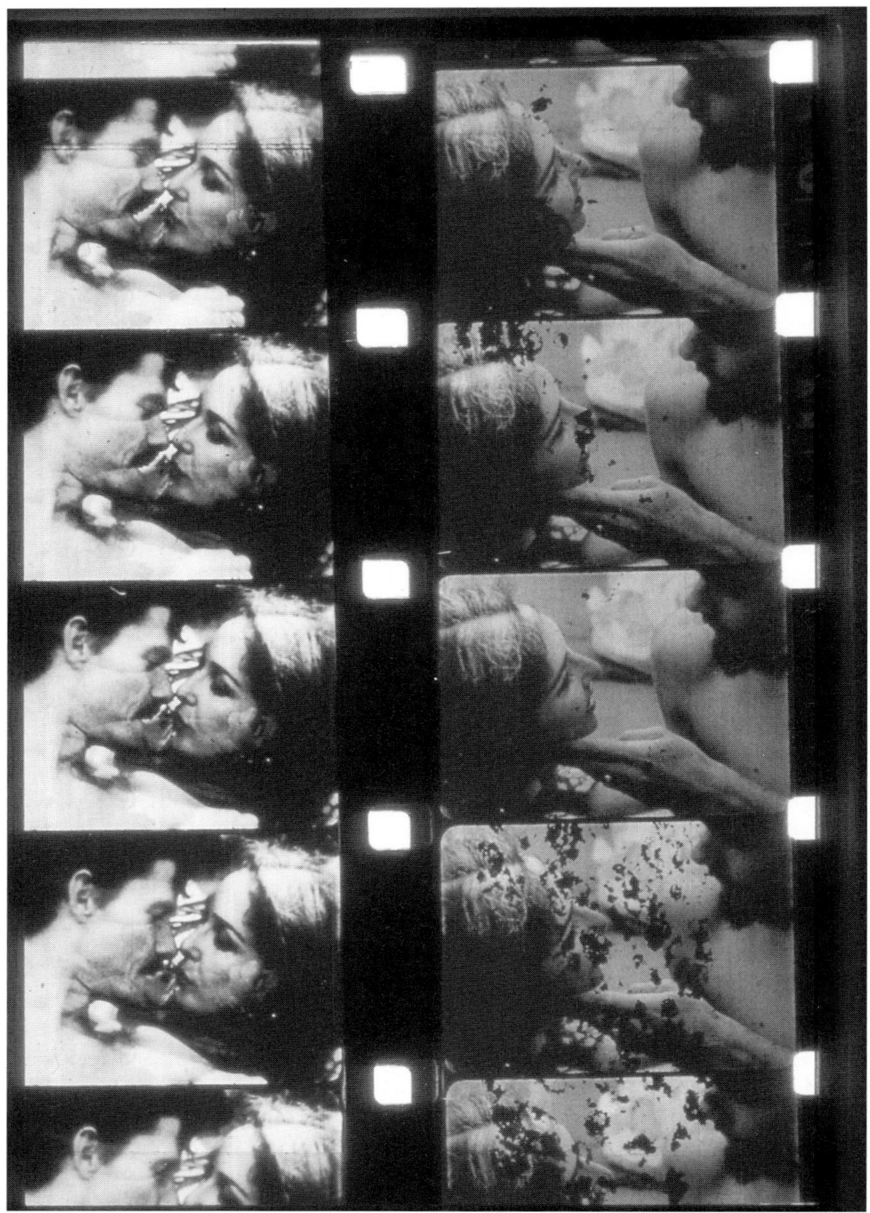

32   Carolee Schneemann and James Tenney practiced an egalitarian form of heterosexuality within and beyond the frame. Their intimacy is visible in these superimposed and collaged images from *Fuses* (Carolee Schneemann, 1964–1967).

but their effect defies static construction. Seasons change as incandescent fields of autumn flowers give way to banks of snow; a body once scored by bikini lines is draped with Christmas tinsel. Under the veil of Schneemann's brush, the meat of the flesh becomes lustrous and deliquescent. Stained with color, and sparkling with flickering light, bodies transcend their boundaries, disintegrate, melt into each other. Hands briefly glimpsed on a steering wheel resume rhythmic stroke of the lips and fur of two 'pussies.' A tree inflamed at dusk bursts into an ironic image of Schneemann's 'burning' bush. The film's parallel montage relishes such witticisms, but it also reminds us of the continuum between inside and outside.

Transfixed by the film's exploration of the *gestalt* of sexuality, we are none-theless blinded by its occluded visions. Images of bodies 'writhing underneath' the 'rippling contours' of the film's skin[119] appear before being submerged again in dark waves of pigment. If we can barely distinguish between male, female and feline flesh before the constantly agitated frame metamorphoses again, it is because the film chooses sensual immersion over scopic mastery. Too densely collaged to run through the laboratory's printer when first completed,[120] *Fuses*'s stunning palimpsest documents sex from the inside of pleasure. Suspended in this throbbing extensivity, I remember poet Stanley Kunitz's admonition to '"live in the layers / not on litter."'[121]

Recurring images of light streaming through a window, changing foliage, and tangled sheets situate sexuality simultaneously in the realm of domestic-ity and the natural world. Yet rather than fetishizing domesticity, Schneemann incorporates typically 'feminine' labors into her process, in such a way that evidences – more authentically than the visual tropes in *Cat's Cradle* – the way in which the formal strategies employed by female artists coincide with other forms of experimentation practiced in a home studio.

Formally astonishing as these aesthetic effects are, however, their power derives from the 'pervasive intensity of the interchange' between Schneemann and Tenney.[122] Working next to each other in adjoining studios – he practicing Ives, Ruggles, Webern and Schoenberg on the piano while she was 'shredding an image source to produce an incremental visual gestalt'[123] – Schneemann and Tenney influenced each other to challenge the limits of the media with which they worked. As a painter 'working with space as if it is time,' Schneemann found, through her close collaboration with Tenney, a way of musically render-ing the space between bodies in the durational media of film. As Schneemann has noted, *Fuses* is a 'painterly, tactile translation' of bodily sensation that is 'edited as a music of frames.'[124]

Schneemann's relationship with Tenney provided a model of male and fe-male collaboration and cohabitation that was relatively unique in the 1950s and 60s. Indeed, Schneemann often wondered whether Brakhage was threatened by the 'sustained and equitable erotic intimacy'[125] in their relationship:

> the accusations [implied by Brakhage] are those which our love is based on and
> which Stan could never bear for himself so he pretends it is also impossible, re-
> ally, for Jim and that I have 'done it'; our equality. And that this equality means
> we share petty things and help each other, which he would never do, and the
> basic orders of domestic routine are suspect by them as we come more and
> more to take them easily and with certain pleasures.[126]

Schneemann employed equivalence as a guiding principle of her editing, which
she used to constantly challenge viewer's 'unconscious attitudes' about the anatomical distinction between the sexes: 'I edited sequences so that whenever
you were looking at the male genital it would dissolve into the female and vice
versa.'[127] As Gene Youngblood observed, this deliberate 'fragmentation not only
prevents narrative continuity,' but 'also closely approximates the actual experience of sex in which the body of one's partner becomes fragmented into tactile
zones and exaggerated mental images.'[128]

Defying the taboo against full frontal male sexuality, Schneemann's camera
lavishes ample attention on her partner's genitals, which are studied in close-up,
from multiple angles, and in various states of excitation. At times hard, slick,
and red, at other times tentative, pink, and probing, the curved shaft of Tenney's
penis in shifting states of tumescence serve as the film's plumb line, even as these
images are matched by Tenney's rapacious exploration of Schneemann's own
body. Schneemann's unabashed fascination with her partner's shape-shifting
genitals – which traditionally could be shown only if they were 'placed within
an idealized mythology'[129] – has had profound effects on viewers, including
(heterosexual male) avant-garde film historian and archivist Robert Haller:

> Your film, to my eyes, does everything Stan's first two did (albeit *Lovemak-*
> *ing* was made after *Fuses*), and also adds other dimensions that are very much
> yours: a political sense (you and Jim are real equals in *Fuses* – the film revels
> in the sexuality of males and females, not just from one point of view, as in
> the works of others: one example is your treatment of the erect penis which
> too many artists still shy away from; you make it, for heterosexual male view-
> ers, such as myself, as erotic and attractive as your own breasts, vagina, your
> whole body).[130]

If the image of male genitalia could startle such seasoned male viewers of experimental cinema as Haller, then I may as well confess that the image that most
astonishes me is a close-up of Schneemann's face as she performs oral sex on
Tenney. Made in the same period that Warhol notoriously withheld such an
explicit image in *Blow Job* (1964), this female-authored shot is historically unprecedented. Not only were blow jobs never represented in what Linda Williams
has described as 'the belated coming of age' of American film (1896–1963), but
before *Deep Throat* (1972) accorded 'mainstream public recognition' to fellatio,

it had often been regarded, along with other non-procreative sexual acts, as abnormal, perverse or even legally punishable sexual behavior.[131]

Debuting five years before *Deep Throat*, Schneemann's depiction of oral sex was all the more remarkable because, unlike a pornographic blockbuster created by a male entrepreneur, *Fuses* is a feminist self-portrait. Although the feminist anti-porn movement did not coalesce until the 1970s, *Fuses* was completed just as feminist discontent with pornography was beginning to surface aboveground. Although it would be ten years before Robin Morgan coined the controversial phrase, 'Pornography is the theory, rape is the practice,' the protests against the 1968 Miss American Pageant, often regarded as inaugurating the feminist anti-porn crusade, were only a year away.[132] By the end of the 1960s, certain radical feminists were already articulating their fear that the sexual desires and pleasures of straight women might be a form of false consciousness that emerged from the conditions of 'compulsory heterosexuality'[133] within patriarchy. As these fears increased in response to the explosion of hard-core pornography in the early 1970s, feminists often critiqued fellatio as an inherently submissive form of sexual behavior. Following the unprecedented success of *Deep Throat*, which celebrated – according to anti-porn crusader Catherine MacKinnon – the 'subordination' of women 'as eager servicing receptacles for male genitalia and ejaculate,' the 'improbable' notion that 'a woman would engage in fellatio of her own accord'[134] seemed increasingly suspicious. Even by 1989, fellatio was still considered controversial enough for porn scholar Linda Williams to ask: 'Are feminists to declare themselves against representations of fellatio, against being on their knees during sex, against anything other than absolutely egalitarian forms of mutual love and affection? Indeed what forms of sex are egalitarian?'[135]

What did it mean in this context for Carolee Schneemann to offer a portrait of herself performing fellatio on her lover? Schneemann has written that, 'There were no aspects of lovemaking which I would avoid … As a painter I had never accepted the visual and tactile taboos concerning specific parts of the body.'[136] Watching this still-searing image, I am struck by Schneemann's bravery. Unlike the well-choreographed, often grotesque facial acrobatics of *Deep Throat*, Schneemann's face suggests a euphoric, unselfconscious sense of erotic abandonment. As in the parallel shots of Tenney performing cunnilingus on Schneemann as her body thrashes in pleasure, moments of awkward discomposure accentuate the image's authenticity. Unlike hard-core pornography, this encounter has *not* been choreographed for 'maximum visibility.'[137] Beautiful as Schneemann is, she is not framed 'to-be-looked-at.'[138] On the contrary, her pleasure breaks the frame. One cannot speak of submission or objectification when lovers have so fully and generously dissolved the boundaries between themselves.

Yet while my own response crystallizes around such moments of intersubjective dissolution, my thinking about *Fuses* is constantly transformed by

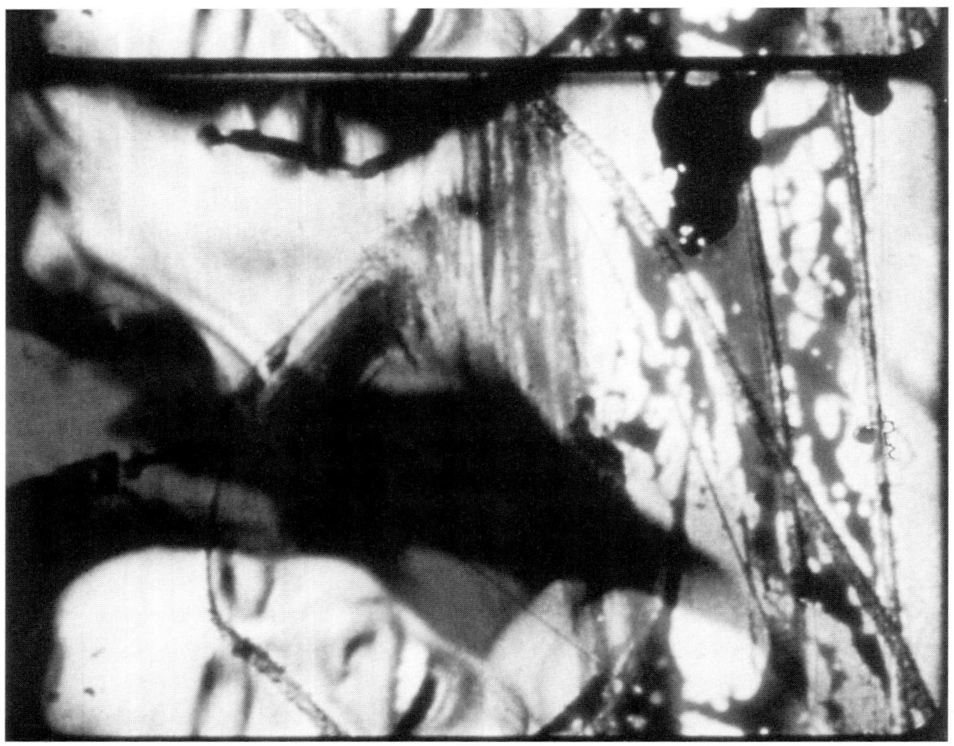

33   Sexual ecstasy, experienced from the inside of pleasure, deconstructs the transparency of the image in Carolee Schneemann's *Fuses* (1964–1967).

my students' reactions. In a recent screening of the film, one of my students expressed disappointment that the 'fuck' promised by Schneemann's writing was not as evident as he had hoped. Though he acknowledged *Fuses*'s images of genital penetration, he argued that its depiction of fucking seemed 'hidden' by Schneemann's painterly and sculptural manipulations. Just as generations of all-male stag film audiences had learned to associate 'meat' exclusively with the genitals, I wondered whether this student had learned to think of fucking as nothing more than genital penetration? How has the unprecedented access to pornography on the internet transformed how we see and don't see sex?

I was relieved to learn that my student had not been put off by the 'invisibility' of sexuality in *Fuses*, but by the film's emphasis on seemingly ideal corporeal encounters. As it turns out, his notion of 'sexual authenticity' pivoted upon both the acknowledgment of failure and the departure from ideal forms of beauty. 'Real' fucking, he insisted, was a lot less formally beautiful and acrobatic than it appears in Schneemann's film. He expressed an earnest desire to see the moments of failed fucking, 'all of the times Tenney's dick didn't work,' and the outtakes when Schneemann leapt into Tenney's standing embrace and *didn't* land in perfect position for penetration.

Historic screenings of *Fuses* have elicited less sympathetic responses. Though Schneemann showed the film as a work in progress as early as 1965 and 1966,[139] it was more regularly screened in its entirety in 1968, 1969, and the early 1970s. When *Fuses* showed at the 'Dialectics of Liberation' conference in London in 1968, Schneemann was yanked out of the projection booth and informed that she would not be defended in the (likely) case of immorality charges.[140] When the film showed at Cannes, 'a great commotion erupted in front of the screen. French men were ripping up the seats with razor blades and screaming because it was not truly pornographic. It wasn't satisfying the predictable erotic, phallocentric sequences they wanted.'[141]

My student's objections have stayed with me as I re-consider how *Fuses*'s intensely haptic representation of sexuality positions us to see and *not* see the sex act. Contrary to my initial presumptions, this student's inability to see the 'fuck' was in part determined by the way current generations of progressive students educated in critical race and gender theory seem to have more trouble seeing, thinking, and speaking about forms of white heterosexual sex than they

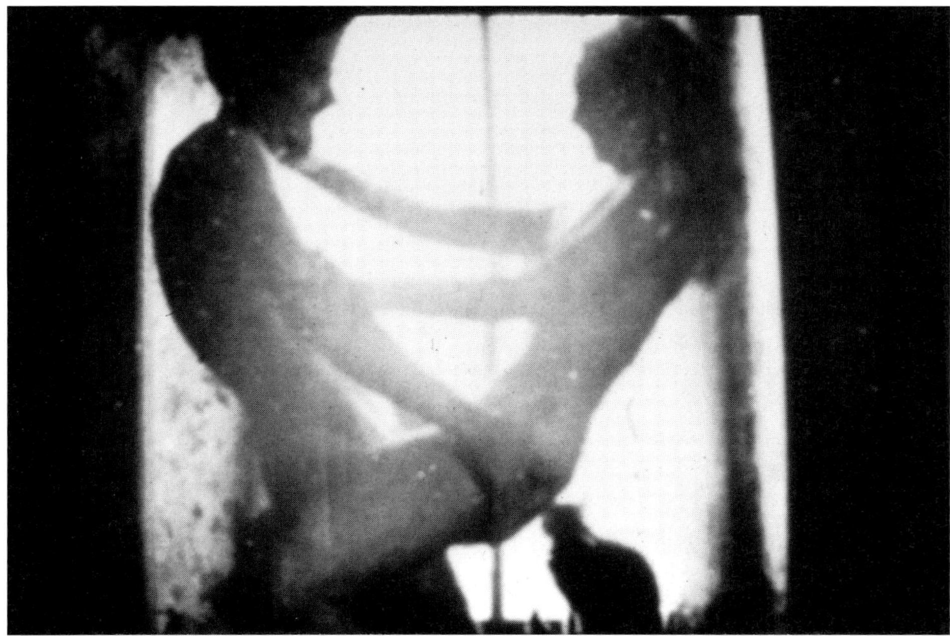

Carolee Schneemann and James Tenney in coital embrace in *Fuses* (Carolee   **34**
Schneemann, 1964–1967). One of my students longed to see the outtakes when such
erotic acrobatics failed.

do about the queer sexuality performed, for example, in the films of Kenneth Anger or Andy Warhol. As such encounters continue, I wonder whether, in our ongoing critique of heteronormativity, we have forgotten how to think critically and affectively about heterosexuality. Has the realm in which so many of us still live, love, and work in solidarity with our queer brothers and sisters remained a blind spot, in which queer films about 'straight' sex are obscured by the damning association of heterosexuality with hegemony?

In her move away from Brakhage's insistence on procreation towards the representation of 'fucking' as a sensual but non-reproductive interpenetration of bodies, Schneemann queered heterosexual sex. At the same time, *Fuses*'s insistently corporeal mode of address implicitly aligned Schneemann's approach with McClure's definition of 'fucking' as a 'personal creative act' generative of new possibilities for the intermingling of self and other:

> Say FUCK, say FUCK, say FUCK, say anything that opens to acts.
>
> Is there any more personal creative act than fucking? Fuck does not mean merely the act of copulation but all ramifications, doings, and movements that give sexual delight to the spiritbeast who is lonely and cold and in need of touch and warmth in his separateness. … Is there a more *personal* and *creative* gesture? When copulation is unearthly it is fucking. Fuck is the old deep word. *Copulation* and *intercourse* are words made up from a dead language. To have intercourse or to copulate is not to fuck. To fuck is to give moments of ease and warmth to another and to accept the same from a loved one, and to join bodies and clear the spirit of its heaviness.[142]

For both Schneemann and McClure, the fuck was not the wham and bam of hard-core porn, but a utopic commingling in which Eros merged with ethos. Though Schneemann's emphasis on the word 'fuck' served as a way of 'eroticizing' her 'guilty culture,'[143] using the word was also, as McClure writes, a method of *opening up* (the self, the body, the other, and the community) *to acts.* 'The fuck,' Schneemann writes, 'was inseparable from an intimacy, an erotic generosity.'[144] Fucking was a way of shattering the limitations of the corporeal and political body, in order to move beyond the psychological and spiritual paralysis of the subject within hegemonic culture. For McClure, even *saying* the word 'fuck' amounted to a political act, a refusal of oppressive state power by an embrace of the 'ob-scenity' of personal experience. As McClure writes, 'Fucking is personal and should be spoken of. Men who say *copulate* or *intercourse* feel removed from their bodies. They use those words to create an illusion of objectivity – as if they look down on the doings of beasts.'[145]

Rather than looking down at the 'doings of beasts,' Schneemann joined them, presenting her vision of herself fucking through the imagined eyebody of her cat Kitch, who 'watches with complete unrestrained interest.' 'We are perceived through the eyes of our cat. By visualizing the cat's point of view I was able to present our coupled images in the context of the rectangles and the seasons surrounding us.'[146] But if *Fuses* aspires to represent the cat's corporeal apprehension of the sex act – through smell, touch, hearing, movement and imperfect sight – my student's response suggests that it also partially obscured the human's. Human vision is, after all, not equivalent with what is *visible*. Although *Fuses* relies on the visual realm to evidence the pleasures of lovemaking, it derives its intensity from the tactile. As Laura Marks has argued about haptic cinema, Schneemann's tactile camera yields to the body of the thing seen, dissolving the boundaries of the seer.[147] Although certain hard-core images of the 'fuck' remain recognizable, the closer the camera gets to the erotic encounter, the less visible the specific machinations of sex become. Filmed by lovers with no intervention by an outside cameraperson,[148] the camera becomes a body whose 'eye' goes in and out of focus. Alternately handheld or affixed to a swinging chandelier, the camera bears chaotic witness to the frenzied motion of the lovers' bodies.

Actively participating rather than passively observing the action, the camera frequently obfuscates the sight of the observer, whose own eye is never permitted to site the body as its target. In her study of motion-picture pornography, Linda Williams analyzes the ubiquitous money shot as a swerving away from more direct forms of genital engagement, by privileging the visual spectacle of male ejaculation over the tactile pleasure of coming inside the woman. 'With this convention,' she writes, 'viewers are asked to believe that the sexual performers within the film want to shift from a tactile to a visual pleasure at the crucial moment of the male's orgasm.'[149] Just as Schneemann is not an artist who *shows* her body, *Fuses* is not a film that *shows* sex but rather a 'lover's discourse,' in which 'description' has been 'replaced by its simulation.'[150] Rather than visual surveillance of the sex act, *Fuses* mimics what Roland Barthes has described as the lover's experience of engulfment and succumbing in which the body's gesture is 'caught in action and not contemplated in repose.'[151] Gene Youngblood was quick to recognize the 'fluid oceanic quality' and sense of boundlessness created by Schneemann's corporeal expansion of cinema: 'She's filming her consciousness, not her orifices. *Fuses* moves beyond the bed to embrace the universe in oceanic orgasm.'[152]

That succumbing to such ecstatic engulfment – as participant/spectator – should involve a degree of immersive blindness is consistent with Schneemann's desire to delve into 'lovemaking's erotic *blinding* core.'[153] It is also consistent with Merleau-Ponty's notion of the 'invisible' as a form of phenomenological apprehension that is situated inside the visible. In love's blinding core, which is always also an abyss, corporeal sensation overwhelms the subject's ability to organize the sensory richness of being into recognizable chunks of information. Schneemann's blinding fuck refuses the artificial parceling of subjectivity into the binary opposition between body and mind: As McClure writes, 'I would rather fuck with my meat body than have intercourse and watch it with my mind – or pretend that my mind-aloof looks down on a divisible body. I will not amputate myself into pieces that stare at one another and snicker.'[154]

If *Fuses* moves to satisfy the spectator/lover's 'craving to be engulfed,'[155] then it does so at the deliberate expense of Western paradigms of vision and Cartesian accounts of subjectivity. Refusing the visual mastery implied by Renaissance perspective, as well as hard-core's fetishistic insistence on maximum visibility, *Fuses* approaches the optical blindness of sexuality as an exquisite 'crisis of engulfment.'[156]

Requiem

Over the years, Schneemann's angst over her friendship with Brakhage came to serve as a model for the fated misrecognitions that so often rupture the political camaraderie between male and female artists. Responding to Clayton Eshleman's suggestion that her work depended upon 'the necessity … to show [her] naked body,'[157] Schneemann repudiated such misogynist theories of sexual difference: 'Brakhage used to drag his Freud all over me… his fraud… do you really believe the cunt/woman IS a wound?'[158] Yet Brakhage's death in 2003 provided Schneemann with an opportunity to come to terms with the frustrations that had long defined their friendship. Recalling some points of contention in her relationship with Brakhage, Schneemann again returned to the apron, which remained a laden symbol of the gender inequities that had been insufficiently dismantled between them.

> As hosts & guests, we struggled over who empties overflowing ashtrays? How do we share? Who shops? Cooks? Washes up? You [Brakhage] announce a profligate devotion to having babies though you had no way to support them. You rage at my abortion: 'That baby belongs to Jim and to me'… I had to paint! For *Cat's Cradle*, you insisted I wear the silly apron Jim's mother had sent for Christmas.[159]

Schneemann's candid recollections illuminate the difficulties involved in artistic collaboration, domestic partnership, and the struggle to define oneself as a female artist within patriarchy. Even within the context of his own radical expansion of the camera eye, Brakhage's adherence to Freudian notions of sexual difference functioned as an ideological blind spot. For Schneemann, Brakhage's blindness extended beyond trivial costume choices:

> And in those years, your objections to my despair over women artists as marginal, tokens – though you championed [Gertrude] Stein, [Maya] Deren, [Marie] Menken, H.D. You and Jane burnt the copy of Simone de Beauvoir's *The Second Sex* I sent for a revelatory (I hoped) 1959 Christmas present. You were

> outraged by my notes on gender exclusions. My letters to you were cut up and
> burnt so that only certain acceptable paragraphs remained in a scrapbook.[160]

In Schneemann's eyes, Brakhage's dismissal of (most) female artists distorted his
perception of her own work. As early as 1959, Schneemann had bitterly noted
Brakhage's indifference to her paintings: 'Stan would show a belated interest
in what Jim really DID, and correspondingly a vigorous resistance to what I
did. This last spring when they first stayed with us: his refusing to see the best
work… .'[161] Schneemann would note these biases throughout her career, accusing Brakhage on different occasions of failing to advocate for or show her work,
neglecting the care of her paintings,[162] and omitting her letters from inclusion
in the *Brakhage Scrapbook*.[163] Yet in spite of these offenses, Schneemann was
loath to lose Brakhage as an artistic kindred spirit. In a letter following a painful
visit in 1959, Schneemann expressed her simultaneous love of Brakhage's art
and her agony about his sexual politics:

> I am afraid we have seen Stan perhaps for the last time. If that is in itself true it
> is terrible with the consequence of not knowing any more about them – where
> they go, how they are, which in my way of never losing love's concern – even
> when the love is not presently active – is a cruelty. And not to see the films. But
> there is a point where it is no longer possible to say it is because of the Art of
> each other that we weather all personal difficulties; it is the person who makes
> the art, but the person first perhaps.[164]

Schneemann's fears about losing Brakhage as an interlocutor suggest the difficulty of coming to terms with the ideological conflicts that emerge even among
artistically kindred spirits. Her reluctant emphasis on 'the person first' also
reveals the extent to which she imagined aesthetics as a necessary and vital
extension of one's ethical relationship to the world. In an era in which the
boundaries between art and other types of experience were collapsing, might
the spiritual value of one's art actually depend on who we are and how we treat
each other beyond the frame of canvas or celluloid? Might this be part of what
Wittgenstein means when he writes that 'ethics and aesthetics are one'? Going
against the 'genius' model of artistic innovation, which subordinates all ethical
and political questions to the supreme value of novelty, Schneemann broaches
the feminist hunch that bad politics might be commensurate with bad form.

Fortunately, Schneemann's elegiac tone proved premature; her friendship
with Brakhage continued for more than forty years. During this time, Brakhage
occasionally responded to Schneemann's accusations. In a letter from 1975,
written after spending a day poring over Schneemann's book *Cézanne, She Was
a Great Painter*, Brakhage acknowledged his friend's charges with a heartfelt
admission: 'I have no argument with your pronouncement apropos "Window
Water Baby Moving" (tho' I think there was a better balance in some of the

later childbirth films); and I am properly shamed by the "his"s which pepper my writing: I've tried to weed them out: it is not always possible.'[165] Addressing Schneemann's allegations about his neglect of her work, however, Brakhage cited the inevitably 'selfish' role of the 'family man' which compelled him to neglect friends in need. While it would be pointless to 'blame' Brakhage for his inability to be all things to all people, his concerns broach the very real crisis of how to balance artistic work and the need to make a living with the care that family members and friends require. In a culture that privileges certain forms of analogy above others (such as the bloodlines of the nuclear family), the crucial correspondences between other kindred beings are often overlooked.

Yet even as Brakhage defended his support of Schneemann's work, he continued to distinguish her from the handful of female filmmakers whose work he *truly* admired:

> As for the guilt – that's confusing … mixed up with the disturbances I have about 'FUSES.' I constantly have supported Maya Deren, Marie Menken (while she was alive, yes) and now Gunvor Nelson. I am enabled to SEE the work of these three women in film; but (while I've never excluded 'FUSES,' have in fact rented it, lectured on it) I do not really see it well.[166]

Brakhage's inability to see *Fuses* as a 'genuine' work of art remained a continual source of pain for Schneemann. However we may protest that there is no accounting for taste, it is difficult to separate Brakhage's aesthetic dismissal of *Fuses* from the context of their embittered relationship. It is also hard to ignore the irony that Brakhage could not 'see' a work whose style and concerns were, in so many ways, commensurate with his own.

One of Brakhage's most poignant responses, however, concerns his identification with the fraught position of women in a patriarchal, capitalist society:

> I remember one of our arguments, when Jane and I first came to visit, began with my insistence that you realize the AWFUL task men have been socially assigned, called 'making a living.' I think we would not argue now. It is all the same… the same enslavement which denies the uniqueness of person. I also have always wished to be SUPPORTED! … as do many women, willing to pay that exorbitant price – a being-nothing-there OTHER than what the supporter wants. The economic supporters (mostly male) most obviously want to destroy the earth. What I'm trying to say is that I feel your book struggles for my freedom as well as your own and that of other women. I am deeply grateful.[167]

In his rage against the constraints of wage earning, Brakhage surely overestimated the benefits of being financially supported: 'being-nothing-there other than what the supporter wants' amounts to a kind of psychological and spiritual death that feminists have rightfully rallied against. But even in these myopic remarks, it is evident that Brakhage was deeply moved by Schneemann's critique of patriarchy. Though Schneemann has rightly insisted that, 'Issues of master /

slave, degree of service / must be described and defined by the persons in the disadvantaged positions,'[168] the Hegelian terms of the master/slave dialectic is an insufficient model for the types of queer friendship with which this book is concerned.

Like Robert Morris's failure to 'recognize' Schneemann, Brakhage's failure to 'see' *Fuses* emerged, at least partially, from his own alienation within a capitalist society that made acceptable masculine industry synonymous with the unceasing pursuit of profit. If the very mode of home movies realized by Brakhage enabled him to create a personal cinema outside of the corporate model of the industry, then it also condemned him – as it did many artists of the period who rejected the commodity system of Art Capitalism – to struggle to support himself through pitifully under-funded venues of distribution and exchange. Brakhage's complaints about having to make a living may sound indulgent to artists in dire pursuit of the kind of university teaching positions he enjoyed. Yet this should not diminish our recognition that the Sisyphean struggle to make non-profitable but emotionally, aesthetically, and politically meaningful art in a capitalist economy often requires shattering sacrifices. In the 1950s, 1960s, and 1970s, conditions of life were precarious for both Schneemann *and* Brakhage; poverty, constant relocation, lack of institutional support, absence of health care, and physical and/or psychological turmoil were ongoing dilemmas.

The fact that institutional venues were far more accessible to male artists like Brakhage and Morris – both of whom managed to acquire permanent teaching jobs[169] – than they were to Schneemann – who wondered in 1986 'if I had gotten dressed after "Eye Body" and stayed in the studio would I have a teaching job by now?'[170] – does not diminish the fact that patriarchal capitalism has deliberately positioned male and female artist-laborers to misrecognize the potential alliances between them. Yet such vexed misrecognitions do not diminish the need for such alliances. For even as Schneemann acknowledged the way patriarchy wrenches our capacity to recognize our ontological kinship with other embodied beings, she continued to yearn for relationships expansive enough to accommodate her complex identity as female artist, lover, friend, and activist. 'The crux of anxiety and energy / image making is that simple,' she wrote, 'I can't work without love / the primacy of work destroys love. Stability, coherence in relationship gives me freedom, spirit to work but makes it impossible to give a man the compliment of my serving-maternal role.'[171]

Yet at the core of these charged collaborations – between Schneemann and Brakhage, and many of the other non-normative 'couples' explored in this book – I see potentially radical forms of identification, solidarity, love, and kinship. Though these alternative forms of relationality remain vulnerable to the hegemonic forces that aim to obliterate the essential analogies between individuals of different genders, classes, races, ethnicities, and nations, they persist. The fact that such analogous relationships could be felt and experienced at all within a society that systematically denies them is a testament to the struggle of these artists to see outside of and beyond the tutored vision of capitalist ideology. For however flawed and incomplete this process was – and nobody recalls its limitations more compellingly than Schneemann – these collaborations were nonetheless poignant, vital attempts to open the eyebody to acknowledge the Other as 'flesh of my flesh.'

Carolee Schneemann's performances and films from the 1960s and 1970s offer a magnificently generous fusion of self and other, spectator and performer, male and female, eye and body, and skin and film. Becoming 'in'-visible in the meat joys of these works, we give ourselves over to the oceanic feeling of radical connectedness that alone can challenge the Western fiction of an impenetrable, sovereign ego and the social divisions it supports. And as we do, the boundaries between our bodies dissolve, and melt away, allowing us the transcendent possibility of moving through this 'bag of meat' and merging with the flesh of the world. As Roland Barthes reminds us, 'we die together from loving each other.'[172] I leave you then to tend your mortal coils.

Notes

1 Claude Lévi-Strauss, *The Raw and the Cooked, Introduction to a Science of Mythology: 1*, Vol. 1 (New York: Harper & Row, 1964), p. 164.

2 The show 'American Supermarket' was held at the Bianchini Gallery, New York City, October 6, 1964 to November 7, 1964. Christopher Grunenberg, 'The American Supermarket,' *Shopping: A Century of Art and Consumer Culture*, ed. Christopher Grunenberg and Max Hollein (Ostfildern: Hatje Cantz Publishers, 2002), pp. 171–178.

3 Schneemann, 'Interior Scroll', in *Imaging Her Erotics* (Cambridge, MA: The MIT Press, 2003), pp. 151–161; p. 159.

4 Jonathan Crary, *Techniques of the Observer* (Cambridge, MA: The MIT Press, 1990), p. 150.

5 Sally Banes, *Greenwich Village 1963: Avant-Garde Performance and the Effervescent Body* (Durham, NC: Duke University Press, 1993), pp. 192, 194.

6 Amelia Jones, *Body Art/Performing the Subject* (Minneapolis, MN: University of Minnesota Press, 1998), p. 10.

7 Carolee Schneemann to Naomi Levinson, May 29, 1959, in *Correspondence Course: An Epistolary History of Carolee Schneemann and Her Circle*, ed. Kristine Stiles (Durham, NC: Duke University Press, 2010), p. 41.

8 Carolee Schneemann, interview by Carl Heyward, 'Interview with Carl Heyward,' in *Imaging Her Erotics*, 1999, originally published in *Art Papers* 17, no. 1 (January–February 1993), pp. 9–16.

9 Kaja Silverman, *Flesh of My Flesh* (Stanford, CA: Stanford University Press, 2009), p. 34.

10 Ibid., p. 26.

11 Ibid., p. 2.

12 Schneemann, 'Mortal Coils', *Imaging Her Erotics*, pp. 278–286.

13 This performance was held at Artists Space in February, 1974. Carolee Schneemann, email to author, June 26, 2012.

14 Schneemann, 'Homage to Ana Mendieta' and 'Mortal Coils,' in *Imaging Her Erotics*, pp. 276–285.

15 Silverman, *Flesh of My Flesh*, p. 4.

16 Schneemann, 'Mortal Coils', in *Imaging her Erotics*, p. 279.

17 Ibid.

18 Ibid., p. 281.

19 Silverman, *Flesh of My Flesh*, p. 35.

20 Schneemann, 'Mortal Coils', in *Imaging her Erotics*, p. 279.

21 Ibid., p. 281.

22 Silverman, *Flesh of My Flesh*, p. 29.

23 Sigmund Freud, *Beyond the Pleasure Principle*, Vol. 18 of *The Standard Edition of the Complete Psychological Works of Sigmund Freud*, trans. James Strachey (London: Hogarth Press, 1943–1974) p. 49, quoted in Silverman, *Flesh of My Flesh*, p. 33.

24 Schneemann, quoted in Robert Riley, 'Infinity Kisses,' in *Imaging her Erotics*, p. 264.

25 Silverman, *Flesh of My Flesh*, p. 26.

26 Schneemann, 'Meat Joy,' in *Imaging her Erotics*, p. 62.

27 Carolee Schneemann to James Tenney, May 30, 1964, in *Correspondence Course*, p. 85.

28 Schneemann, 'Meat Joy,' in *Imaging her Erotics*, p. 61.

29 Carolee Schneemann to Wolf Vostell, January 22, 1965, in *Correspondence Course*, pp. 94–95.

30 Carolee Schneemann to Kristine Stiles, December 28–29, 1985, in *Correspondence Course*, p. 360.

31 Ibid., p. 361.

32 Michael McClure, 'Phi Upsilon Kappa,' in *Meat Science Essays*, 2nd ed. (San Francisco, CA: City Lights Books, 1963), p. 8.

33 Ibid., p. 14.

34 Ibid., p. 13.

35 Ibid., p. 15.

36 Ibid., p. 14.

37 Linda Williams, 'Porn Studies: Proliferating Pornographies On/Scene: An Introduction,' *Porn Studies*, ed. Linda Williams (Durham, NC: Duke University Press, 2004), pp. 4–5.

38 McClure, 'Phi Upsilon Kappa,' in *Meat Science Essays*, p. 18.

39 Carolee Schneemann, interview by Linda Montano, 'Interview with Linda Montano,' in *Imaging her Erotics*, p. 131.

40 Carolee Schneemann, interview by Carl Heyward, in *Imaging her Erotics*, p. 202.

41 Carolee Schneemann to Naomi Levinson, March 30, 1959, in *Correspondence Course*, p. 32.

42 Carolee Schneemann to Stan Brakhage, April 4, 1957, *Correspondence Course*, p. 9.

43 André Bazin, 'The Ontology of the Photographic Image,' *What is Cinema?* trans. Hugh Gray, Vol. 1 (Berkeley, CA: University of California Press, 1967), pp. 9–16.

44   Carolee Schneemann, 'Eye Body: 36 Transformative Actions,' in *Imaging her Erotics*, p. 55.

45   Schneemann to Eshleman, 24 October 1975, *Correspondence Course*, p. 261.

46   Schneemann to Naomi Levinson, 30 March 1959, *Correspondence Course*, p. 32.

47   Carolee Schneemann, email message to the author, June 26, 2012.

48   Schneemann, 'Eye Body: 36 Transformative Actions,' in *Imaging her Erotics*, p. 55.

49   Linda Williams, *Hard Core: Power, Pleasure, and the 'Frenzy of the Visible'* (Berkeley, CA: University of California Press, 1989), p. 72.

50   Ibid., p. 73.

51   Schneemann, 'Interior Scroll,' in *Imaging her Erotics*, p. 155.

52   In *Hard Core*, Williams argues that the fetishistic inclusion of shots of the ejaculating penis in hard-core pornography (known as 'money shots') is a compensatory device for the stubborn 'invisibility' of female sexual pleasure. In earlier forms of moving image pornography, like stag films, 'meat shots' (shots of genital penetration) were considered adequate evidence of genital activity. Williams, *Hard Core*, pp. 58–92, 93–119.

53   Ibid., 93.

54   This character is actually based upon avant-garde film theorist and co-founder of *October* journal, Annette Michelson. Carolee Schneemann, interview by Scott MacDonald, in *A Critical Cinema: Interviews with Independent Filmmakers* (Berkeley, CA: University of California Press, 1988), p. 143, quoted in David Levi Strauss, 'Love Rides Aristotle Through the Audience: Body, Image, and Idea in the Work of Carolee Schneemann,' in *Up To and Including Her Limits* (New York: New Museum of Contemporary Art, 1996), p. 29.

55   'he told me he had lived with / a "sculptress" i asked does / that make me a "filmmakeress"? / "Oh no," he said. "We think of you / as a dancer."' For the full text of the performance see, Schneemann, 'Interior Scroll,' in *Imaging her Erotics*, pp. 156–160.

56   Ibid., p. 159.

57   Ibid.

58   Ibid.

59   Ibid.

60   Ibid.

61   Jones, *Body Art*, p. 3.

62   Schneemann, 'Interior Scroll,' in *Imaging her Erotics*, p. 153.

63   Ibid., p. 154.

64   Ibid.

65   Schneemann, 'Meat Joy,' in *Imaging her Erotics*, p. 62.

66   Jones, *Body Art*, pp. 53–102.

67   Michael Fried, 'Art and Objecthood,' in *Art in Theory 1900–1990: An Anthology of Changing Ideas*, ed. Charles Harrison and Paul Wood (Oxford: Blackwell, 1992), p. 825, originally published as Fried, 'Art and Objecthood,' *Artforum* (Summer 1967), pp. 12–23.

68   Ibid., p. 826.

69   Carolee Schneemann, interview by Odili Donald Odita, 'Conversation with Carolee Schneemann, Part 1,' *Plexus* (web magazine), 1997, www.plexus.org/connect/texts/interviews/texts/1.html (accessed May 5, 2011).

70 Eunice Lipton, *Alias Olympia: A Woman's Search for Manet's Model and Her Own Desire* (Ithaca, NY: Cornell University Press, 1999).

71 John Berger, *Ways of Seeing* (London: British Broadcasting Corporation and Penguin Books, 1972), pp. 45–64.

72 Lorraine O'Grady, 'Olympia's Maid: Reclaiming Black Female Subjectivity,' *The Feminism and Visual Culture Reader*, ed. Amelia Jones, 2nd ed. (London: Routledge, 2003), p. 209.

73 'Primary Structures' was the name given to an exhibition of Minimalist Art held from April to June 1966 at the Jewish Museum in New York. Morris, 'Notes on Sculpture 1–3,' in *Art in Theory 1900–1990*, ed. Charles Harrison and Paul Wood (Oxford: Blackwell Publisher, 1992), pp. 813–822.

74 Donald Judd, 'Specific Objects,' in *Art in Theory 1900–1990*, p. 809, originally published as 'Specific Objects,' *Arts Yearbook*, 8 (1965), pp. 74–82.

75 Yvonne Rainer, *Feelings Are Facts: A Life* (Cambridge, MA: The MIT Press, 2006), p. 235. Rainer describes 'Morris's 1962 Living Theater "presentation" in which a rectangular gray column stood for some minutes, then toppled over and lay on the floor for the same duration.'

76 Schneemann, interview by Odili Donald Odita, 'Conversation with Carolee Schneemann, Part 1.'

77 Harold Bloom, *The Anxiety of Influence: A Theory of Poetry*, 2nd ed. (Oxford: Oxford University Press, 1997).

78 Carolee Schneemann, email message to the author, June 26, 2012.

79 Francesca Coppa, 'The Body Immaterial: Magicians' Assistants and the Performance of Labor,' *Performing Magic on the Western Stage: From the Eighteenth Century to the Present*, ed. Francesca Coppa, Lawrence Hass and James Peck (New York: Palgrave Macmillan, 2008), pp. 85–106.

80 Robert Morris, 'Subjective Histories of Sculpture II: Robert Morris,' lecture at The New School, New York, April 7, 2008.

81 Rainer, *Feelings Are Facts*, p. 244.

82 Banes, *Greenwich Village 1963*, p. 226.

83 Carolee Schneemann, 'Interview with Linda Montano,' in *Imaging her Erotics*, p. 133.

84 Schneemann to Mona Mellis, February 2, 1960, in *Correspondence Course*, p. 43.

85 Ibid.

86 P. Adams Sitney, *Visionary Film: The American Avant-Garde, 1943–2000*, 3rd ed. (Oxford: Oxford University Press, 2002), pp. 164–165. Brakhage considered ending the film *Anticipation of the Night* with his own suicide.

87 Kristine Stiles, 'The Painter as an Instrument of Real Time,' in *Imaging her Erotics*, p. 4.

88 Carolee Schneemann, 'Eye Body: 36 Transformative Actions,' in *Imaging her Erotics*, p. 55.

89 Stan Brakhage, 'The Camera Eye,' in *The Essential Brakhage: Selected Writings on Filmmaking*, ed. Bruce McPherson (Kingston, NY: McPherson & Company / Documentext, 2001), p. 15.

90 Laura U. Marks, *The Skin of the Film: Intercultural Cinema, Embodiment, and the Senses* (Durham, NC: Duke University Press, 2000), p. xi.

91 Ibid.

92 Carolee Schneemann, 'From the Notebooks,' in *Imaging her Erotics*, p. 27.

93 Carolee Schneemann to Robert Haller, October 23, 1977, in *Correspondence Course*, p. 288.

94 Carolee Schneemann, email message to author, June 26, 2012.

95 Ibid.

96 Carolee Schneemann to Stan Brakhage, September 7, 1975, in *Correspondence Course*, pp. 255–256.

97 Sitney, *Visionary Film*, pp. 143, 159.

98 Carolee Schneemann to Robert Haller, October 23, 1977, in *Correspondence Course*, p. 287.

99 Ibid.

100 Carolee Schneemann to Naomi Levinson, May 29, 1959, in *Correspondence Course*, p. 38.

101 Carolee Schneemann to Robert Haller, October 23, 1977, in *Correspondence Course*, p. 287.

102 Carolee Schneemann to Naomi Levinson, May 28, 1958, in *Correspondence Course*, p. 28.

103 Ibid., p. 25.

104 Ibid.

105 Ibid., p. 26.

106 Ibid., pp. 26–27.

107 Carolee Schneemann, 'It is Painting,' in *Stan Brakhage Filmmaker*, ed. David E. James (Philadelphia, PA: Temple University Press, 2005), pp. 78–87; p. 83.

108 James Tenney to Stan Brakhage, June 24, 1957, box 17, folder 1, James Stanley Brakhage Collection, University of Colorado at Boulder Libraries.

109 Schneemann, 'It is Painting,' p. 81.

110 James Tenney to Stan Brakhage, July 18, 1957, box 17, folder 1, James Stanley Brakhage Collection, University of Colorado at Boulder Libraries.

111 Claude Lévi-Strauss, *Elementary Structures of Kinship*, trans. James Harle Bell and John Richard von Sturmer, ed. Rodney Needham (Boston, MA: Beacon Press, 1969).

112 Eve Kosofsky Sedgwick, *Between Men: English Literature and Male Homosocial Desire* (New York: Columbia University Press, 1985).

113 Carolee Schneemann to Robert Haller, October 23, 1977, in *Correspondence Course*, p. 287.

114 Ibid.

115 Schneemann, 'It is Painting,' p. 83.

116 Lee Edelman, *No Future: Queer Theory and the Death Drive* (Durham, NC: Duke University Press, 2004), p. 27.

117 Carolee Schneemann to Wolf Vostell, January 22, 1965, in *Correspondence Course*, p. 95.

118 Amelia Jones, 'Screen Eroticisms: Exploring Female Desire in the Work of Carolee Schneemann and Pipilotti Rist,' *Screen/Space: The Projected Image in Contemporary Art*, ed. Tamara Trodd (Manchester: Manchester University Press, 2011), pp. 126–144; p. 129.

119 Ibid.

120 Carolee Schneemann, 'Interview with Kate Haug,' in *Imaging Her Erotics*, p. 43.

121 Stanley Kunitz, 'The Layers,' in *The Collected Poems* (New York: W.W Norton, 2000), pp. 217–218; p. 218.

122 Carolee Schneemann, email message to the author, July 20, 2012.

123 Ibid.

124 Carolee Schneemann, 'Interview with Kate Haug,' in *Imaging Her Erotics*, p. 43.

125 Carolee Schneemann to Robert Haller, October 23, 1977, in *Correspondence Course*, p. 287.

126 Carolee Schneemann to Naomi Levinson, May 29, 1959, in *Correspondence Course*, p. 39.

127 Schneemann, 'Interview with Kate Haug,' in *Imaging her Erotics*, p. 33.

128 Gene Youngblood, 'Synaesthetic Cinema and Polymorphous Eroticism,' in *Expanded Cinema* (New York: E. P. Dutton), p. 119.

129 Carolee Schneemann, 'The Lebanon Series,' in *Imaging her Erotics*, pp. 186–195; p. 193.

130 Robert Haller to Carolee Schneemann, October 28, 1977, in *Correspondence Course*, p. 289.

131 Linda Williams argues that although 'fellatio was certainly not invented by the generation of the seventies,' it was nonetheless not a sex act that had much public recognition before this decade. Williams, *Screening Sex* (Durham, NC: Duke University Press, 2008), p. 137.

132 Alice Echols, *Daring to Be Bad: Radical Feminism in America 1967–1975* (Minneapolis, MN: University of Minnesota Press, 1989), pp. 92–101.

133 Adrienne Rich, *Compulsory Heterosexuality and Lesbian Existence* (Antelope, CA: Antelope Publications, 1982).

134 Catherine MacKinnon, quoted in Lisa Duggan, Nan Hunter, and Carole S. Vance, 'False Promises: Feminist Antipornography Legislation in the U.S.,' in *Women Against Censorship*, ed. Varda Burstyn (Vancouver: Douglas & MacIntyre, 1985), p. 138.

135 Williams, *Hard Core*, p. 25.

136 Carolee Schneemann, 'Notes on *Fuses*,' in *Imaging Her Erotics*, p. 45.

137 Williams, *Hard Core*, pp. 48–49.

138 Laura Mulvey, 'Visual Pleasure and Narrative Cinema,' *Screen* 16, no. 9 (Autumn 1975), p. 11.

139 Schneemann, 'Interview with Kate Haug,' in *Imaging Her Erotics*, p. 23.

140 James M. Harding, 'Between Dialectics, Decorum, and Collage: Sabotaging Schneemann at the Dialectics of Liberation Congress, London 1967,' in *Cutting Performances: Collage Events, Feminist Artists, and the American Avant-Garde* (Ann Arbor, MI: University of Michigan Press, 2010), p. 134.

141 Carolee Schneemann, interview by Aviva Rahmani, 'On Censorship: Interview with Aviva Rahmani,' in *Imaging Her Erotics*, p. 211, originally published in *M/E/A/N/I/N/G Journal* (1989), pp. 3–7.

142 McClure, 'Phi Upsilon Kappa,' in *Meat Science Essays*, pp. 19–20.

143 Schneemann, 'Interview with Linda Montano,' in *Imaging Her Erotics*, p. 123.

144 Schneemann, 'Interview with Kate Haug,' in *Imaging Her Erotics*, p. 26.

145 McClure, 'Phi Upsilon Kappa,' in *Meat Science Essays*, p. 20.

146 Schneemann, 'Notes on *Fuses*,' in *Imaging Her Erotics*, p. 45.

147 Marks, *The Skin of the Film*, p. 132.

148 Schneemann, 'Interview with Kate Haug,' *Imaging Her Erotics*, p. 42.

149 Williams, *Hard Core*, p. 101.

150 Roland Barthes, *A Lover's Discourse: Fragments*, trans. Richard Howard (New York: Hill & Wang, 1978), p. 3.

151 Ibid., pp. 10–12, 4.

152 Youngblood, 'Synaesthetic Cinema and Polymorphous Eroticism,' p. 121.

153 Schneemann, 'It is Painting,' p. 83, emphasis added.

154 McClure, 'Phi Upsilon Kappa,' in *Meat Science Essays*, p. 20.

155 Barthes, *Lover's Discourse*, p. 10.

156 Ibid., p. 11.

157 Clayton Eshleman to Carolee Schneemann, September 11, 1975, in *Correspondence Course*, p. 256.

158 Carolee Schneemann to Clayton Eshleman, October 24, 1975, in *Correspondence Course*, p. 261.

159 Schneemann, 'It is Painting,' p. 81.

160 Ibid., p. 83.

161 Carolee Schneemann to Naomi Levinson, May 29, 1959, in *Correspondence Course*, p. 35.

162 Carolee Schneemann to Stan Brakhage, June 21, 1982, in *Correspondence Course*, p. 337.

163 Ibid., p. 336.

164 Carolee Schneemann to Naomi Levinson, May 29, 1959, in *Correspondence Course*, p. 37.

165 Stan Brakhage to Carolee Schneemann, August 11, 1975, in *Correspondence Course*, p. 251.

166 Ibid., p. 252.

167 Ibid., p. 252.

168 Schneemann to Eshleman, September 12, 1975, in *Correspondence Course*, p. 259.

169 Brakhage was a professor at the University of Colorado, Boulder from 1981 to 2002, as well as a lecturer at the Art Institute of Chicago. Robert Morris has been a professor of art at Hunter College, CUNY, since 1964.

170 Carolee Schneemann to Henry Sayre, July 15, 1986, in *Correspondence Course*, p. 367.

171 Schneemann to Eshleman, September 21, 1971, in *Correspondence Course*, p. 182.

172 Barthes, *Lover's Discourse*, p. 11.

It is a winter morning in Montreal. The neighbor has already begun her daily marathon of Christmas music; 'So this is Christmas / And what have you done?' More than forty years ago, in another room in this same frigid city, Yoko Ono and John Lennon staged their *Bed-In* for peace. I am beginning to understand why they didn't want to get up. Why is it so difficult to write about work you love? Why can't this chapter on Yoko Ono, like so many of her own projects, remain unrealized? I have, after all, followed my own instructions for engagement to my personal satisfaction:

> Watch Yoko Ono's films.
> Watch them until you can touch them.
> Read everything.
> Shake it all up and think about it.
> Enjoy the mess in your mind.

This has proved a reliable method for leading an intellectually rich life. But it is hard to translate this mess telepathically, to clear away space for someone else to crawl in. For this, we need writing, a different set of instructions. So I try the following:

> Start with a memory.
> Use it to cut a hole in what you think you know.

I erase thirty years. It is still winter. I am four years old, at a huge protest against nuclear power in Central Park. I can't possibly know then but this will be the first of many protests; later, I will discover that they, too, are good ingredients for a rich life.

I assume that my parents tried to explain nuclear power to me, but I can't remember. What I *do* remember vividly are monsters walking around with huge *papier-mâché* skeleton masks covering their heads. What a terrifying, magnificent sight! This – and a commercial for god-knows-what that showed a seemingly endless loop of cloud-filled sky – constitutes my earliest conception of death. One was a political *danse macabre*. The other, I realize years later, could have been from a film by Yoko Ono.

When we return home that day, my parents tell my sister and me to draw our impressions for our 'conscientious-objector files.' In case we grow up in a war-torn world where women (or little girls?) are drafted: You need to prove that you have a history of non-violence. Decades later, I will wonder where on earth these files went. Perhaps one day I will make my own children make drawings for their files. But for now, there is only the dog and she refuses to do anything that I say.

For years, whenever I think of John Lennon's murder, these *papier-mâché* death heads come to mind. I am not sure why but my memories of these two events have fused so completely that I never think of one without the other. Suddenly, while reading the last interview completed before Lennon's death, I come across the following detail: 'In the kitchen [of their NYC Dakota apartment], the radio blurted a news report about a demonstration outside New York City against nuclear power.'[1] The resurrection of this lost moment astounds me. I suddenly understand: Lennon was inside while we were outside. A few days later, he was dead. At three years old, I could not understand why the whole world suddenly unraveled.

I do now. For in addition to their respective careers – in music, visual art, performance, literature, and cinema – Yoko Ono and John Lennon pioneered new forms of heterosexuality that were vastly influential on a generation of people looking for more egalitarian and eccentric forms of coupling. In spite of the tragedy that ended Lennon's life, their relationship served as a model for the inter-subjective redefinition of racial, gender, sexual, and professional roles that could be practiced between men and women. Not only was their relationship one of the most visible interracial, and inter-national relationships in the postwar period, but it also expanded the definition of acceptable forms of femininity, masculinity, and coupledom. As Kristine Stiles has argued, 'their union' provided 'a unique cultural model for ways in which gender and racial equality' could be 'constructed in heterosexual relations.'[2] Thinking back, I can understand why my parents – who practiced their own kind of radical unconventionality – saw kindred spirits in Ono and Lennon.

Ono and Lennon's relationship publicly performed a new way of being together that was informed but not determined by the many forms of racism, classism, and misogyny they encountered. As this chapter will demonstrate, Yoko Ono's films and performances pioneered equally compelling ways of incorporating and critically responding to violence. As Stiles has observed, elements of destruction have been visible in Ono's work since the late 1950s.[3] Yet rather than forging a nihilistic relation to the world, I argue that the constant oscillation between sadism, masochism, and voyeurism in Ono's work produces forms of eccentric embodiment that allow the viewer to transcend his or her seeming entrapment in non-egalitarian or abusive relations of power. In this chapter, I look at the ways in which the still, vulnerable, assaulted or prone body figures as a site of resistance in several of Ono's films and performance pieces from the Vietnam era, including *Cut Piece* (1964), *No. 4* (a.k.a. *Bottoms*, 1966), and *Fly* (1970, with John Lennon). More specifically, I consider the subversive potential of Ono's investigation of the gendered, racialized body in works structured by stringent performance imperatives, prescribed conditions of spectatorship, and/or injunctions of the apparatus. By examining the relationship between the surveillance gaze and the disciplined body, I investigate the racial, sexual, political, and affective implications of Ono's strategic use of such sadomasochistic structures of engagement.

As a conceptual artist, performer, and musician well known in American, British, and Japanese avant-garde communities, Ono was deeply involved in, and influential upon, the mixed-media practices of the 1960s. It was through her association with the aesthetic and philosophical tenets of Fluxus, as well as her close friendship with its founder, George Maciunas, that Ono began making films in 1966. Like her work in other media, Ono's film projects from 1966 to 1971 are deeply conceptual, rooted in the notion that once articulated, an idea could and should be carried out by any number of individuals other than the idea's 'author.' Many of Ono's most compelling works remain unrealized as tangible objects, existing instead as written instructions that can be completed through either the participant's imagination or actions.

By creating an intimate link between the artist and the viewer-participant, Ono forged an insistently corporeal mode of address in which the distinction between the tactile and visual apprehension of the art object collapsed. To fully 'experience' Ono's art, one cannot merely watch, but must give one's body over to it. Defying Descartes's *cogito*, Ono routes conceptual art through the body, demonstrating the ways in which thinking is inseparable from corporeality. By conceiving works that can only be realized through the observer's bodily engagement with the art object or performer, Ono creates artworks meant to touch and be touched. In doing so, she challenges the Kantian ideal of disinterested, distanced spectatorship[4] while insisting upon the 'text' as an embodied interface in the process of constant material transformation. Many of Ono's projects, including *Beat Piece* (1965) in which audience members are invited to come onto a stage and lay down on each other's bodies and listen, focus on intimate corporeal exchanges. Other pieces, like *Bag Piece* (a.k.a. *Stone Piece*, 1964), in which couples climb into a giant black muslin bag, remove their clothing, and perform various unknowable actions, privilege the tactility of the bodily encounter while simultaneously rebuffing the scopic desire of the non-participating viewer.[5] Even in her unrealized works, in which the fulfillment of her instructions is imagined rather than enacted, Ono conceives of the body as the 'scar' of the mind,[6] or the site where the individual wound of subjectivity takes shape.

Like much conceptual art of the 1960s and 1970s, the corporeal forms of engagement practiced by Ono deconstruct the notion of the artwork as a precious object, and erode the distinction between artist and observer. Yet this collapse of boundaries, between subject and object, author and text, and artist/performer and spectator, often had distressing implications for feminist artists who used their own body to make abusive relations of power visible. Ono's projects from this period frequently involve the viewer in troubling forms of violence directed against women's bodies, including her own. This is most explicit in *Cut Piece*, which Ono performed publicly between 1964 and 1966 in various venues in Kyoto, Tokyo, London, and New York.[7]

Cut Piece

According to Amelia Jones, the 1960s performances of Yoko Ono, Carolee Schneemann, and Japanese artist Yayoi Kusama inaugurated the critical feminist practice of body art.[8] Certainly, nude female bodies had already been used in the increasingly explicit artistic spectacles of mid-century and postwar art. For his series *Anthropometries* in 1960, Yves Klein instructed several nude women to cover their bodies with wet paint in his signature color, YKB (Yves Klein Blue), and lie 'like live brushes'[9] across large sheets of paper that covered the floor. Engaging what Jones has described as the 'Pollockian performative,' Klein used women as mark-making tools who performed the action of painting while the male artist, invoking the 'author function Pollock,' remained detached from the physical work but nonetheless received all of the credit.[10] The female body was also employed as an instrument of splatter that same year in Alfred Hitchcock's *Psycho* (1960), which displaced the ejaculatory vulnerability of the male subject onto a woman as she was slashed to pieces in the film's famous shower scene. Shifting the castration anxiety of the male viewer (and male artist) onto the female body, *Psycho* made a spectacle of female powerlessness in order to defend male subjectivity from its own lack.[11] By compelling female bodies to 'ejaculate' blood or paint (or in the case of *Psycho*, Bosco's chocolate syrup), male artists disavowed the non-transcendent corporeality of the male body, whose own spastic emissions might have seemed – until their glorification in *Deep Throat* – as the ultimate sign of out-of-control vulnerability.

In different ways, Klein and Hitchcock constructed ejaculatory female bodies in order to reiterate 'the norms of masculine genius' at women's expense.[12] Working against these heightened forms of misogynistic spectacle, Ono and Schneemann revolutionized the use of the female body as a non-phallic tool of artistic expression and political discourse. Wielding their own bodies to confront the violence of the male gaze, and the imperialist, racist, patriarchal culture that authorizes it, these artists used the body, as Jones has argued, to explode the myth of the disinterested interpretation of the female nude.[13] Yet

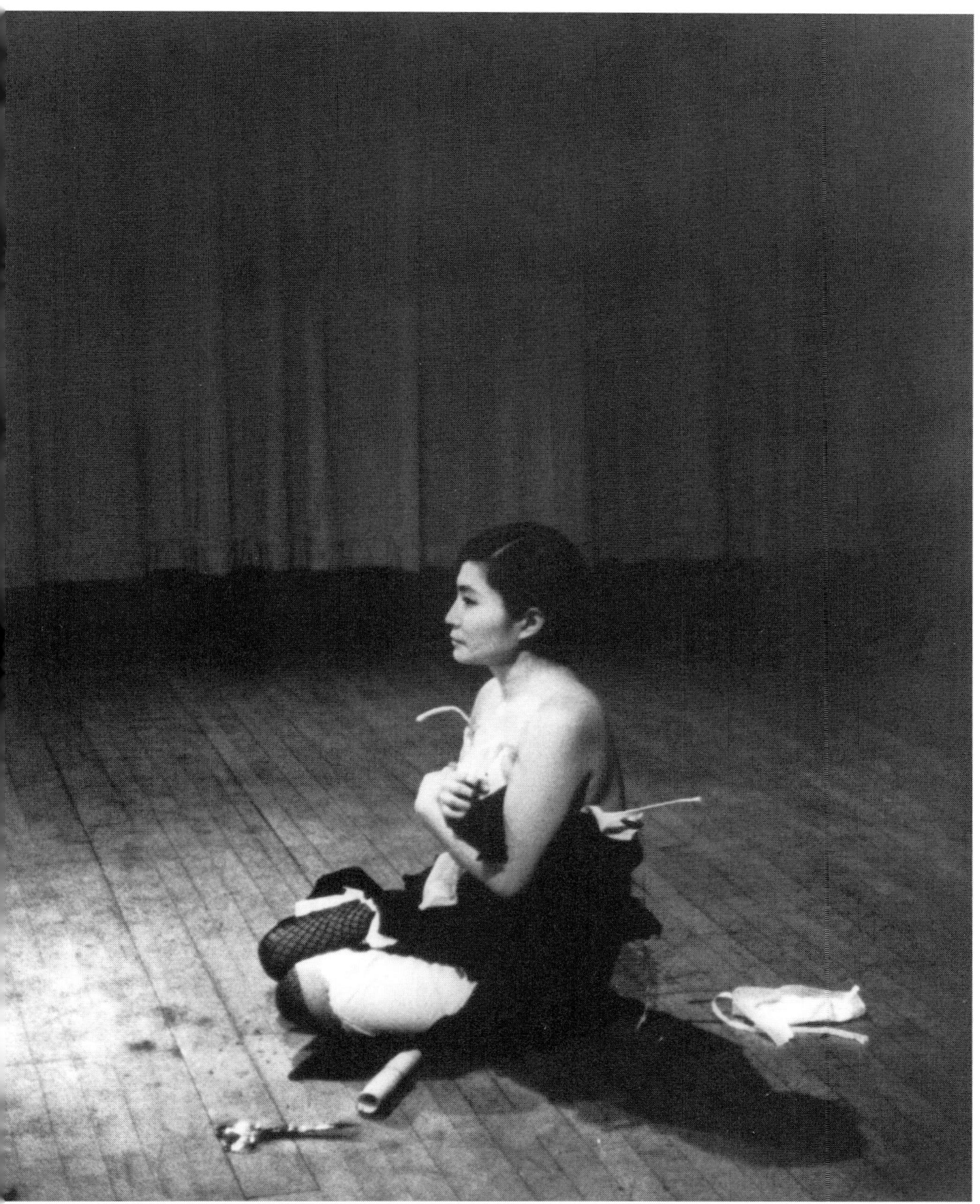

In Yoko Ono's *Cut Piece* (1964), members of the audience are invited to cut away the   **35**
pieces of the artist's clothing they do not like.

while much of Schneemann's work from the 1960s depends upon the expressive gestures of Abstract Expressionism even as it feminizes and re-signifies them, Ono employs the still body as a locus of immobility that catalyzed action around it. Rather than channeling the interiority of the artist through the frenetic movement of the body (Pollock, Schneemann), Ono choreographed performative lacuna that could only be filled by the actions of others.

In *Cut Piece*, the artist, wearing her best clothes,[14] kneeled on the concert-hall stage with her knees folded beneath her and a scissor placed in front of her on the floor. Members of the audience were then invited to approach the stage one at a time and cut a piece of her clothing away, which they were allowed to keep.

Ono described her violent denuding as follows:

> People went on cutting the parts they do not like of me finally there was only the stone remained of me that was in me but they were still not satisfied and wanted to know what it's like in the stone.[15]

According to the score, the performer was expected to remain motionless throughout the piece, which would end at the performer's request. In this way, Ono retained control over the piece's duration. Yet the fact that Ono's own body was also featured as the object on display represented a significant, perilous relinquishment of control. Not only could Ono not anticipate how participants would behave, or prevent it, but the piece itself would only be 'completed' when Ono had been 'undone' by other author-observers.

As in many of Ono's pieces, *Cut Piece* pivots upon the mutability of objects, which can be rent, segmented, marked, exposed, penetrated, or re-situated to create vastly different meanings. Like the canvas left on the floor in her 1960 piece *Painting to Be Stepped On*, or the white board ready to be pounded in *Painting to Hammer a Nail* (1961/1966), Ono's body becomes the raw material upon which viewers were invited to leave their mark. Like many of Ono's other interventions during this period, *Cut Piece* invites acts of laceration that literalize the 'incisive potential of the gaze to puncture and wound, to cut away at that which is observed.'[16]

Ono was not the first artist to rupture the typically smooth surface of painting through incision. Beginning in 1949, Italian-Argentine artist Lucio Fontana pioneered the slashed canvas in order to create a mysterious sense of illusion and depth in a medium then celebrated, by American art critic Clement Greenberg, for its two-dimensionality.[17] On the other side of the world, in Ono's native Japan, members of the Gutai group had been thrusting their bodies against and through all sorts of supports – including packing paper, canvas, and screens – since the mid-1950s.[18] But in pieces like *Painting to Shake Hands* (1961), *Painting to See a Room Through* (1961), *Painting to See the Skies* (1961), and *Painting for the Wind* (1961), Ono moves beyond Fontana's superficial wounds towards a more profound investigation of the inter-subjectivity of the artwork which, as Jones has theorized, is 'contingent' upon its relation to others.[19] In her conceptual cut pieces, Ono demonstrates how lacerating stretched canvas not only re-orients the relationship between positive and negative space, but actually opens up the fixed dimensions of traditional easel painting and its typically reverential mode of reception to more radical forms of relationality. These works are not merely innovative compositions, but means of revitalizing collective experience. Decimating the distinction between painting and performance, Ono's cuts render the forbiddingly visual medium of painting tactile and interactive, inviting the viewer to puncture the rarified art object. Celebrating what Walter Benjamin has ambivalently described as the destruction of the art work's 'aura,'[20] Ono turns the collective experience of reception into an opportunity for dialectical engagement.

But if Ono's work suspends the traditional subjection of the spectator, then it also reveals the ways in which this suspension can produce even more troubling forms of subjugation. Female artists who stage their own vulnerability by posing 'passively' on the stage, gallery, or street often find themselves transformed into the ritual sacrifices of an emboldened group. Yet rather than merely demonstrate what Wilhelm Reich, Gustav Le Bon, and Sigmund Freud[21] have each anatomized as the psychopathology of the madding crowd, Ono's experiments attempt to overcome the crowd's instincts towards fascism through charged encounters with the sexualized body. Posing her own, or others', bodies as sacrificial victims, Ono demonstrates how sadomasochistic performance strategies can make visible and challenge the instrumentalization of the Other in a non-egalitarian society determined by sexual and racial difference. This is nowhere more evident than in Ono and Lennon's film *Rape* (1969), in which a two-man camera crew relentlessly stalks and records an unsuspecting woman until she collapses in distress.[22]

In her staging of ritual sacrifice, Ono often provocatively insists upon the interchangeability of bodies and other forms of matter. The instructions for an unrealized film project, entitled *Film Script 3*, are remarkably similar to those of *Cut Piece*:

> Ask audience to cut the part of the image on
> the screen that they don't like.
> Supply scissors.[23]

Here, the screen functions as a prosthetic extension of the implicitly female body upon which the audience member can project their fantasies of dismemberment. By encouraging viewers to dissect it, Ono supplants the flesh of the sacrificial body with the skin of the film screen. In doing so, she calls upon the material supports of cinema to function as proxies for the human body in the sadistic processes of projective identification that, as psychoanalyst Melanie

Klein has theorized, defines our earliest relation to others.[24] Like Klein, Ono envisions the female, maternal body as the aim of the subject's desire to rend and destroy. And like Klein, Ono pioneered forms of play in which subjects could act out their aggression towards others. When Ono performs *Cut Piece*, she replaces the screen with her own body. Troubling Ono's rhetorical insistence on the equivalence between bodies and other objects, the lacerations made in Ono's clothing publically expose the flesh of a body doubly marginalized by race and gender.

In a filmed documentary by the Maysles brothers of the 1965 Carnegie Recital Hall performance of *Cut Piece*, Ono is perfectly composed as audience members begin to slice away her clothing. Seemingly intimidated by the prospect of violating the artist, the earliest participants are careful to crop only insignificant scraps of her apparel. Trimming the neckline of her blouse along the axis of her shoulders, or respectfully shortening its sleeves, the participants seem reluctant to go further. Watching this section, I am embarrassed to admit the frivolous details that distract me. Why, for example, am I so surprised by the propriety of Ono's outfit and her kempt hair? Combed and neatly tied back, it's a far cry from the wild mane she will sport later, with Lennon, during the *Bed-In for Peace*, or on the cover of *Two Virgins*, where the paleness of both of their naked bodies is interrupted by four shocks of hair. Skinflint that I am, I ponder the idiot dilemma of how Ono was willing to have her favorite bra snipped. This, unworthily, astounds me.

Finally, a man comes up to the stage and delicately snips away a fragment of Ono's shirt that covers her nipple. To his dismay, her breast remains veiled by both a brassiere and a corset-like undergarment that looks borrowed from my grandmother's closet. Unlike later canonical performances in which feminist artists present their nude bodies to a public audience – Marina Abramović's *Rhythm 0* (1974) and Ana Mendieta's *Rape Scene* (1973) come to mind – I am pricked by the suggestion of a modesty which will come to seem out of place in body art of subsequent decades.

Yet Ono's modesty seems to abet further transgression, as the man's encroachment sets the stage for further violation. The next participant is eager to surpass this relatively mild provocation. Smugly warning the audience that his efforts 'might take a while,' he enthusiastically cuts away the part of Ono's garment that covers her breasts. As the front of shirt falls away, he slices away her corset, pushing Ono's limp limbs aside to achieve better access. Still dissatisfied, he retreats behind the crouching woman and slashes the straps of her bra with the scissors. Ono, who appears increasingly apprehensive as the man progresses, responds to this final desecration by holding the now unsupported cups of her bra over her breasts with her hands. Nearly forty minutes after the performance begins, it ends with Ono sitting on the stage naked, her lips trembling and her hands partially covering her breasts and groin.

Bearing witness to Ono's strategic subjugation, the Maysles's documentary reveals the increasing sadism of the audience. I am appalled but not surprised to watch as a timid group of observers is transformed into an aggressive crowd of assailants; this is Mob Psychology 101. Contrary to Ono's later film *Rape*, here the audience, rather than the filmmaker, assumes the metaphoric role of rapist. Nonetheless, the sadomasochistic dynamic that emerges feels just as imprisoning. In *Cut Piece*, there is no neutral position to occupy. Instead, one is offered three repellant possibilities of identification: 1) with the masochistic subject who consents to abuse, 2) with the participant whose sadistic desire to penetrate the woman assumes the form of physical violence, or 3) with the curious onlooker who does nothing to prevent the woman's violation. Considering these miserable options, I am astounded by the overwhelming force Ono's motionlessness exerts upon the audience. Her passivity constructs us all.

My own jaded response, which has come to treat Ono's body as just one thing among others (worrying, for a moment, more about her bra than about her safety), is hardly more empathetic. Having encountered different records of this canonical piece for nearly half my life, I realize that I have stopped *seeing* it. Or rather, I have come *only* to *see* it, and have forgotten how to *feel* it. Overexposure to female nudity in performance art of the intervening decades has turned Ono's body into an object of scopic curiosity. Writing about *Cut Piece* more than forty years after it was first performed, it is impossible to experience it 'the way it really was';[25] you cannot, as both Heraclites and Benjamin remind us, step in the same river twice, even when it flows with blood.

In his prophetic 'Theses on the Philosophy of History,' written just before he committed suicide on the French-Spanish border while trying to escape the Nazis, Walter Benjamin recognized the urgent need to arrest thinking in order to salvage an endangered image of the past, which would otherwise be lost to the flow of 'homogenous, empty time':

> Thinking involves not only the flow of thoughts, but their arrest as well. Where thinking suddenly stops in a configuration pregnant with tensions, it gives that configuration a shock, by which it crystallizes into a monad. A historical materialist approaches a historical subject only where he encounters it as a monad. In this structure he recognizes the sign of a Messianic cessation of happening, or, put differently, a revolutionary chance in the fight for the oppressed past.[26]

This book couldn't have been written without the unpredictable appearance of such monads. Although sites like YouTube and ubuweb have made records of once obscure performances readily available, the mind-numbing rituals of websurfing are nothing if not attuned to the pace of homogeneous, empty time. Coming back to my thoughts on *Cut Piece*, I am disturbed to discover it a lifeless object, a weighty art historical *thing*. This all changes for me in a flash, when I watch, in horror, a video of a peaceful line of protesting students at the

University of California, Davis on November 18, 2011 as an indifferent police officer in paramilitary gear pepper-sprays them in the face. The occupation of the UC Davis campus was part of an international wave of Occupy protests that began in New York in the autumn of 2011 in partial response to the liberation movements of the previous Arab Spring. Watching these students brutalized at close range as they non-violently resist the increasing costs and diminishing accessibility of education, I am incredibly moved by their extraordinary fortitude – and vulnerability. What courage it takes to *passively* resist a potentially deadly police force that abjures all ethical responsibility in the name of defending the property of the capitalist state. The appearance of this monad returns me, transfixed, to the stage upon which Yoko Ono once sat – nearly but not entirely motionless.

For the first time in nearly a decade, I am overwhelmed by what it must have meant for Ono to sit upon that stage and ask audience members to cut away the parts they didn't like. My body is shocked back into visceral empathy. I taste the fear she must have felt as she waited, uncertain as to whether anyone would critically or even fatally assault her. After all, there was nothing actually stopping anyone from attacking her body with the scissors she had provided. Indeed, when Ono performed the work in Kyoto in July 1964, a man came on stage and raised the scissors over Ono's head threatening to stab her before eventually dropping his arm to cut her clothing instead of her flesh.[27] Such violent responses to Ono's body far outnumber the few instances of empathy practiced by audience members, as when one man comes up to the stage and, 'with shaking hands,' stitches his handkerchief to the tatters of Ono's 'fiercely chopped' dress to cover her naked breast that had been savagely revealed by the previous participant.[28]

In the face of such dangers, I am heartened by Ono's dismissive comment, 'Men have an unusual talent for making a bore out of everything they touch.'[29] One must only think of Warhol's films to remember that boredom was one of the primary strategies mobilized by the postwar avant-garde. As many critics have noted, boring an audience was not only a way of refusing the ideologically complicit escapism of mass entertainment, but also of sexually teasing an audience, putting them in their place, or, more generously, enabling them to see 'nothing' differently. (For Warhol, boring an audience was also a way of branding blankness as a highly privileged form of cultural capital.) But boredom also, etymologically, emerges from the notion of boring a hole, cutting with a sharp tool, perforating or piercing an object. In a culture in which violence against women is so naturalized that it is often regarded with complete indifference, there is nothing more 'boring' than a man boring a woman to death. One must only think of the murder of Kitty Genovese, raped and stabbed to death on the streets of Ono's adopted home of New York City on March 13, 1964, a mere three months before the debut of *Cut Piece*. According to what has become an infamous *New York Times* report,[30] none of the thirty-eight people who heard her screams called the police or otherwise provided assistance. Though these claims have since been disputed, for American audiences after Kennedy's assassination, this story of callous indifference embodied what had become an altogether predictable response to the spectacle of violence. It even, as psychology students know, has a psychological phenomenon named after it: often described as the 'Genovese syndrome,' the 'bystander effect' denotes the diffusion of responsibility that occurs when a group witnesses an act of violence.[31] Ono's work emerges from the double-edged sense of 'boredom' so horrifically demonstrated by the murder of Genovese: the boredom of patriarchal violence, and its endless and therefore unremarkable boring of and into women.

For Walter Benjamin, Bertolt Brecht, Antonin Artaud, and many other theorists of modernity, shock was a necessary instrument of awakening a public who had been lulled into political inertia by self-perpetuating forms of bourgeois mystification. Yet after five decades of performance art in which abject alterity has become something of a norm,[32] why does Ono's relatively modest performance remain so staggering? Retrospectively, the modesty of Ono's pose has become all the more provocative – and effective – for waking us from the anesthesia of complacency. What *really* pricks me – what Roland Barthes would call the 'punctum' of the piece[33] – are not the cuts sustained by Ono or the violent, all-too-predictable response of an audience given license to violate, but Ono's minimal gesture of self-defense.

Perhaps it is the cynic in me, but I can't help but wonder whether Ono's gesture of covering her breasts is an affect meant to heighten the sense of violation, or an authentic, un-premeditated reflex of self-protection. According to Kristine Stiles, Ono 'covered her breasts at the moment of unbosoming' when she performed *Cut Piece* in both New York and London.[34] But how does this gesture of self-concealment signify? Referring specifically to the work of Hannah Wilke, Amelia Jones has described feminist body art of the 1970s as animated by a 'radical narcissism' which stages the beautiful female body as a way of phenomenologically exploring the 'constitution of the gendered, racialized, and sexualized self in relation to others.'[35] In order to redeem Wilke's work, which is often dismissed as uncritically narcissistic, Jones draws upon Craig Owens's concept of the 'rhetoric of the pose.'[36] In his 1984 article 'The Medusa Effect,' Owens (channeling Lacan) argues, 'to strike a pose is to present oneself to the gaze of the other as if one were already frozen, immobilized – that is, already a picture.' For Lacan, the pose has 'a strategic value': By strategically 'mimicking the immobility induced by the gaze,' the pose is able to reflect 'power back on itself,' forcing it 'to surrender.' 'Confronted with a pose,' Owens writes, 'the gaze itself is immobilized, brought to a standstill.'[37] But what is the rhetoric of Ono's pose?

In a patriarchal culture in which female value is contingent upon physical beauty, it is no wonder that the avant-garde has mined the visual contrast between pulchritude and disfiguration. The sadistic desire to deface the beautiful woman and watch her suffer is certainly an animating trope of mainstream visual culture; Janet Leigh's brutal murder in *Psycho* is but one example. In this context, it is not surprising that feminist artists aim to re-activate this paradox in order to critique a patriarchal order that insists, simultaneously, on the fetishistic objectification and destruction of women. The rhetoric of Ono's pose deliberately exposes the sadomasochistic dynamic of gendered looking, making visible the way in which the woman's bearing of the (male-inflicted) wound sutures women into a position of immobility. In the terms Laura Mulvey would articulate ten years after *Cut Piece* was first performed, Ono reveals the sadistic male gaze that maintains the fictive opposition between active masculinity and female passivity. Yet while *Cut Piece* places the body within the cult of female beauty, it does not fully align itself with its conventions.

Unlike Wilke, who operated within the codes of ideal beauty in order to solicit the desire of the spectator and thereby dispel the myth of aesthetic disinterest, Ono avoids exaggerating her beauty. Of course, Ono's beautiful Asian body was not received in the United States and Europe in the same way as Wilke's beautiful Caucasian body. In Western culture, beautiful women are, of course, presumed to white.[38] As John Lennon described, 'it was hard for Yoko to understand, having been recognized all her life as one of the most beautiful and intelligent women in Japan … Having been brought up in the genteel poverty of a lower-middle-class environment, I should not have been surprised by the outpouring of race-hatred and anti-female malice to which we were subjected,' Lennon reflected, but it was, nevertheless, 'humiliating and painful for both of us to have her described as ugly and yellow and other derogatory garbage.'[39]

Within a few years of performing *Cut Piece*, Western fears of miscegenation were turned full force on Yoko Ono, who, as Joseph Jonghyun Jeon has argued, came to represent a new form of 'yellow peril' in an era of increased globalization. These anxieties were projected onto Ono's body, which was made to bear the 'virulent enmity'[40] of a range of racist and sexist stereotypes, including what scholar Celine Parreñas Shimizu has described as the fantasized 'hypersexuality' of Asian femininity, as well as the frequent description of Ono as the 'dragon lady' who broke up the Beatles.[41] Although Ono would force audiences to confront these stereotypes head-on in several of her pieces – including the controversial nude portrait of she and Lennon that graced the cover of their 1968 album *Two Virgins*, and the *Bed-In for Peace* that they held to celebrate their marriage – in *Cut Piece*, she does not accent her sexuality. But it is only 1964. Not yet a 'hate object,' Ono is still just what Jeon has described as a 'racial thing,' an inscrutable, illegible blank.[42]

Although wearing her 'best clothes,' Ono does not aim to seduce. On the contrary, she is desexualized by her matronly black costume and prim underwear. Unlike Wilke and Abramović later, Ono does not wear lipstick or show off her substantial mane of hair. By resisting 'making herself up' as an object of desire, Ono's pose refuses to compensate for the (racist, Western, male) lack that her body will be compelled to signify. Yet even as it denies the balm of the female fetish to the castration-anxious males in the audience, the rhetoric of Ono's pose is not confrontational. Compare Ono's pose to Marina Abramović, who borrows from *Cut Piece* in *Rhythm 0* (1974) when she invites audience members to use any of the seventy-two instruments she has supplied, including a whip, scalpel, a gun and a single bullet, upon her body. Whereas Abramović challenges the spectator through her erect body and fierce expression, Ono's body assumes the position. Although Ono abides the violent interventions of participants, her expression does not dare audiences to transgress. Instead, Ono's minimalist pose is devoid of histrionics. Simultaneously avoiding overt feminist bravado or the bathos of the violated beauty queen, Ono refuses to theatricalize either her strength or her vulnerability. Yet by reducing her compendium of gestures to a minimum, Ono demonstrates the audacity of passivity in the face of violence. Her limbs are still but supple; her body prepares to be undone. Denying the solace of anonymity to her oppressors, Ono stares straight ahead. But she is not Medusa, and her gaze will not immobilize her audience. Knowing this, she waits.

In the description of *Cut Piece* published in the 1971 re-edition of *Grapefruit*, Ono concluded with the statement that, 'the performer, however, does not have to be a woman.' She also did not specify that the performer must be Asian. Be this as it may – and many non-Asian men and women *have* performed the piece to powerful, albeit different effect – it is important to remember the particular codes of race, gender, and nationality that framed the reception of Ono's body when she performed *Cut Piece* in New York and London in the mid-1960s. As with Kitty Genovese, whose own lesbianism was never acknowledged by the media,[43] it is impossible to analyze the responses of Ono's audience without paying attention to her identity. Rather than theorizing the indifference of bystanders to acts of violence as *universal,* we must recognize how the alterity of particular bodies informs the responses of spectator-participants in both scenarios. For no matter how difference is effaced or repressed, our perception of it shapes the way we think, act, and identify.[44]

Although her insights were unheeded by the media, and her identity as Kitty Genovese's lover erased by the more neutral designation 'roommate,' Mary Ann Zielonko believed that their neighbors' homophobic suspicions of Genovese's lesbianism played a significant role in their indifference to her deadly assault. In spite of the fact that there were no culturally acceptable terms to describe either Genovese's sexual identity or the prejudice against it, these differences were legible within the community in which she lived and died. Remembering Genovese, and so many other victims of hate crimes, I insist that the specificity of Ono's Asian female body is essential to the affective and political charge of her performances. Indeed, I argue that it was Ono's femaleness and Asianness that made it seem acceptable for participants to violate her while other spectators watched without doing anything about it. The 'bystander effect' is not necessarily an identity-neutral category.

But if the public reception of Ono's pose is inextricable from the perception of her sexual and racial difference, then the act of sitting *seiza*, the traditional way of sitting in Japan, also distinguishes Ono's ethnic and national difference from the majority of her European and American audiences. In the mid-1960s, the spectacle of an Asian woman kneeling upon a stage and being aggressively denuded by a nearly all-white audience would have been inextricable from the audience's perception of the growing crisis in Vietnam, in spite of the fact that Ono was not, of course, Southeast Asian. American military presence in Vietnam escalated throughout the Kennedy (1960–1963) and Johnson (1963–1969) administrations. In 1964, the Gulf of Tonkin Resolution gave then President Johnson power to conduct military operations in Southeast Asia without declaring war, and a widespread bombing campaign against North Vietnam ensued. By March 21, 1965, when Ono performed *Cut Piece* in New York's Carnegie Hall, 3,500 Marines had just been deployed to South Vietnam, marking the beginning of the American ground war.[45]

In particular, Ono's pose pays tribute to the self-immolation of Buddhist monks in protest of the oppressive conditions in Vietnam. In June 1963, Thích Quàng Dúc, a Vietnamese Mahayana monk, burned himself to death at a busy Saigon intersection in order to protest the persecution of Buddhists by South Vietnam's Roman Catholic government, led by Ngô Dinh Diêm.[46] Dúc's protest was excruciatingly, modestly choreographed: he emerged from a car, sat on a cushion in the street in the traditional Buddhist meditation lotus position, was drenched in gasoline by a colleague, recited a prayer, and dropped a lit match upon himself. American journalist David Halberstam, who watched as flames consumed Dúc's robe and flesh, described the martyr's unflappable posture: 'As he burned he never moved a muscle, never uttered a sound, his outward composure in sharp contrast to the wailing people around him.'[47]

Photographs of Dúc's self-immolation by journalist Malcolm Browne were published on the front pages of newspapers worldwide, bringing critical attention to the oppressive policies of the Diêm regime. President John F. Kennedy, whose administration was Diêm's main sponsor, later remarked that, 'no news picture in history has generated so much emotion around the world as that one.'[48] Throughout the 1960s, the photos were sold on the streets of Europe as postcards, and China distributed millions of copies throughout Asia and Africa as evidence of American imperialism.[49] In spite of the fact that violence against oneself was prohibited by most interpretations of Buddhist doctrine, there is a long tradition of self-immolation as a form of radical political protest. Following Dúc's example, many Buddhist monks, as well as some American citizens, self-immolated in protest of the war in Vietnam. These actions also helped inspire the 2010–2011 Arab Spring, as the Tunisian revolution was at least partially catalyzed by the self-immolation of a street vendor named Mohamed Bouazizi, who set himself on fire in protest against continued harassment by a municipal officer.[50]

Craig Owens has described how woman 'turns herself into a picture in order to compel the surrender of the male gaze' by submitting to it.[51] Ono, Dúc, and Bouazizi also turned themselves into pictures in order to demand the surrender of the forces that oppress them. But if Ono turns herself into a picture by remaining still for nearly the entire performance, the duration of her motionless was not, strictly speaking, picturesque. Unfolding for almost an hour, her performance reminds us of those temporal aspects of corporeality that a still picture *cannot* capture. Watching Ono's performance develop, we cannot help but realize that her position is an exercise in endurance. Maintaining this position over time, and in spite of the violent interventions of others, Ono demonstrates the remarkable fortitude required to assume and maintain the position. Composing her body through an act of extraordinary discipline, Ono produces herself as both body and mind, thereby subverting, as Jones has argued about feminist body art, 'the Cartesian separation of *cogito* and *corpus* that sustains the masculinist myth of transcendence.'[52]

And then, without warning, Ono's frozen body cracks, her impassive posture instantly de-composed by the raising of her hands and the covering of her breasts. But unlike the myth of Pygmalion and Galatea, in which the sculpture of a woman is kissed into corporeality by the smitten male sculptor who created her, Ono's sudden vivification does not gratify the prurient gaze of the male beholder. Rather, this sudden gesture of self-protection shatters what Owens has theorized as 'the Medusa effect,' by rupturing the conditions of ideal picturehood. Ono's gesture reminds us that this manhandled and abused object is also a subject. Suddenly the picture becomes a person.

In the face of the complete apathy of the audience, the artist is compelled to protect herself from being further victimized. One cannot, as it turns out, depend upon the kindness of strangers. Yet, by staging her violation by others, Ono suggests that women's supposed castration is not a biologically inherent lack, as Freud so misogynistically claimed, but a socially produced process whereby men attempt to demonstrate their own fictive coherence through the sadistic mastery of culturally disenfranchised others. Authorizing her own violation, Ono resists objectification by voluntarily submitting to it.

By covering her breasts, Ono breaks her own rules of engagement, which explicitly specify the immobility of the performer. Regardless of whether her gesture represents an involuntary reflex, conditioned response or pre-meditated decision, it is a startling breach of form. This is neither action as what Amelia Jones would call a 'claim to transcendence,' nor what Douglas Crimp might describe as a manifestation of shame.[53] Rather, Ono's gesture makes the audience's complicity in her violation explicit by suggesting the proximity of a limit. Staging the failures of our empathy towards each other, Ono unveils the aesthetic ideal of Kantian detachment not only as fictive, but – more urgently – as a violation of the sacred bonds between us.

Like Buddhist monk Thích Quàng Dúc, Ono saw her action less as a damnation of her audience than as an act of compassion. Dúc's last words, documented in a letter he had left, pleaded with Diêm to 'take a mind of compassion towards the people of the nation and implement religious equality.'[54] Ono also conceives of *Cut Piece* in terms of compassion and generosity. She explains her own strategy of non-violent resistance as a gift that could open up a pathway to enhanced perception and awareness: 'It was a form of giving, giving and taking. It was a kind of criticism against artists, who are always giving what they want to give. I wanted people to take whatever they wanted to, so it was very important to say you can cut wherever you want to.' Ono recounts an allegory in which the Buddha:

> left his castle with his wife and children and was walking towards a mountain to go into meditation. As he was walking along, a man said that he wanted Buddha's children because he wanted to sell them or something. So Buddha gave him his children. Then someone said he wanted Buddha's wife and he gave him his wife. Someone calls that he is cold, so Buddha gives him his clothes. Finally a tiger comes along and says he wants to eat him and Buddha lets the tiger eat him. And in the moment the tiger eats him, it became enlightened.[55]

This form of total giving, as 'opposed to reasonable giving like "logically you deserve this" or "I think this is good, therefore I am giving this to you"'[56] allowed the Buddha to transcend the binary oppositions that circumscribe the relations between self and other. By allowing himself to be consumed, the Buddha dissolved the corporeal boundaries that prevent recognition of one another as of the same flesh. Yoko Ono continued to dissolve these boundaries in her filmic work.

Eccentric embodiment

Along with Andy Warhol, Yoko Ono was one of the most significant harbingers of the 'structural' turn in experimental cinema. Bridging Underground cinema's emphasis on the flesh with structural cinema's deployment of fixed preconditions of framing, editing and duration,[57] Ono's cinema brought a conceptual rigor to the cinematic investigation of the body. Like Warhol's early films, many of Ono's films were single-shot, minimalist studies of the body in motion. Indeed, Ono's films *No. 1 Eyeblink* (1966), *No. 4* (a.k.a. *Bottoms*, 1966), *Film No. 5* (a.k.a. *Smile*, 1968), *Up Your Legs Forever* (1970), and *Freedom* (1970) bear a great formal resemblance to Warhol's cinema in their enthrallment with the corporeal part object and their experimentation with duration and/or slow motion.

Although Ono wrote many instructions for film projects, including a series of film scores intended for other filmmakers, she also made a number of realized 'cinema objects.' The first of these were initiated through her participation in Fluxus. Started in 1961 by Lithuanian émigré George Maciunas and composer La Monte Young, Fluxus was an interdisciplinary, internationalist art movement that united visual artists, performers, musicians, dancers, filmmakers and poets.[58] In several Fluxus Manifestos – which all of the members including its author refused to sign – Maciunas advanced some of the tenets of the movement.[59] These included the notion of cheap mass production and circulation, the use of everyday experience, the celebration of amateurization, the democratic leveling of the artist, the utopian model of collective work and life, and the constant need for change, or flux.[60] Inspired by Soviet constructivism, Zen Buddhism, and John Cage's enormously influential electronic music class at the New School, Fluxus was internationalist in its approach as well as its membership. While Fluxus also resembled Pop Art in its celebration of low-cost multiples, its genuine philosophy of accessibility as well as the truly pro-Soviet politics of its leader were incompatible with the unapologetic capitalism of Pop, which was turning out increasingly expensive collectors' items by the early 1960s.[61] As a self-proclaimed low or anti-art movement, Fluxus was also particularly 'fascinated by bodily processes, from ingestion to excretion.'[62] As Sally Banes has explained, the very name 'Fluxus' borrowed not only from the common definition of the word 'flux' (change), but also from its medical meaning, which described a fluid discharge from the bowels or other parts of the body's lower strata.[63]

On January 22, 1966, Maciunas invited Ono and other Fluxus artists including Shiomi Mieko, Joe Jones, and Pieter Vanderbeek to filmmaker Peter Moore's New York apartment to make short films using a high-speed camera that operated at 2,000 frames per second rather than the standard 24. Since the camera, which was originally intended to shoot scientific subjects, had a fixed-frame lens that could not be altered once set up, it was mandatory that the artists film simple actions.[64] Many of these 'Fluxfilms' were minimalist motion studies that concentrated on human bodies, or parts of human bodies, as they performed simple activities. Ono's two contributions, *Match* (1966) and *Eyeblink*, slowed nearly imperceptible actions to the point that they became not only visible, but seemingly motionless as well. *Match* (*No. 1*) was a five-minute black-and-white silent film depicting a match, held by two fingers, being struck and left to burn. Whereas in real time, this action would have only lasted a few seconds, Ono's film temporally expanded it to last several minutes. *Eyeblink*, Ono's second single-shot film, recorded the involuntary blink of the artist's own eye. Although

Ono's eye is centered in the middle of the frame, and thus situated to directly acknowledge the viewer, it does not return the viewer's gaze. Removed from the context of the face, the eye becomes an object rather than an instrument of vision, a site of enrapturement whose slowly descending lid both invites and forecloses the possibility of penetration. These tensions, between motion and stillness, and between the visibility of the body and the impossibility of its possession, were central motifs in both Ono and Warhol's filmic experiments.

In a culture in which media spectacles of obscene violence were becoming normalized while the on-screen representation of sexuality remained *verboten*, Ono and Warhol were kindred provocateurs. Their work reminds us how watching the body – any body – perform ordinary movements could catalyze expanded forms of consciousness. Yet in a society with ever more forms of distraction, the concentration required for such transformative perception demanded disciplinary intervention. For both Warhol and Ono, these interventions often took the form of imposing visual and temporal limits on what the viewer could see and know. Like Warhol's *Blow Job* (1964), Ono's *Up Your Legs Forever* and *Freedom* flirt with viewer's expectations about what could and could not be shown on-screen. As in *Blow Job*, both of these films titillate the viewer with the genitals' seemingly imminent exposure, while their immanent limitations conspicuously interrupt or preclude the desired revelation.

Ono's film *Freedom*, which provides a slow motion, frontal view of the artist's nearly nude torso as her hands struggle to unclasp her bra, ends just before her uncontained breasts might be exposed to the camera. In *Up Your Legs Forever*, a compendium of 333 pairs of nude legs, an unfixed camera pans up the length of the legs to the upper-most limits of the thigh before systematically cutting to the next pair of legs. As in *Freedom*, Ono pressures the limits of the visible to suggest what remains out of frame, or literally 'ob-scene.' In *Up Your Legs Forever*, the upward momentum of the camera implants the desire and expectation to see the performers' genitals. As a result of the insistently repetitive structure of the film, desire remains permanently suspended between activation and fulfillment, as its object is constantly suggested by the proximity of the apparatus but held 'forever' out of reach.

Like *Erection* (1971), Ono and Lennon's suggestively titled film about the gradual construction of a building being raised in London, these films play, visually and linguistically, upon the unfulfilled promise of genital revelation. Although Ono and Lennon would in fact deliver the sight of the genitals in several of their films, including *Self Portrait* (1969) an approximately forty-minute slow-motion film of Lennon's penis in a semi-erect state, their rapt attention to other parts of the body dismantled the hierarchical valuation of the body, and thereby resist what Herbert Marcuse had described as genital supremacy.[65] At a time when feminists were becoming increasingly critical of mass media images that sliced the female body into bits, Ono's partitive approach to corporeal representation exposed the body's social construction and affective territorialization by patriarchy. But Ono's egalitarian celebration of non-genital corporeal part objects also posits an alternative libidinal economy in which it is possible to re-imagine viewers' affective relationships to visual and erotic pleasure, as well as to each other.

Bottoms (a.k.a *No. 4*, 1966)

Ono's approach to corporeal representation is mobilized by this desire to affectively engage with other bodies. Yet as in Warhol's cinema, the bodies recorded by Ono's camera frequently belong to celebrities in the art, music, and literary worlds. By using a battery of formal techniques and structural imperatives, Ono's films play celebrity and corporeality against each other in ways that mutually obscure and illuminate the body on display. For Ono's most famous film, *No. 4*, she catalogued the naked, moving buttocks of hundreds of London's art-world luminaries.

The film exists in two versions. The first, *Fluxfilm #16*, is a five-and-a-half-minute silent film, which Ono made with her second husband Anthony Cox a few months after the session at the Moores's apartment. Using a conventional-speed 16mm camera, Ono followed the naked buttocks of a group of artists and friends from the Fluxus community, including Geoffrey Hendricks, Carolee Schneemann, and James Tenney, as well as herself, Cox, and their daughter Kyoko as they walked.[66] Each bottom is filmed in a single, continuous shot, and is followed, without interruption, by another unidentified bottom. Along with *Match* and *Eyeblink*, this short version was included in the *FluxFilm Program*, which premiered at the Film-Maker's Cinematheque in New York in 1966.

Soon after completing the first *No. 4*, Ono made an eighty-minute sound version of the same concept while she was in London. Unlike the earlier silent film, this version includes a soundtrack that consists of the voices of different, unidentified participants, describing their experiences while making the film. In this second version, Ono aimed to film 365 participants, theoretically offering a different bottom for each day of the year. Having constructed a special measuring instrument that insured that each set of buttocks remained in the frame, as well as a kind of treadmill so that her subjects' buttocks would consistently fill the screen as they walked, Ono returned to the minimalism of early cinema's motion studies.[67]

Yet unlike the early motion studies by Eadweard Muybrige, Ono's motion studies do not fetishize sexual difference but treat male and female bodies identically.[68] Indeed, among the myriad fat, lean, smooth, hairy, lumpy, pert, sagging, round, and flat asses that are included in the film, it is often difficult to assess the sex of the person to which each pair of buttocks belong. By focusing on a gender-neutral body part, Ono avoided the crisis of gendered identification, and encouraged viewers to enjoy temporary, mobile attractions to a constantly renewed supply of egalitarian objects. Furthermore, by including recordings of the participants' conversations as well as her own interviews with the British press out of sync with the images, Ono not only actively promoted the misidentification of each ass but disabled the viewer's voyeuristic instinct towards visual mastery. Unbinding both the voices and the bottoms from the bodies to which they 'belonged,' Ono posed a fluid conception of identity that was not based upon a fictive notion of coherent subjectivity, but upon an ever-changing, contingent play of momentary proximities and associations.

Rather than dramatizing sexual difference, Ono's focus on bottoms invites the spectator to enjoy the spectacle of androgynous bodily form and everyday motion. Furthermore, Ono's deliberately disorienting misalignment of auditory and visual indicators of identity celebrates rather than bemoans the limits of our perceptual knowledge. These limitations to what we can see and know are not experienced as an agonizing lack, but as a form of sensory abundance and erotic plenitude that lends itself to fluid and peripatetic forms of identification.

Characterized by a non-hierarchical, non-fetishistic approach to bodies and a polyphonous, deliberately incoherent representation of identity, *No. 4* is, in many ways, a send-up of the Warholian *Screen Test*. The *Screen Tests*, which employed comparably minimalist strategies to frame their famous subjects from the art, literary, and music worlds, tended to freeze their subjects in the embalming silence of Warhol's camera. By depriving his subjects of their voices, and commanding them to remain motionless, Warhol sadistically ratcheted up the movie producer's demand for his stars to distinguish themselves by making a spectacle of their exceptionality. Relieving her famous subjects of the obligation to perform their cultural capital for the camera, Ono demystifies the cult of personality upon which Warhol's work depends.

Though *No. 4* includes the names of countless art world celebrities in its lengthy credits, *Bottoms* parodies the conventions of the traditional portrait by focusing solely on a comically unrecognizable part of her subjects' bodies. By transforming the ass into an image as enthralling and expressive as the face itself, Ono's extensive catalogue of ordinary but startlingly various bottoms celebrates the body as body. In doing so, Ono helps us to imagine a visual pleasure of corporeality not structured by the libidinal economy of patriarchal capitalism.

Contemporary sex manuals

For all of their mutually illuminating parallels, however, Ono's films are ultimately quite different from Warhol's. Unlike the 'cockteaser' Warhol, Ono employed the limits of film structure and duration to invite more participatory forms of eccentric embodiment. The critical distinction between their approaches is made explicit in Ono's *Unrealized Film Script for Film No. 5*, 'A Contemporary Sexual Manual (366 sexual positions)' of 1968, which boasts a cast of three (a woman, a man, and a child):

> The whole film takes place in a bedroom with a large double bed in the center and a window at the foot of the bed. The film is a family scene of a quiet couple and a four year old daughter lying on the bed for the whole night. All they do is just sleep, and the 366 sexual positions are all in the mind of the audience. But this is not Andy Warhol: in a sense this is basically a clean, healthy hetero-sexual scene spared from boredom.[69]

As in many of Ono's conceptual pieces, 'Contemporary Sexual Manual' pivots upon the participant's imagination, which can produce forms of intimacy that cannot always be enacted in the world.[70] Written in 1968, the same year that Warhol fulfilled his own dream of making a film purely about fucking with *Blue Movie*, Ono's 'Contemporary Sexual Manual' retrieves the heterosexual couple from the realm of obsolescence. At a time when heterosexuality and childrear-ing were increasingly regarded by feminists as compulsory mantles that needed to be resisted, Ono demonstrates how modes of artistic and spiritual kinship could redefine the nuclear family. Rejecting a Warholian politics of boredom, Ono proposed supple, more inclusive forms of engagement that do not depend upon the exclusion of women from desire's *mise-en-scène*.

In their most well-known collaborative performance, Yoko Ono and John Lennon publicly enact what could be described as a version of Ono's 'Contem-porary Sexual Manual.' As has been well documented, Ono met John Lennon in 1966 at her show at the Indica Gallery in London. They began to live together in 1968, and married on March 20, 1969. To celebrate their honeymoon, they staged a week long *Bed-In for Peace* at the Amsterdam Hilton, in which they conducted interviews for ten hours a day to protest violence.[71] Like Warhol's *Blue Movie*, Ono and Lennon's *Bed-In* transforms the private bedroom into a public site where resistance to the war could be enacted through corporeal intimacy and discursive interrogation. After the U.S. government prevented them from restaging the *Bed-In* in New York, Ono and Lennon repeated their performance at the Queen Elizabeth Hotel in Montreal in May of 1969, con-ducting more than 60 radio interviews during the process.

Performed at a time when racial hatred against Ono was so common as to seem almost fashionable,[72] the *Bed-In* both invites and deflects prurient curi-osity about the private life of the mixed-race, inter-national, and inter-class couple. Yet like the 'Contemporary Sexual Manual,' the *Bed-In* is a picture of innocence. Afloat on plush white linens and surrounded by white flowers, the couple enacts a 'clean, healthy heterosexual scene' of familial intimacy for the public eye. John wears two-tone white pajamas, Yoko is covered from neck to toe by a floor-length white nightgown with long sleeves and a high collar, and

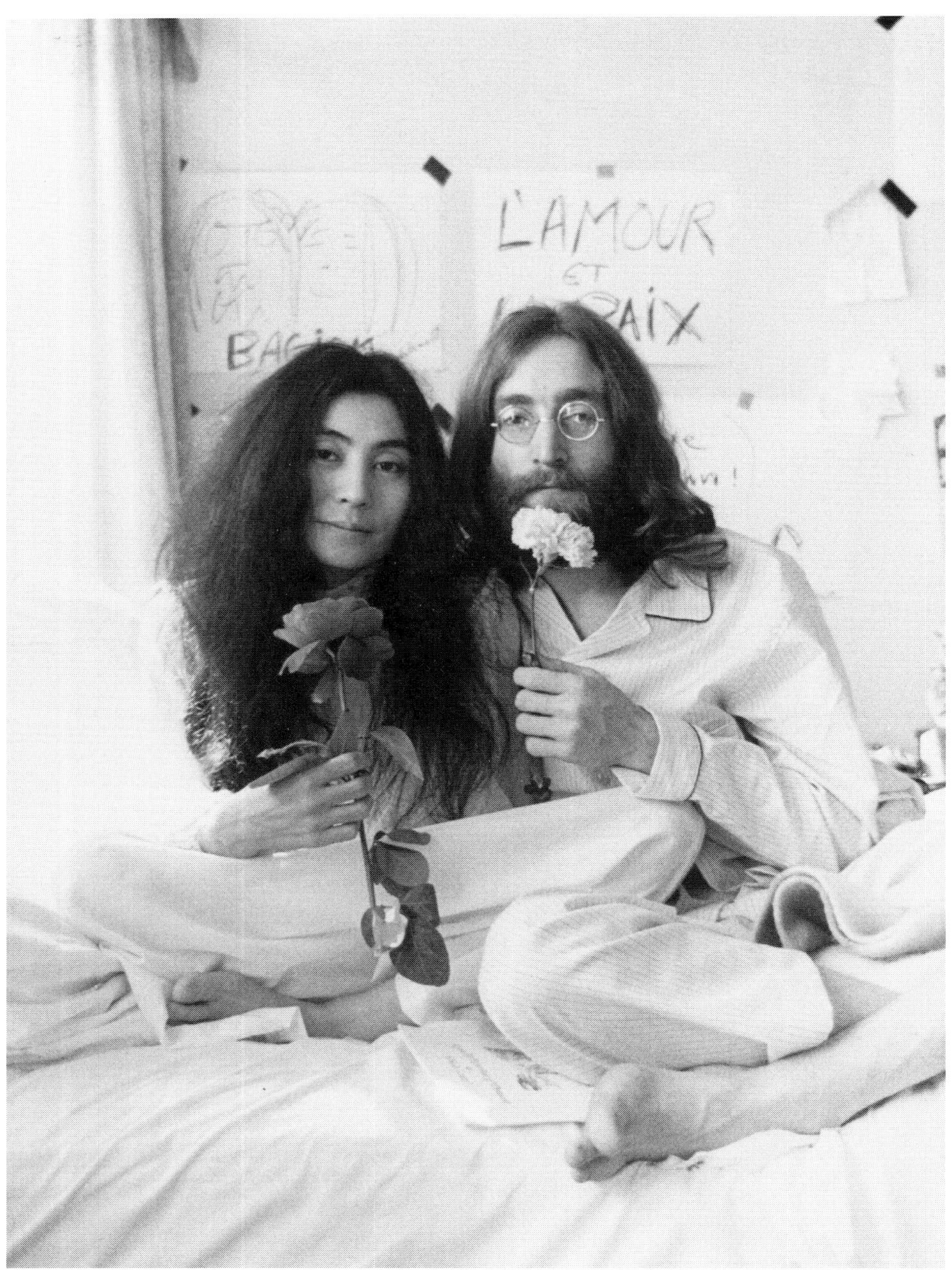

36   Yoko Ono and John Lennon transform their honeymoon suite into a public site where resistance to the war is enacted through interracial intimacy in *Bed-In for Peace*. First performed in Amsterdam and then in Montreal in 1969.

Ono's daughter Kyoko plays between them in her underwear. Journalists crowd around them, jamming cameras and microphones in their faces. As John Lennon recalled, 'Who could forget the sight of half the world's press pushing and trampling each other at the door of our bedroom in the vain hope of seeing the Beatle and his nigger doing it for Peace in the Amsterdam Hilton's Honeymoon suite? Or the sighs of disappointment when it dawned on them that there was to be no sex and we weren't even naked.'[73] By publicizing 'the intimacy of the nuptial bed as a metaphor for cultural transformation'[74] in the midst of the Vietnam War, Ono and Lennon demonstrated how 'white' bodies and 'yellow' bodies might come together in pacifist solidarity, rather than as agents of mutual destruction. Playing on the public's desire to witness the scandal of interracial sex, Ono and Lennon instead model how the bedroom might be used as a space of egalitarian intimacy and non-violent resistance. Returning to the site of the bedroom in their 1970 film *Fly*, Ono and Lennon explore how inter-special intimacy could serve as a model for even more expanded – and troubling – forms of relationality.

Fly (1970)

> Circulation is the secret to freedom and the key to fly.
>
> (Yoko Ono)

Flying was, for Ono, a primary metaphor for freedom. In the mid-1960s, Ono performed 'Fly Piece' as part of her 'Music of the Mind' concerts[75] in Kyoto in 1964,[76] and in London, between 1967 and 1968.[77] For 'Fly Piece,' audience members were invited to 'fly' on stage by jumping off real ladders that Ono had prepared for them or by coming up with alternative ways. Not surprisingly, most people declined to physically participate.[78] For as anyone who has woken from a dream of soaring to the disappointing heaviness of one's earthbound body knows, flying can be difficult. Just look at the wreck made by Ilya Kabakov's *The Man Who Flew into Space from His Apartment* (1984).

In order to ease the transition from land to air, Ono composed the following instructions.

> How to Fly
> 1) Make sure that your mind is not clogged with heavy burdens such as: resentment, anger, secrets and the past. They can be heavy.
> 2) Make sure that your body is not clogged with excess fat and excrements.
> 3) Make sure that your wings are light and free. This is the most difficult proposition. Your wings cannot be free unless the whole world is free, because you are part of the world. However, there is a way for the whole world to be free. Just like your body, all it needs is to be unclogged and have good

circulation. Circulation is the secret to freedom and the key to fly.

4)   When the whole world is in good circulation we will all fly together.

5)   Meanwhile, give wings to things around you so they will circulate.[79]

If flying was, for Ono, a method of improved circulation, in which the burdens of the earthbound world could be temporarily suspended, then it was also an explicitly feminist form of institutional critique. Flies and flying were the subject of an unauthorized exhibition Ono arranged for herself at New York's Museum of Modern Art in December 1971, the same year art historian Linda Nochlin published her groundbreaking feminist essay, 'Why Have There Been No Great Women Artists?'[80] For the event, Ono filled a large glass container with flies. She then placed this container, which was 'equal in volume to her own body and sponged with the perfume she typically used,' in the center of the museum's garden and opened the lid. Participants were invited to join the artist in following the trajectory of the fly, a task supposedly made possible by the distinct odor of the flies.[81]

In 1968, Yoko Ono penned the following instructions for *Fly* (a.k.a. *Film No. 13*): 'Let a fly walk on a woman's body from toe to head and fly out of the window.'[82] Shot over two frigid days in the middle of December 1969 in a Bowery loft, *Fly* turned into a twenty-five-minute color, sound film in which the proverbial 'fly on the wall' of direct cinema abandoned its supposedly objective perch and descended upon the body of a supine, nude woman, played by actress Virginia Lust. Ono's own corporeality manifests in the film's vocal soundtrack, which she composed and performed by imagining herself as the fly, a sympathetic, implicitly female personality whose movements match the extreme gradations of the author's voice.

As it turned out, the project was more difficult to execute than Ono's minimal instructions suggest. According to cinematographer Steve Gebhardt, Lust was knocked out on heroin during the forty straight hours it took to shoot the film so that she would remain perfectly still while the two of them filmed flies on 'every imaginable part of her body.'[83] Although numerous 'gophers' had tried and failed to obtain enough flies for the film's production from the basement cellar of a Horn & Hardart automat restaurant on 23rd Street in New York's Chelsea neighborhood, the flies were eventually purchased, in jars of 100, from a scientific lab on Long Island. But the problem with flies is that the minute you open the vat, they fly away. In order to be able to shoot them on the body, Gebhardt and his partner Bob Fries attempted to paint Lust's body with a sugar water mixture to attract the insects to her skin. When this failed, they decided 'out of necessity' to 'compromise' the flies through the use of chemical warfare by stunning them with carbon dioxide – which either temporarily knocked them out or killed them. Working quickly, Gebhardt and Fries placed the gas-stunned survivors on various parts of Lust's body and filmed them as they were awakening. Learning this, I can't help but picture the absurd cruelty of an army of insect slaves, bumping into each other in the trenches of the art world. To think what a fly must go through just to meet a Beatle! Though many flies died in the process, Gebhardt and Fries were eventually able to film enough coming back to life to acquire the necessary footage.

Fly begins with a hazy image of a pale color field, accompanied by the mellifluous sound of a human voice singing, sighing, and humming. Soon the camera pans, a fly comes into focus, and the recorded sound becomes shrill and mercurial. A fly perches nonchalantly on human flesh. Shot in almost scientific close-up with a sophisticated Macro-Kilar lens,[84] the finespun body of an ordinary housefly becomes a magnificent kinetic sculpture. Rubbing its front legs together fastidiously, it produces a symphony of motion whose tenor is echoed by Ono's fitful vocals. At first, it is unclear what parts of the body are being shown, as the camera's extreme close-ups transform the flesh into otherworldly landscapes. Gentle folds and creases suggest corporeality but refuse to indicate anatomical specificity. The first recognizable body part that comes into view is a cluster of meaty toes whose momentary appearance quickly transfers our sense of place from Mars to the morgue. Though immobile, this cadaverous foot carries us to the site of death, whose macabre aura will henceforth dialogue with the sensuality evoked by Ono's images of inter-special congress.

Beauty returns in the image of the female flank silhouetted against a pale blue ground. Here is the apotheosis of the body as exquisite terrain, safely aestheticized. A few moments later, however, the pubis appears, its sudden shock of frizzled hair disrupting the marble line of flesh. This image is followed abruptly by a frontal, close-up shot of a woman's crotch, her parted legs exposing what Gustave Courbet had called *l'origine du monde*, but what then-contemporary audiences might have less poetically described as 'a beaver.' As Ono's voice raises to a pitch alarming enough to send my dog scurrying under the covers in a fit of whimpers, I catch sight of the fly perched on the woman's vaginal lips, its dark, tiny body nearly obscured by the wool of her labia. Ono's voice careens in an acoustic rendering of what is presumably the teeny trespasser's sensorial bliss. And then, seemingly in response to this 'innocent' but nonetheless startling transgression, her vagina subtly but visibly clenches, the stillness of the geographic body ruptured by the seismic volition of cognizant flesh. *So she is not quite dead after all*, I have remarked in my notes. Later, when the fly tarries over the woman's lips, they too tremble. Given the woman's sedation, these reflexive, involuntary gestures startle. Falling beyond the purview of conscious control, these kinetic traces of pure feeling seem revelatory. It is no wonder that early film theorist Béla Balázs considered involuntary spasms guarantors of authenticity capable of revealing the 'hidden life of little things.'[85]

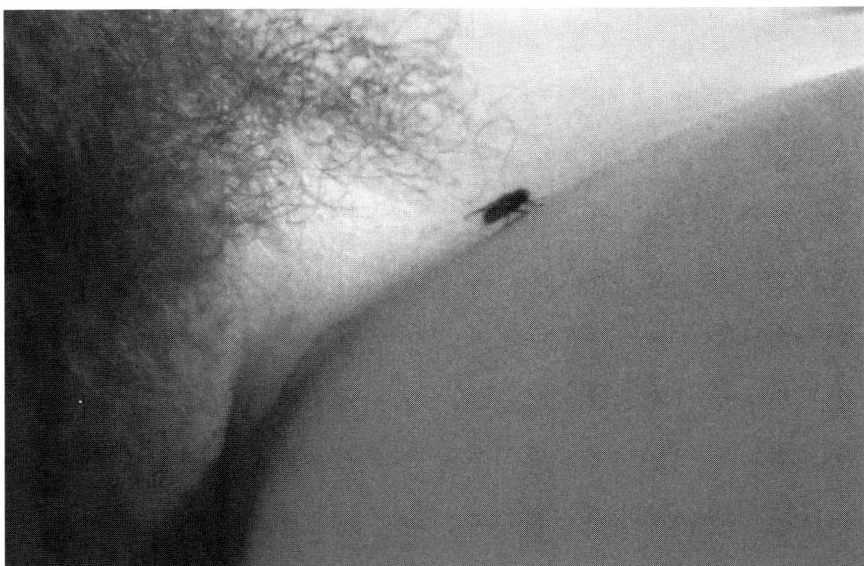

37   Though the fly does not distinguish between human genitals and other parts of the corporeal terrain upon which it crawls, spectators of Yoko Ono's film *Fly* (1970) tend to experience these distinctions quite viscerally.

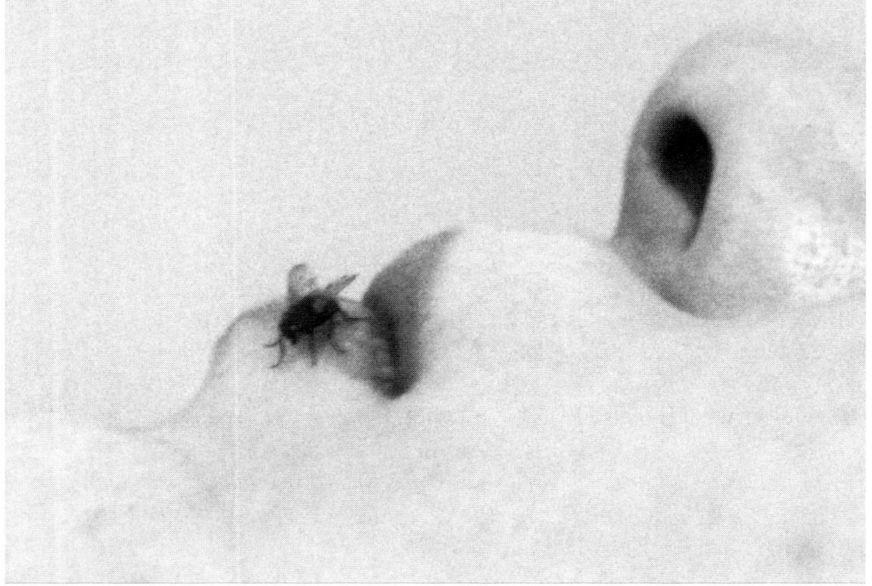

38   The slightest shudder in response to the fly's caress indicates that the otherwise motionless woman in Yoko Ono's *Fly* (1970) is indeed alive. But is she conscious?

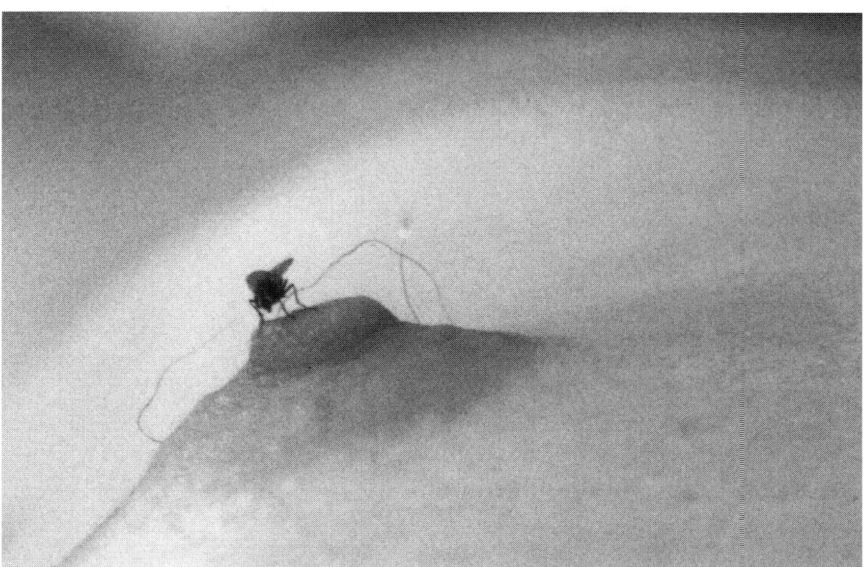

Shot in scientific close-up to capture the intricacies of both human and animal flesh,   **39**
Fly (Yoko Ono, 1970) nonetheless abrogates the viewer's desire for visual mastery.

By showing the fly crawling across intimate regions of the body known for acute sensitivity to touch and pressure, Ono makes it impossible for the spectator to remain oblivious to the vitality of the terrain the insect traverses. Though the fly remains indifferent to the significance of the genitals and other hypersensitive erogenous membranes, the spectator cannot help but respond corporeally to its exploration of these privileged regions. Considering the nearly universal cultural emphasis on the genitals, it is no surprise that these moments are among the film's most visceral. When watching the film, it is difficult to suspend one's learned sexual and psychological hierarchies. Thus, when the fly nonchalantly moors on the woman's nipple – a pink mesa encircled by a decadent thread of hair – or penetrates the inviolable crevice between her legs, it seems more intrusive than when the fly explores neutral zones of the body. For as much as breasts may resemble sloping hills, the fly's journey reminds the viewer what it feels like to be touched – how even the slightest weight and movement on the skin can be pleasurable, ticklish, painful, arousing, or unbearable. Whether we are repulsed, titillated, or affronted, we are *moved* by these images. Watching *Fly*, our skin crawls.

Yet while the fly's dispassionate investigation of the genitals confronts us with our own culturally conditioned anxieties, then the very fact of its meandering sets us free. If the rhythms of pornography are determined in part by vigorous thrust and rush to climax, then the temporality of *Fly* is appropriately that of the crawl. Like Roland Barthes's amorous reader, we linger, entranced by the pleasures of the corporeal text: the filigree of the fly's delicate armature, the variable textures of even this most porcelain skin, the luxurious curtain that lashes the human eye. Unlike more conventional examples of 'body genres,' which typically subsume all ancillary corporeal sensations to some type of orgasmic climax – be it the ubiquitous 'money shot' of hard-core pornography or the explosive bloodletting of the slasher film[86] – in *Fly*, we become exquisitely attuned to other particularities of bodyhood – the woman's, the fly's, and our own. The camera may follow the random trajectory of the fly, but each viewer responds individually and idiosyncratically to the various legs of the fly's journey. In this way, the fly affectively maps our own secret spots, the specificity of the viewer's own body dictating the sensory charge of each encounter.

Inching slowly across the topography of flesh, the fly proves itself the consummate lover. Rather than rapidly traversing reproductively irrelevant parts of the body in a rush towards genital penetration, Ono's fly is polymorphous perverse. Indifferent to the territorialization of the body and its incumbent symbolization, the fly explores the body in all of its perceptible richness. For the first fifteen minutes of the film, Ono presents us with what Giles Deleuze and Félix Guattari, following Antonin Artaud, famously described as a 'body without organs.'[87] In place of the Freudian model, which subsumes desire under a set of binary choices and binds anatomy to destiny, the 'body without organs' provides 'a model of desire as pure, self-begetting positivity untrammeled by lack or absence.'[88] Moving freely across the flesh, the fly's haptic journey across the flesh un-structures and disorganizes the body, thereby increasing its intensity. According to critic Amos Vogel, who saw the film with Ono and Lennon when it premiered at Cannes in 1971, the effect of *Fly* was 'hypnotic.' 'The audience sat transfixed at this juxtaposition of predatory animal and beautiful body, with neither party performing according to rules and thereby disrupting the reality game.'[89]

Following the fly, the camera abjures its usually scopophilic relation to the female body. For the film's gaze is not, *at least not yet*, intent on surveying or sexually objectifying the body from afar. Rather, the nearly tactile proximity of the lens to the body on display, as well as the trembling, erratic inclination of the handheld camera, privileges a haptic model of looking. Fostering an erotic, but non-fetishistic relation to the image, Ono invites us to become the fly, and thereby liberate ourselves from identifying with either the subject or object of the oppressive male gaze. Through the 'untutored' eye[90] of the insect, the body's symbolic value slips away.

Yet around fifteen minutes into *Fly*, the tone of the film changes. Notes of electronic music become interspersed with the organic yowl of Ono's voice. This more explicit reference to cinema as a mechanical apparatus serves to remind the viewer that the encounter between the woman and the fly has been mediated all along. Oddly, it is only at this moment when I register the non-vocal music that I am shocked that I am no longer 'alone' with this woman. But of course I have never been! The sudden interruption of non-diegetic music transforms this private encounter into a public one. Like the orchestral swell that announces the imminence of a Hollywood kiss, the machine-made music interpellates the participant as that particularly Pavlovian creature, the moviegoer.

Emerging details of the film's sparse *mise-en-scène* contribute to the increasing sense of threat that permeates the rest of the film. The brief sight of silver nail polish on the woman's fingers and toes transforms her nudity – classical, idealized – into nakedness.[91] Until now, nothing was visible that was not intrinsic to their bodies. Nail polish particularizes the woman as a historical subject, implicating the viewer in an act of looking that can never be neutral. This is not *anybody*, a body without organs, but *somebody*, a human subject living in a particular time and place. This forensically dense detail evidences the world *out there*, thereby interrupting the film's free play of intensity and instantly restructuring the flesh into an over-determined set of signifiers.

On its way to becoming a cadaver, the woman first becomes a victim. She is no longer any woman, but a certain *kind* of woman. The kind of woman who wears silver nail polish. The kind of woman who might be raped and discarded. The kind of woman whose corporeal details will be itemized and anatomized by a criminal institution that regards her as just another Jane Doe. What Roland Barthes has described as the 'punctum' arrives in the guise of 'studium' and knocks me out cold.[92]

Around the nineteen-minute mark, the camera begins to pull back, revealing larger swathes of the human body in a montage of shots taken from different angles and distances. To our horror, we suddenly see *two* flies, conferencing together on the woman's abdomen like a pair of co-conspirators. The shock of their revelation can only be compared to the nauseating sense of betrayal when one first realizes that one's lover has taken another. But it doesn't stay a threesome for long. As the shots become wider, our love affair becomes an orgy. Three, four, five, six flies are seen cavorting on the woman's exposed body, which suddenly, in the words of Chrissie Iles, appears 'corpselike and repellant.'[93] The camera, as it turns out, has not been following a single explorer but a platoon of necrophilic offenders. After a montage of partial views, the camera finally reveals the entirety of the woman, lying spread-eagled on a mattress in a bare room with a single, open window. Perfectly still, and covered in vermin, she suddenly seems the victim of sexual assault. As in Ana Mendieta's 1973 performance piece, *Rape Scene*, the appearance of (previously invisible) props like the bed and open window narrativize the woman, placing her mute, naked body in a chamber play of patriarchal violence. This isn't a movie; it's a crime scene. Or perhaps, like Ono's film *Rape*, it is both. No longer identifying with the fly as the agent of our own inquisitive exploration, the spectator becomes complicit with a patriarchal order that perversely insists, with Edgar Allen Poe, on the beauty of violated women.

As Iles has argued, with the change in the camera's point of view, 'the viewer's attitude toward the fly shifts from identification and empathy to disgust.'[94] The horizontality of the woman's recumbent body renders her abject; like the corpse, the woman appears 'removed from the (vertical) province of the human.'[95] Although the fly's encounter with the woman had seemed symbiotic, when the camera draws back, the flies appear parasitic, signaling filth and decay. 'The voyeuristic low-angle camera shot of the woman's impassive naked body lying on the mattress, the pubic region suddenly prominent, hands the fly's (Ono's) enjoyment of the female body over to an invisible male oppressor.'[96]

As the shot widens, the film's mode of address metamorphoses from a 'haptic' to an 'optic' image. Feminist film theorists from the 1970s, including Laura Mulvey, argued that the cinematic partition of the body was material evidence of the violent, scopophilic drive that animated mainstream cinema. Again, one must only remember the infamous shower scene in Alfred Hitchcock's *Psycho* to recall how often the sadism of Hollywood's male gaze comes in the form of

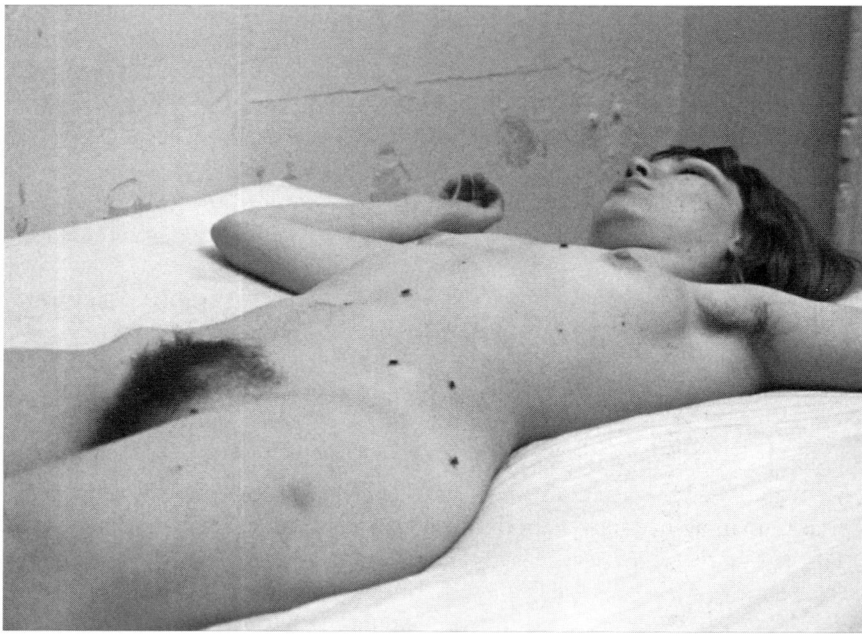

40   Around nineteen minutes into *Fly* (Yoko Ono, 1970) the film cuts to wider images of actress Virginia Lust's body. Splayed out on a bed in an empty room, and photographed from above, the representation of the woman changes from a sensorily rich 'haptic' image to an objectifying 'optic' image.

the cut, which assimilates the splice of celluloid to the incision of female flesh. Contrary to this tendency, however, here it is the sight of the woman's entire body that initiates the sense of violation. When portrayed as an assortment of corporeal fragments – a body without organs – the body seemed safe from scopic violence. Yet as the focus of the film changes from part to whole object, hierarchies that had been suspended are re-implanted. Woman, it turns out, is more than the sum of her parts; her body cannot be divorced from relations of power. When recomposed, she turns into a passive, lifeless object, and the typical quandary of the female spectator returns. If this is the point of the film, it is a cynical one.

Iles's interpretation of the film's abrupt switch in tone is apt. However, what is not often mentioned in criticism of the film is its ending. The film, after all, does *not* conclude with the sight of the woman's motionless body, and the spectator paralyzed between sadistic complicity and masochistic identification. The last few shots of the film are significant. After a wide-angle shot that shows a sliver of the woman's body on the bed, the film cuts to a close-up of her limp hand. Two flies alight upon its slack fingers, swathed in a brume of bluish light. And then, in a crucial gesture, the focus racks: The hand becomes a mere blur in the foreground while the background comes into view as the outline of a brick building at dusk. The camera lingers on the image long enough for the viewer to note the ornamental brickwork before it pans to the right, revealing more silhouetted structures against an early evening sky. For anyone who has lived in a modern metropolis, this crepuscular city scene is a familiar one; the roof-tops of the buildings just across the way suggest the nearby presence of other voices and other rooms, in spite of the fact that the film has gone temporarily, eerily mute. After this brief pause, it comes as a relief when the fly resumes its melody. The camera pans up as the last building drops out of view. For a few glorious moments, we float weightlessly in the periwinkle firmament. And then, as abruptly as it appeared, the image vanishes.

This ending reminds us that *Fly* is a *double entendre*, referring simultaneously to the winged insect and the act of soaring. This duality is essential to understanding the film. For unlike Ono and Lennon's film *Rape*, which relentlessly insists upon the complicity of viewers with the violent apparatus of cinema, *Fly* permits the viewer to float and flutter amongst various identifications. We are, as Ono imagined herself, both the fly *and* the woman and, simultaneously, neither of them. Owing to the film's disorienting camerawork, as well as Ono's capricious vocals, these identifications remain mobile and unfixed. Ono employs the visual and aural instrument of cinema not to survey and record, but as a conduit to the tactile. Addressed as haptical rather than optical beings, we are touched by the skin of the film. Watching *Fly*, my body is suspended in pure sensation. I am no longer male or female, human or animal, but flesh itself, magnificently feeling.

When normative power relations are suspended, as they are in *Fly*, it is impossible to distinguish the toucher from the touched. For whether she is conscious or not, the woman touches the fly as much as the fly touches the woman. Perceiving this haptic encounter, we identify not with the initiating agent, but with the point of contact, with touch itself. Yet by the end of the film, the stakes have changed. The image of an entire subject, rather than an intensified continuum of flesh, returns us to the prison house of patriarchy, in which woman is, as Ono observed, 'the nigger of the world.'[97] But how to extricate oneself from this predicament?

In her essay, 'The Feminization of Society,' published in 1971, Ono responds to this crisis. Her strategy involves turning the myth of female passivity against the oppressor. 'Active passivity' employs the semiotics of vulnerability as a form of resistance. In *Fly*, this strategy is first mobilized by linguistic play. After all, 'fly' not only denotes the film's eponymous insect, but an imperative to take wing. Throughout most of the film, the first definition predominates; the insect is the focus of our attention. Yet at the very end of the film, Ono turns the noun designated by the title back into a verb, inviting us to soar beyond the crisis of gendered spectatorship and oppressive power relations. Having sated itself on the flesh of the body, the fly sails through the window and departs the scene. By taking wing with the fly, we release ourselves from the dynamic of sadomasochistic identification, the impossible dilemma of being this woman or violently surveying her. This is Ono's lesson in circulation: she is teaching us how to unburden ourselves by practicing eccentric forms of embodiment. Out the window and away we go.

Notes

1   David Sheff, introduction to section 17 of *The Playboy Interviews with John Lennon and Yoko Ono*, ed. G. Barry Golson (New York: Playboy Press, 1981), p. 96.
2   Kristine Stiles, 'Unbosoming Lennon: The Politics of Yoko Ono's Experience,' *Art Criticism*, 7, no. 2 (1992), pp. 21–54; p. 22.
3   Ibid., p. 39.
4   Amelia Jones, *Body Art/Performing the Subject* (Minneapolis, MN: University of Minnesota Press, 1998), pp. 3–5.
5   Stiles, 'Unbosoming Lennon,' p. 29.
6   Midori Yoshimoto, *Into Performance: Japanese Women Artists in New York* (New Brunswick, NJ: Rutgers University Press, 2005), p. 101. Yoshimoto reports that: 'In later performances of *Cut Piece*, she [Ono] held a scrolled poster with the words, "My body is the scar of my mind."'
7   The first two performances took place in Kyoto and Tokyo in July and August 1964. The third performance was presented at Carnegie Recital Hall in New York City in March 1965. The fourth and fifth performances were offered as part of the

Destruction in Art Symposium presentation of Two Evenings with Yoko Ono at the Africa Centre in London in September 1966.

8   Jones, *Body Art*, pp. 1–9.

9   Ibid., p. 86.

10   Ibid., p. 89.

11   Kaja Silverman, 'Suture', in *The Subject of Semiotics* (Oxford: Oxford University Press, 1984), pp. 194–236; Kaja Silverman, 'Lost Objects and Mistaken Subjects: A Prologue', in *The Acoustic Mirror: The Female Voice in Psychoanalysis and Cinema* (Bloomington, IN: Indiana University Press, 1988), pp. 1–41.

12   Jones, *Body Art*, p. 89.

13   Ibid., p. 166.

14   Yoko Ono, 'If I Don't Give Birth Now, I Will Never Be Able To', in *Just Me! The Very First Autobiographical Essay by the World's Most Famous Japanese Woman* (Tokyo: Kodansha International, 1986), pp. 34–36, quoted in Kevin Concannon, 'Yoko Ono's CUT PIECE: From Text to Performance and Back Again', *PAJ: A Journal of Performance and Art*, 30, (September 2008), pp. 81–93, http://imaginepeace. com/archives/2680 (accessed on 14 August, 2013).

15   Yoko Ono, 'Statement', *Village Voice*, October 7, 1971, p. 20.

16   Kristine Stiles, 'Cut Piece, 1964', in *Yes Yoko Ono* (New York: Japan Society; New York: Harry N. Abrams, 2000), pp. 158–159: p. 158.

17   Anthony White, 'Spatial Concept: 'The Holes', 1949–1953', in *Lucio Fontana: Between Utopia and Kitsch* (Cambridge, MA: The MIT Press, October Books, 2011).

18   Shinichiro Osaki, 'Body and Place: Action in Postwar Art in Japan', *Out of Actions: Between Performance and the Object 1949–1979*, ed. Paul Schimmel (London: Thames & Hudson, 1998), pp. 121–157.

19   Jones, *Body Art*, p. 166.

20   Walter Benjamin, 'The Work of Art in the Age of Mechanical Reproduction', *Illuminations: Essays and Reflections* trans. Harry Zohn, ed. Hannah Arendt (New York: Schocken Books, 1968), p. 222–224 .

21   Gustave LeBon, *Psychologie des foules* (Paris: Alcan, 1895); Sigmund Freud, *Group Psychology and the Analysis of the Ego*, trans. James Strachey (London: The International Psycho-Analytical Press, 1922); Wilhelm Reich, *The Mass Psychology of Fascism*, trans. Theodore P. Wolf (New York: Orgone Institute Press, 1946).

22   Joan Hawkins, 'Exploitation Meets Direct Cinema: Yoko Ono's *Rape* and the Trash Cinema of Michael and Roberta Findlay', *Cutting Edge: Art-Horror and the Horrific Avant-Garde* (Minneapolis, MN: University of Minnesota Press, 2000), pp. 117–140.

23   Yoko Ono, 'FILM SCRIPT 3', in *Grapefruit: A Book of Instructions and Drawings by Yoko Ono*, intro. John Lennon (New York: Simon & Schuster, 2000; Tokyo: Wunternaum Press, 1964), section 6.

24   Melanie Klein, 'The Psychological Principles of Infant Analysis' [1926] and 'A Contribution to the Psychogenesis of Manic-Depressive States' [1935], in *The Selected Melanie Klein*, ed. Juliet Mitchell (New York: The Free Press, 1986), pp. 57–68, pp. 115–145.

25 Walter Benjamin, 'Theses on the Philosophy of History', in *Illuminations*, p. 255.

26 Ibid., pp. 262–263.

27 Stiles, 'Cut Piece, 1964,' p. 158.

28 This event occurred when Ono performed *Cut Piece* in London in 1966 as part of the three day Destruction in Art Symposium (DIAS). Brenda Jordan, 'DIAS,' *Resurgence* 1, no. 4 (1966), pp. 18–21, quoted in Yoshimoto, *Into Performance*, p. 107.

29 Yoko Ono, 'On Film No. 4 (in taking the bottoms of 365 saints of our time)', in *Grapefruit*, section 9.

30 Martin Gansberg, 'Thirty Eight Who Saw Murder Didn't Call the Police,' *New York Times*, March 27, 1964.

31 John Darley and Bibb Latané, 'Bystander Intervention in Emergencies: Diffusion of Responsibility,' *Journal of Personality and Social Psychology*, 8, no. 4 (April 1968), pp. 377–383; Carrie Rentschler, 'An Urban Physiognomy of the 1964 Kitty Genovese Murder', *Space & Culture* 14, no. 3 (August 2011), pp. 310–329; Carrie Rentschler, 'The Physiognomic Turn', *International Journal of Communication* 4 (2010), pp. 1–6.

32 Hal Foster, *The Return of the Real: The Avant-Garde at the End of the Century* (Cambridge, MA: The MIT Press, 1996), pp. 152–168.

33 Roland Barthes, *Camera Lucida: Reflections on Photography*, 1st American ed. (New York: Hill and Wang, 1981), p. 25. Barthes describes the 'punctum' of an image as the contingent, unintentional detail that stings, pricks, or punctures the viewer.

34 Stiles, 'Unbosoming Lennon,' p. 35.

35 Jones, *Body Art*, p. 195.

36 Ibid., pp. 151–195 (pp. 153, 153–164, 299 n.5); Craig Owens, 'The Medusa Effect; or, The Spectacular Ruse,' in *Beyond Recognition: Representation, Power, and Culture*, ed. Scott Bryson et al. (Los Angeles, CA: University of California Press, 1992), p. 192.

37 Owens, 'The Medusa Effect,' p. 198.

38 Richard Dyer, *White* (New York: Routledge, 1997), chap. 2.

39 John Lennon, 'The Ballad of John and Yoko,' *Skywriting by Word of Mouth And Other Writing, Including The Ballad of John and Yoko* (New York: Harper Perennial, 1996), p. 15.

40 Joseph Jonghyun Jeon, *Racial Things, Racial Forms: Objecthood in Avant-Garde Asian American Poetry* (Iowa City: University of Iowa Press, 2012), p. 144.

41 Celine Parreñas Shimizu, *The Hypersexuality of Race: Performing Asian/American Women on Screen and on Scene* (Durham, NC: Duke University Press, 2007); Jeon, *Racial Things*, pp. xvi–xvii, 144–148, 151–152, 184 n.5.

42 Jeon, *Racial Things*, p. xvii.

43 Carrie A. Rentschler, *Second Wounds: Victims' Rights and the Media in the U.S.* (Durham, NC: Duke University Press, 2011), pp. 4–5; Mary Ann Zielonko, 'Remembering Kitty Genovese,' an interview by *Sound Portraits.org*, broadcast with introduction by Scott Simon, *Weekend Edition*, Saturday, March 13, 2004, www.soundportraits.org/on-air/remembering_kitty_genovese (accessed on August 14, 2013).

44 Amelia Jones, *Seeing Differently: A History and Theory of Identification in the Visual Arts* (New York: Routledge, 2012).

45 Irwin Unger, 'Vietnam and Its Opponents,' in *The Sixties* (Boston, MA: Prentice Hall, 2011), pp. 70–87.

46 Unger, *The Sixties*, pp. 16–23.

47 David Halberstam, *The Making of a Quagmire* (New York: Random House, 1965), p. 211.

48 Seth Jacobs, *Cold War Mandarin: Ngo Dinh Diem and the Origins of America's War in Vietnam, 1950–1963* (Lanham, MD: Rowman & Littlefield, 2006), p. 149.

49 William Prochnau, *Once upon a Distant War* (New York: Times Books, 1995), p. 309.

50 Kareem Fahim, 'Slap to a Man's Pride Set Off Tumult in Tunisia,' *The New York Times*, January 21, 2011.

51 Owens, 'The Medusa Effect,' p. 198.

52 Jones, *Body Art*, p. 157.

53 Ibid., pp. 122–123, pp. 152–153; Crimp, *Our Kind of Movie*, pp. 20–36.

54 Nhị Tường, *Tiểu Sử Bồ Tát Thích Quảng Đức* (Fawker: Quang Duc Monastery, 2005), www.quangduc.com/BoTatQuangDuc/09tieusu.html (accessed on August 20, 2007).

55 Roger Perry and Tony Elliott, 'Yoko Ono,' *Unit* (December 1967), pp. 26–27, quoted in Concannon, 'Yoko Ono's CUT PIECE,' p. 88.

56 Concannon, 'Yoko Ono's CUT PIECE,' p. 89.

57 P. Adams Sitney, 'Structural Film,' in *Visionary Film: The American Avant-Garde 1943–2000*, 3rd ed. (Oxford: Oxford University Press, 2002), pp. 347–370. Sitney cites Warhol as a precursor to structural film, but never mentions Ono in the book.

58 Sally Banes, *Greenwich Village 1963: Avant-Garde Performance and the Effervescent Body* (Durham, NC: Duke University Press, 1993), p. 60.

59 Ken Friedman, 'Explaining Fluxus,' *White Walls* 16 (Spring 1987), pp. 12–29; p. 17.

60 Jon Hendricks, ed. *Fluxus Etc.: The Gilbert and Lila Silverman Collection* (New York: Ink &, 1983; Pasadena: Baxter Art Gallery, 1983).

61 Banes, *Greenwich Village 1963*, p. 61.

62 Ibid., p. 202.

63 Ibid., p. 61.

64 Chrissie Iles, 'Erotic Conceptualism: The Films of Yoko Ono', in *Yes Yoko Ono*, p. 202.

65 Herbert Marcuse, *Eros and Civilization: A Philosophical Inquiry into Freud* (Abingdon: Routledge, 1998), p. 201.

66 Iles, 'Erotic Conceptualism,' p. 203.

67 Scott MacDonald, 'Yoko Ono: *No. 4 (Bottoms)*', in *Avant-Garde Film Motion Studies* (Cambridge: Cambridge University Press, 1993), pp. 19–27.

68 Linda Williams, 'Film Body: An Implantation of Perversions', in *Narrative, Apparatus, Ideology: A Film Theory Reader*, ed. Philip Rosen (New York: Columbia University Press, 1986), pp. 198–209.

69 Yoko Ono, *Yoko Ono: Arias and Objects*, ed. Barbara Haskell and John G. Hanhardt (Salt Lake City, UT: Gibbs Smith, 1991), p. 102.

70 Ono's daughter Kyoko (with her second husband, the American musician Anthony Cox) had been born in 1963 and would have been around four or five years old at the time Ono wrote the instructions for the piece. After Cox and Ono's separation, a bitter legal battle ensued and Ono was awarded full custody. Kyoko was kidnapped by Cox in 1971 and did not resume relations with Ono until 1994.

71 Stiles, 'Unbosoming Lennon,' p. 37.

72 Jeon, *Racial Things*, pp. 143–162; p. 145.

73 Lennon, *Skywriting by Word of Mouth*, p. 21.

74 Kristine Stiles, '*Bed In*, 1969', in *Yes Yoko Ono*, p. 172.

75 Barabara Haskell and John G. Hanhardt, 'Music of the Mind', in Ono, *Arias and Objects*, p. 48.

76 Midori Yoshimoto, '*!*, 1964', in *Yes Yoko Ono*, p. 156; Ono, 'Fly Piece,' in *Grapefruit*, section titled 'INFORMATION.'

77 Ono, *Arias and Objects*, p. 87.

78 Yoshimoto, '*!*, 1964', p. 156.

79 Ono, *Arias and Objects*, p. 85.

80 Linda Nochlin, 'Why Have There Been No Great Women Artists?,' *ARTnews*, 69 (January 1971), pp. 22–39.

81 Kevin Concannon, 'Museum of Modern [F]art', *Yes Yoko Ono*, p. 194.

82 Ono, *Arias and Objects*, p. 87.

83 Steve Gebhardt, telephone conversation with the author, January 5, 2012.

84 Ibid.

85 Béla Balázs, *Theory of the Film: Character and Growth of a New Art* (New York: Dover, 1970), pp. 54–55, 57.

86 Linda Williams, 'Film Bodies: Gender, Genre, and Excess', in *Film Genre Reader II*, ed. Barry Keith Grant (Austin, TX: University of Texas Press, 1995), pp. 141–159; p. 142.

87 Elena del Río, 'Choreographies of Affect', in *Deleuze and the Cinemas of Performance: Powers of Affection* (Edinburgh: Edinburgh University Press, 2008), pp. 67–112.

88 Gilles Deleuze and Félix Guattari, *Anti-Oedipus*, trans. Robert Hurley, Mark Seem, and Helen R. Lane (Minneapolis, MN: University of Minnesota Press, 1983), p. 26; and del Río, *Deleuze and the Cinemas of Performance*, p. 69.

89 Amos Vogel, '"I made a glass hammer": John and Yoko at Cannes', *The Village Voice*, June 24, 1971.

90 Stan Brakhage, 'Metaphors on Vision', in *The Essential Brakhage: Selected Writings on Filmmaking*, ed. Bruce McPherson (Kingston, NY: McPherson & Company / Documentext, 2001), p. 12.

91 Kenneth Clark, *The Nude: A Study in Ideal Form* (New York: Pantheon, 1956); cited in John Berger, *Ways of Seeing* (London: British Broadcasting Corporation and Penguin Books, 1972), pp. 45–64.

92 Barthes, *Camera Lucida*, pp. 25–28. Barthes describes the 'studium' as the cultural information embedded in every image.

93   Iles, 'Erotic Conceptualism', p. 205.

94   Ibid.

95   Jones, *Body Art*, p. 191. Jones uses this phrase to describe a photograph from Hannah Wilke's series *Intra Venus* (c. 1992–1993).

96   Iles, 'Erotic Conceptualism', 205.

97   Yoko Ono and John Lennon, 'Woman is the Nigger of the World.' Song included on *Some Time in New York City*, 1972.

Paul Sharits,
beyond the pleasure principle

destroy destroy destroy destroy distraught distraught distraught his straw his straw his stroll this girl this girl this girl his scrod his droll his stroll its drill his girl his girl his girl has dropped his scrod his straw his straw he stroy he stroy this girl had dropped his straw his draws his draws this girl has cut off his straw this girl was cut off his straw his straw his scroll his scraw his scraw this girl has stirred up his skull his skull its throw its throw up its throw up its throw up
(A fragment of what I heard when listening to the soundtrack of
Paul Sharits's *T,O,U,C,H,I,N,G*)

I have always struggled to find the right words to describe the cinema of Paul Sharits. Maybe that is because, as Sharits wrote to Stan Brakhage, 'words are ass-holes.'[1] Witness, or rather listen to, what happens to the word 'destroy' when it is repeated over and over again on the soundtrack of Sharits's 1968 film *T,O,U,C,H,I,N,G*. Like assholes, words are the site where meaning is turned into shit. As we fumble our way through the acoustic scene of the crime, the imperative 'Destroy!' swerves from its linguistic function and metamorphoses into semantic debris. Repetition destroys the listener's ability to distinguish between sounds, as well as the word's capacity to signify consistently. Yet this detonation also opens the listener up to the evocative associations generated by the 'signifying chains'[2] of the unconscious: 'this girl has cut off his straw this girl was cut off his straw his straw his scroll his scraw his scraw this girl has stirred up his skull his skull its throw its throw up.' Watching and listening to Sharits's films, we are moved into a perceptual zone beyond normative itera-tion and representation. Welcome to the place where words, like orifices and eyeballs, get fucked.

Violently confronting us with what we have been 'trained to ignore,'[3] Sharits staged his cinematic revolution at the level of the film frame, concentrating on the relationship between the materiality of celluloid and the process of projec-tion. Best known as a pioneer of 'flicker' films, in which pulsating flashes of color and/or black-and-white frames disrupt the illusion of continuous on-screen motion and create uncanny optical effects for the viewer, Sharits explodes the conventional grammar of cinema. Mining the potential of the flickering frame to wreak havoc on the perceptual apparatus of the human body, Sharits dismembers cinema and besieges the spectator. Designed to expand our capacity for perception, Sharits's films produce hallucinogenic, often startling effects of color, sound, and light that convulse the spectator into a heightened awareness of physiological and filmic sensation.

Yet owing to his ongoing reputation as the pure colorist and geometrician of American experimental cinema, the pornographic content and invasive approach of much of Sharits's work is difficult to reconcile with the critical tendency to regard structural film as the epitome of cool modernism. Though legendary avant-garde film theorist P. Adams Sitney had Sharits's work in mind when he defined 'structural film' as a cinema 'in which the shape of the whole film is predetermined and simplified' and content is 'minimal and subsidiary to the outline,'[4] this description hardly speaks to the breathtaking, brain-throbbing experience of taking Sharits's films in the eye and ear. By flashing intermittent images of eye surgery, epileptic seizures, coitus, mutilation, and attempted suicide in his films, Sharits put typical strategies of structural film into dialogue with obscene representations of the body. In doing so, he shapes a filmic practice informed by the fuck *and* the flicker, both of which demand a heightened physiological response from the viewer. By choosing to examine films that incorporate representational content, I aim not only to trouble any lingering distinction between abstraction and figuration in Sharits's work, but to challenge the persistent notion that structural cinema represented a turn away from the more conspicuously corporeal experiments of the early 1960s.[5]

In their original celebrations of artists like Sharits, Hollis Frampton, and Michael Snow, critics like Sitney, Annette Michelson, and Rosalind Krauss minimize the extent to which strategies of structural cinema are bound up with the physiological body that served as both disciplined conduit and predictable foil for the structuralists' filmic experiments. Defying the myth of analytical detachment privileged by modernism as the ideal condition of viewership, structural filmmakers aim their films at subjects whose bodies cannot fail to react to the optical and auditory stimulations of the screen. Under-theorized as it has been, the corporeal and affective besiegement of the spectator is essential to understanding Sharits's engagement with film form. As Sharits knew all too well, bodies are fragile forms easily torn asunder by cinema's affective forces: 'The projector is an audio-visual pistol, the retinal screen is a target,' he wrote; 'Goal: the temporary assassination of the viewer's normative consciousness.'[6] As any student who has endured a screening of Warhol's *Empire* (1964), Tony Conrad's *The Flicker* (1966), Michael Snow's *Wavelength* (1967), or Ernie Gehr's *Serene Velocity* (1970) knows, the potentially ecstatic experience of enhanced perception is inseparable from the experience of a sore ass, pulsing eyeballs or a throbbing migraine. It's not for nothing that Jonas Mekas tied an audience member to a chair to prevent him from leaving a screening of Warhol's films.[7]

But while the stubborn mess of bodies is difficult to address within the geometry of structural film, then the personal experience of its filmmakers has proved even more troublesome. Shunning what is often described as the 'biographical fallacy,' the first historical critics of Sharits's work avoid consideration of the relationship between his visual poetics and his own physical and psychic trauma. Sharits noted the evasion: 'There was a problem in the 60's and even in 70's of a lot of intimidating artists into avoiding emotional motivations for their work, the dominant criticism then pursued everything in terms of impersonal, formal, structural analysis…'[8]

More than any other filmmaker associated with the 1960s American avant-garde, Sharits created a cinema of pain. Moving beyond the pleasure principle towards the death drive, Sharits sought the potential for expanded perception in 'damaged-diseased'[9] eyes and broken bodies. In doing so, he troubled the relationship between ethics and aesthetics through an expanded cinema practice that approaches spiritual enlightenment through what often seems like sadomasochistic means. Exploring the vision of the blind, the enlightened, the intoxicated, and the disabled, Paul Sharits used the filmic apparatus to both produce and mimic the physiological responses of shattered bodies. Yet far from trying to overwhelm the spectator's perceptual thresholds in the pursuit of cruelty, Sharits strived to create an empathic relationship between his films and his spectators.

By aggressively 'touching' the flesh of the body and the celluloid, Sharits's films create a meditational space for the viewer in which it becomes possible to forge expanded forms of relationality between and with abjected subjects. By contextualizing Sharits's optical ballistics within his own acute experience of suffering – occasioned through family trauma, physical assault, drug and alcohol abuse, chronic anxiety, and depression – this chapter examines the convulsive strategies that Sharits uses to represent corporeal, psychological, and neurological anguish. After broaching the taboo subject of the artist's biography, the chapter proceeds with analyses of *Piece Mandala / End War* (1966) and *T,O,U,C,H,I,N,G* (1968), two 'flicker' films from the mid- and late 1960s, in which the abstract language of light and color is interspersed with explicit representational imagery of the mutilated or sexually stimulated body. With the help of psychoanalytic theory, I argue that the mandala-like structure of these films attempts to manage the overwhelming stimulation of trauma. Theorizing a cinema beyond the 'pleasure principle,' I consider how Sharits's use of repetition, looping, 'isotropic' form, and sadomasochistic visual display struggle to bind devastation to cinematic structure. By the late 1960s, however, Sharits renounced the mandalic form and began to pioneer forms of multiple and loop projection that subjected the body to alternative regimes of duration and duress. I conclude this chapter by considering the ethical and political risks involved in Sharits's attempt, in his first 'locational' piece *Epileptic Seizure Comparison* (1976), to redeem suffering through the creation of an empathic architecture.

Geometries of suffering: the Mandala films

Structure   without life   is dead.   But Life   without
structure   is un-seen   .   Pure life
expresses itself   within   and through structure.
(John Cage, 'Lecture on Nothing')

Merging biographical information with art criticism has a long and vexed history. While certain more personal or confessional modes – particularly those practiced by female, non-white, non-heterosexual, or non-Western artists – are often approached via a consideration of identity politics, there is a long-standing taboo against the exegesis of modernist form through feeling. Daring to write 'personally' about so-called 'structural' film, nearly all of which were made by white, Western, heterosexual males, and which were often treated as the apotheosis of Greenbergian modernism in cinema, is bound to flare with danger. It is 'into this furnace' that 'I ask you now to venture.'[10]

Paul Jeffrey Sharits was born in Denver in 1943 to a half-Italian, lower-middle-class family with working-class roots. Two years later, his brother Greg was born. Their father was a politically conservative, devout Roman Catholic who was often away from home working as a traveling salesman supplying military commissaries throughout the Midwest. Their mother suffered from severe depression and alcoholism.

Between 1957 and 1960, Sharits went to South Denver High School, where, unbeknownst to him at the time, experimental filmmakers Stan Brakhage and Larry Jordan had attended ten years earlier. Though Sharits retrospectively referred to himself as a juvenile delinquent and high school dropout, other than smoking and drinking with his friends in self-conscious imitation of the 'beatnik' lifestyle, his interests at this time were primarily painting and making psycho-dramatic 8mm films about juvenile sexual frustration.[11]

In 1960, Sharits married Frances Trujillo (later Sharits, then Niekerk) whom he had met at a Catholic church dance. He also began to study painting at University of Denver, where he earned a BFA in Fine Arts. Working in a context where representational painting was treated as a sin, Sharits deliberately emptied figurative content from his work. After becoming exposed to Brakhage's films, whose importance he 'immediately recognized,'[12] Sharits began to pour the messy excess of his being into cinema. In 1962, he founded the Denver Experimental Film Society in order to expose himself to underground 'oddities' and rent classics from the Museum of Modern Art film collection.[13] After giving up Catholicism, Sharits adopted Wassily Kandinsky's 1911 text *Concerning the*

Spiritual in Art as his 'bible.' Indeed, Kandinsky's ideas about the relationship between music and painting, and the 'psychic effect' of color which could create both palpable physiological responses and 'spiritual vibrations'[14] within the viewer, are indispensable to the development of Sharits's aesthetic.

With its long history of narrative, film originally appealed to Sharits as a medium in which he could explore sexual neuroses and other corporeal concerns that were banished from mid-century painting. Initially, Sharits intended to keep his work in film private, maintaining it as a pastime distinct from the more public discipline of painting. Yet Sharits soon abandoned the psycho-dramatic content of his early films. He began to do graph drawings and set to work on the abstract, pure color flicker film that would become *Ray Gun Virus* (1966).

In 1964, Sharits began an MFA at Indiana University, where he founded the Indiana University Experimental Cinema Group. That same year, Sharits's beloved maternal grandmother passed away. In March of 1965, Paul and Frances Sharits had a son, Christopher. Only a few months later, in July of 1965, Sharits's mother Florence committed suicide by psychiatric medical overdose. At the time of her death, Florence was in Frances's care. The combined force of his mother's suicide and the responsibilities of new parenthood catapulted Sharits into a deep emotional crisis. During this time, Sharits 'felt like committing suicide' but decided that if he 'pretended that the "I" had already died,' then he could do whatever he wished in film.[15]

Florence Romeo Sharits's suicide was the turning point in Paul Sharits's artistic career as well as his emotional life. From this point on, Sharits used film, as Kandinsky had used paint, as a spiritual 'exercise' in which the 'impression of varied colour' could serve as the 'starting point of a whole chain of related sensations' and emotional discoveries.[16] Recognizing that the creation of visual conflict through the alternation of color could involve, as Kandinsky described, either a movement towards 'eternal discord' with the possibility for future rebirth *or* 'absolute discord' that was 'devoid' of such possibilities,[17] Sharits embarked on a new phase of creation that approached flicker as the musical orchestration of color. Sharits abandoned his earlier black-and-white psycho-dramatic films, and burned most of the evidence, accidentally leaving a single film *Wintercourse* (1962) intact. Finally feeling free enough to make a film without actors, Sharits began experimenting with color structure and the modular, rectangular shapes that were constitutive of both graph paper and the filmstrip. *Ray Gun Virus* represented an attempt to move his tormented consciousness towards and through 'mental suicide' to rebirth.[18]

Critics and other filmmakers soon recognized Sharits's modular experiments as exemplifying a particularly rigorous (and implicitly non-corporeal and non-emotional) trend in structural film. In a career-making assessment of Sharits's work, art historian and *October* co-founder Rosalind Krauss explained the filmmaker's 'strength' as 'his capacity for, and commitment to abstraction.'[19]

Fellow filmmaker Hollis Frampton also described Sharits as 'the most rigorous excluder of referential and personal content around.'[20] Long-time advocate Annette Michelson praised him with the following distinction: 'Of all the film-makers of this last decade, Sharits has made the most systematic attempt to explore and objectify the dynamics of the recording process and the materiality of film.'[21] Like many of her contemporaries, Michelson fetishized the 'empty' or 'image-free' film frame as the height of cinematic achievement. In keeping with the mid-century modernist rhetoric of media self-reflexivity, Michelson recognized the rich capacity of the 'image-free' frame to allegorize the specific materiality and ontology of cinema.

> Black or light – or color-filled, subliminal or aggressive in effect, weak or saturated, grainy or dense, it [the empty frame] signals most immediately ac-knowledgement of shape and surface, of the boundaries and luminescence of the screen itself, its impossibility of emptiness, the irreducibility of the projec-tive situation. … I will now indeed propose it as *the icon and the emblem of advanced film-making in this country as it has matured into the energetic and refined exploration of the epistemology of filmic enterprise in all its aspects and parameters.*[22]

For Sharits, commercial cinema's quest for illusion insufficiently explored the potential of 'cinematics'[23] to transform perception. Sharits's extensive research into phenomenology helped him formulate a new approach to cinema, which abandoned purely mimetic aspirations in favor of an investigation of the principles of vision. In his statement for the Knokke-le-Zoute experimental film festival in 1967, Sharits explains:

> I wish to abandon imitation and illusion and enter directly into the higher drama of: celluloid, two dimensional strips; individual rectangular frames; the nature of sprockets and emulsion; projector operations; the three dimensional reflective screen surface; the retinal screen; optic nerve and individual psycho-physical subjectivities of consciousness.[24]

Determined to reveal the material basis of cinema, Sharits explores the essential duality of film – as the physical object of celluloid, and the temporal process of projection – in works that insisted on film's unique ontology. Acknowledging that it is almost impossible for viewers to 'distinguish "the movie" from "the projection,"' Sharits recognizes that film was both 'corpuscular' (the cell-like qualities of each film frame) and 'wave-like' (the directional, temporal drive of the film strip).[25]

Sharits's *Frozen Film Frame* series (1960s–1970s), in which strips of celluloid are serially arranged between sheets of plexiglass,[26] reveal in their extraordinary modular arrangements of color the material basis for the optical pulsations experienced by viewers of his flicker films. They also provide tangible evidence of the relationship between vision and audition theorized by Kandinsky and practiced by Sharits. 'My early "flicker" films,' Sharits writes, 'wherein clusters of differentiated single frames of color can appear to almost blend or, each frame insisting upon its discreteness, can appear to aggressively vibrate – are filled with attempts to allow vision to function in ways particular to hearing.'[27] As Sharits discovered, rapidly alternating color frames could 'generate in vision, horizontal-temporal chords (as well as the more expected "melodic lines" and "tonal centers").'[28] Illustrating the musical structure of Sharits's cinema, the frozen frames also demonstrate how film – which Sharits contends is both 'dead' and 'alive' – carries the capacity for frenzied motion within its inert objecthood. In order to reanimate the deadness of celluloid, Sharits uses 'optical sensation' to strike what Kandinsky had described as color's 'inner spiritual chords – "der inner klange."'[29]

But even as he was celebrated for his pioneering work in non-narrative cinema, Sharits remained uninterested in the 'traditional abstract film'[30] and often chose to incorporate images of the human body in his work. In short, Sharits's frames were not always image-free. In 1966, Sharits completed *Ray Gun Virus* and *Piece Mandala / End War,* a color flicker film that incorporates pornographic images of him and his wife in various positions of sexual intercourse. Merging figuration and abstraction, *Piece Mandala* follows the path towards 'spiritual revolution'[31] imagined by Kandinsky. Writing in 1911, as the geometrical visions of Cubism were being lauded as the first structural art form antithetical to emotionalism,[32] Kandinsky warns against the banishment of 'material objects' from painting. 'As every word spoken rouses an inner vibration,' Kandinsky writes, 'so likewise does every object represented. To deprive oneself of this possibility is to limit one's powers of expression.'[33] Throughout his career, Sharits continued to be pulled in these two 'presumably different directions,' towards 'the formal (musical) world of abstraction and towards the psychological/emotional world of figuration.'[34]

Clement Greenberg's insistence that an artwork should interrogate the limits of its own ontological conditions rather than strive to create an illusion beyond its natural purview[35] was a mixed blessing for an artist whose films merged the techniques of painting and music. Working to expand this potentially stultifying modernist rubric, Sharits recognized that even the 'purest' cinema could include the pro-filmic event that the camera was designed to record. Sharits explains, 'Film, "motion picture" and "still" film, unlike painting and sculpture, can achieve an autonomous presence without negating iconic reference because the phenomenology of the system includes "recording" as a physical fact.'[36] Arguing that 'pure' cinema does not have to exclude imagery, Sharits also refuses to eliminate considerations of the temporality of narrative, which were built into cinema as a time-based medium. Though he dispensed with the conventional notion of a story with a beginning, middle, and end, Sharits complicates the typical relationship between duration and expectation that linear, single-screen cinema engages. By pioneering forms of multiple and loop projection that subject the body to alternative regimes of duration and anticipation, Sharits supplants the implied finitude of the 'arrow model of time'[37] with a notion of filmic constancy.

In the period immediately following his mother's suicide – the period bracketed by *Ray Gun Virus* and *T,O,U,C,H,I,N,G* – Sharits attempted to create films that maintained intense sensation at a consistent level. According to Frampton, Sharits longed to make a film that was fully 'isotropic' in the sense that 'wherever you sliced it, it would be pretty much the same.'[38] The 'mandala' films from the late 1960s were 'not only completely symmetrical but also – by implication or as a way of promoting isometrics – circular, so that it could be arranged, presumably, as a vast loop and run on forever.'[39] Sharits explains his logic:

> My interest in creating temporal analogues of Tibetan mandalas, evoking their circularity and inverse symmetrical balance, led me to making what are basically two vector, symmetric works in which the first part's forward directed structure is countered by the second part's retrograde direction. A complex form of this vectorial approach, which issues a sense of isotropic homogeneity rather than a sense of developmental directiveness, can be obtained by overlapping or regularly intersecting two opposing vectors (i.e., superimpose a forward progression 'over' a backwards progression); the whole work is, so to speak, a conceptual 'lap dissolve' and will have the curious quality of constant but *directionless* motion.[40]

Through his use of the mandala structure, Sharits attempts to relieve the temporal anxiety typical of dramatic narrative film.[41] But these circularly organized flicker films also strive to transcend the psychologically paralyzing model of his mother's suicide by finding a form capable of supplanting linear models of time with a sense of undiminished presence and constancy. Yet while Sharits's flicker films are often experienced as an unrelenting intensity of stroboscopic, visual patterns of color, as Sitney observes, they also 'mold' and 'punctuate' the viewer's attention by incorporating 'linear signs for determining how much of the film's time has expired, how much is yet to come.'[42] These temporal markers, which often take the form of images of the human body or other material objects, punctuate the seemingly endless alternation of color with startling representations of finitude.

Sharits's refusal to eliminate images of the body originally troubled the most influential champions of his work. In his groundbreaking study *Visionary Film*, first published in 1974, P. Adams Sitney damned Sharits's increasing reliance on representation as a failure to live up to the abstract promise of his flickering (image-free) color fields:

> The dilemma of Sharits's art has turned on the failure of the imagery to sustain its authority in the very powerful matrix of the structures he provides. His search for metaphors and icons for the particular kind of cinematic experience that his films engender has not been as successful as his invention of markers to reflect the duration of his films … . These metaphors either lack the immediacy of the color flickers or the scratches around them, or they overpower their matrix, as in *T,O,U,C,H,I,N,G*, and instigate a psychological vector which the form cannot accommodate as satisfactorily as the trance film or mythopoeic film.[43]

Sitney's assessment of Sharits's failure to merge figurative imagery with the more recognizable elements of structural films (which he famously itemized as fixed camera position, the flicker effect, loop printing, and re-photography off the screen)[44] suggests a deep suspicion of illusionistic forms. In retrospect, it is difficult to separate Sitney's aversion from the *types* of images Sharits typically uses: nude bodies, close-ups of genitals, gruesome images of surgery, and other explicit forms of corporeal rupture. Rather than confronting the particular sensations produced by such provocative images, Sitney disavows them.

Considering that Sitney was the first and most important scholar to argue for the significance of postwar experimental cinema as an art form as significant as poetry, his reluctance to address Sharits's pornographic impulses is understandable. Unfortunately, however, Sitney's original critical diminishment of the pornographic content and corporeal mode of address of structural film has led to an enduring misunderstanding of how central the body, in all of what Sally Banes has described as its 'effervescence,'[45] is to postwar experimental cinema.

Let us turn to Sharits's *Piece Mandala / End War* (1966) as an example. In this five-minute silent film, blank color frequencies are interspersed with black and white still images of heterosexual intercourse. In this film, Sharits appears naked with his wife Frances in a variety of sexual positions against a background split horizontally into black and white color fields. In some of these images, Frances lies supine as Paul kneels between her legs with his face dipping towards her crotch. In others, Paul is seen *in media res* climbing onto Frances in missionary position. Yet the distinctions between these positions are clear only if you study the film as a series of 'frozen' frames. At its normal projected speed, the superimposition of their bodies forms a blur of frenetic sexual action in which figure and ground merge in a metronomic throb. Both Paul's and Frances's heads appear nearly simultaneously at both the right and left edges of the frame. Merged together through the dream of cinema, the couple becomes a four-headed, multi-limbed Hindu deity, a Brahma, the infinite, the source of all space, time, causation, name and form.

Midway through the film, Paul Sharits appears in medium close-up, clothed and staring directly into the camera. Holding a small gun in his right hand, he moves his arm in an arc that brings the gun to the side of his head. This image

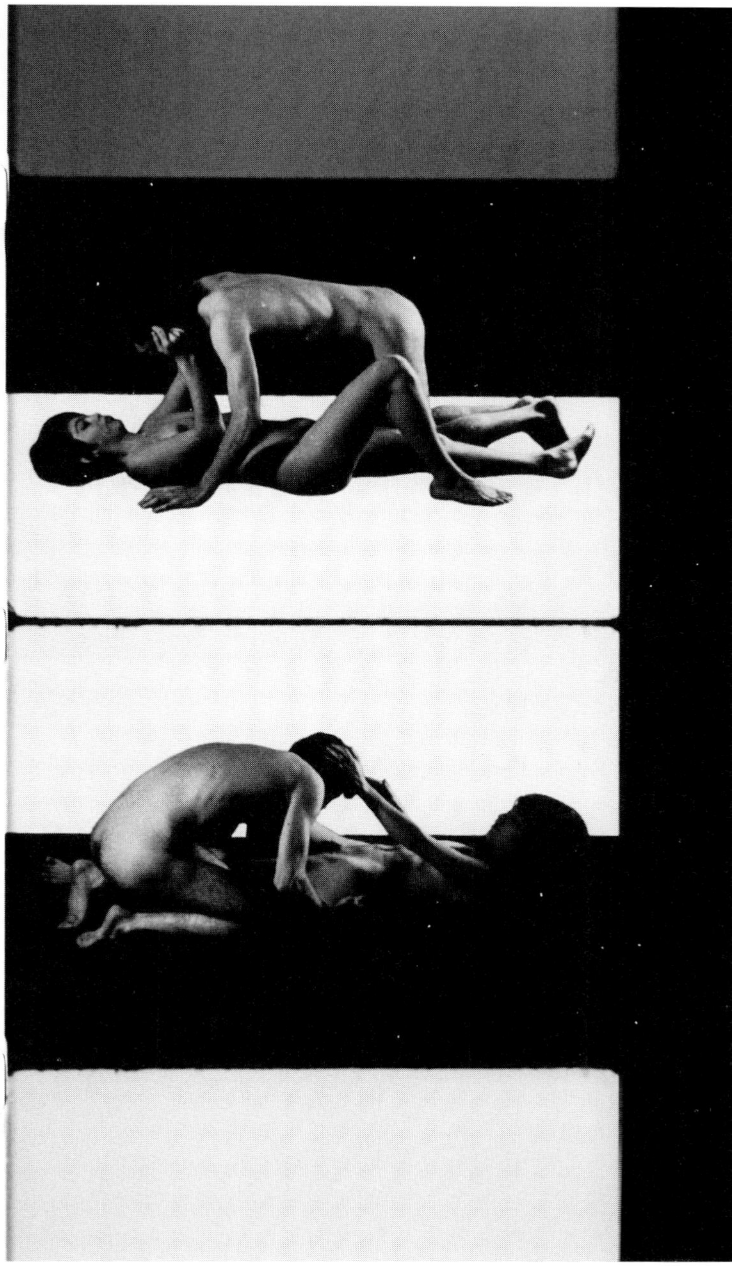

Images of Paul and Frances Sharits making love are intercut with color flicker in Paul   **41**
Sharits's *Piece Mandala / End War* (1966). The pornographic content of many of Sharits's
films have been difficult to reconcile with his reputation as a structural filmmaker.

of threatened suicide disappears a few moments later, and the frenzied sex re-sumes. Soon, the suicide re-appears and is 'consummated.' An animated white dash line indicates the direction of an imaginary fired ballistic, whose impact with Sharits's head is comically implied by the splattering of cartoon white droplets. Though his eyes are closed at the time of the impact, they re-open as Sharits returns the gun to its original position and the flicker fuck resumes. In the second half of the film, pinks, vermilions, oranges, reds, and golds abound, punctuated by an occasional burst of bright royal blue. As the film approaches the end, the preliminary sexual gestures of the first half are 'completed.' Her arms reach toward his face and head, the couple makes love while kissing on the mouth, he buries his face in her crotch.

In his single-line description of the film in *Visionary Film*, Sitney neglects to mention that the color flickers in *Piece Mandala* are intercut with explicit images of a man and a woman fucking. Yet far from being gratuitous or incon-gruous, the film's depiction of sexual communion complements the alternation of the color flickers, which are maintained in their own constant state of inter-course. Both 'attractions'[46] convulse the spectator's body into a state of corpo-real excitation. This is not pleasure so much as ecstasy, a rapture of heightened sensation always on the verge of painful overstimulation. Were we to slow the film down, and watch it frame by frame, the magic would disappear, leaving a series of stillborn, not-so-dirty pictures and minimalist color fields in its wake. When projected, *Piece Mandala* calls attention to the exquisite mysteries that occur between bodies and frames as they move in rhythm. But while projection catalyzes the collision of bodies on the viewer's retina, the flicker reminds us that these moments of perfect beauty are ephemeral. Any attempt to fix them destroys them; there is no fuck without the flicker. Orgasm, which comes in the cartoon form of an ejaculating pistol rather than hard-core porn's ejaculat-ing penis, is part of the drive towards extinction. But if the suicidal impulses of a war-mongering civilization are glimpsed here in the form of Sharits's own fantasized self-destruction, then their logic does not obtain for long. As in the popular mantra of the day, Sharits makes love to end war through the life-giving movement of cinema.

Upon seeing the film, Stan Brakhage thanked Sharits for giving him 'that cut to the bone of some matter that does really concern me: how a man and a woman meet nakedly head-on among the colors.'[47] In his own writings, Sharits also treated the film as a 'magical' or 'charmed object':

> PIECE MANDALA had a great deal to do with my relationship with my wife
> at that particular time – we are separated now – at that time we had been sepa-
> rated for a short while and we got back together. Then the form crystallized to
> me: how could I make a film that would have a magical effect in our relation-
> ship – just my wife and myself.[48]

At the time of making the film, Sharits and his wife had just reconciled after splitting up – they would divorce permanently in 1969 – and the construction of the film was of the 'deepest significance' in the temporary reconstruction of their marriage.[49] Sharits realized that the film was 'properly' dedicated to his wife:

> seeing, at last, your mind as it must be at times in unendurable anguish, a series of events leading to that sense of self as burden, Artaud making art of it, misery, saw your minding of such in my own horror, shocked, shaking my head to get a feeling for what is dream and what is not, my head a crazy catalogue of images, classical symbols, cartoons of grief – but it is not always so and it is that lack of it which has to stand in for joy in the absence of blessings – and there are, in rare instances, blessings and you are often there at those places and I have a total sense of sense and you are absolutely cream, having to step on plastic flowers, my mind bursting, blossoming – someday I will tell you my dreams when it is quiet and I am more willing to let the tragic have its due warmth – that comes later; now I am content that my dreams were dreams.[50]

Embracing Artaud's use of cruelty as a bludgeon with which to shatter the surfaces of reality and move through the wreckage towards deeper truths,[51] Sharits describes joy not as occasions of pleasure ('blessings') but as the management of pain's 'cartoons of grief.' As the following analyses will demonstrate, Sharits's attempt to manage grief would take many forms, from his theorization of cinema as a form of cutting, to his own masochistic propensity for mutilation, to the repetitive structures and violent imagery that abound in his work.

Razor blades

For Sharits, the 'magic' of cinema is inextricable from its ability to incise the filmmaker and the spectator through acts of penetration. Cutting and scratching, both of which are dynamic motifs in Sharits's *oeuvre*, function as tangible traces of the mutual and often violent inscription of bodies upon each other. Recalling Walter Benjamin's famous analogy between the filmmaker and the surgeon, Sharits's invasive approach to 'cinematics' literalizes the analogy between the editor's cut and the scalpel's incision. 'How does the cameraman compare with the painter?' Benjamin asks in his seminal 1936 essay, 'The Work of Art in the Age of Mechanical Reproduction':

> To answer this we take recourse to an analogy with a surgical operation. The surgeon represents the polar opposite of the magician. The magician heals a sick person by the laying on of hands; the surgeon cuts into the patient's body. The magician maintains the natural distance between the patient and himself; though he reduces it very slightly by the laying on of hands, he greatly increases it by virtue of his authority. The surgeon does exactly the reverse; he

greatly diminishes the distance between himself and the patient by penetrating into the patient's body, and increases it but little by the caution with which his hands moves among the organs. In short, in contrast to the magician – who is still hidden in the medical practitioner – the surgeon at the decisive moment abstains from facing the patient man to man; rather, it is through the operation that he penetrates into him. Magician and surgeon compare to painter and cameraman. The painter maintains in his work a natural distance from reality, the cameraman penetrates deeply into its web. There is a tremendous difference between the pictures they obtain…[52]

Perhaps unwittingly channeling Benjamin, Sharits acknowledged the surgical might of the filmmaker's cut and the implicit corporeality of celluloid. He was, by his own admission, '*tormented* by the implications of film as a physical strip'[53] whose body was vulnerable to assault, decay, and obsolescence. 'It's sort of hard to say,' he told Hollis Frampton, but 'I'm beginning to feel that film grain is about as personal to me as an image I might take of my child.'[54]

By 1970, Sharits confessed that he could no longer refer to his 'impolite cutting as "editing."'[55] But whereas Benjamin had seen the approach of the surgeon and the magician as diametrically opposed, Sharits bridges the spiritual healing techniques of the shaman with the invasive approach of the scalpel. Following Benjamin's analogy literally, it would be too easy to suggest that this was because Sharits was both a painter and a cameraman. By approaching film as a magical object, Sharits enables spectators to transcend the constraints of ordinary perception. He accomplishes this 'magical' aim by treating the filmstrip as an analytical tool, which can be surgically partitioned and manipulated in order to reveal its inner nature. Merging the lessons of science and spirituality, Sharits pierces the skin of the filmstrip in order to heal the spectator.

Rather than approaching the filmmaker's interventions on the filmstrip as a unidirectional force, however, Sharits came to appreciate the reciprocal energy of the razor's edge. In his 1971 film *S:TREAM:S:S:ECTION:S:ECTION:S:S:EC TIONED*, Sharits engraves deep scratches on the emulsion of the celluloid to create the impression of a running incision whose movement parallels the film's recorded images of flowing water. But while these scratches are produced on the surface of the image, they also inflict an equivalent wound on the filmmaker. Like a boomerang, the scratches hurl their own penetrative force back at their maker. As if film itself possesses embodied and animate force – Sharits describes celluloid as a 'dying medium' in the sense of both its increasing technological obsolescence and its ontological relation to the always-dying organism – the scratch scratches the scratcher. 'The filmy surface,' Sharits reflects, 'seems to be incising itself into me … an unexpected feedback being penetrated so passionately in removed clarity, "like" being puzzled thru an endless razor blade, love wounds jaggedly blossoming onto the back of my sensitive edges!'[56]

Sharits's reference to razor blades is hardly surprising; every experimental filmmaker of the era used them as a primary editing tool. What does startle, however, is his allusion to their effects as 'love wounds.' Such provocative references to razor blades abound in Sharits's work of this period. His thirty-second *Wirst Trick* (*Fluxfilm #28*, 1965) rapidly edited 'before,' 'during,' and 'after' images of hands and razors to create the impression of a suicide by wrist slashing. Furthermore, between 1965 and 1968, Sharits made a two-screen installation film called *Razor Blades*, which showed, amongst more psychedelic graphics, 'hideous'[57] images of a man slashing his wrist, a nude female body, a monkey fetus being removed from its mother's womb, raw meat being sliced by a razor, a man shaving, and a penis in various stages of tumescence.

Linking sexual desire with surgical penetration, Sharits's razor blades expose the fleshiness of the body as meat to be sliced. But as the quintessential artistic tool for the film editor, they also symbolize the incisive will of the artist, which can nonetheless be laid waste by emotional paralysis. Consider the following quote, in which Sharits despairingly describes 'the *sickness* of never being able to write down the properly expressive cluster of thoughts which so rapidly alter "their" foundations, to be rotting away like a pile of razor blades which have lost the time to cut even jagged figures – *this* must be Perfect Joy!! – this is what the decaying system of "Cinema" can optimistically formulate.'[58] While citing the 'sickness' of unused, rotting razor blades as a surrogate for the afflicted artist, Sharits morbidly describes this situation as 'Perfect Joy.' The pursuit of art is here conceived in relation to the death drive; 'perfect joy' emerges beyond pleasure in the realm of pathology. In the following outpouring, Eros has bled completely into Thanatos:

> feelings of death provoke my only sense of humor … *bliss slashes across 'my wrists'*, little flower of joy (fetal, stir, fear) go spinning 'out' entropically (the false elation of feeling 'somewhere') away from 'my center', microcosms of a frighteningly expanding universe, 'leaving me' punctuated with uncertain, badly placed pauses, as if their departure increased rather than decreased the total mass of my emptiness, 'sorrow' EVENTUAL 'stupidity', and so on .. [59]

In his attempt to deal with the terrors of such a frighteningly expanding universe, Sharits moves beyond what Freud described as the 'pleasure principle' towards a reckoning with profound abjection, mutilation, and death.

Beyond the pleasure principle

In Freud's 1920 study *Beyond the Pleasure Principle*, he grapples with the challenge posed by traumatized veterans of the World War I to his theory of the 'pleasure principle.' If dreams are a form of wish fulfillment, as Freud argued twenty years earlier in *The Interpretation of Dreams*,[60] why did shell-shocked veterans, neurotics and anxious children compulsively return to instances of 'unpleasure,' in which the sudden increase of excitation could demolish the individual's already precarious ability to protect himself against stimuli? As Freud discovered, repetition is a way of mastering the trauma occasioned by overwhelming sensations by binding and transforming them.[61]

What is most surprising in Freud's attempt to explain 'the mysterious masochistic trends of the ego,'[62] is his insistence that pleasure is not defined by an *increase* in stimulation – as might be expected – but by keeping excitation 'as low as possible or at least to keep it constant.'[63] This principle of constancy provided a working method for subjects besieged by intense levels of perceptual sensation. For Sharits, the repetition and binding of distress was a survival strategy of the greatest urgency.

In *Beyond the Pleasure Principle*, Freud associates trauma with unpredictable stimuli, and imagines a possible resolution through corporeal mutilation: 'In the case of the ordinary traumatic neuroses two characteristics emerge prominently: first, that the chief weight in their causation seems to rest upon the factor of surprise, of fright: and secondly, that a wound or injury inflicted simultaneously works as a rule against the development of a neurosis.'[64] Noting how preparedness constitutes the subject's only line of defense against stimuli, Freud argues that the lack of such preparedness can prove the key factor in producing traumatic neurosis.[65] For while Freud associates unpleasure with an intensification of stimuli and pleasure with its diminution, he regards the main distinction between them as the capacity of energy to be 'bound.'[66] 'Binding' stimuli is a kind of sewing-up or placing of sensation within a framework where it can be managed. Maintaining that an injury sustained simultaneously with the apperception of increased stimuli works 'as a rule against the development of a neurosis,'[67] Freud argues that the wound binds up the 'excess of excitation' 'by calling for a narcissistic hypercathexis of the injured organ.'[68] That this 'placing' occurs on the body is gruesome but not surprising; the physical wound offers the war veteran a literal site where trauma can be sutured and healed. If loss and failure leave 'behind them a permanent injury to self-regard in the form of a narcissistic scar'[69] then an actual flesh wound has the capacity to change this traumatic energy from a free-flowing and unpredictable provocation into a dependable state of quiescence.[70]

Freud's insights about the efficacy of the wound offer a way of understanding Sharits's own proclivity towards corporeal ruination; he was, as his son, Christopher, has described, 'accident prone.'[71] Over the course of his adult life, Sharits broke his hip and knee while trying to jump from the roof into the window of a friend's home, sustained chronic back injuries in a car accident, broke his ankle roller skating, and was stabbed by a prostitute. In 1980, Paul Sharits's brother Greg Sharits was shot and killed by police while coming out of a jewelry store in Berkeley, California with a pointed gun in his hand. Paul was devastated.[72] Two years later, Paul Sharits was shot in the abdomen with a shotgun at a bar in Buffalo, New York after being mistaken for another patron. 'I've been in a lot of surgery,' he mused in 1983, and 'I started to view the entire world as being a medical problem.'[73] In 1990, Sharits was charged with menacing and criminal possession of a weapon after producing a jackknife in an argument over parking. Of course not all of Sharits's accidents were of his own making, and many occurred while the artist was intoxicated. Yet is it possible that Sharits's courtship of injury was an attempt to site the unexpected shock of his mother's suicide upon his own body and thereby bind its overwhelming energy to matter?

Sharits's courtship of physical trauma extends to an exploration of masochistic ecstasy in his work. Indeed, one of the reasons Sharits's cinema remains so provocative in a visual culture organized by the sadistic male gaze upon the female 'object' is because of his relentless exploration of the taboo of male abjection. In his 1968 film *T,O,U,C,H,I,N,G*, Sharits constructs a primal scene around 'taking it in the eye,' or what Carol Clover theorizes as a masochistic fantasy of ocular overwhelming in which the subject identifies through embattled vision with the dismembered body.[74] Completed two years after the redemptive love-making of *Piece Mandala / End War*, this anguished film about the mutilation of the male subject is an attempt to allow the tragic 'its due warmth' by divesting the 'burden' of self through acts of radical dismemberment.

Dismembered cinema: *T,O,U,C,H,I,N,G* (1968)

> Colour is the keyboard, the eyes are the hammers, the soul is the piano with many strings. The artist is the hand which plays, touching one key to another, to cause vibrations in the soul.
>
> (Wassily Kandinsky, *Concerning the Spiritual in Art*)[75]

> TOUCHING (the most clear statement of my nearly schizoid obsession with extreme polarities: sex/ death, rebirth through death, etc.)
>
> (Paul Sharits)[76]

I cannot remember where I was the first time I saw *T,O,U,C,H,I,N,G* but I distinctly recall that I did not enter the room. Instead, I cowered against the doorjamb as if this threshold could offer some protection from the film's incessant flicker. Though I instinctively did not want this film to touch me, my resistance turned out to be futile. For just as one's own heart beats in maudlin synchronicity with the latest pop song blasted at a dance club, so too do one's own eyes and ears unwittingly rehearse Sharits's premeditated tricks. Mistaking an architectural threshold for a perceptual one, I strove to protect the latter by hovering at the former. But as Sharits's films remind us, eyes are as vulnerable to penetration as any other orifice. Sliced and spliced by the image, the assaulted eye becomes a body, an 'organ of touch.'[77] The film entered me. My body became the contingency whose inevitable physiological response completed the circuit of the filmic apparatus.

Sharits, who was deeply attuned to the significance of the threshold in both transgression and trauma, perches his films at the limits of the tolerable. He explains, 'a lot of the work deals with perceptual thresholds. It brings us to the limits of our perceptual abilities so that often one cannot tell whether or not what one is experiencing is in the work or in oneself.'[78] Even in the space of the movie theater, Sharits's cinema inhabits the body, transforming one's own corporeality into physiological antechamber. Although the projection of celluloid always depends upon human optics to animate its collection of still frames, when watching Sharits's work we become physically cognizant of how cinema's rhythms are tapped out on our organs.

In the manner of a child's early reader, *T,O,U,C,H,I,N,G* begins with the letter T. As the film progresses, the entire word is spelled out, letter by letter, from T to G, in a series of rapid color flickers. As each letter breaks away from the others, and thus disrupts the syntactical relationship between them, the word 'TOUCHING' dissolves into incoherence. In this schizophrenic dissection of language's capacity to signify, language acquires a projective force; rather than semantically processing the word, we are assaulted by it. This is only the first of *T,O,U,C,H,I,N,G*'s lessons in dismemberment.

Punctuated by the regular appearance of these throbbing letters, single frame shots of a shirtless young man with cascading brown hair flash by in a series of positive and negative, and color and black-and-white images. These portrait shots are interspersed with stroboscopic passages of color flicker and the occasional intrusion of graphic photographic images of the penetrated body, including eye surgery, close-ups of genitals engaged in sexual intercourse, and an image of the bottom half of a supine nude female body with her legs spread open in a pose reminiscent of Gustave Courbet's 1866 painting *L'Origine du monde*. Throughout the film, the word 'destroy' is repeated incessantly on the soundtrack.

Though he bears uncanny resemblance to Sharits, the portrait is of the filmmaker's best friend, the poet David Franks (1948–2010). Throughout almost the entirety of the film, Franks appears with his eyes closed in medium shot, sometimes in various poses of mutilation. In the film's most memorable instance, a closed-eye Franks appears holding a pair of open scissors around his extended tongue as if he is about to snip it off. Balancing this suggestion of auto-mutilation are other recurring images of sadomasochistic violence. Over and over we see Franks's face being scratched by the long talons of a female hand that invades the frame from the left side. In a trick borrowed from Sergei Eisenstein, primitive animation produces the illusion of movement, in which the rapid succession of 'before' and 'after' images leaves the impression of bloody scratch wounds across the subject's face.[79]

As the film passes the halfway mark of six minutes, the sharp instruments that threaten Franks begin to withdraw, although the original images of penetration also recur. In some images, the long-taloned hand appears further away from Franks's face; in others, the still-opened scissors drop below his chin. Beginning in the last sixth of the film, which coincides with the appearance of the letter 'N' and the ten-minute mark, Franks no longer appears with his eyes closed, but stares intently into the camera. These images continue, now only interrupted by flickering color frames, some of which have a differently colored rectangle positioned inside of them. Finally, around the twelve-minute mark, the letter 'G' appears and the film ends.

In *T,O,U,C,H,I,N,G*, dismemberment assumes many forms, from the film's deconstruction of the acoustic and linguistic signifier, to its vivisection of the filmstrip into minuscule fragments of color, to its graphic images of bodily mutilation. Using the same principle of optics as the thaumatrope – a nineteenth-century visual toy in which a two-sided disc with different images on each side is spun to give the illusion of their overlapping – Sharits relies on the persistence of vision to create an anxious palimpsest of castration. Castration anxiety is not only evident in the film's recurring image of Franks's extended tongue as it is about to be severed (an obvious metaphor for genital dismemberment), but in the many images of female clawing, ocular mutilation, and genital penetration. Yet, as my interrogation of the film's aesthetics of trauma shall demonstrate, the film's castration anxiety does not derive from male angst over sexual difference, as in Freud's misogynistic account, but from the artist's recognition of the vulnerability of all subjects to various forms of shattering.

For Sharits, perception renders all bodies vulnerable to penetration. By rhythmically cutting between images of optical and vaginal penetration and facial mutilation, *T,O,U,C,H,I,N,G* produces a chain of equivalence that binds the besieged spectator to the subject of the film in a mutual acknowledgement of castration. As an organ that can be penetrated and physically stimulated, the eye was, for Sharits, deeply related to sexuality.[80] Yet *T,O,U,C,H,I,N,G*'s condensation of eye surgery and sexual intercourse is not a mere anagram for Freud's theories of female insufficiency, in which the woman's lack of a penis attests to her inferiority and restricts her access to the symbolic.[81] As in Jacques Lacan's account of the inability of *any* corporeal being to command the gaze,[82] Sharits suggests how the limitations of the mortal body inform a profound castration that afflicts *all* subjects regardless of their gender. When images of female genitals appear in Sharits's film, it is not then as a symbol of the dreaded mutilation of the penis, but of a world over-determined by lack.

For Sharits, lack signifies most profoundly through the devastating loss of his mother. Sharits plays out his own filial drama of loss and recovery, of

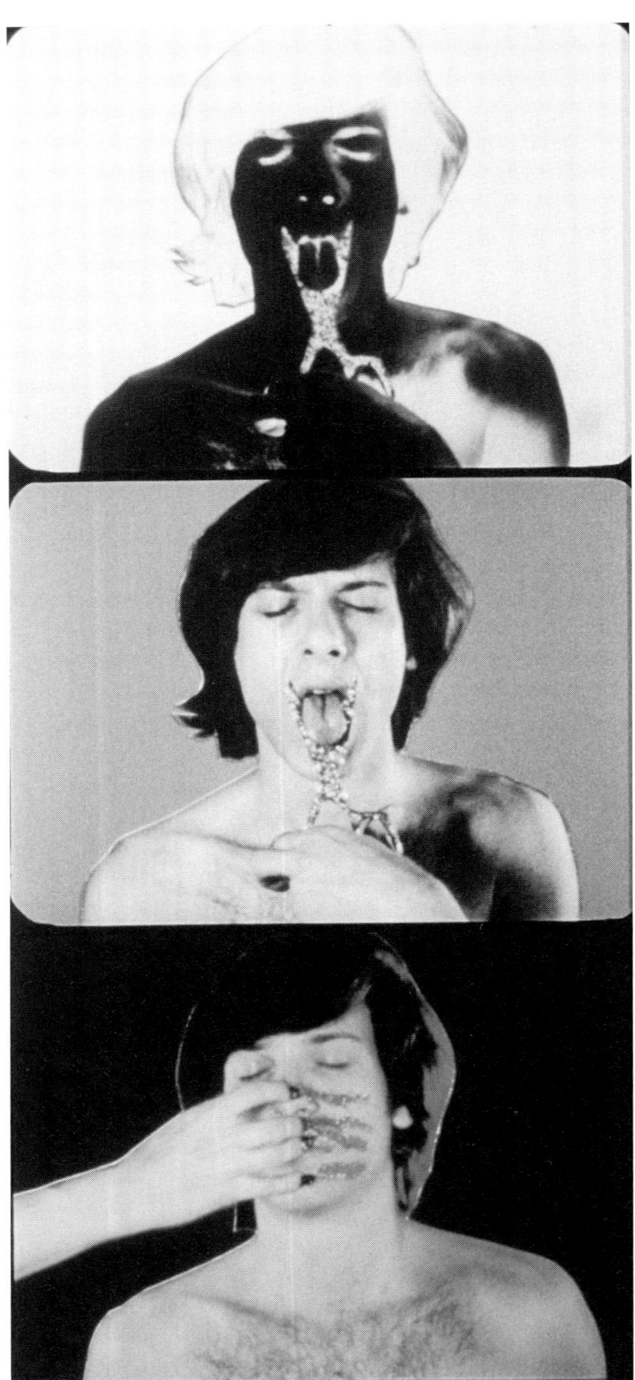

42
Images of bodily mutilation abound in Paul Sharits's *T,O,U,C,H,I,N,G* (1968). In the first two frames, poet David Franks threatens to snip off his tongue; in the third, a woman's fingernails leave the impressions of long scratch marks on his face.

pain and palliation, in the compulsively repetitive rhythms of *T,O,U,C,H,I,N,G*. As in the childhood game of *fort/da*, in which Freud observed his grandson stage the disappearance and reappearance of his mother and even himself,[83] *T,O,U,C,H,I,N,G* rehearses and repeats the distress caused by maternal absence through the emergence and evaporation of color blocks, as well as frequent disappearances of the filmmaker's surrogate, David Franks.

Sharits himself recognized the 'irrational' structures at work in his own use of repetition. 'To repeat, monotonously, some common word, until the sound ceased to convey any idea to the mind, to lose all sense of motion or physical existence' is a major '(ir)rationale of the soundtracks of both *T,O,U,C,H,I,N,G* and *S:S:S:S:S:S*.'[84] This compulsion to repeat is nowhere better illustrated than in *T,O,U,C,H,I,N,G*'s constant reiteration of the word 'destroy.' To make the soundtrack, Sharits recorded Franks speaking, and then removed the normative pauses between words that make language decipherable.[85] When edited into a constant, uninterrupted stream, the ear refuses to register the enunciated word, which begins to sound like a multitude of other sounds and phrases.[86] Like many of Sharits's techniques, this trick was learned from Kandinsky, who advised that, 'frequent repetition of a word … deprives the word of its original external meaning …'[87]

Yet as Sharits discovered, repetition of sound does not function in the same way as the repetition of color flicker. Because of the shutter of the projector, and the physiological event in the nervous system that it activates, the viewer thinks that she is 'seeing a continuous light' when 'in fact the light really is not on screen all the time because the shutter comes in a lot and there's a lot of blank, black moments.' On the other hand, as Sharits explains, the sound track is 'not interrupted by a shutter. The sound is continuous. And so the sound can act in a way that the image cannot; the image cannot be on the screen continually.'[88] While the soundtrack maintains a level of acoustic constancy, the illuminations on the screen emerge and vanish. To couch this phenomenon of projection in Freud's terms, illuminated frames are 'da' (there) one moment and 'fort' (gone) the next. Yet the fact that the human subject is not typically able to perceive this difference perceptually erases the distinction between there and gone. In this way, the animation of projection strives to erase the trauma of absence, by artificially reconciling the impossibility of being both here and elsewhere (or nowhere). Sharits's use of color flicker restores the perception of 'gone' by making us physiologically aware of the disappearing image. In this way, his films enable the viewer to apprehend the absence that defines presence and thereby recognize the existence of death within life.

Sharits's cinematic exploration of castration does not depend, as Freud's, on a divisive and misogynistic construction of anatomical difference but upon an anguished empathetic identification with the other. By recognizing his (m)other's body as an extension of his own, Sharits radically inverts the terms of the Oedipus crisis, which pivot upon the son's failure to recognize his mother as kindred. This 'blindness' of the son to the mother is critical to normative accounts of masculinity. In Freud's account, the severance of the identificatory bond between mother and son occurs after the 'revelation' of castration, in which the once-phallic mother suddenly appears mutilated and devalued. For Freud, this disassociation is key to the successful resolution of the Oedipus complex and the assurance of heteronormativity, because it encourages the son's identification with the parent of the same sex. By switching his primary identification from the mother to the father, the male child is inaugurated as a privileged subject in the phallogocentric culture of patriarchy.

Paul Sharits's mother's suicide completed the son's agonized physical separation from the mother that commences at birth and is recapitulated during the Oedipus crisis. But it also threatened to compel Sharits – the son and new father – to masochistically surrender to the death culture of patriarchy. For Sharits, identification with his mother was restored rather then negated through the tragedy of her suicide, which enabled him to recognize the abiding, albeit devastating terms of their kinship.

T,O,U,C,H,I,N,G is Sharits's first cinematic attempt to identify with this thrice-lost mother, by sharing in rather than reviling or recoiling from her suffering. For Julia Kristeva, who described the corpse as 'the utmost of abjection,' the abject was inextricably linked to the maternal, for its appearance signifies the moment of separation when boundaries between the self and the 'm(other)' are established.[89] What Kristeva describes as the 'horror' of the abject stems from the perception that these boundaries – between self and other, human and animal, or life and death – are always on the verge of collapse. Following Kristeva's logic, nothing could be more abject than the mother's corpse. Yet for all of the distress it generates, *T,O,U,C,H,I,N,G* does not elicit this horror. Rather, the film's metronomic barrage shatters the illusory boundaries that separate the flesh of the body from the flesh of the world, and thereby enables the crucial recognition of the self in the abjected other. Empathy depends upon this recognition. As Kaja Silverman argues, empathy involves the embrace of abjection and a profound sense of ontological kinship with the other.[90] However, this kind of identification comes with substantial risk for the subject, for it pivots upon the recognition of the inevitability of corporeal ruination and death.

As the filmmaker's biography suggests, the cost of recognition proved to be fatal: in *T,O,U,C,H,I,N,G*, Paul Sharits gives himself up for dead. Sharits's empathy with his mother's pain would eventually involve the ultimate act of identification. Unable to extricate himself from the mandalic structure of genetic mental illness, Paul Sharits committed suicide at the age of fifty on July 8, 1993. Choosing his favorite holiday weekend as well as the same month as his mother's suicide, Sharits deliberately overdosed on thorazine, an antipsychotic drug used to treat schizophrenia and severe bipolar disorder.[91] Years earlier, Sharits had told his daughter-in-law that he would eventually overdose on this date. His son Christopher had grown up with his father's threats of suicide, and has described the paradox of never being able to believe it, and simultaneously knowing that he would never be able to prevent it.[92] It is of course possible that in making these threats, Paul Sharits was trying to prepare his child for the trauma of losing a parent by providing a temporal marker that would help him anticipate the end.

Twenty-five years before enacting his final communion with his mother, Sharits labored to move through his acknowledgment of their mutual suicidal despair by giving himself up to psychic and physical dismemberment. Trying to distance himself from the kind of suicide where 'one succeeds in physically eliminating oneself', Sharits improvises 'other forms of suicide' that might 'allow a re-birth.'[93] Such penultimate forms of suicide could, he hoped, 'negate certain forms of negation' and thereby enable the subject to empathize with the other's suffering without destroying himself completely. Refuting critical claims that *T,O,U,C,H,I,N,G* was a 'sadistic work', Sharits describes it instead as an 'anti-sadistic', 'empathetic' film about 'healing.'

The cathartic arc of *T,O,U,C,H,I,N,G* is perhaps most evident in the transformation from a shut-eyed to an open-eyed Franks in the last sixth of the film. Shutting down or closing oneself off to stimuli does not prove to be an adequate response to trauma. For just as the viewer cannot escape the flicker's throb by closing one's eyes to its source, Franks cannot protect himself from the dangers of perception by cutting off his tongue or shielding his eyes. As Brakhage theorized in *Metaphors on Vision*, the phenomena of the visual world continue to be received by the closed eye, as the skin of the eyelid becomes another screen through which vision is mediated. Perhaps when Franks finally opens his eyes at the end of the film it signals not the triumph over suicide and the resumption of consciousness, but an acknowledgment that in the face of our potentially fatal vulnerability to stimuli, it is better to open oneself to it, to prepare oneself for penetration. This is Sharits's philosophy of pain in the making.

Eventually, Sharits began to recognize his mother's suicide as her decision to release herself from tension and enter a 'serenity' beyond pleasure. 'To decide to commit suicide is to relax', Sharits reflected:

> And I mean [that] really definitively: like the day that my mother committed suicide, she'd been nervous, depressed all week. Then, one day, a very pleasant day she was as serene as an angel. A few hours later, she was dead. And through making that decision, she became very serene. Well, I had made that decision. I became relaxed enough so I thought: Well, wait a minute, at this point, anything I do is okay because I'll probably commit suicide anyway.[94]

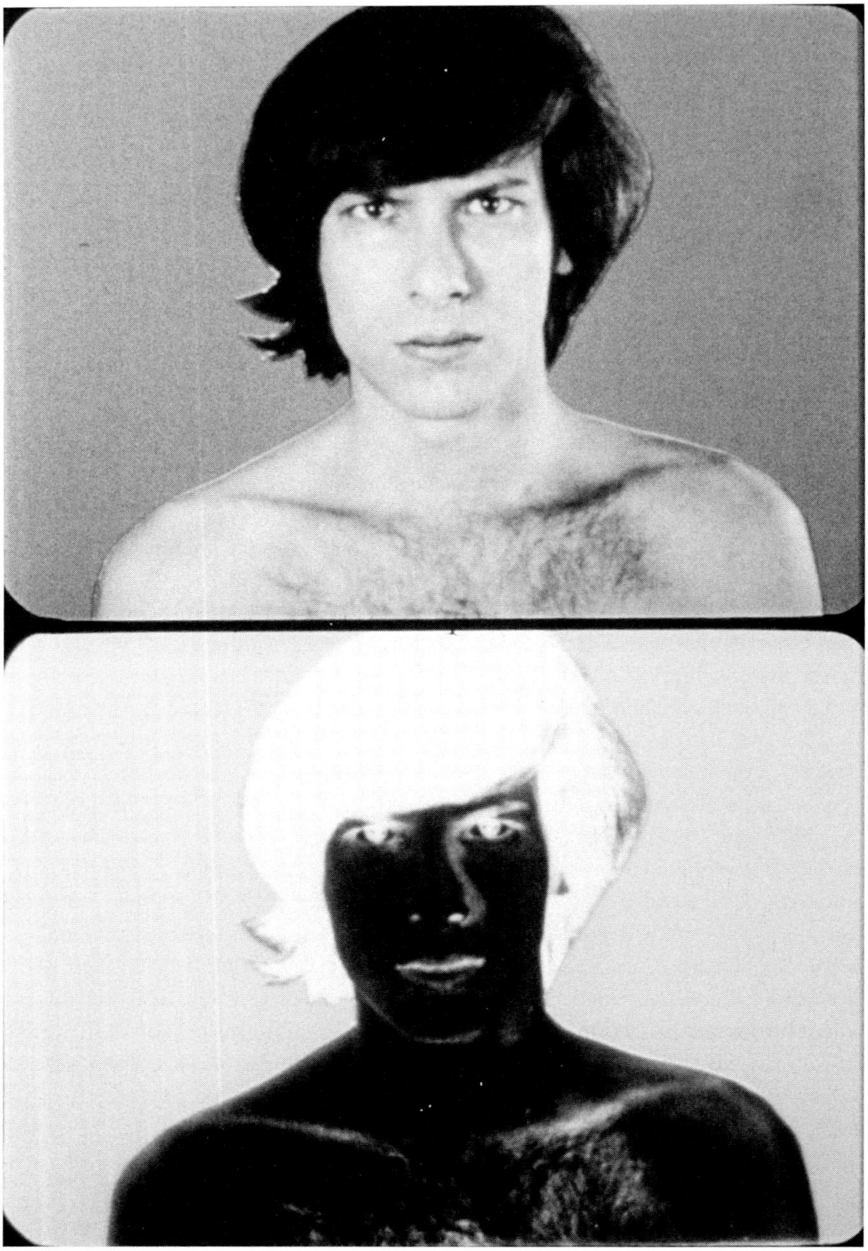

43   Near the end of Paul Sharits's *T,O,U,C,H,I,N,G* David Franks stares at the camera with newly opened eyes.

Preparing for his own suicide by accepting its eventuality, Sharits entered a new phase of cinema that didn't require the graphic staging of his own dismemberment.

The completion of *T,O,U,C,H,I,N,G* marks the end of the first serious phase of Sharits's filmmaking career. It also occasions the artist's second purge of raw emotional content from his films, and an attempt to expunge the violence that animated it. 'After years of anxiety and agony,' he writes,

> I feel like I've come somewhat full cycle (that agony, cyclic/ symmetric/ polarity/ struggle, has consciously and, I'm sure, non-consciously formed itself in all the work I've done after RAY GUN VIRUS) and will be ready, after finishing TOUCHING (the most clear statement of my nearly schizoid obsession with extreme polarities: sex/death, rebirth through death, etc.) to get on with non-symmetrically balanced 'ode of/to pure joy' … somehow life is coming to that point, non-manic but vital feelings of being alive & becoming.[95]

Sharits's attempt to sever his films from the agony of temporal expectation and inevitable disappointment involved a thorough renovation of his conception of isotropic film structure, as well as a move away from representational imagery. 'I was free at last,' Sharits wrote, 'to make works which would celebrate the life process rather than dramatize the anxieties of death.'[96] In 1968, Sharits decided to abandon mandalic structure and instead work 'with a single vector form rather than dualistically balanced vectors: I have come to believe that while they provide discrete experiences, the latter are too closed and death-evoking in their over-stressing of "beginning" and "ending" are, in this sense, models of closed systems.'[97]

Sharits vowed to end his filmic 'appeal to the cruder emotions,' and began to pursue a cinema practice 'more distant' from theatrics.[98] After 1968, Sharits recalls, 'I wanted to remove from the work literary structures and dramatic-psychological themes. In relation to the removals of painting and literary elements, color rhythms which evoked or produced senses of emotionality also should be eliminated …'[99] Yet this dramatic disavowal of 'emotional' cinema must be contextualized in relation to the devastations of his personal life during this period. By his own admission, Sharits made *T,O,U,C,H,I,N,G* in the middle of his own 'season of hell.' By the summer of 1969, his marriage to Frances had collapsed, and Sharits found himself in a 'terrifying and depressing state of being.'[100] He had already manifested symptoms of mental illness and was taking lithium for manic depression, which ran deep in his maternal family.[101] During this pivotal crisis, Sharits acknowledged that

> personal and esthetic transvaluations had to be performed but during nearly every moment of that time the most prominent and often violently exaggerated concern was with what was 'real' and what was ethical … I had never been able

to really separate the esthetic and the ethical (Wittgenstein) and this new set of crises undercut my every confidence.

Epileptic Seizure Comparison (1976)

			Structure is	
simple	be-cause	it can be thought out,	figured out,	
measured	.	It is a discipline	which,	
accepted,	in return	accepts whatever	, even those	
rare moments	of ecstasy,	which, as sugar loaves train horses,		
train us	to make what we make	.		

(John Cage, 'Lecture on Nothing')

Sharits came to reconsider his renunciation of mandalic form, and the 'desperate need to forcibly invoke order' that it embodied: 'The overall (crystalline) form was "perfect" for the (dis)content of my self of "life" and it is only in retrospect that i see it was my own obsessiveness, and not the "mandala structure", that was limiting, that needed to be transcended.' Through 'enormous emotional struggle', Sharits developed 'more fluid, [and] open' formulations of 'filmic architecture.'[102] The first of the artist's 'locational' pieces, *Epileptic Seizure Comparison* (1976) entailed the construction of an architectural space within the gallery that would effectively submerge the besieged viewer in a cocoon of convulsive experience. Although the piece is not always experienced this way, Sharits's stated goal was to produce feelings of empathy in the viewer through a violent barrage of optical and auditory sensation.

Like many of Sharits's works from the late 1960s, *Epileptic Seizure Comparison* (1976) is mobilized by the paradoxical impulse 'to portray the tortured self and provide also an experience for ecstatic feelings and transcendent emotions.'[103] Made in the same year that Sharits was stabbed in the back during an argument, it was the first of the artist's work that featured representational images after a hiatus of nearly six years:

> The issue of 'ontology' has receded from the position of being a high priority and concerns with behavioral psychology and medical pathology have become increasingly prominent; human images, given up for images of various filmstrips in 1968, returned to my work in 1976.[104]

This return of corporeal imagery corresponded to the artist's different 'states of consciousness and feeling.' 'When I feel calmer and more relaxed in the world,' Sharits writes, 'I tend probably to do more formal work, and when I'm feeling more, what shall we say, hysterical, I tend to work with images and rhythms that are more emotional and psychological.'[105] A two-channel film installation that features found footage of patients suffering medically induced seizures

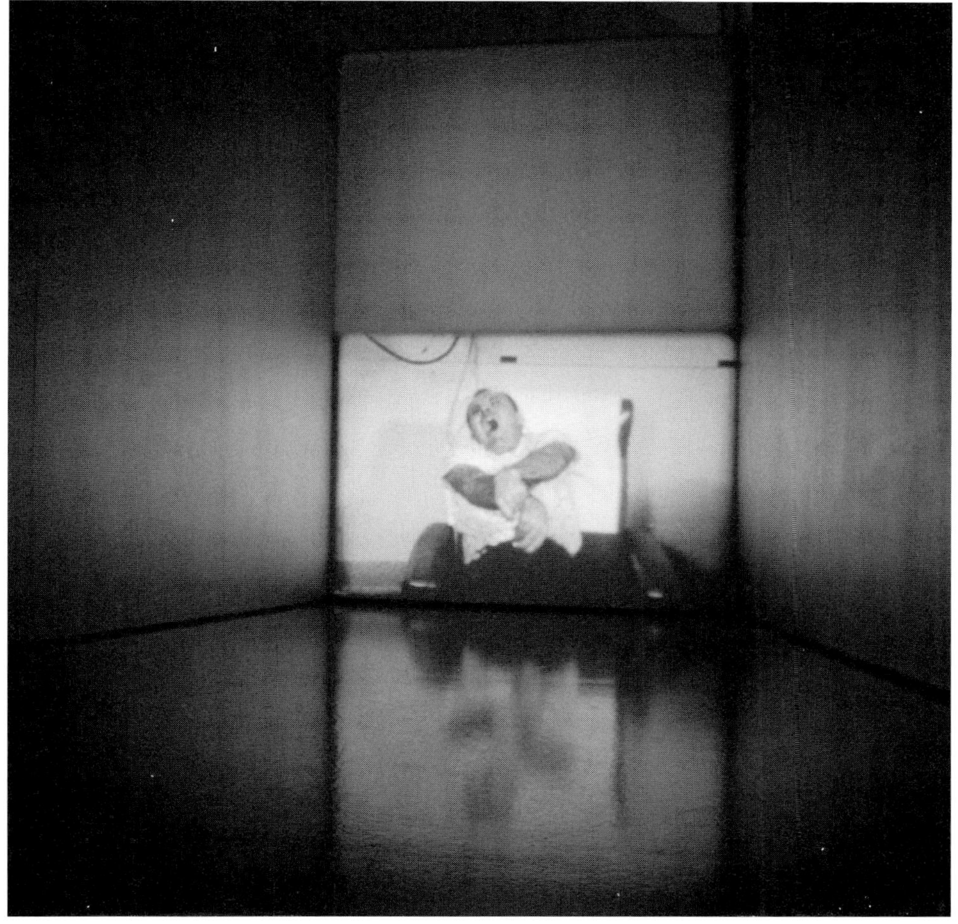

Installation shot of Paul Sharits's first 'locational' piece *Epileptic Seizure Comparison*   **44**
(1976).

interspersed with color flicker, *Epileptic Seizure Comparison* is the artist's most
devastating and effective representation of corporeal agony. It is also one of the
masterpieces of film installation of the postwar period.

The creation of an empathic architecture was integral to Sharits's pursuit of
more expansive forms of vision and relationality. *Epileptic Seizure Comparison*
was originally created as a double screen, quadraphonic 'locational' installation
shown at the M. L. D'Arc Gallery on East 57th Street in New York City. In its
original iteration, the top screen featured footage of a male patient suffering
from a *grand mal* seizure, which is caused by abnormal electric activity throughout the brain and typically involves loss of consciousness and violent muscle

contractions. Simultaneously, the bottom screen presented footage of another male patient jolting from a seizure induced by photic stimulation, or flashes of light. Situated in a trapezoidal-shaped gallery space with reflective aluminum painted walls designed to 'exaggerate the frenetic pulsing' of the moving images, the effect of the images was further enhanced by the stereo sound, which enfolded viewers in a deliberately 'convulsive space.'[106]

The top two speakers delivered the natural vocal sounds made by the subjects while entering their respective seizures, while the bottom two featured soundtracks composed on a sound synthesizer at the Buffalo Media Center in New York. Both 'bottom' tracks were based on the rhythm and structure of

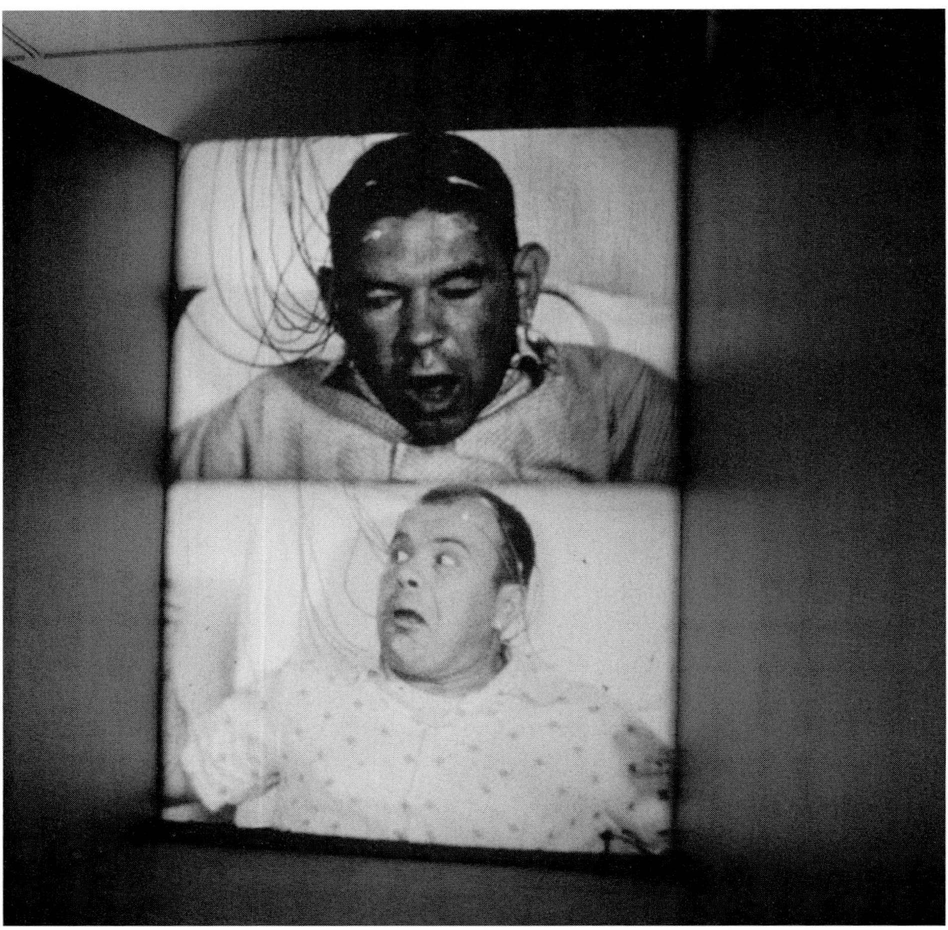

45   Footage of medical patients suffering induced epileptic seizures are intercut with color flicker in Paul Sharits's *Epileptic Seizure Comparison* (1976).

EEGs (electroencephalographs, or recordings of brain wave patterns) taken during the two types of seizures.[107]

Visualizing André Breton's injunction that 'beauty shall be convulsive,' *Epileptic Seizure Comparison* proffers the gruesome, uncontrollable spasms of human medical subjects as they suffer induced epileptic fits. With their heads wired to some kind of recording device, the patients are jolted by seizures that hideously contort their facial expressions, roll their eyes, transform their mouths into anguished grimaces, flail their limbs, and quake their bodies. These images are interrupted by the silent, still pauses between jolts, when the spent patients slump over lifelessly. As the screen throbs with intermittent color flickers, the guttural, feral moans recorded on the film's audio track confirm this impression of exceptional bodily distress. At times, the bodies are shaken so forcefully that the subjects look as if they will fall off the bed or chair where they are confined. Other times, their faces register what looks like tremendous fear.

In spite of the appearance of extreme discomfort, Sharits maintained that convulsive forms of epilepsy were 'not in themselves painful,' although sufferers could unwittingly injure themselves while in the throes of a fit.[108] Yet the fact that the hideous animation we witness bears no relation to the pain it visually signifies seems to only further evacuate the subjects of their agency and intentionality. Displaying the body throbbing in what seems like spasms of death, *Epileptic Seizure Comparison* transforms the frenetic motions of the anguished body into a pornographic spectacle. Watching the film, I can't help but recall the gruesome sight of the 'dancing chicken,' a now obsolete relic of the arcades in New York City's Chinatown, in which a sorry caged bird would involuntarily shimmy to the throb of an electrified floor. Dancing like this, one might as well lose one's head.

These are not, as we know, ideal conditions for identification. Yet how might immersion in a visually and acoustically throbbing architectural space mitigate the specularization of the abject, disabled body? I would like to take a brief detour to consider the type of optical and epistemological relationship that Sharits may have been trying to avoid in his decision to submerge the viewer in an epileptic chamber. I do so by way of another architecturally minded filmmaker, Michelangelo Antonioni, whose early, aborted attempt to document psychiatric patients underscores the dangerous relations of power that inevitably exist between filmmakers and their subjects.

> The first time I put an eye behind a camera, it was in a lunatic asylum. … A number of my friends and myself had decided to make a documentary on the insane. The director of the asylum was most anxious to be of service, he even went so far as to roll himself over the floor to show us how his patients reacted under certain provocations. But I was determined to make a documentary that would include the inmates them-

selves; I was so insistent on this point that he finally said: 'Okay, let's try it.'

So we set up the camera, got the lights ready and placed the inmates around the room in preparation for the first shot. I must say that they were very cooperative in following our instructions and extremely careful not to make any mistakes. They helped us move things around and I was really quite surprised by their efficiency and good will.

Finally, I gave the order to turn on the lights. I was a bit nervous and anxious. Suddenly, the room was flooded with light, and for an instant the inmates remained absolutely stationary as though they were petrified. I have never seen such expressions of total fear on the faces of any actors. The scene that followed is indescribable. The inmates started screaming, twisting, and rolling themselves over the floor – just as the head of the asylum had demonstrated earlier. In no time at all the room became an inferno. The inmates tried to desperately to get away from the lights as if they were being attacked by some kind of prehistoric monster. The same faces that had kept madness within human bounds in the preceding calm, were now crumpled and devastated. And this time we were the ones who stood petrified at the sight. The cameraman didn't even have the strength to turn on the motor, nor I to give an order. It was the head of the asylum who yelled, 'Stop, off the lights!' And as the room became silent and subdued, we saw a slow and feeble movement of bodies which seemed to be in their final states of agony.

I have never forgotten that scene. And it was around this scene that we unconsciously started talking about neorealism.[109]

As is evident from his reminiscences, Antonioni's first cinematic crisis pivots around his failure to anticipate the violent power of the apparatus upon the incarcerated subjects he wished to film. Sharits's own consideration of the apparatus's projective force extends beyond the relationship between the filmmaker and his subjects in the production process to a consideration of the ways in which the architectural spaces of reception help shape the relationship between spectators and films. Yet in spite of their different approaches to imaging the disabled, however, the description of Antonioni's writhing patients sounds remarkably like the out-of-control flailing of bodies that we witness in Sharits's *Epileptic Seizure Comparison*. To what extent is it possible to transform such dehumanizing footage of suffering into a medium for expanded forms of identification?

In his pursuit of more empathic filmic practice, Paul Sharits conjured a long, albeit marginalized tradition of re-thinking architectural form through feeling. Although the term 'empathy' did not gain psychological importance until the late 1950s, in the late nineteenth and early twentieth century, empathy was the primary theoretical concept in aesthetics and art history used to link the perceiving subject to the object of perception.[110] Aesthetician Robert

Vischer coined the term empathy, *einfühlung*, in 1873. In its original German, the term literally means 'in feeling.' Vischer's notion of empathy was rooted in his own ideas of mental projection and the physiology of sensation,[111] and although physiology has receded in our colloquial understanding of empathy, it was central to the theorization of an affectively expanded architectural practice in the late nineteenth and early twentieth centuries.[112] Heavily influenced by the father of experimental psychology Wilhelm Wundt's 1874 text *Principles of Physiological Psychology*,[113] psychologists and aesthetic theorists began to apply theories of empathy to architecture simultaneous with the development of the technologies of cinema. Wundt was, in fact, the teacher of Hugo Munsterberg, one of the first theorists of the new medium. According to Heinrich Wölfflin, the best-known architectural form psychologist, in empathy, the viewer's feelings enter the object as a projection of bodily identification. Wölfflin described how in relation to the 'architectural body' the 'effect of yielding to an oppressive weight is sometimes so powerful that we imagine that the forms affected are actually suffering.'[114] In the work of aesthetic theorists such as August Schmarsow and Wilhelm Worringer, space itself was conceived as a receptacle for projected feelings.[115]

Unlike sympathy, which depends upon the distinction between subject and object in spite of their parallelism, empathy denotes such a complex transference of one's ego into the object that the subject and object become fused. Architect Richard Neutra recognized this fusion in an unpublished 1940s essay entitled 'Empathy-Infeeling' that is quoted at length in Sylvia Lavin's eye-opening study *Form Follows Libido*. Neutra writes:

> A suitable definition for love, and probably even for all incipient steps of personal 'infeeling' which lead to this culminating phenomenon, is: 'Being favorably stimulated by the recognition that one is oneself a stimulus to the other individual.' …
>
> Empathy is quite generally a constitutional potential concretely developed by exercise and accidental or purposeful conditioning. It is perhaps similar to sympathy, but at any rate quite surpasses it in emotive identification with the other individual. Empathy means in fact a far reaching physiological functioning (with many neuro-cerebral implications) 'as if' … one were that other individual.[116]

But if empathy linked the body to space by projecting feelings that were inside the subject onto the outside of phenomenal objects, then it should come as no surprise that empathic space was not always pleasurable. As Lavin writes, 'the space of the world does not produce sensations of pleasure but rather threatens to overwhelm, consume, and absorb.'[117]

The feeling of being overwhelmed is a common response to Sharits's work, particularly *Epileptic Seizure Comparison*. Reviewing the installation in the *Village Voice*, Jonas Mekas writes: 'the image didn't exactly come at me. But the room, the space did. I found the shape of the room very unpleasant. It offended my aesthetic senses. It oppressed me. It disturbed me. I wanted out of it, and out I went … The "V" shape left me miserable. Nobody will every drag me again into a "V"-shaped room; I promise you.'[118]

Mekas's aversion to *Epileptic Seizure Comparison* pivoted upon its aggressive mode of architectural address, which transformed the exhibition space into a perceptual torture chamber. His impression of the room's architecture was anything but empathetic. Not all visitors to the gallery were as repulsed as Mekas. Calling the piece 'superb,' filmmaker Leslie Thornton wrote to Sharits that it had:

> been ages since I've been that overtaken by something new … The fascination it held for me stemmed from its root in paradox – the seduction of horror, the rapid negation of the initial seduction through formal structure, the mitigation thru repetition & duo image – and then more subjective responses of almost identification with the subjects, disorientation, loss of contact, sense of being manipulated & wanting to be … But all came down to an event that was bizarrely beautiful.[119]

Using repetition to 'mitigate' the horror of the images, Sharits strives to create physiological empathy between the subjects of the film and its spectators. Whether or not viewers find this compulsory identification gruesome or gratifying, they tend to acknowledge the film's convulsive effects on their own bodies.

In its profound embrace of abjection, *Epileptic Seizure Comparison* engages its viewers in involuntary, corporeal identification with anonymous, medically disposable subjects of chronic neurological disease. As someone who also suffered from an inherited illness, Sharits seized upon the disease's alternative history as a pathway to ecstasy, catharsis and insight. For precisely the same reasons Sharits considered epilepsy a 'sad malady' – because seizures were 'unexpected, uncontrollable, and involve a lapse of consciousness'[120] – he realized its potential for inspiring creative elation. Since brain waves reach an abnormally high altitude during seizure at the same time that their frequencies slow down, Sharits considered the convulsive epileptic state akin to certain practices in Zen meditation and Shamanism, which strive to increase brain activity along similar axes. Similar to Hungarian film theorist Béla Balázs's notion that ungovernable facial spasms could reveal intimate *psychological* truths about film's subjects,[121] Sharits deemed the involuntary muscular spasms of epilepsy a form of higher consciousness.

Since seizures could be induced by 'photic' stimulation, which can occur in anything from light reflections and flashes in everyday environments to the regular but usually unperceived rhythms of film and television, Sharits regarded epileptic reactions as uniquely compatible with the light-based medium of cinema.[122] Furthermore, since exposing patients to light flickers had been one of the primary, and most effective methods of researching the disease, Sharits's signature flicker effect is particularly well suited to exploring the phenomenology of the disease.

Even when converted into a single screen, color, sound film, *Epileptic Seizure Comparison* preserves the essential duality of the original composition. Sharits arranged the two reels sequentially so that the footage of the photic seizure followed images of the *grand mal* seizure. Furthermore, Sharits intercut this medical footage with abstract imagery of a color roll and a black-and-white roll of a synthesizer's simulation of brain wave patterns, whose pulsations were used to 'emphasize the contortions and movements of the figure.'[123] Although the spectator could not be fully immersed in the space of seizure, as in the original installation, the film fulfills Sharits's goal of 'creating a sound-image-space situation wherein sympathetic observers ... [could] begin to identify with the convulsive epileptic.'[124]

Like the 'body genres' that Linda Williams and Carol Clover have theorized (pornography, horror, and melodrama),[125]*Epileptic Seizure Comparison* provokes the spectator to physiologically mimic the involuntary gestures of the bodies on screen. Knowing that photic epileptics might be unable to stop their brain waves from 'falling into synchronous relationship' with the film's 'external stimuli,' Sharits dissuaded them from entering such an intense 'field of excitation.'[126] Yet even if we are immune to such compulsory neurological mirroring, our own bodies cannot help but bear psychological and physiological witness to the apocalyptic orgasm of pain that explodes on screen. By displaying the body throbbing in what seems like spasms of death, *Epileptic Seizure Comparison* transforms the frenetic motions of the anguished body into a pornographic spectacle. What types of knowledge do such provocative images claim to produce and what are the implications of our participation in the production of such morbid ecstasy?

At several points, the camera zooms in and out as the patient's mouth emits a horrific (though inaudible) scream; it seems as if the approach of the camera itself, or the person wielding it, is an object of terror. In such moments, we recognize how our own perception is aligned with the menace of the apparatus, since we are only privy to such images as a result of its disciplinary interrogations. As in the famous Milgram study conducted only five years earlier, in which test subjects overwhelmingly consented to the electric-shock torture of seemingly anguished 'patients' by white-coated 'doctors' (unbeknownst to them, both roles were played by actors),[127] *Epileptic Seizure Comparison* implicates viewers in the production of, and consensual participation in, the gruesome spectacle proffered by its 'medical' footage. Not only is there no evidence of the identity of the film's subjects – are they voluntary or coerced patients, or just actors? – but the film never indicates the genealogy of Sharits's presumably (but not necessarily) found footage. Watching this film, it is impossible to determine whether Sharits's sadistic assault on the spectator is a further exploitation of authentically disabled patients, or a radical, visceral critique of a medical and cinematic apparatus that instrumentalizes and dehumanizes its subjects. For even as we are confronted with the apparent pain of these others, our inability to verify its authenticity problematizes any ready, prefabricated response to the spectacle of suffering.[128]

Sharits was cognizant of the film's difficulty. 'The problem that I see is that possibly these inclinations [towards representing the tortured self and providing a transcendent experience for the viewer] could work against each other and cancel each other out.' Speaking specifically about *Epileptic Seizure Comparison*, Sharits recognizes that, 'for some people, the nature of the subject is too revolting or frightening for them to allow themselves to feel the kind of release that I want.'[129] While acknowledging his desire to experience the 'state of exultation just prior to the seizure,' Sharits wondered about the film's dubious ethics, and whether he 'should be tampering with images of a certain form of human disability.'[130]

Sharits had good reason to fret. Cinema's own history of documenting epilepsy is atrocious. Beginning at the turn of the century, filming the seizures of epileptic patients had been one of the key objectives of European and American neurologists and psychiatrists. In the United States, the tradition of filming epileptic seizure dates back to at least 1905, when the Craig Colony for Epileptics in New York began subjecting its patients to constant cinematic surveillance in an effort to record every seizure at the facility.[131] Since seizures were unpredictable, and medical students could thus rarely study them, the technologies of cinematic recording were instrumental to the medical interrogation of epilepsy in spite of the fact that, as visual culture theorist Lisa Cartwright has explained, these fetishistic images of nude writhing bodies produced no knowledge of the disease's etiology.[132] Yet as becomes evident in the Nazi regime, which used filmic records of seizure to support the sterilization and extermination of the disabled,[133] the cinematic interrogation of epilepsy has been historically inseparable from the eugenic project of racial purification. Although seizures were not induced for the purpose of study at the Craig Colony as they were by the Nazis, these studies share a mutual fascination with fetishistic images of the out-of-control body. Furthermore, both regimes construct epilepsy as a form of corporeal excess that could be used to taxonomize and discipline 'pathological' forms of human locomotion and the subjects who involuntarily performed them.

Rapt attention to the frenzied body also animates *Epileptic Seizure Comparison*. Nonetheless, Sharits claimed that the film's goal was not to further pathologize these radically othered subjects, but create a visceral means of corporeal identification with them: 'Seizure Comparison is an attempt to orchestrate sound and light rhythms in an intimate and proportional space, an ongoing location where-in non-epileptic persons may begin to experience, under controlled conditions, what Dr. [W. Grey] Walter calls the majestic potentials of convulsive seizure.'[134] Yet in spite of Sharits's avowed feelings of 'warmth and compassion' towards his subjects,[135] they are inevitably de-personalized through their convulsive gestures. Disciplined by science, and 're-mastered' by art, the bodies of these epileptic patients have been doubly transformed into prurient objects of morbid curiosity. In spite of Sharits's embrace of film's cathartic potential, there is no assurance that art can redeem these subjects from ontological banishment. Troubled by this paradox, Sharits questioned his own propensity towards cruelty:

> There's also the possibility of including there the dematerialization of images by taking someone's face and interspersing colors between shots of the face so as to break it up, to dissolve it, to fragment it in time and with color. I recognize that these elements exist and I'm not sure if the motivation on my part is perverse or sadistic. I don't feel that it is. Nevertheless, the evidence seems to be such that I am in some way malicious, aggressive.[136]

Regarding the pain of others

How do we reconcile the film's own abusiveness – of the on-screen subject, as well as the spectator – with the filmmaker's stated intentions to produce an empathetic and transcendent experience? Furthermore, does formal intervention absolve the filmmaker of ethical responsibility? These questions were paramount for Sharits, who wondered, '"What is my attitude toward the subject of the film?" "What am I trying to do to the audience that sees the film?"' Wary of representations of torture designed to shock audiences, Sharits critiqued the tendency to disguise aggression as empathy.[137]

In her study of sadomasochistic art, poet Maggie Nelson challenges Antonin Artaud's presumption in the *Theater of Cruelty* that violent art can 'restore us, or deliver us anew, to an unalienated, unmediated flow of existence characterized by a more authentic relation to the so-called real.'[138] But even as Nelson embraces more compassionate forms of performance, she concedes a place for artworks that are 'intelligently,' rather than 'stupidly' cruel, in which brutality is not 'being used as a bluff, or a bludgeon.'[139] Of course Artaud did not have color flicker in mind when he theorized the need for cruelty in art. Only in the ivory tower do we dare complain that color hurts! On the other hand, perhaps only those who have endured Sharits's films have the right to maintain that it can and it does. While it is important to distinguish films that occasion optical duress with works that stage the actual mutilation of bodies – Nelson returns repeatedly to examples by the Viennese Actionists – *Epileptic Seizure Comparison* collapses this distinction.

Merging the pain occasioned by color flicker with footage documenting the exploitation of presumably real medical subjects, *Epileptic Seizure Comparison* broaches important questions about the relationship between anguish and enlightenment. Although postwar art is rife with the types of atrocities that Artaud advocated in *The Theater of Cruelty*, I wonder whether it is possible to make empathetic art that pivots on such cruelty or spiritually enlightened work that relies upon the body's shattering. Moved as I am by many of postwar art's cruel indulgences, I have always been suspicious of the instrumentalization of the body for metaphysical effect. Relying upon the fraught distinction between the body and the soul, epistemological regimes that claim to detour through the body in order to access a 'higher' truth have been notorious abusers of the very bodies they are so keen to transcend. On the other hand, programs for spiritual enlightenment that disavow the body are hopeless. How might we ever hope to transcend anguish if we don't have access to it?

Writing the end of a book that I have housed in my body for nearly a decade, I find myself suspended in ambivalence. Perched on the threshold between endurable and unendurable stimuli, Sharits's films link their creator to the viewer through a luminescent current of pain. While I am tempted to say that the incessant throb of Sharits's flicker viscerally bridges the gap between us – *we are in it together, aren't we?* – I am reminded of Susan Sontag's admonition that 'no "we" should be taken for granted when the subject is looking at other people's pain.'[140] Though he employs the types of visceral shock that Artaud advocated, Sharits does not allow us to become habituated to the pain he represents; even after years of watching, thinking, and feeling his films, I have never been able to accustom my body to their nauseating assault, nor to master the affect they produce. While I hoped that writing about *Epileptic Seizure Comparison* would be cathartic, I discover that my empathy with these subjects has not absolved me of the excruciating burden of my responsibility towards them. The film haunts me.

Is it possible that what feels like sadomasochistic cruelty might be a radical form of empathy? The now outdated physiologically based notion of empathy in *fin-de-siècle* psychological, aesthetic, and architectural theory is a crucial tool for comprehending the seeming contradictions in Sharits's assaulting, empathetic work. Acknowledging the bodily substrate of psychic functions, *Epileptic Seizure Comparison* approaches empathy as a kind of physiological conditioning. Though such conditioning is not, for the most part, pleasurable, this abject 'unmastering' of the viewer is the key to Sharits's ethical and aesthetic project. Subjected to the same type of perceptual barrage as the film's subjects, we are decomposed and eviscerated. Try as we may, we cannot physiologically overcome or become habituated to the painful stimulation of Sharits's work. Entering us with projective force, the other's abjection expands and remakes us. Such mimesis enables us to acknowledge our mutual precarity, and by doing so, become more fully human. The 'higher consciousness' we achieve in *Epileptic Seizure Comparison* is not some state of incorporeal bliss, but a recognition that it is only when we move beyond the pleasure principle into pain that we become fully cognizant of our inescapable immersion in the flesh of the world.

Notes

1 Paul Sharits to Stan Brakhage, June 11, 1966, in *Buffalo Heads: Media Study, Media Practice, Media Pioneers, 1973–1990*, ed. Woody Vasulka and Peter Weibel (Karlsruhe: Center for Art and Media Karlsruhe, 2008; Cambridge, MA: The MIT Press, 2008), p. 258.

2 Jacques Lacan, 'The Instance of the Letter in the Unconscious, or Reason Since Freud', *Écrits: The First Complete Edition in English*, trans. Bruce Fink (New York: W.W. Norton, 2007), pp. 412–444.

3 Paul Sharits to Stan Brakhage, June 3, 1966, in *Buffalo Heads*, pp. 256–257; p. 257.

4 P. Adams Sitney, *Visionary Film: The American Avant-Garde 1943–2000*, 3rd ed. (Oxford: Oxford University Press, 2002), p. 348.

5 Sitney, *Visionary Film*, pp. 347–370; Annette Michelson, 'Toward Snow', *Artforum* (June 1971), pp. 30–37. In his chapter on 'Pure Film', David James writes that 'structural film marks a categorical break with the aesthetic and social project of the underground', through its 'general subordination in interests in representation'. David E. James, *Allegories of Cinema: American Film in the Sixties* (Princeton, NJ: Princeton University Press, 1989), pp. 240, 241.

6 Paul Sharits, 'Notes on Films, 1966–1968', *Film Culture*, 47 (1969), pp. 13–16.

7 Andy Warhol and Pat Hackett, *POPism: The Warhol Sixties* (New York: Harcourt Brace Jovanovich, 1980), p. 50.

8 Paul Sharits, 'Interview with Paul Sharits', interview by Jean-Claude Lebensztejn, June 12 and 14, 1983, trans. Sandra Reid, *Paul Sharits*, ed. yann beauvais (Dijon: Les presses du réel, 2008), pp. 71–101, p. 90.

9 Paul Sharits, 'My painting (& film) for Galerie A,' in *Paul Sharits*, pp. 163–167, p. 165.

10 Leonard Cohen, 'The Old Revolution', *Songs from a Room*, Sony Music Entertainment, 1969.

11 Paul Sharits, 'My painting (& film) for Galerie A,' p. 163.

12 Ibid., p. 164.

13 Ibid.

14 Wassily Kandinsky, *Concerning the Spiritual in Art*, trans. M.T.H. Sadler (New York: Dover Publications, 1977), p. 24.

15 Paul Sharits, 'My painting (& film) for Galerie A,' p. 165.

16 Kandinsky, *Concerning the Spiritual*, pp. 36, 23.

17 Ibid., p. 37.

18 Paul Sharits, 'My painting (& film) for Galerie A,' p. 165.

19 Rosalind Krauss, 'Paul Sharits', in *Paul Sharits*, pp. 47–55; pp. 47, 54.

20 Hollis Frampton, 'Interview with Paul Sharits,' March 1, 1973, in *Buffalo Heads*, pp. 280–291; p. 280.

21 Annette Michelson, 'Paul Sharits and the Critique of Illusionism: An Introduction', *Film Culture*, no. 65–66 (1978), pp. 83–89; p. 87; originally published in *Projected Images: Peter Campus, Rockne Krebs, Paul Sharits, Michael Snow, Ted Victoria, Robert Whitman* (Minneapolis, MN: Walker Art Center, 1974).

22 Ibid., p. 84, emphasis added.

23 Sharits uses the term 'cinematics' to describe a practice of making and viewing films that critique 'natural-naïve conceptions of cinema.' Paul Sharits, 'A Cinematics Model for Film Studies in Higher Education,' *Film Studies*, no. 65–66 (1978), pp. 43–68; p. 44.

24 Sharits, 'Notes on Films,' p. 13, quoted in Stuart Liebman, 'Apparent Motion and Film Structure: Paul Sharits's *Shutter Interface*', *Millennium Film Journal*, 1, no. 2 (Spring–Summer 1978), pp. 101–109; p. 105.

25 Paul Sharits, 'Postscript as Preface,' *Film Culture*, no. 65–66 (1978), pp. 1–6; p. 5.

26 Paul Sharits, 'Exhibition / Frozen Frames: Regarding the "Frozen Film Frame" Series: A Statement for the "5th International Experimental Film Festival," Knokke, December 1974,' *Film Culture*, no. 65–66 (1978), pp. 81–83; p. 81.

27 Paul Sharits, 'Hearing: Seeing,' *Film Culture* no. 65–66 (1978), pp. 69–75; pp. 70–71.

28 Ibid.

29 Paul Sharits to Stan Brakhage, [late November/early December] 1966, in *Buffalo Heads*, p. 259.

30 Paul Sharits, 'Unpublished interview with John du Cane and Simon Field, London 1970', 1970, www.paulsharits.com/canepart1.htm (accessed 21 August 2011).

31 Kandinsky, *Concerning the Spiritual*, p. 14.

32 M.T.H. Sadler, introduction to Kandinsky, *Concerning the Spiritual in Art*, p. xx.

33 Kandinsky, *Concerning the Spiritual*, p. 32.

34 Sharits, 'My painting (& film) for Galerie A,' p. 163.

35 Clement Greenberg, 'Towards a New Laocoon,' [1940], 'Abstract Art' [1944], and 'Abstract and Representational' [1954], *Art in Theory 1900–1990: An Anthology of Changing Ideas*, ed. Charles Harrison and Paul Wood (Oxford: Blackwell, 1993), pp. 554–560.

36 Paul Sharits, 'Words per Page,' in *Buffalo Heads*, p. 272.

37 Frampton, 'Interview with Paul Sharits,' p. 283.

38 Ibid.

39 Ibid.

40 Paul Sharits, 'Postscript as Preface,' pp. 5–6.

41 Paul Sharits, 'An Interview with Paul Sharits,' interview by Linda Cathcart, *Film Culture*, no. 65–66 (1978), pp. 103–108; p. 107, originally published in *Paul Sharits: Dream Displacement and Other Projects* (Buffalo, NY: Albright-Knox Gallery, 1976).

42 Sitney, *Visionary Film*, p. 361.

43 Ibid., pp. 362, 363–364.

44 Ibid., p. 344.

45 Sally Banes, *Greenwich Village 1963: Avant-Garde Performance and the Effervescent Body* (Durham, NC: Duke University Press, 1993).

46 Thomas Gunning, 'The Cinema of Attractions: Early Film, Its Spectator and the Avant-Garde', in *Early Cinema: Space, Frame, Narrative*, ed. Thomas Elsaesser (London: BFI, 1990), pp. 56–62; Gunning, 'An Aesthetic of Astonishment: Early Film and the (In)Credulous Spectator,' *Art and Text* 34 (Spring 1989).

47 Quoted in 'Paul Sharits films,' *Mikehoolboom.com*, 'Writings on Artists,' www.mikehoolboom.com/?p=39#essay_452 (accessed August 29, 2013).

48 Paul Sharits, 'Mental Funerals: An Interview with Paul Sharits by John du Cane and Simon Field,' 1970, on *Mikehoolboom.com*, 'Writings on Artists,' www.mikehoolboom.com/?p=39#essay_468 (accessed August 29, 2013).

49 Sharits, 'Notes on Films.'

50 Ibid.

51 Antonin Artaud, 'The Theatre of Cruelty (First Manifesto)' and 'The Theater of Cruelty (Second Manifesto),' in *The Theater and Its Double*, trans. Mary C. Richard (New York: Grove Press, 1994), pp. 89–100, 122–132.

52 Walter Benjamin, 'The Work of Art in the Age of Mechanical Reproduction,' in *Illuminations*, trans. Harry Zohn, ed. Hannah Arendt (New York: Schocken Books, 1968), pp. 217–251; pp. 233–234.

53 Sharits, 'Postscript as Preface,' p. 2, emphasis added.

54 Frampton, 'Interview with Paul Sharits,' p. 280.

55 Paul Sharits, '-UR(i)N(ul)LS:TREAM:S:S:ECTION:S:SECTION:-S:S:ECTIONED (A)(lysis)JO: "1968–70,"' *Film Culture*, no. 65–66 (1978), pp. 7–28; p. 19.

56 Ibid., p. 24.

57 Sharits, 'Paul Sharits Films' on *Mikehoolbloom.com*.

58 Sharits, '-UR(i)N(ul)LS:TREAM:S:S:ECTION:S:SECTION:-S:S:ECTIONED(A)(lysis)JO: "1968–70,"' p. 18.

59 Ibid., p. 17, emphasis added.

60 Sigmund Freud, *The Interpretation of Dreams*, trans. and ed. James Strachey (New York: Basic Books, 1955).

61 Sigmund Freud, *Beyond the Pleasure Principle*, trans. and ed. James Strachey (New York: W.W. Norton, 1961), pp. 4, 25, 33–38.

62 Ibid., p. 12.

63 Ibid., p. 5.

64 Ibid., p. 11.

65 Ibid., p. 36.

66 Ibid., p. 4.

67 Ibid., p. 11.

68 Ibid., p. 38.

69 Ibid., p. 22.

70 Ibid., p. 35.

71 Christopher Sharits, 'About Paul,' email message to the author, August 8, 2011.

72 Christopher Sharits, 'About Paul,' email message to the author, July 11, 2011.

73 Paul Sharits, 'Interview with Paul Sharits,' interview by Jean-Claude Lebensztejn, p. 97.

74 Carol Clover, *Men, Women, and Chain Saws: Gender in the Modern Horror Film.* (Princeton, NJ: Princeton University Press, 1993).

75 Kandinsky, *Concerning the Spiritual*, p. 25.

76 Sharits to Brakhage, April 18, 1968, *Buffalo Heads*, p. 261.

77 Laura Marks, *The Skin of the Film: Intercultural Cinema, Embodiment, and the Senses* (Durham, NC: Duke University Press, 2000), p. 162.

78 Sharits, 'An Interview with Paul Sharits,' interview by Linda Cathcart, p. 106.

79 These artificial 'wounds' were made with streaks of glitter rather than blood. Sharits, 'Unpublished interview with John du Cane and Simon Field, London 1970.'

80 Ibid.

81 Sigmund Freud, 'Some Psychical Consequences of the Anatomical Distinction Between the Sexes,' in *The Freud Reader*, ed. Peter Gay (New York: W.W. Norton, 1989), pp. 670–678.

82 Jacques Lacan, 'The Split Between the Eye and the Gaze,' in *Four Fundamental Concepts of Psychoanalysis*, trans. Alan Sheridan (New York: Karnac, 1977); Kaja Silverman, 'Fassbinder and Lacan: A Reconsideration of Gaze, Look and Image,' *Camera Obscura*, 7, no.1 (January, 1989), pp. 54–85.

83 Freud, *Beyond the Pleasure Principle*, chapter 2.

84 Sharits, '-UR(i)N(ul)LS:TREAM:S:S:ECTION:S:SECTION:-S:S:ECTIONED(A)(lysis)JO: "1968–70,"' p. 23.

85 Ibid., p. 15.

86 Sitney, *Visionary Film*, p. 389.

87 Kandinsky, *Concerning the Spiritual*, p. 15.

88 Sharits, 'Unpublished interview with John du Cane and Simon Field, London 1970.'

89 Julia Kristeva, 'Approaching Abjection,' in *Powers of Horror: An Essay on Abjection*, trans. Leon S. Roudiez (New York: Columbia University Press, 1982), p. 4.

90 Kaja Silverman, *Flesh of My Flesh* (Stanford, CA: Stanford University Press, 2009).

91 'Paul J. Sharits, 50, dies; avant-garde filmmaker,' *The Buffalo News*, July 14, 1993. C7.

92 Christopher Sharits, 'About Paul,' email message to the author, August 8, 2011.

93 Sharits, 'Unpublished interview with John du Cane and Simon Field, London 1970.'

94 Frampton, 'Interview with Paul Sharits,' p. 290.

95 Sharits to Stan Brakhage, April 18, 1968, in *Buffalo Heads*, p. 261.

96 Sharits, '-UR(i)N(ul)LS:TREAM:S:S:ECTION:S:SECTION:-S:S:ECTIONED(A)(lysis)JO: "1968–70,"' p. 11.

97 Sharits, 'Postscript as Preface,' p. 6.

98 Sharits, 'Unpublished interview with John du Cane and Simon Field, London 1970.'

99 Sharits, 'Hearing: Seeing,' p. 72.

100 Sharits, 'Postscript as Preface,' p. 2.

101 According to Christopher Sharits, two of Florence Romeo's siblings also committed suicide.

102 Paul Sharits, ' – UR(i)N(ul)LS:TREAM:S:S:ECTION:S:SECTION:-S:S:ECTIONED(A)(lysis)JO: '1968–70,' p. 12.

103 Sharits 'Interview with Paul Sharits,' interview by Jean-Claude Lebensztejn, p. 89.

104 Paul Sharits, 'Statement Regarding Multiple Screen/Sound "Locational" Film Environments – Installations (1976),' *Film Culture*, no. 65–66 (1978), pp.79–80; p. 80.

105 Sharits, 'Interview with Paul Sharits,' interview by Jean-Claude Lebensztejn, p. 81.

106 Paul Sharits, 'Locational Film Pieces,' *Film Culture*, no. 65–66 (1978), p. 124.

107 Ibid., pp. 123–124.

108 Ibid., p. 123.

109 Michelangelo Antonioni, 'Making a Film is My Way of Life,' *Architecture of Vision: Writings and Interviews on Cinema* (New York: Marsilio Publishers, 1996), pp. 14–17.

110 Sylvia Lavin, *Form Follows Libido: Architecture and Richard Neutra in a Psychoanalytic Culture* (Cambridge, MA: The MIT Press, 2007), p. 35.

111 Ibid., p. 36.

112 Ibid., p. 33.

113 Wilhelm Max Wundt, *Principles of Physiological Psychology*, trans. Edward Bradford Titchener (New York: Macmillan, 1910).

114 Wölfflin, Heinrich, *Renaissance and Baroque*, trans. Kathrin Simon (London: Collins, 1964), p. 45.

115 Lavin, *Form Follows Libido*, 36.

116 Richard Neutra, 'Empathy-Infeeling,' 'Ideas' folder, box 193, vol. 1, Richard J. Neutra Archives, Charles E. Young Research Library, University of California, quoted in Lavin, *Form Follows Libido*, p. 34.

117 Lavin, *Form Follows Libido*, p. 37.

118 Jonas Mekas, 'Movie Journal,' *The Village Voice*, July 15, 1976.

119 Leslie Thornton to Paul Sharits, May 22, 1976, Paul Sharits Collection, WYN Artist Archives, Burchfield Penney Art Center.

120 Sharits, 'Locational Film Pieces,' p. 123.

121 Béla Balázs, 'The Face of Man,' in *Theory of the Film: Character and Growth of a New Art*, trans. Edith Bone (London: Denis Dobson, 1952), pp. 60–88.

122 Sharits, 'Locational Film Pieces,' p. 123.

123 Sharits, 'Interview with Paul Sharits,' interview by Jean-Claude Lebensztejn, p. 81.

124 Sharits, 'Locational Film Pieces,' p. 124.

125 Linda Williams, 'Film Bodies: Gender, Genre, and Excess,' in *Film Genre Reader II*, ed. Barry Keith Grant (Austin: University of Texas, 2003), pp. 141–159; Clover, *Men, Women and Chain Saws*.

126 Sharits, 'Interview with Paul Sharits,' interview by Jean-Claude Lebensztejn, p. 92.

127 Stanley Milgram, *Obedience to Authority: An Experimental View*. New York: Harper & Row, 1974.

128 Susan Sontag, *Regarding the Pain of Others* (New York: Picador, 2003).

129 Sharits, 'Interview with Paul Sharits,' interview by Jean-Claude Lebensztejn, p. 89.

130 Ibid.

131 Lisa Cartwright, *Screening the Body: Tracing Medicine's Visual Culture* (Minneapolis: University of Minnesota Press 1995), pp. 56–58.

132 Ibid.

133 Ulf Schmidt, *Medical Films, Ethics and Euthanasia in Nazi Germany: The History of Medical Research and Teaching Films of the Reich Office for Educational Films /*

Reich Institute for Films in Science and Education, 1933–1945 (Husum: Matthiesen Verlag, 2002), p. 201.

134   Sharits, 'Locational Film Pieces,' p. 124. Dr. W. Grey Walter was a brain surgeon and pioneer of electroencephalography who used flicker (stroboscopic light) in the study of epilepsy. W. Grey Walter, *The Living Brain* (New York: W. W. Norton, 1953), p. 60.

135   Sharits, 'Locational Film Pieces,' p. 124.

136   Sharits, 'Interview with Paul Sharits,' interview by Jean-Claude Lebensztejn, p. 88.

137   Ibid., p. 90.

138   Maggie Nelson, *The Art of Cruelty: A Reckoning* (New York: W.W. Norton, 2011), p. 9.

139   Ibid., p. 10.

140   Sontag, *Regarding the Pain of Others*, p. 7.

Conclusion

I began thinking seriously about the films discussed in this book when I was nineteen. As I write this, the umpteenth draft of my conclusion, I am thirty-five years old. I have lived with the films and characters in this book for my entire adult life. In the process of writing it, I've fallen in and out of love a handful of times, become estranged from friends, changed jobs, lost a parent, emigrated to a new country, misplaced and rediscovered my own capacity for making art, grown up, and grown older. It is as much a history of a particular period in American experimental cinema, as it is a record of my own coming to terms with how bodies are changed by the vicissitudes of living and dying.

As I mention in Chapter 1, when I first saw *Christmas on Earth*, I was roughly Barbara Rubin's age when she made it. The film, upon first viewing, blew me away. To be less colloquial, it opened me to the recognition of the radical creative potential of sexual desire unbound by convention. The film's energy, canned decades before, leapt out at me from the screen and moved me across time and space. It was more alive than anything I had ever seen before in a movie theater. In retrospect, I have come to see this encounter as one of those rare moments of recognition that changes the course of one's life. Which is not to say that my sense of recognition was mimetic; I *still* have not experienced all of the types of sexual pleasure that are documented in Rubin's extraordinary film! Nonetheless, watching it, I felt my own nascent sense of myself as a sexual being expand and refract, like seeing an ordinary landscape turn to jewelry through the lens of a kaleidoscope. I knew that anything was possible. It was a conversion experience, whose impact I interpreted then as the spiritual calling to live ecstatically, to give one's body over to pleasure, to pursue 'Christmas on Earth.' And I also realized that everything I had ever learned or assumed about avant-garde cinema (which, in retrospect, was not yet that much) was wrong. Experimental film wasn't elitist or boring or purely about difficulty. It was, as Sitney promised, *visionary*.

I am no longer the girl that I was when I first watched *Christmas on Earth*. When this book is finally published, I will be older than Barbara Rubin was when she died. Though my body has not yet been transformed by childbirth, as hers was a half-dozen times, it has been shattered by other corporeal experiences. I have witnessed firsthand the hazards of being a body, and I know that nobody will be spared. These things are hard to talk about, and the end of a book is not an ideal place to broach such heavy subjects. Here, then, are just a few things I learned from caring for a dying parent: That lifting a body from a bed is a dance, a balance of differently weighted beings. (It is what *Site* never was, and couldn't be.) That empathy is about the recognition that my body is your body, and vice versa. It is, then, a form of analogy, as is all representation. And finally, that although we die different deaths at different moments, the fact that we all eventually go up the chimney is what binds us together – irrevocably. As Roland Barthes writes, 'we die together by loving each other.'[1]

I do not underestimate the power of these experiences to bring different aspects of the films discussed in this volume into focus. I now recognize that empathy – as much as ecstasy – motivates the 'chiasmic intertwinings'[2] of bodies witnessed in Rubin's *Christmas on Earth*, Carolee Schneemann's *Fuses*, and Paul Sharits's *Piece Mandala / End War*. As these filmmakers knew so well, intimacy is always about sensuality *and* loss, and bliss is just another form of dissolution. Bodies made for love must nonetheless learn death; that's one of the lessons of the image of the beautiful corpse with the bikini tan in Brakhage's *The Act of Seeing With One's Own Eyes*. 'What just was' is no longer. And yes, we have to see with our *own* eyes, feel with our *own* bodies, and give ourselves over to the tension between plenitude and decay. This tension can feel like a physiological assault, as it does in Sharits's *Epileptic Seizure Comparison*, but it can also feel uncannily liberating, as it does when we overcome our initial disgust and begin to identify with Yoko Ono's eponymous *Fly*. The best art spills over with this knowledge, and invites us to experience this paradox.

Writing this book has provided a space to explore the turmoil occasioned by bodies, and their relentless and often wrenching transformations. After all of these years, I cannot help but feel that my relationships to the figures discussed in this book has amounted to a kind of friendship, no less affective for being virtual. If the films discussed in this volume served, as I argue, as a way for their makers to explore the embodied contradictions of their own lives, then they have served a similar function for me. As I've grown older, I've learned different things from them and the relationships that inspired them. Which is why I suppose I'm not too sorry that writing the book has taken as long as it did. For in that time, I realized that the relationships we have with each other behind the scenes of our artistic or professional lives are not a form of degraded knowledge – as gossip is often characterized – but a critical form of thinking and creating. In the ten years that it took me to write this book amidst my own explorations of other forms of creativity and kinship, I've developed the courage to insist that the textures of people's lives matter. Not only is friendship a suitable pursuit for scholarly writing, but it is also one of the most significant sources of art and meaning.

Coming to 'terms'

When I first undertook the study of American avant-garde cinema, I was a doctoral student at the University of California, Berkeley, pining for New York City, where I had grown up and where my family still lived. I felt a profound sense of alienation. If such a thing is possible, I was not only nostalgic for a particular place, but also for a time I had never experienced firsthand. I endeavored to write this book as a way of imaginatively re-living New York in the 1960s, the time and place in which my parents had come of age, met, and married. I had questions about their identities and relationships that either I could not ask them, or they could not satisfactorily explain. I had the strange idea that watching avant-garde films could somehow help answer some of these questions. They did and they didn't. Of course it is never that simple.

My father had 'come out of the closet' in my early teen years, but had never shared with me the details of his sexuality before he married my mother. I was always curious about his past, particularly about how he identified in his early adulthood. Although I have never had the courage to directly ask him when and how he first had sex with men and women, on the occasions that I have inquired whether he was 'gay' before he and my mother married, his answers always seemed evasive. He wasn't unwilling to discuss his sexuality; on the contrary, if there was any timidity in these conversations, it was my own. Nevertheless, I sensed some kind of communication block or generation gap that prevented me from understanding what my father's sexuality was and had been, at least in the terms that I offered. He seemed uncomfortable with using the word 'gay,' not out of shame, but because it seemed an inappropriate way to describe his erotic experiences as a young man. When he tried to explain that people were not 'gay' in the early 1960s the way they were in the 1990s, I had trouble understanding what he meant. Although I had read Foucault's *History of Sexuality*, I suppose I still had trouble grasping the ways in which sexuality is constructed through discourse when it was presented to me as family history.

It was only when I started watching experimental films made in the 1960s that I began to understand the alternative constructions of sexuality during this period. In films by Rubin, Jack Smith, Warhol, Schneemann, Brakhage, and Ono, bodies were ambiguously gendered, uncooperative, difficult to discern. One can no more discern the gender of the person to whom each pair of buttocks belongs in Ono's *Bottoms* than one can distinguish between authentic and performative sexual moments in Brakhage's *Lovemaking*. Much as we might insist otherwise, desire is not stable. How we act in one situation does not determine how we might act in another. Lovemaking is queer, whether it happens between a man and a woman, two men, a group of people eating bananas, or a bunch of dogs. Relationships are in flux and unpredictable, but it is this instability that enables us to experience expanded forms of being that are capable of dissolving the boundaries between oneself and others. This expansion can be ecstatic – as it is *Christmas on Earth* and *Fuses* – but it can also entail a wrenching vulnerability as it does in *Epileptic Seizure Comparison*. As Yoko Ono so bravely demonstrates in *Cut Piece*, giving of ourselves involves exposing ourselves to the threat of pain, dissolution, and death.

Watching the fleshy films discussed in this book has been as titillating – and as painful – as touching. The facile oppositions between sexual repression and liberation, heterosexuality and homosexuality, or distress and ecstasy, do not go very far to explain the ever-shifting entanglements unfolding on these screens. Like relationships themselves, these films shattered my illusions, challenged my prejudices, expanded my boundaries, bruised and scarred me. Like all kindred spirits through whose lives we walk, these filmmakers have left their mark on me. I am, as Stanley Kunitz writes, 'not who I was, / though some principle of being / abides, from which I struggle / not to stray.'[3]

As Warhol, Brakhage, and Sharits all demonstrate in their documents of lovemaking, sex is hard work. Moments of erotic intermingling are often shot through with awkwardness, tension, and difficulty. Even the most intimate sexual encounters are haunted by others, whether they take the literal form of bodies in the room, or the phantasmatic shape of the many versions of ourselves that we are, have been, and may become. Strive as we may to experience our own bodies and others in ways that are not determined by ideology, even in the moments of our most intense transcendence, our focus cannot help but rack between the mystery of being and the ways we have been disciplined to mind the distinction between self and other. Though we may not have the same opportunities for re-invention in 'real life' that each change of the reel provides in a film like *Couch*, I've learned from these films that we must nonetheless strive to create friendships capacious enough to accommodate the caterpillar changes of our intellectual, spiritual and erotic lives. Seeing with one's own eyes is an 'act' that can mobilize us to pursue more expanded ways of being.

If the filmmakers discussed in this book work so hard to defamiliarize the conventional ways of seeing the body – by scratching or painting on the film stock, crowding the *mise-en-scène*, flickering or superimposing the image, or creating unexpected frames – it is because their aim is, I argue, to use film to create alternative ways of being together. Yet even when the mastering gaze of the apparatus is diverted and distorted through what the filmmaker imagines to be the more visionary perspective of animals, children, the primitive 'other' or the diseased, the tensions of normal life leak through. This seepage of everyday dystopia into the utopian energy of these filmic visions is what accounts for their extraordinary poignancy as documents of the difficulties of artistic and erotic commingling.

Studying American experimental cinema was a way not only of seeing my parents' relationship anew, but also of discovering alternatives to what I think I knew about sexuality and its discontents. I began to wonder whether my father had seen films like Warhol's *Haircut* or *Blow Job*, and whether they had influenced or informed his own emergent desires. Although I do not know whether he actually saw these titles since he remembers only that he watched some films where 'nothing happened,' I imagine that in the space where nothing happened, something may indeed have happened. This is obviously not to say that my father 'became' gay as a result of any singular experience, least of all a film screening. However, by watching experimental films during this period, I suspect that my father, like many other members of his generation, may have had his first encounters with the public presentation of non-normative sexualities. In a perverse way, watching these films was a way of getting to know him better, regardless of their potentially fictional place in his life.

For a narcissist, grand historical events are frequently interpreted through the prism of their own narrow experiences. Even after years of studying the 1960s, my understandings of this decade are inextricable from my curiosity about my parents. My father met my mother on Manhattan Beach in Brooklyn over Memorial Day weekend in 1968. They were married two years later by a reformed rabbi on a rain-soaked rooftop on the Upper East Side. My mother wore white pancake make-up, white eye shadow, white lipstick, an old white dress with new white buttons, and flats because my father was shorter than her. They had, I think, a monogamous heterosexual relationship that lasted for over twenty years. When my father 'came out' (oh Foucault!), they stayed married, continued to share a house and spent a lot of time with each other. Both of them had other Significant Others until my mother died from cancer in 2009. During her illness, I watched my parents' friendship evolve into new forms of intimacy. I was amazed to discover how even as a body is brutally undone, there are opportunities for expanded ways of being. By the time of my mother's death, my parents had been married for forty years. Devastated as I am by her loss, I am glad that I was able to witness my mother's transformation in the last few years of her life from an outlaw to a shaman. A lot of what she taught me about love has made its way into this book.

If this study originally served as way of understanding the type of queer coupling practiced by my parents, then it ended up becoming as much about my own relationships as it was about theirs. As the intimacies of my life have become comparably if not identically queer, my questions have changed from erotic to ethical ones. Or rather, to be more accurate, I have found that erotic questions are often ethical as well. What happens to desire for others, and our relationship to our selves when our bodies grow older, get tired, witness death and are remade by loss? How can we reconcile the radical and often unruly forms that love and desire take within marriage or other forms of commitment? How can long-term closeness to another person not only survive but actually enable new kinds of creativity and freedom? How can we dispossess ourselves of the urge to possess others? Can exhaustion and familiarity ever affirm our sense of being alive as intensely as vigor and novelty? And, to be more practical, how can we make a living without sacrificing the openness and flexibility with which one may prefer to approach the world, time, and relationships? How do we practice queer forms of friendship with our students, our colleagues, and the various others that we encounter in our professional lives?

Studying the films in this book hasn't answered these questions, but it has helped me to understand the complex, multiple, and eternally evolving ways that we exist in relation to each other. Sex is obviously one form of this kinship, but of course it is not the only one. Having once watched experimental films looking for the dirty parts, I now see their moments of explicit imagery in dialogue with other types of entanglement that are as profound, and potentially as shattering, as sex. Relinquishing a sense of optical mastery is perhaps only the first step we might take towards activating a deeper sense of empathy with others, but it is an important one. The films discussed in this book explore this, and other paths towards more equitable and intense communion.

I originally thought that the debut of feature-length pornography in the United States in the early 1970s heralded the end of this era of sexually explicit experimental cinema. How absurd such a causal sense of history now seems! Of course, the corporeal impulses of American experimental film often took new form after the 1960s and early 1970s. Many of the filmmakers associated with this period, like Paul Sharits, increasingly began showing their films in gallery spaces rather than the more traditional venues of experimental cinema. By the late 1960s and early 1970s, other filmmakers emerged who pursued explorations of the body and sexuality that would not have been possible without the rise of second-wave feminism and other forms of identity politics: Yvonne Rainer, Barbara Hammer, and Martha Rosler's moving-image work exists on a continuum with the films described in this volume. As the 1970s wore on, many artists interested in using moving images in their exploration of bodies chose video rather than film as a more affordable medium; certainly the performance and video works of artists like Vito Acconci, Joan Jonas, Marina Abramović, Gary Hill, and Chris Burden – to name just a few – are politically if not aesthetically kindred with the films discussed here. Of course, certain filmmakers, like Barbara Rubin and Andy Warhol, simply stopped making films at the end of the 1960s because of profound corporeal and spiritual transformations that made the pursuit of filmmaking less necessary in their creative lives. Still others, like Yoko Ono and Carolee Schneemann, continue to explore questions of corporeality, sexuality, and gender in other media. And of course a handful of the practitioners of the fleshy cinema described in this book, like Stan Brakhage, continued their devotion to the particularities of celluloid even as their interests in embodiment evolved in ways that are less visibly concurrent with their early film practices.

Recent experimental film, video art, and performance have been profoundly influenced by the corporeal turn of American avant-garde cinema in the 1960s. Nonetheless, while many of these recent works have important affinities with the films produced in this period, their textures and concerns are nonetheless inevitably distinct. This has as much to do with the transformations of technology and the evolving social and political landscape as it does with the changes in distribution and exhibition that have occurred in the last few decades. While I do believe that the spirit that animates Flesh Cinema persists in contemporary art forms, I nonetheless recognize that the institutional and community structures that sustained this particularly intense period of corporeal exploration in cinema have changed dramatically.

My mother used to tell me that the best we can hope for in relationships is to float together for a while, like bits of driftwood bobbing together in a great sea, before drifting apart to pursue our own erratic course in the unfathomable depths. Since her death, I cannot help but recognize that the reverberations from these encounters might well last a lifetime. I am ready, at long last, to let this book drift from me.

Notes

1 Roland Barthes, *A Lover's Discourse, Fragments*, trans. Richard Howard (New York: Hill & Wang, 1978), p. 11.
2 Maurice Merleau-Ponty. *The Visible and the Invisible*, ed. Claude Lefort, trans. Alphonso Lingis (Evanston, IL: Northwestern University Press, 1968), pp. 130–155.
3 Stanley Kunitz, 'The Layers.' In *The Collected Poems* (New York: W.W. Norton, 2000), pp. 217–218; p. 218.

Bibliography

Agamben, Giorgio, *Homo Sacer: Sovereign Power and Bare Life*, trans. Daniel Heller-Roazen (Stanford, CA: Stanford University Press, 1998).

Althusser, Louis, 'Ideology and Ideological State Apparatuses', in *Lenin and Philosophy and Other Essays*, trans. Ben Brewster (London: NLB, 1971), pp. 121–173.

Altieri, Charles, 'Contingency and Sociality in American Poetry of the Fifties', *Freedom and Form: Essays in Contemporary American Poetry*, ed. Esther Giger and Agnieska Salska (Lodz: Wydawnictwo University Press, 1998), pp. 27–35.

Altieri, Charles, 'The Sensuous Dimension of Literary Experience: An Alternative to Materialist Theory', *New Literary History*, 38 (2007), pp. 71–98.

Angell, Callie, *Andy Warhol Screen Tests: The Films of Andy Warhol Catalogue Raisonné*, Vol. 1 (New York: Harry Abrams, 2006).

Angell, Callie, *The Films of Andy Warhol: Part II* (New York: Whitney Museum of American Art, 1994), published in conjunction with an exhibition of the same name, New York, Whitney Museum of American Art, March 30 to April 24, 1994.

Anger, Kenneth, Kenneth Anger to Stan Brakhage, September 26, 1972, box 1, folder 12, James Stanley Brakhage Collection, University of Colorado at Boulder Libraries.

Antin, David, 'Warhol: The Silver Tenement', *Art News* 65 (Summer 1966).

Antonioni, Michelangelo, 'Making a Film is My Way of Life', *Architecture of Vision: Writings and Interviews on Cinema* (New York: Marsilio Publishers, 1996), pp. 14–17.

Aronowitz, Brett, telephone interview with the author (Summer 2004).

Artaud, Antonin, *The Theater and Its Double*, trans. Mary C. Richard (New York: Grove Press, 1994).

Arthur, Paul, '"A Panorama Compounded of Great Human Suffering and Ecstatic Filmic Representation": Texts on Ken Jacobs', in *Optic Antics: The Cinema of Ken Jacobs*, ed. Michele Pierson, David E. James, and Paul Arthur (Oxford: Oxford University Press, 2011), pp. 25–37.

Balázs, Béla, *Theory of the Film: Character and Growth of a New Art* (New York: Dover, 1970).

Ball, Gordon, *66 Frames* (Minneapolis, MN: Coffee House Press, 1999).

Ball, Gordon, interview with the author (January 2009).

Banes, Sally, *Greenwich Village 1963: Avant-Garde Performance and the Effervescent Body* (Durham, NC: Duke University Press, 1993).

Barthes, Roland, *Camera Lucida: Reflections on Photography*, 1st American ed. (New York: Hill and Wang, 1981).

Barthes, Roland, *A Lover's Discourse: Fragments*, trans. Richard Howard (New York: Hill & Wang, 1978).

Bazin, André, *What is Cinema?*, ed. and trans. Hugh Gray, Vol. 1 (Berkeley: University of California Press, 1967).

Belasco, Daniel, 'A Vanished Prodigy,' *Barbara Rubin: Christmas on Earth* (New York: Boo Hooray Gallery, 2012), published in conjunction with an exhibition of the same name, New York, Boo Hooray Gallery, December 18, 2012 – January 15, 2013, originally published in *Art in America*, December 2005, pp. 61–67.

Benjamin, Walter, 'Theses on the Philosophy of History,' *Illuminations: Essays and Reflections*, ed. Hannah Arendt (New York: Schocken Books, 1968), pp. 253–264.

Benjamin, Walter, 'The Work of Art in the Age of Mechanical Reproduction,' in *Illuminations*, trans. Harry Zohn, ed. Hannah Arendt (New York: Schocken Books, 1968), pp. 217–251.

Berger, John, *Ways of Seeing* (London: British Broadcasting Corporation and Penguin Books, 1972).

Bersani, Leo, *The Freudian Body: Psychoanalysis and Art* (New York: Columbia University Press, 1986).

Bersani, Leo, *Is the Rectum a Grave? and Other Essays* (Chicago, IL: University of Chicago Press, 2009).

Bloom, Harold, *The Anxiety of Influence: A Theory of Poetry*, 2nd ed. (Oxford: Oxford University Press, 1997).

Bockris, Victor, *The Life and Death of Andy Warhol* (New York: Bantam, 1989).

Bornstein, Stephen, telephone interview with the author (February 2009).

Bourdon, David, *Warhol* (New York: Harry Abrams, 1989).

Brakhage, Jane, 'The Birth Film,' in *The Film Culture Reader*, ed. P. Adams Sitney (New York: Praeger, 1970), pp. 230–233.

Brakhage, Marilyn, email message to the author (February 11, 2013).

Brakhage, Stan, *Brakhage Scrapbook: Collected Writings*, ed. Robert A. Haller (New Paltz, NY: Documentext, 1982).

Brakhage, Stan, *The Essential Brakhage: Selected Writings on Filmmaking* ed. Bruce McPherson (Kingston, NY: McPherson & Company / Documentext, 2001).

Brakhage, Stan, 'In Defense of the Amateur Filmmaker,' *Filmmakers Newsletter*, 4, no. 9–10 (July–August 1971), pp. 20–25.

Brakhage, Stan, letter to Annette Michelson, November 8, 1971, box 12A, folder 'Michelson, Annette 1969–1985,' James Stanley Brakhage Collection, University of Colorado at Boulder Libraries.

Brakhage, Stan, letter to Barney Rosset, June 23, 1974, box 23, folder 11 'Grove Press Correspondence,' James Stanley Brakhage Collection, University of Colorado at Boulder Libraries.

Brakhage, Stan, letter to Ed Dorn, November 24, 1971, box 5A, folder 11, James Stanley Brakhage Collection, University of Colorado at Boulder Libraries.

Brakhage, Stan, letter to Eugene Verrier, dated 'early' December 1969, box 30, folders 14–15, James Stanley Brakhage Collection, University of Colorado at Boulder Libraries.

Brakhage, Stan, letter to Hollis Frampton, November 22, 1971, box 6A, folder 'Frampton, Hollis 1971–9/72,' James Stanley Brakhage Collection, University of Colorado at Boulder Libraries.

Brakhage, Stan, letter to James Broughton, November 10, 1971, box 2A, folder 'Broughton, James 1955–1972,' James Stanley Brakhage Collection, University of Colorado at Boulder Libraries.

Brakhage, Stan, letter to Jane Brakhage, dated '2nd Tues in Pittsburgh,' September 1971, box 36, folder 10, James Stanley Brakhage Collection, University of Colorado at Boulder Libraries.

Brakhage, Stan, letter to Jerome Hill, dated 'near end June 1969,' box 8, James Stanley Brakhage Collection, University of Colorado at Boulder Libraries.

Brakhage, Stan, letter to Jonas Mekas, June 30, 1973, box 12, folder 6, James Stanley Brakhage Collection, University of Colorado at Boulder Libraries.

Brakhage, Stan, letter to Jonas Mekas, July 2, 1982, box 12a, James Stanley Brakhage Archive, University of Colorado at Boulder Libraries.

Brakhage, Stan, letter to Paul Sharits, dated 'early August' 1968, Brakhage File, Anthology Film Archives.

Brakhage, Stan, letter to Paul Sharits, dated 'near end April, 1968,' Brakhage File, Anthology Film Archives.

Brakhage, Stan, letter to Paul Sharits, April 6, 1974, Brakhage File, Anthology Film Archives.

Brakhage, Stan, letter to Robert Creeley, November 22, 1971, box 4, folder 'Creeley, Robert 1966–1973,' James Stanley Brakhage Collection, University of Colorado at Boulder Libraries.

Brakhage, Stan, letter to Robert Creeley, November 22, 1973, box 4, folder 'Creeley, Robert 1966–1973,' James Stanley Brakhage Collection, University at Colorado at Boulder Libraries.

Brakhage, Stan, letter to Sally Dixon, dated 'early' January 1971, box 5, folder 'Dixon, Sally 1970–1971,' James Stanley Brakhage Collection, University of Colorado at Boulder Libraries.

Bram, Shachar, *Charles Olson and Alfred North Whitehead: An Essay on Poetry* (Lewisburg, PA: Bucknell University Press, 2004).

Brecht, Bertolt, *Brecht on Theater: The Development of an Aesthetic*, ed. and trans. John Willett (New York: Hill and Wang, 2001).

Buchloh, Benjamin H.D., 'Andy Warhol's One Dimensional Art: 1956–1966,' in *Andy Warhol*, ed. Annette Michelson (Cambridge, MA: The MIT Press, 2001), pp. 1–48.

The Buffalo News, 'Paul J. Sharits, 50, dies; avant-garde filmmaker,' July 14, 1993, C7.

Camper, Fred, email message to author (February 22, 2012).

Camper, Fred, 'About the Films,' liner notes for *by Brakhage: An Anthology*, Vol. 1 (Criterion Collection, 2003), DVD.

Canby, Vincent, 'Warhol's Red Hot and 'Blue Movie,' *The New York Times*, August 10, 1969.

Canby, Vincent, 'Where the Naked Truth Was Born,' *The New York Times*, May 18, 1969.

Cartwright, Lisa, *Screening the Body: Tracing Medicine's Visual Culture* (Minneapolis: University of Minnesota Press 1995), pp. 56–58.

Clark, Kenneth, *The Nude: A Study in Ideal Form* (New York: Pantheon, 1956).

Clover, Carol, *Men, Women, and Chain Saws: Gender in the Modern Horror Film* (Princeton, NJ: Princeton University Press, 1993).

Cohen, Leonard, 'The Old Revolution,' *Songs from a Room*, Sony Music Entertainment, 1969.

Comolli, Jean-Louis, 'Machines of the Visible', in *The Cinematic Apparatus*, ed. Teresa De Lauretis and S. Heath (New York: St. Martin's Press, 1981), pp. 121–142.

Concannon, Kevin, 'Museum of Modern [F]art', *Yes Yoko Ono* (New York: Japan Society; New York: Harry N. Abrams, 2000), pp. 194–195.

Concannon, Kevin, 'Yoko Ono's CUT PIECE: From Text to Performance and Back Again', *PAJ: A Journal of Performance and Art*, 30, (September 2008), pp. 81–93, http://imaginepeace.com/archives/2680 (accessed on 14 August, 2013).

Coppa, Francesca, 'The Body Immaterial: Magicians' Assistants and the Performance of Labor', *Performing Magic on the Western Stage: From the Eighteenth Century to the Present*, ed. Francesca Coppa, Lawrence Hass and James Peck (New York: Palgrave Macmillan, 2008), pp. 85–106.

Corliss, Richard, 'Film and Other Four-Letter Words', *National Review*, July 29, 1969, pp. 760–761.

Courtney, Susan, *Hollywood Fantasies of Miscegenation: Spectacular Narratives of Gender and Race 1903–1967* (Princeton, NJ: Princeton University Press, 2005).

Crandall, Jordan, 'Andy Warhol' [1986], in *I'll Be Your Mirror: The Selected Andy Warhol Interviews 1962–1987. Thirty-Seven Conversations with the Pop Master*, ed. Kenneth Goldsmith (New York: Carroll & Graf Publishers, 2004), pp. 348–381.

Crary, Jonathan, 'Modernizing Vision', *Viewing Positions: Ways of Seeing Film*, ed. Linda Williams (New Brunswick, NJ: Rutgers University Press, 1994), pp. 23–35.

Crary, Jonathan, *Techniques of the Observer* (Cambridge, MA: The MIT Press, 1990).

Crimp, Douglas, *'Our Kind of Movie': The Films of Andy Warhol* (Cambridge, MA: The MIT Press, 2012).

Crimp, Douglas, 'Spacious', *October* 132 (Spring 2010), pp. 5–24.

Darley, John, and Bibb Latané, 'Bystander Intervention in Emergencies: Diffusion of Responsibility', *Journal of Personality and Social Psychology*, 8, no. 4 (April 1968), pp. 377–383.

Davenport, Guy, letter to Stan Brakhage, July 13, 1968, box 1, James Stanley Brakhage Collection, University of Colorado at Boulder Libraries.

Davenport, Guy, letter to Stan Brakhage, dated 'Birthday of John Clare', 1968, box 4, folder 6, James Stanley Brakhage Collection, University of Colorado at Boulder Libraries.

Davenport, Guy, letter to Stan and Jane Brakhage, dated 'Birthday of Joyce Cary' 1968, box 4, folder 6, James Stanley Brakhage Collection, University of Colorado at Boulder Libraries.

Davenport, Guy, 'Statement Concerning Stan Brakhage's Film Love-Making', box 4, folder 6, James Stanley Brakhage Collection, University of Colorado at Boulder Libraries, emphasis added.

DeGrazia, Edward and Roger K. Newman, *Banned Films: Movies, Censors & The First Amendment* (New York: R. R. Bowker, 1982).

del Río, Elena, *Deleuze and the Cinemas of Performance: Powers of Affection* (Edinburgh: Edinburgh University Press, 2008).

Deleuze, Gilles, and Félix Guattari, *Anti-Oedipus*, trans. Robert Hurley, Mark Seem, and Helen R. Lane (Minneapolis, MN: University of Minnesota Press, 1983).

Denver Post, 'Sex-Film Showing OKd for Teacher', May 23, 1974.

Dixon, Wheeler Winston, *The Exploding Eye: Re-Visionary History of 1960s American Experimental Cinema* (Albany: SUNY Press, 1997).

Doubiago, Sharon, 'The Art of Seeing with One's Own Eyes,' in *The Book of Seeing with One's Own Eyes* (Saint Paul, MN: Graywolf Press, 1988), pp. 76–97.

Doyle, Jennifer, 'Between Friends,' in *A Companion to Lesbian, Gay, Bisexual, Transgender and Queer Studies*, ed. George E. Haggerty and Molly McGarry (Malden, MA: Blackwell, 2007), pp. 325–340.

Doyle, Jennifer, '"I Must Be Boring Someone:" Women in Warhol's Films,' in *Sex Objects: Art and the Dialectic of Desire* (Minneapolis, MN: University of Minnesota Press, 2006), pp. 71–96.

Duggan, Lisa, Nan Hunter, and Carole S. Vance, 'False Promises: Feminist Antipornography Legislation in the U.S.,' in *Women Against Censorship*, ed. Varda Burstyn (Vancouver, ON: Douglas & MacIntyre, 1985).

Durham, Michael, *Powerful Days: The Civil Rights Photography of Charles Moore* (Tuscaloosa, AL: University of Alabama Press, 2005; New York: Stewart, Tabori & Chang, 1991).

Dyer, Richard, *White* (New York: Routledge, 1997).

Dylan, Bob, 'Desolation Row,' *Highway 61 Revisited*, prod. Bob Johnston (Columbia Records, 1965).

Echols, Alice, *Daring to Be Bad: Radical Feminism in America 1967–1975* (Minneapolis, MN: University of Minnesota Press, 1989).

Edelman, Lee, *No Future: Queer Theory and the Death Drive* (Durham, NC: Duke University Press, 2004).

Eisenhower, Dwight, *Public Papers of the Presidents* (1960), 1035–1040.

Eisenstein, Sergei, 'Methods of Montage,' in *Film Form: Essays in Film Theory*, trans. and ed. Jay Leyda (New York: Harcourt Brace & Company, 1949), pp. 72–83.

Eve, Even, 'Glossary of Keristan English (abridged)', *Kerista: Scientific Utopianism and the Humanities*, 1, no. 4 (Spring 1985), part 1, www.kerista.com/kerdocs/glossary. html (accessed on August 13, 2013).

Fahim, Kareem, 'Slap to a Man's Pride Set Off Tumult in Tunisia,' *The New York Times*, January 21, 2011.

Feliu, Rosebud (Pettet), telephone interview with the author (Summer 2004).

Flatley, Guy, 'How to Be Very Viva: A Bedroom Farce,' *The New York Times*, November 9, 1969.

Flatley, Jonathan, 'Like: Collecting and Collectivity,' *October* 132 (Spring 2010), pp. 71–98.

Foster, Hal, *The Return of the Real: The Avant-Garde at the End of the Century* (Cambridge, MA: The MIT Press, 1996).

Foucault, Michel, *The History of Sexuality*, Volume 1: *An Introduction*, trans. Robert Hurley (New York: Vintage Press, 1990).

Foucault, Michel, interview by R. de Ceccaty, J. Danet, and J. Le Bitoux, trans. John Johnston, *Ethics: Subjectivity and Truth*, ed. Paul Rabinow (New York: The New Press, 1994), pp. 135–140.

Frampton, Hollis, letter to Stan Brakhage, January 26, 1972, James Stanley Brakhage Collection, University of Colorado at Boulder Libraries.

Frampton, Hollis, 'Interview with Paul Sharits,' March 1, 1973, in *Buffalo Heads: Media Study, Media Practice, Media Pioneers, 1973–1990*, ed. Woody Vasulka and Peter Weibel (Karlsruhe: Center for Art and Media Karlsruhe, 2008; Cambridge, MA: The MIT Press, 2008), pp. 280–291.

Freud, Sigmund, *Beyond the Pleasure Principle*, Vol. 18 of *The Standard Edition of the Complete Psychological Works of Sigmund Freud*, trans. James Strachey (London: Hogarth Press, 1943–1974).

Freud, Sigmund, *Group Psychology and the Analysis of the Ego*, trans. James Strachey (London: The International Psycho-Analytical Press, 1922).

Freud, Sigmund, *The Interpretation of Dreams*, trans. and ed. James Strachey, (New York: Basic Books, 1955).

Freud, Sigmund, 'Some Psychical Consequences of the Anatomical Distinction Between the Sexes', in *The Freud Reader*, ed. Peter Gay (New York: W.W. Norton, 1989), pp. 670–678.

Freud, Sigmund, *Three Essays on the Theory of Civilization* [1905], trans. James Strachey (New York: Basic Books, 2000).

Freud, Sigmund, *Three Essays on the Theory of Sexuality*, in *The Standard Edition of the Complete Psychological Works*, trans. James Strachey, Vol. 7 (London: Hogarth Press, 1953).

Fried, Michael, 'Art and Objecthood', *Artforum* (Summer 1967), pp. 12–23.

Friedan, Betty, *The Feminine Mystique* (New York: W.W. Norton, 1963).

Friedman, Ken, 'Explaining Fluxus', *White Walls* 16 (Spring 1987), pp. 12–29.

Fuck You 8, no. 5 (March 1965).

Furlong, John, to Stan Brakhage, August 1974, box 17a (unprocessed at the time of writing), James Stanley Brakhage Collection, University of Colorado at Boulder Libraries.

Gansberg, Martin, 'Thirty Eight Who Saw Murder Didn't Call the Police,' *New York Times*, March 27, 1964.

Gebhardt, Steve, telephone conversation with the author (January 5, 2012).

Ginsberg, Allen, interview with Paul Carroll, 'The Playboy Interview: Allen Ginsberg.' Originally published in *Playboy*, April 1969, pp. 81–92, 236–244. Reprinted in *Allen Ginsberg, Spontaneous Mind, Selected Interviews 1958–1996*, ed. David Carter (New York: Harper Collins, 2001), pp. 159–199.

Ginsberg, Allen, *The Letters of Allen Ginsberg*, ed. Bill Morgan (Philadelphia, PA: Da Capo Press, 2008).

Graw, Isabelle, 'When Life Goes to Work: Andy Warhol,' *October* 132 (Spring 2010), pp. 99–113.

Greenberg, Clement, 'Abstract Art', *The Nation* (15 April 1944).

Greenberg, Clement, 'Towards a Newer Laocoon,' [1940], *Art in Theory 1900–1990: An Anthology of Changing Ideas*, ed. Charles Harrison and Paul Wood (Oxford: Blackwell, 1993), pp. 554–560.

Grunenberg, Christopher, 'The American Supermarket,' in *Shopping: A Century of Art and Consumer Culture*, ed. Christopher Grunenberg and Max Hollein (Ostfildern: Hatje Cantz Publishers, 2002), pp. 171–178.

Gunning, Thomas, 'An Aesthetic of Astonishment: Early Film and the (In)Credulous Spectator,' *Art and Text* 34 (Spring 1989).

Gunning, Thomas, 'The Cinema of Attractions: Early Film, Its Spectator and the Avant-Garde,' *Early Cinema: Space, Frame, Narrative*, ed. Thomas Elsaesser (London: BFI, 1990), pp. 56–62.

Halberstam, David, *The Making of a Quagmire* (New York: Random House, 1965).

Halberstam, Judith, *The Queer Art of Failure* (Durham, NC: Duke University Press, 2011).

Haller, Robert, *Crossroads: Avant-Garde Film in Pittsburgh in the 1970s* (New York: Anthology Film Archives, 2005).

Harding, James M., *Cutting Performances: Collage Events, Feminist Artists, and the American Avant-Garde* (Ann Arbor, MI: University of Michigan Press, 2010).

Hawkins, Joan, 'Exploitation Meets Direct Cinema: Yoko Ono's *Rape* and the Trash Cinema of Michael and Roberta Findlay,' *Cutting Edge: Art-Horror and the Horrific Avant-Garde* (Minneapolis, MN: University of Minnesota Press, 2000), pp. 117–140.

Hendricks, Jon, ed., *Fluxus Etc.: The Gilbert and Lila Silverman Collection* (New York: Ink &, 1983; Pasadena, CA: Baxter Art Gallery, 1983).

Henry, Claire, conversation with the author (May 25, 2012).

Hoberman, J., *On Jack Smith's Flaming Creatures (and Other Secret Flix of Cinemaroc)* (New York: Granary Books, 2001).

Hoberman, J. and Edward Leffingwell, eds, *Wait for Me at the Bottom of the Pool: The Writings of Jack Smith* (New York: High Risk Books, 1997).

Horrigan, Bill, 'Program Guide to the 5th New York Lesbian and Gay Experimental Film Festival,' 1991.

Iles, Chrissie, 'Erotic Conceptualism: The Films of Yoko Ono,' in *Yes Yoko Ono* (New York: Japan Society; New York: Harry N. Abrams, 2000), pp. 201–207.

Jacobs, Ken, telephone interview with the author (January 2009).

Jacobs, Ken and Flo Jacobs, interview with the author (Winter 2008).

Jacobs, Seth, *Cold War Mandarin: Ngo Dinh Diem and the Origins of America's War in Vietnam, 1950–1963* (Lanham, MD: Rowman & Littlefield, 2006).

James, David E., *Allegories of Cinema: American Film in the Sixties* (Princeton, NJ: Princeton University Press, 1989).

James, David E., ed., *To Free the Cinema: Jonas Mekas and the New York Underground, 1992* (Princeton, NJ: Princeton University Press, 1992).

Jeon, Joseph Jonghyun, *Racial Things, Racial Forms: Objecthood in Avant-Garde Asian American Poetry* (Iowa City: University of Iowa Press, 2012).

Johnson, Dominic, *Glorious Catastrophe: Jack Smith, Performance and Visual Culture* (Manchester: Manchester University Press, 2012).

Johnson, Joyce, *Minor Characters: A Beat Memoir* (New York: Penguin, 1999).

Jones, Amelia, *Body Art / Performing the Subject* (Minneapolis, MN: University of Minnesota Press, 1998).

Jones, Amelia, 'Screen Eroticisms: Exploring Female Desire in the Work of Carolee Schneemann and Pipilotti Rist,' *Screen/Space: The Projected Image in Contemporary Art*, ed. Tamara Trodd (Manchester: Manchester University Press, 2011), pp. 126–144.

Jones, Amelia, *Seeing Differently: A History and Theory of Identification in the Visual Arts* (New York: Routledge, 2012).

Jordan, Brenda, 'DIAS,' *Resurgence* 1, no. 4 (1966), pp. 18–21.

Joseph, Branden, '1962,' *October* 132 (Spring 2010), pp. 114–134.

Judd, Donald 'Specific Objects,' *Arts Yearbook*, 8 (1965), pp. 74–82.

Kandinsky, Wassily, *Concerning the Spiritual in Art*, trans. M.T.H. Sadler (New York: Dover Publications, 1977).

Kaplan, Morris, 'Film by Warhol is Ruled Obscene: 3 Judges Call "Blue Movie" Hard-Core Pornography,' *The New York Times*, September 18, 1969.

Kaplan, Morris, 'New Warhol Film Seized by Police: Theater Staff Arrested After Showing of "Blue Movie,"' *The New York Times*, August 2, 1969.

Kaplan, Morris, 'Professor Defends Warhol "Blue Movie" As "Not Stimulating,"' *The New York Times*, September 17, 1969.

Katz, David, '"Angels are Just One More Species": David Katz Meets Lionel Ziprin, Mystic, Maven and Maverick of New York's Lower East Side', *Jewish Quarterly*, no. 204 (Winter 2006/2007).

Keller, Marjorie, *The Untutored Eye: Childhood in the Films of Cocteau, Cornell, and Brakhage* (Rutherford, NJ: Fairleigh Dickinson University Press, 1986).

Kennedy, Dennis, transcription of telephone conversation with Gloria Bartek, June 21, 1974, box 17a (unprocessed at the time of writing), James Stanley Brakhage Collection, University of Colorado at Boulder Libraries.

'Kerista Commune Home Page', *Kerista Commune*, www.kerista.com (accessed September 5, 2012).

Klarl, Joseph, 'Barbara Rubin: Christmas on Earth', *The Brooklyn Rail* (February 2013), www.brooklynrail.org/2013/02/artseen/barbara-rubin-christmas-on-earth (accessed on August 13, 2013).

Klein, Melanie, 'A Contribution to the Psychogenesis of Manic-Depressive States' [1935], *The Selected Melanie Klein*, ed. Juliet Mitchell (New York: The Free Press, 1986), pp. 115–145.

Klein, Melanie, *The Psycho-Analysis of Children*, trans. Alix Strachey (New York: Delacorte Press, 1975).

Klein, Melanie, 'The Psychological Principles of Infant Analysis' [1926], *The Selected Melanie Klein*, ed. Juliet Mitchell (New York: The Free Press, 1986), pp. 57–68.

Koestenbaum, Wayne, *Andy Warhol* (New York: Viking Penguin, 2001).

Kracauer, Siegfried, 'The Mass Ornament', *The Mass Ornament Weimar Essays*, ed. and trans. Thomas Y. Levin (Cambridge, MA: Harvard University Press, 1995), pp. 75–86.

Kramer, Marcia, *Andy Warhol et al.: The FBI File on Andy Warhol* (New York: UnSub Press, 1988).

Kraus, Chris, *I Love Dick*, Semiotext(e) Native Agents Series (Cambridge, MA: The MIT Press, 2006).

Krauss, Rosalind, 'Paul Sharits', in *Paul Sharits*, ed. yann beauvais (Dijon: Les presses du réel, 2008), pp. 47–55.

Kristeva, Julia, *Powers of Horror: An Essay on Abjection*, trans. Leon S. Roudiez (New York: Columbia University Press, 1982).

Kunitz, Stanley, *The Collected Poems* (New York: W.W. Norton, 2000).

Lacan, Jacques, *Écrits*: The First Complete Edition in English, trans. Bruce Fink (New York: W.W. Norton, 2007).

Lacan, Jacques, *Four Fundamental Concepts of Psychoanalysis* (The Seminar of Jacques Lacan Book 11), ed. Jacques-Alain Miller, trans. Alan Sheridan (New York: W.W. Norton, 1998).

Lavin, Sylvia, *Form Follows Libido: Architecture and Richard Neutra in a Psychoanalytic Culture* (Cambridge, MA: The MIT Press, 2007).

LeBon, Gustave, *Psychologie des foules* (Paris: Alcan, 1895).

Leffingwell, Edward, Carole Kismaric, and Marvin Heiferman, eds, *Flaming Creature: Jack Smith, His Amazing Life and Times* (Long Island City, NY: The Institute for Contemporary Art, P.S. 1 Museum, 1997).

Lennon, John, *Skywriting by Word of Mouth And Other Writing, Including The Ballad of John and Yoko* (New York: Harper Perennial, 1996).

Lévi-Strauss, Claude, *Elementary Structures of Kinship*, trans. James Harle Bell and John Richard von Sturmer, ed. Rodney Needham (Boston, MA: Beacon Press, 1969).

Lévi-Strauss, Claude, *The Raw and the Cooked: Introduction to a Science of Mythology: 1*, Vol. 1 (New York: Harper & Row, 1964).

Lewis, Jon, *American Film: A History* (New York: W.W. Norton, 2008).

Lewis, Jon, *Hollywood v. Hard Core: How the Struggle over Censorship Saved the Modern Film Industry* (New York: New York University Press, 2000).

Liebman, Stuart, 'Apparent Motion and Film Structure: Paul Sharits's *Shutter Interface*,' *Millennium Film Journal* 1, no. 2 (Spring–Summer 1978), pp. 101–109.

Lipton, Eunice, *Alias Olympia: A Woman's Search for Manet's Model and Her Own Desire* (Ithaca, NY: Cornell University Press, 1999).

MacDonald, Scott, *Avant-Garde Film Motion Studies* (Cambridge: Cambridge University Press, 1993).

MacDonald, Scott, *Cinema 16: Documents Toward a History of the Film Society* (Philadelphia, PA: Temple University Press, 2002).

Malanga, Gerard, e-mail message to the author (July 12, 2012).

Marcuse, Herbert, [1955] *Eros and Civilization: A Philosophical Inquiry into Freud* (Abingdon: Routledge, 1998).

Marks, Laura U., *The Skin of the Film: Intercultural Cinema, Embodiment, and the Senses* (Durham, NC: Duke University Press, 2000).

McClure, Michael, *Meat Science Essays*, 2nd ed. (San Francisco, CA: City Lights Books, 1963).

Mekas, Jonas, 'Baudelairean Cinema,' in *Movie Journal: The Rise of New American Cinema* (New York: Collier Books, 1972), pp. 85–86.

Mekas, Jonas, 'First Statement of New American Cinema Group,' in *Film Culture Reader*, ed. P. Adams Sitney (New York: Praeger Publisher, 1970).

Mekas, Jonas, interview by Vincent Canby, 'Where the Naked Truth was Born,' *The New York Times*, May 18, 1969, p. 24.

Mekas, Jonas, letter to Stan Brakhage, November 30, 1977, box 12, folder 5, James Stanley Brakhage Collection, University of Colorado at Boulder Libraries.

Mekas, Jonas, 'Movie Journal', *The Village Voice*, July 15, 1976.

Mekas, Jonas, *Movie Journal: The Rise of a New American Cinema, 1959–1971* (New York: Macmillan, 1972).

Mekas, Jonas, 'Notes on Some New Movies and Happiness,' in *Film Culture Reader*, ed. P. Adams Sitney (New York: Praeger, 1970), pp. 317–325.

Mekas, Jonas, 'To the Editor. Motion Pictures. NY Times,' May 19, 1969, box 12, James Stanley Brakhage Collection, University of Colorado at Boulder Libraries.

Merleau-Ponty, Maurice, *The Visible and the Invisible*, ed. Claude Lefort, trans. Alphonso Lingis (Evanston, IL: Northwestern University Press, 1968).

Metz, Christian, *The Imaginary Signifier: Psychoanalysis and the Cinema*, trans. Ben Brewster (Bloomington, IN: Indiana University Press, 1986).

Michelson, Annette, 'Camera Lucida / Camera Obscura,' *ArtForum* 10, no. 5 (January 1973), pp. 30–37.

Michelson, Annette, 'Paul Sharits and the Critique of Illusionism: An Introduction,' *Film Culture*, no. 65–66 (1978), pp. 83–89.

Michelson, Annette, 'Toward Snow,' *Artforum* (June 1971), pp. 30–37.

Michelson, Annette, '"Where is Your Rupture?" Mass Culture and the *Gesamtkunstwerk*,' in *Andy Warhol*, ed. Annette Michelson (Cambridge, MA: The MIT Press, 2001).

Michelson, Peter, *Speaking the Unspeakable: A Poetics of Obscenity*, SUNY Series, The Margins of Literature (Albany, NY: State University of New York Press).

Miles, Barry, *Ginsberg: A Biography* (New York: Simon & Schuster, 1989).

Miles, Barry, telephone interview with the author (February 2009).

Milgram, Stanley, *Obedience to Authority: An Experimental View* (New York: Harper & Row, 1974).

Morgan, Bill, *I Celebrate Myself: The Somewhat Private Life of Allen Ginsberg* (London: Penguin, 2006).

Morris, Robert, 'Notes on Sculpture 1–3,' in *Art in Theory 1900–1990*, ed. Charles Harrison and Paul Wood (Oxford: Blackwell Publishers, 1992), pp. 813–822.

Morris, Robert, 'Subjective Histories of Sculpture II: Robert Morris,' lecture at The New School, New York, April 7, 2008.

Mulvey, Laura, 'Visual Pleasure and Narrative Cinema,' *Screen* 16, no. 9 (Autumn 1975).

Name, Billy, phone conversation with the author (May 16, 2012).

Nelson, Maggie, *The Art of Cruelty: A Reckoning* (New York: W.W. Norton, 2011).

Nesthus, Marie, 'The "Document" Correspondences of Stan Brakhage,' *Chicago Review* 47, no. 4 (Winter 2001), pp. 133–156.

Nochlin, Linda, 'Why Have There Been No Great Women Artists?' *ARTnews* 69 (January 1971), pp. 22–39.

O'Brien, Devora, telephone interview with the author (February 2009).

O'Grady, Lorraine, 'Olympia's Maid: Reclaiming Black Female Subjectivity,' *The Feminism and Visual Culture Reader*, ed. Amelia Jones, 2nd ed. (London: Routledge, 2003), pp. 174–187.

Olson, Charles, *The Maximus Poems*, ed. George F. Butterick (Berkeley, CA: University of California Press, 1984).

Ono, Yoko, *Grapefruit: A Book of Instructions and Drawings by Yoko Ono*, intro. John Lennon (New York: Simon & Schuster, 2000; Tokyo: Wunternaum Press, 1964).

Ono, Yoko, *Just Me! The Very First Autobiographical Essay by the World's Most Famous Japanese Woman* (Tokyo: Kodansha International, 1986).

Ono, Yoko, 'Statement,' *Village Voice*, October 7, 1971, p. 20.

Ono, Yoko, *Yoko Ono: Arias and Objects*, ed. Barbara Haskell and John G. Hanhardt (Salt Lake City, UT: Gibbs Smith, 1991).

Ono, Yoko, and John Lennon, 'Woman is the Nigger of the World.' Song included on *Some Time in New York City*, 1972.

Osaki, Shinichiro, 'Body and Place: Action in Postwar Art in Japan,' *Out of Actions: Between Performance and the Object 1949–1979*, ed. Paul Schimmel (London: Thames & Hudson, 1998), pp. 121–157.

Osterweil, Ara, *Flesh Cinema: The Corporeal Avant-Garde, 1959–1979* (Ann Arbor, MI: UMI Dissertation Services, 2005).

Osterweil, Ara, 'Queer Coupling, or The Stain of the Bearded Woman,' *Framework* 51, no. 1 (Spring 2010), pp. 33–60.

Osterweil, Ara and David Baumflek, 'Emergent Bodies: Human, All Too Human, Posthuman,' in *The Anatomy of Body Worlds: Critical Essays on the Plastinated Cadavers of Gunther von Hagens*, ed. T. Christine Jespersen, Alicita Rodríguez, and Joseph Starr (London: McFarland & Company, 2009), pp. 240–258.

Owens, Craig, *Beyond Recognition: Representation, Power, and Culture*, ed. Scott Bryson et al. (Los Angeles, CA: University of California Press, 1992).

Perry, Roger, and Tony Elliott, 'Yoko Ono,' *Unit* (December 1967), pp. 26–27.

Poe, Edgar Allan, 'A Philosophy of Composition,' *Graham's Magazine* 28, no. 4 (April 1846), pp. 163–167.

Prochnau, William, *Once upon a Distant War* (New York: Times Books, 1995).

Rainer, Yvonne, *Feelings Are Facts: A Life* (Cambridge, MA: The MIT Press, 2006).

Reich, Wilhelm, *The Mass Psychology of Fascism*, trans. Theodore P. Wolf (New York: Orgone Institute Press, 1946).

Rentschler, Carrie, 'The Physiognomic Turn,' *International Journal of Communication* 4 (2010), pp. 1–6.

Rentschler, Carrie, *Second Wounds: Victims' Rights and the Media in the U.S.* (Durham, NC: Duke University Press, 2011).

Rentschler, Carrie, 'An Urban Physiognomy of the 1964 Kitty Genovese Murder,' *Space & Culture* 14, no. 3 (August 2011), pp. 310–329.

Rich, Adrienne, *Compulsory Heterosexuality and Lesbian Existence* (Antelope, CA: Antelope Publications, 1982).

Richie, Donald, titled only 'Brakhage/Richie,' n.d., Brakhage File, Anthology Film Archives.

Riley, Robert, 'Infinity Kisses,' in *Imaging Her Erotics*, ed. Carolee Schneemann (Cambridge, MA: The MIT Press, 2003), p. 263.

Rimbaud, Jean Nicholas Arthur, *Rimbaud: Complete Works, Selected Letters*, bilingual edition, trans. Wallace Fowlie (Chicago, IL: University of Chicago Press, 2005), p. 362.

Rosen, Abigail, 'Interview with Abigail Rosen (McGrath),' interview by Gary Comenas, December 2007, Warholstars.org, www.warholstars.org/articles/abigailrosen/abigailrosen.html (accessed June 20, 2012).

Rubin, Gayle S., 'Thinking Sex: Notes for a Radical Theory of the Politics of Sexuality,' *The Lesbian and Gay Studies Reader*, ed. Henry Abelove, Michèle Aina Barale, and David M. Halperin (New York: Routledge, 1993), pp. 3–44.

RufusCollins.org, www.rufuscollins.org/little_known.html (accessed July 5, 2010).

Sarris, Andrew, 'Westward Ho-Ho with Warhol,' *The Village Voice*, May 8, 1969.

Schmidt, Ulf, *Medical Films, Ethics and Euthanasia in Nazi Germany: The History of Medical Research and Teaching Films of the Reich Office for Educational Films / Reich Institute for Films in Science and Education, 1933–1945* (Husum: Matthiesen Verlag, 2002).

Schneemann, Carolee, *Correspondence Course: An Epistolary History of Carolee Schneemann and Her Circle*, ed. Kristine Stiles (Durham, NC: Duke University Press, 2010).

Schneemann, Carolee, email message to author (June 26, 2012).

Schnee mann, Carolee, email message to author (July 20, 2012).

Schneemann, Carolee, 'Eye Body: 36 Transformative Actions,' in *Imaging Her Erotics*, (Cambridge, MA: The MIT Press, 2003), pp. 55–59.

Schneemann, Carolee, 'From the Notebooks,' in *Imaging Her Erotics*, (Cambridge, MA: The MIT Press, 2003), pp. 46–51.

Schneemann, Carolee, 'Homage to Ana Mendieta,' in *Imaging Her Erotics*, (Cambridge, MA: MIT Press, 2003), pp. 276–277.

Schneemann, Carolee, 'Interior Scroll,' in *Imaging Her Erotics*, (Cambridge, MA: The MIT Press, 2003), pp. 151–161.

Schneemann, Carolee, 'On Censorship: Interview with Aviva Rahmani,' in *Imaging Her Erotics*, (Cambridge, MA: The MIT Press, 2003), pp. 211–216.

Schneemann, Carolee, 'Interview with Carl Heyward,' in *Imaging Her Erotics*, (Cambridge, MA: The MIT Press, 2003), pp. 196–207.

Schneemann, Carolee, 'Interview with Kate Haug,' in *Imaging Her Erotics*, (Cambridge, MA: The MIT Press, 2003), pp. 21–44.

Schneemann, Carolee, 'Interview with Linda Montano,' in *Imaging Her Erotics*, (Cambridge, MA: The MIT Press, 2003), pp. 131–134.

Schneemann, Carolee, interview by Odili Donald Odita, 'Conversation with Carolee Schneemann, Part 1', *Plexus* (web magazine), 1997, www.plexus.org/connect/texts/interviews/texts/1.html (accessed May 5, 2011).

Schneemann, Carolee, interview by Scott MacDonald, *A Critical Cinema: Interviews with Independent Filmmakers* (Berkeley, CA: University of California Press, 1988), pp. 134–151 .

Schneemann, Carolee, 'It is Painting,' in *Stan Brakhage Filmmaker*, ed. David E. James (Philadelphia, PA: Temple University Press, 2005), pp. 78–87.

Schneemann, Carolee, 'The Lebanon Series,' in *Imaging Her Erotics*, (Cambridge, MA: The MIT Press, 2003), pp. 186–195.

Schneemann, Carolee, 'Meat Joy,' in *Imaging Her Erotics*, (Cambridge, MA: The MIT Press, 2003), pp. 60–73.

Schneemann, Carolee, 'Mortal Coils,' in *Imaging Her Erotics*, (Cambridge, MA: The MIT Press, 2003), pp. 278–285.

Schneemann, Carolee, 'Notes on Fuses,' in *Imaging Her Erotics*, (Cambridge, MA: The MIT Press, 2003), p. 45.

Sedgwick, Eve Kosofsky, *Between Men: English Literature and Male Homosocial Desire* (New York: Columbia University Press, 1985).

Sewall-Ruskin, Yvonne, *High on Rebellion: Inside the Underground at Max's Kansas City* (New York: Thunders Mouth Press, 1998).

Sharits, Christopher, 'About Paul,' email message to the author (August 8, 2011).

Sharits, Christopher, 'About Paul,' email message to the author (July 11, 2011).

Sharits, Paul, 'A Cinematics Model for Film Studies in Higher Education,' *Film Studies*, no. 65–66 (1978), pp. 43–68.

Sharits, Paul, 'Exhibition / Frozen Frames: Regarding the "Frozen Film Frame" Series: A Statement for the "5th International Experimental Film Festival," Knokke, December 1974,' *Film Culture*, no. 65–66 (1978), pp. 81–83.

Sharits, Paul, 'Hearing: Seeing,' *Film Culture* no. 65–66 (1978), pp. 69–75.

Sharits, Paul, 'Interview with Paul Sharits,' interview by Jean-Claude Lebensztejn, June 12 and 14, 1983, trans. Sandra Reid, in *Paul Sharits*, ed. yann beauvais (Dijon: Les presses du réel, 2008), pp. 77–101.

Sharits, Paul, 'An Interview with Paul Sharits,' interview by Linda Cathcart, *Film Culture*, no. 65–66 (1978), pp. 103–108.

Sharits, Paul, 'Locational Film Pieces,' *Film Culture*, 65–66 (1978), pp. 121–124.

Sharits, Paul, 'My painting (& film) for Galerie A', in *Paul Sharits*, ed. yann beauvais (Dijon: Les presses du réel, 2008), pp. 163–167.

Sharits, Paul, 'Notes on Films, 1966–1968', *Film Culture*, 47 (1969), pp. 13–16.

Sharits, Paul, letter to Stan Brakhage, January 14, 1974, Brakhage Files, Anthology Film Archives.

Sharits, Paul, letter to Stan Brakhage, February 11, 1971, Brakhage File, Anthology Film Archives.

Sharits, Paul, letter to Stan Brakhage, dated 'Friday' 1968, Brakhage File, Anthology Film Archives.

Sharits, Paul, 'Postscript as Preface', *Film Culture*, no. 65–66 (1978), pp. 1–6.

Sharits, Paul, 'Statement Regarding Multiple Screen/Sound "Locational" Film Environments – Installations (1976)', *Film Culture*, no. 65–66 (1978), pp. 79–80.

Sharits, Paul, 'Unpublished interview with John du Cane and Simon Field, London 1970', www.paulsharits.com/caneparti.htm.

Sharits, Paul, '-UR(i)N(ul)LS:TREAM:S:S:ECTION:S:SECTION:-S:S:ECTIONED(A) (lysis)JO: "1968–70,"' *Film Culture*, no. 65–66 (1978), pp. 7–25.

Sharits, Paul, 'Words per Page', in *Buffalo Heads: Media Study, Media Practice, Media Pioneers, 1973–1990*, ed. Woody Vasulka and Peter Weibel (Karlsruhe: Center for Art and Media Karlsruhe, 2008; Cambridge, MA: The MIT Press, 2008).

Sheff, David, introduction to section 17 of *The Playboy Interviews with John Lennon and Yoko Ono*, ed. G. Barry Golson (New York: Playboy Press, 1981).

Shimizu, Celine Parreñas, *The Hypersexuality of Race: Performing Asian/American Women on Screen and on Scene* (Durham, NC: Duke University Press, 2007).

Shklovsky, Viktor, 'Art as Technique', *Art in Theory 1900–1990: An Anthology of Changing Ideas*, ed. Charles Harrison and Paul Wood (Oxford: Blackwell, 1992), pp. 274–278.

Siegel, Marc, 'Documentary That Dare/Not Speak Its Name: Jack Smith's *Flaming Creatures*,' in *Between the Sheets, In the Streets: Queer, Lesbian, Gay Documentary*, ed. Chris Holmlund and Cynthia Fuchs (Minneapolis, MN: University of Minnesota Press, 1997).

Silverman, Kaja, 'Fassbinder and Lacan: A Reconsideration of Gaze, Look and Image', *Camera Obscura*, 7, no.1 (January, 1989), pp. 54–85.

Silverman, Kaja, *Flesh of My Flesh* (Stanford, CA: Stanford University Press, 2009).

Silverman, Kaja, 'Lost Objects and Mistaken Subjects: A Prologue', in *The Acoustic Mirror: The Female Voice in Psychoanalysis and Cinema* (Bloomington, IN: Indiana University Press, 1988), pp. 1–41.

Silverman, Kaja, *Male Subjectivity at the Margins* (New York: Routledge, 1992).

Silverman, Kaja, 'Suture', in *The Subject of Semiotics* (Oxford: Oxford University Press, 1984), pp. 194–236.

Sitney, P. Adams, *Eyes Upside Down: Visionary Filmmakers and the Heritage of Emerson* (Oxford: Oxford University Press, 2008).

Sitney, P. Adams, telephone conversation with the author (February 22, 2012).

Sitney, P. Adams, telephone interview with the author (Spring 2004).

Sitney, P. Adams, *Visionary Film: The American Avant-Garde, 1943–2000*, 3rd ed. (Oxford: Oxford University Press, 2002).

Smith, Jack, '"The Adorable and Pasty Creatures…": Journal Notes on the Uses of Pornography', in *Wait for Me at the Bottom of the Pool: The Writings of Jack Smith*, ed. J. Hoberman and Edward Leffingwell (New York: High Risk Books, 1997), pp. 77–80.

Sontag, Susan, *Regarding the Pain of Others* (New York: Picador, 2003).
Steinberg, Leo, 'Reflections on the State of Criticism,' in *Robert Rauschenberg*, ed. Branden W. Joseph (Cambridge, MA: The MIT Press, 2002).
Stiles, Kristine, 'Bed In, 1969,' in *Yes Yoko Ono* (New York: Japan Society; New York: Harry N. Abrams, 2000), pp. 172–173.
Stiles, Kristine, 'Cut Piece, 1964,' *Yes Yoko Ono* (New York: Japan Society; New York: Harry N. Abrams, 2000), pp. 158–159.
Stiles, Kristine, 'The Painter as an Instrument of Real Time,' in *Imaging Her Erotics*, ed. Carolee Schneemann (Cambridge, MA: The MIT Press, 2003), pp. 2–16.
Stiles, Kristine, 'Unbosoming Lennon: The Politics of Yoko Ono's Experience,' *Art Criticism*, 7, no. 2 (1992), pp. 21–54.
Stockton, Kathryn Bond, *The Queer Child: Or Growing Sideways in the Twentieth Century*, Series Q (Durham, NC: Duke University Press, 2009).
Strauss, David Levi, 'Love Rides Aristotle Through the Audience: Body, Image, and Idea in the Work of Carolee Schneemann,' in *Up To and Including Her Limits* (New York: New Museum of Contemporary Art, 1996).
Suárez, Juan A., *Bike Boys, Drag Queens and Superstars: Avant-Garde, Mass Culture, and Gay Identities in the 1960s Underground Cinema* (Bloomington, IN: Indiana University Press, 1996).
Taubin, Amy, 'Afterglow,' *Film Comment*, 42, no. 1 (January 2006), pp. 58–59.
Taubin, Amy, 'Christmas on Earth,' Barbara Rubin File, Anthology Film Archives.
Taubin, Amy, interview with the author (Winter 2008–2009).
Taubin, Amy, telephone interview with the author (Winter 2009).
Tavel, Ronald, interview by Patrick Smith, in *Andy Warhol's Art and Films* (Ann Arbor, MI: UMI Research Press, 1986), pp. 484–503.
Tenney, James, letter to Stan Brakhage, June 24, 1957, box 17, folder 1, James Stanley Brakhage Collection, University of Colorado at Boulder Libraries.
Tenney, James, letter to Stan Brakhage, July 18, 1957, box 17, folder 1, James Stanley Brakhage Collection, University of Colorado at Boulder Libraries.
Thornon, Leslie, letter to Paul Sharits, May 22, 1976, Paul Sharits Collection, WYN Artist Archives, Burchfield Penney Art Center.
Tường, Nhị, *Tiểu Sử Bồ Tát Thích Quảng Đức* (Fawker: Quang Duc Monastery, 2005), www.quangduc.com/BoTatQuangDuc/09tieusu.html (accessed on August 20, 2007).
Tyler, Parker, *Underground Film: A Critical History* (New York: Da Capo Press, 1995).
Unger, Irwin, *The Sixties* (Boston, MA: Prentice Hall, 2011).
Variety, 'Blue Movie, or F**K: Warhol Makes Even Sex a Bore,' *Variety*, June 25, 1969.
Variety, 'Warhol's "Blue Movie" The Bluest of 'Em All, If and When Released' (June 18, 1969).
Vasulka, Woody and Peter Weibel, eds., *Buffalo Heads: Media Study, Media Practice, Media Pioneers, 1973–1990* (Karlsruhe: Center for Art and Media Karlsruhe, 2008; Cambridge, MA: The MIT Press, 2008).
Vaughan, Jimmy, letter to Stan Brakhage, September 24, [1969 or 1972], box 29, folder 7, James Stanley Brakhage Collection, University of Colorado at Boulder Libraries.
Verrier, Eugene, letter to Brakhage, June 17, 1969, box 30, folders 14–15, James Stanley Stan Brakhage Collection, University of Colorado at Boulder Libraries.
Vogel, Amos, *Film as a Subversive Art* (New York, Random House, 1974).

Vogel, Amos, "'I made a glass hammer": John and Yoko at Cannes,' *The Village Voice*, June 24, 1971.

Walter, W. Grey, *The Living Brain* (New York: W. W. Norton, 1953).

Warhol, Andy, *The Philosophy of Andy Warhol (From A to B and Back Again)* (New York: Harcourt Brace Jovanovich, 1975).

Warhol, Andy and Pat Hackett, *POPism: The Warhol Sixties* (New York: Harcourt Brace Jovanovich, 1980).

Warholstars.org, 'Andy Warhol's Couch at St. Marks Church,' *Andy Warhol Chronology*, www.warholstars.org/chron/couch.html (accessed July 7, 2010).

Watson, Steven, *Factory Made: Warhol and the Sixties* (New York: Pantheon, 2003).

Waugh, Thomas, 'Cockteaser,' in *Pop Out: Queer Warhol*, ed. Jennifer Doyle, Jonathan Flatley, and José Esteban Muñoz (Durham, NC: Duke University Press, 1996), pp. 51–77.

Waugh, Thomas, *Hard to Imagine: Gay Male Eroticism in Photography and Film from Their Beginnings to Stonewall* (New York: Columbia University Press, 1996).

White, Anthony, *Lucio Fontana: Between Utopia and Kitsch* (Cambridge, MA: The MIT Press, October Books, 2011).

Williams, Forrest, letter to Stan Brakhage, dated only 'August 23', box 18, folder 2, James Stanley Brakhage Collection, University of Colorado at Boulder Libraries.

Williams, Linda, 'Film Bodies: Gender, Genre, and Excess,' in *Film Genre Reader II*, ed. Barry Keith Grant (Austin, TX: University of Texas Press, 1995), pp. 141–159.

Williams, Linda, 'Film Body: An Implantation of Perversions,' in *Narrative, Apparatus, Ideology: A Film Theory Reader*, ed. Philip Rosen (New York: Columbia University Press, 1986).

Williams, Linda, *Hard Core: Power, Pleasure, and the 'Frenzy of the Visible'* (Berkeley, CA: University of California Press, 1989).

Williams, Linda, 'Porn Studies: Proliferating Pornographies On/Scene: An Introduction', in *Porn Studies*, ed. Linda Williams (Durham, NC: Duke University Press, 2004), pp. 1–23.

Williams, Linda, *Screening Sex* (Durham, NC: Duke University Press, 2008).

Williams, Linda, 'Skin Flicks on the Racial Border: Pornography, Exploitation, and Interracial Lust,' *Porn Studies*, ed. Linda Williams (Durham, NC: Duke University Press, 2004), pp. 271–308.

Williams, Liza, *Los Angeles Free Press*, 7 November 1969.

Wolf, Reva, *Andy Warhol, Poetry, and Gossip in the 1960s* (Chicago, IL: University of Chicago, 1997).

Wölfflin, Heinrich, *Renaissance and Baroque*, trans. Kathrin Simon (Collins: The Fontana Library, 1964).

Wundt, Wilhelm Max, *Principles of Physiological Psychology*, trans. Edward Bradford Titchener (New York: Macmillan, 1910).

York, Michelle, 'Sharon Springs Journal: Like the Water, Grand Plans Buoy Spirits at a Vacation Spot From a Bygone Era,' *New York Times*, June 5, 2008.

Yoshimoto, Midori, '!, 1964,' in *Yes Yoko Ono* (New York: Japan Society; New York: Harry N. Abrams, 2000), p. 156.

Yoshimoto, Midori, *Into Performance: Japanese Women Artists in New York* (New Brunswick: Rutgers University Press, 2005).

Youngblood, Gene, *Expanded Cinema* (New York: E.P. Dutton, 1970).

Youngblood, Gene, Intermedia, *Los Angeles Free Press*, March 7, 1969.

Zelizer, Viviana, *Pricing the Priceless Child: The Changing Social Value of Children* (Princeton, NJ: Princeton University Press, 1985).

Zielonko, Mary Ann, 'Remembering Kitty Genovese,' an interview by *Sound Portraits. org*, broadcast with introduction by Scott Simon, *Weekend Edition*, Saturday, March 13, 2004, www.soundportraits.org/on-air/remembering_kitty_genovese (accessed on August 14, 2013).